THE TRAGEDY OF LIBERATION

THE TRAGEDY OF LIBERATION

A HISTORY OF THE CHINESE REVOLUTION, 1945–57

FRANK DIKÖTTER

BLOOMSBURY PRESS

NEW YORK · LONDON · NEW DELHI · SYDNEY

Copyright © 2013 by Frank Dikötter

Map by ML Design

All rights reserved. No part of this book may be used or reproduced in any manner
whatsoever without written permission from the publisher except in the case of brief
quotations embodied in critical articles or reviews. For information address Bloomsbury Press,
1385 Broadway, New York, NY 10018.

Every reasonable effort has been made to trace copyright holders of material reproduced
in this book, but if any have been inadvertently overlooked the publishers would be glad
to hear from them.

Published by Bloomsbury Press, New York

All papers used by Bloomsbury Press are natural, recyclable products made from wood
grown in well-managed forests. The manufacturing processes conform to the
environmental regulations of the country of origin.

LIBRARY OF CONGRESS CATALOGING-IN-PUBLICATION DATA HAS BEEN APPLIED FOR

ISBN: 978-1-62040-347-1

First U.S. Edition 2013

1 3 5 7 9 10 8 6 4 2

Typeset by Hewer Text UK Ltd, Edinburgh
Printed and bound in the U.S.A. by Thomson-Shore Inc., Dexter, Michigan

'[W]in over the majority, oppose the minority and crush all enemies separately.'

Mao Zedong

CONTENTS

Preface

The Chinese Communist Party refers to its victory in 1949 as a 'liberation'. The term brings to mind jubilant crowds taking to the streets to celebrate their newly won freedom, but in China the story of liberation and the revolution that followed is not one of peace, liberty and justice. It is first and foremost a history of calculated terror and systematic violence.

The Second World War in China had been a bloody affair, but the civil war from 1945 to 1949 also claimed hundreds of thousands of civilian lives – not counting military casualties. As the communists tried to wrest the country from Chiang Kai-shek and the nationalists, they laid siege to one city after another, starving them into submission. Changchun, in the middle of the vast Manchurian plain north of the Great Wall of China, was blockaded for five months in 1948. Lin Biao, the commander in charge of the communist troops, ordered that it be turned into a 'city of death'. He placed sentries every 50 metres along a perimeter around the city and prohibited starving civilians from leaving, putting more pressure on the grain reserves of the nationalists. People tried to survive by eating grass, insects and tree bark. A few turned to human flesh. Anti-aircraft guns and heavy artillery bombarded the city day and night. At least 160,000 people died of hunger and disease during the siege.

A few months later, the People's Liberation Army moved into Beijing unopposed. Other cities also fell without firing a shot, unwilling to endure a prolonged blockade. In parts of the country, sympathetic crowds even welcomed the communists, relieved that the war had come to an end and hopeful of a better future. Across the country people accepted liberation with a mixture of fear, hope and resignation.

In the countryside, land reform followed liberation. Farmers were given a plot of land in exchange for overthrowing their leaders. Violence was an indispensable feature of land distribution, implicating a majority in the murder of a carefully designated minority. Work teams were given quotas of people who had to be denounced, humiliated, beaten, dispossessed and then killed by the villagers, who were assembled in their hundreds in an atmosphere charged with hatred. In a pact sealed in blood between the party and the poor, close to 2 million so-called 'landlords', often hardly any better off than their neighbours, were liquidated. From Hebei, Liu Shaoqi, the second-in-command, reported that some of them had been buried alive, tied up and dismembered, shot or throttled to death. Some children were slaughtered as 'little landlords'.

Less than a year after liberation came a Great Terror, designed to eliminate all the enemies of the party. Mao handed down a killing quota of one per thousand, but in many parts of the country two or three times as many people were executed, often on the flimsiest of pretexts. Entire villages were razed to the ground. Schoolchildren as young as six were accused of spying for the enemy and tortured to death. Sometimes cadres simply picked a few prisoners at random and had them shot to meet their quota. By the end of 1951, close to 2 million people had been murdered, sometimes during public rallies in stadiums, but more often than not away from the public eye, in forests, ravines, beside rivers, alone or in batches. A vast network of prisons scattered across the length and breadth of the country swallowed up many more.

Violence *was* the revolution, to paraphrase Simon Schama's observation about the French Revolution. But violence needed to be inflicted only occasionally to be effective. Fear and intimidation were its trusted companions, and they were widely used. People were encouraged to transform themselves into what the communists called 'New People'. Everywhere, in government offices, factories, workshops, schools and universities, they were 're-educated' and made to study newspapers and textbooks, learning the right answers, the right ideas and the right slogans. While the violence abated after a few years, thought reform never ended, as people were compelled to scrutinise their every belief, suppressing the transitory impressions that might reveal hidden bourgeois thoughts behind a mask of socialist conformity. Again and again, in front of assembled crowds or in study sessions under strict supervision, they had to write confessions, denounce their friends, justify their past activities and answer queries about their political reliability. One victim called it a 'carefully cultivated Auschwitz of the mind'.

Yet much of the regime was founded on far more than mere violence and intimidation. The history of communism in China is also a history of promises made and promises broken. The communists wanted to woo before they tried to control. Like Lenin and the Bolsheviks, Mao achieved power by promising every disaffected group what they wanted most: land for the farmers, independence for all minorities, freedom for intellectuals, protection of private property for businessmen, higher living standards for the workers. The Chinese Communist Party rallied a majority under the banner of the New Democracy, a slogan promising co-operation with all except the most hardened enemies of the regime. Under the façade of a 'united front', a number of non-communist organisations such as the Democratic Party were co-opted into power, although they remained under the leadership of the communist party.

One by one these promises were broken. Mao was a master of strategy: 'win over the majority, oppose the minority and crush all enemies separately'. One by one a whole range of opponents were eliminated with the unwitting help of the enemies of tomorrow, those who were cajoled into co-operating with the authorities. Immediately after the bloody terror of 1951, the regime turned against the former government servants it had asked to stay on a few years earlier. Their services no longer needed; over a million of them were sacked from their jobs or thrown in gaol.

The business community was attacked in 1952. Entrepreneurs were dragged to denunciation meetings where they had to confront their employees, who were worked up into a fever pitch of hatred – real or feigned. In a mere two months, more than 600 entrepreneurs, businessmen and shopkeepers killed themselves in Shanghai alone. Many others were ruined. Everything that stood between the entrepreneur and the state was eliminated. All existing laws and judicial organs were abolished, replaced by a legal system inspired by the Soviet Union. Free speech was curtailed. Independent courts were replaced by people's tribunals. Autonomous chambers of commerce were taken over by local branches of the state-controlled All-China Federation of Industry and Commerce. In 1956 the government expropriated all private enterprises – whether small shops or large industries – under the so-called 'redemption-purchase policy', although the policy entailed neither purchase nor redemption.

In the countryside, despite fierce resistance to collectivisation and the devastation it produced, in 1956 farmers lost their tools, their land and their livestock. They also lost their freedom of movement and were compelled to sell their grain to the state at prices mandated by the state. They became bonded labourers at the beck and call of local cadres. Already by 1954, by the admission of the regime itself, farmers had a third less food to eat compared to the years before liberation. Almost everybody in the countryside was on a starvation diet.

When Mao turned against intellectuals in 1957, sending half a million of them to the gulag, it was the culmination of a series of drives by the party to eliminate all opposition, whether it came from ethnic minorities, religious groups, farmers, artisans, entrepreneurs, industrialists, teachers and scholars or doubters within the ranks of the party itself. After a decade of communist rule, there was hardly anybody left to oppose the Chairman.

But even as every promise was broken, the party kept on gaining followers. Many were idealists, some were opportunists, others thugs. They displayed astonishing faith and almost fanatical conviction, sometimes even after they themselves had ended up being devoured by the party machinery. A few party intellectuals purged in 1957 actually volunteered to work in the Great Northern Wilderness, a vast swamp infected with mosquitoes where prisoners were sent to reclaim wasteland. They saw it as an opportunity to redeem themselves and seek self-renewal in the hope of being allowed to serve the party again.

'Is there *any* good that the Chinese Communists have done?' Valentin Chu asked in a landmark book entitled *The Inside Story of Communist China*, published a decade after the communist conquest. His answer was that a single act or a single programme, when isolated from the broader picture, may very well have been invaluable: a dam that worked, a nursery where children fared well, a prison where the inmates were treated humanely. The campaign to eliminate illiteracy in the countryside was laudable, until it was given up. But when seen in the overall context of what happened to the country between 1949 and 1957, these isolated achievements did not amount to a broad trend towards equality, justice and freedom, the proclaimed values of the regime itself.

People from all walks of life were caught up in this huge tragedy, and they are at the heart of this book. Their experiences have often been silenced, not least by the official propaganda that produced a seemingly endless flow of pronouncements from the leadership. The propaganda was about the world in the making, not about the reality on the ground. It was a world of plans, blueprints and models, featuring model workers and model peasants, not real people of flesh and blood.

Historians, too, have sometimes confused the abstract world presented by propaganda with the complicated individual tragedies of revolution, buying all too readily into the gleaming image that the regime so carefully projected to the rest of the world. Some have called the years of liberation a 'Golden Age' or a 'Honeymoon Period', in contrast to the cataclysm of the Cultural Revolution that started in 1966. On a more popular level, keepers of the faith continue to portray the Chinese revolution as one of the greatest events in world history, all the more so as other communist dictators, Russia's Joseph Stalin, Cambodia's Pol Pot and North Korea's Kim Il-sung, have lost much of their credibility. But, as this book shows, the first decade of Maoism was one of the worst tyrannies in the history of the twentieth century, sending to an early grave at least 5 million civilians and bringing misery to countless more.

The bulk of the evidence presented in this book comes from party archives in China. Over the past few years vast amounts of material have become available, and I draw on hundreds of previously classified documents, including secret police reports, unexpurgated versions of important leadership speeches, confessions extracted during thought-reform campaigns, inquiries into rebellions in the countryside, detailed statistics on the victims of the Great Terror, surveys of working conditions in factories and workshops, letters of complaint written by ordinary people, and much more. Other sources include personal memoirs, letters and diaries, as well as eyewitness accounts from people who lived through the revolution. Sympathisers of the regime have unjustly discarded many of the claims of these earlier eyewitnesses, but these can now be corroborated by archival evidence, giving them a new lease of life. Taken as a whole, these sources offer us an unprecedented opportunity to probe beyond the shiny surface of propaganda and retrieve the stories of the ordinary men and women who were both the main protagonists and the main victims of the revolution.

The Tragedy of Liberation is the second volume of the *People's Trilogy*. It precedes chronologically an earlier volume, *Mao's Great Famine*, which looks at the man-made catastrophe that claimed tens of millions of lives between 1958 and 1962. A third and final volume on the Cultural Revolution will follow in due course. The nature of the archival evidence that underpins the *People's Trilogy* is explained in greater detail in an essay on the sources in *Mao's Great Famine*.

Chronology

6 and 9 August 1945:
Atomic bombs are dropped on Hiroshima and Nagasaki.

8 August 1945:
Stalin declares war on Japan and Soviet troops invade Manchuria.

21 August 1945:
A formal surrender ceremony between China and Japan concludes the Second World War in the Pacific.

April 1946:
Soviet troops withdraw from Manchuria after allowing the communists to take over the countryside.

May 1946:
Mao calls for radical land distribution and all-out class struggle in the countryside.

June 1946:
The nationalists pursue the communists all the way to the northern border of Manchuria, but are forced to halt their advance as George Marshall, President Truman's envoy, imposes a ceasefire. The communist troops regroup and are trained by the Soviets.

September 1946–July 1947:
Truman imposes an arms embargo.

December 1946–December 1947:
The nationalists keep on pouring their best troops into Manchuria, which turns into a death trap.

December 1947–November 1948:
The communists win the battle of Manchuria after blockading all major cities.

22 January 1949:

Beijing surrenders to the communists after a forty-day siege.

November 1948–January 1949:

The nationalists lose the battle of Xuzhou in central China, opening up the Yangzi Valley and all of the south to communist conquest.

April–May 1949:

Nanjing, the nationalist capital on the south bank of the Yangzi, falls to the communists. After a protracted siege, the communists conquer Shanghai.

30 June 1949:

On the twenty-eighth anniversary of the Chinese Communist Party, Mao announces that China should 'lean to one side' and embrace the Soviet Union.

1 October 1949:

Mao Zedong proclaims the People's Republic of China on Tiananmen Square in Beijing.

10 December 1949:

After the fall of Chongqing, Chiang Kai-shek abandons China and flees to Taiwan.

December 1949–January 1950:

Mao is in Moscow to obtain recognition and help from Stalin. On 14 February 1950 China signs a Treaty of Friendship, Alliance and Mutual Assistance with the Soviet Union.

June 1950–October 1952:

The communists implement land reform in the south.

25 June 1950:

North Korea invades South Korea, drawing condemnation from the United Nations Security Council and a counter-offensive under General Douglas MacArthur.

7 October 1950:

The People's Liberation Army invades Tibet.

10 October 1950–October 1951:

A Great Terror unfolds, called the 'Campaign to Suppress Counter-Revolutionaries'.

18 October 1950:

China enters the Korean War.

November 1950:

Start of a campaign to 'Resist America, Aid Korea'.

1951–1953:

Once the land has been redistributed, villagers are pooled into 'mutual-aid teams' in which they have to share their tools, working animals and labour.

October 1951–June 1952:

A 'Three-Anti Campaign' aims to purge the ranks of the government.

October 1951:

Start of a thought-reform campaign designed to regiment and absorb the educated elite into the state bureaucracy.

January–June 1952:

Mao declares war on the private sector in a campaign known as the 'Five-Anti Campaign'.

February–April 1952:

Beijing alleges that the United States is waging germ warfare.

5 March 1953:

Stalin dies.

27 July 1953:

A ceasefire brings an end to the Korean War.

November 1953:

Introduction of a state monopoly over grain, as cultivators are forced to sell all 'surplus' grain to the state at prices determined by the state.

1953–1955:

The mutual-aid teams are turned into co-operatives, with tools, working animals and labour now shared on a permanent basis and the land pooled.

February 1954–May 1955:

Gao Gang and other senior leaders are purged for 'treachery' and 'splitting the party'.

April–December 1955:

Hu Feng and other intellectuals are denounced for heading a 'counter-revolutionary' clique. More than 770,000 people are arrested in a campaign against counter-revolutionaries.

June 1955:

A household-registration system restricts the movement of people in the countryside.

Summer 1955–spring 1956:

As part of a push to accelerate the collectivisation of the countryside, called the 'Socialist High Tide', farmers are herded into collectives in which they no longer own the land. In the cities most industry and commerce are nationalised.

February 1956:

Khrushchev denounces Stalin and the cult of personality in a secret speech in Moscow. Criticism of Stalin's disastrous campaign of collectivisation strengthens the position of those opposed to the Socialist High Tide in China. Mao perceives deStalinisation as a challenge to his own authority.

September 1956:

A reference to 'Mao Zedong Thought' is removed from the party constitution, the principle of collective leadership is lauded and the cult of personality is decried. The Socialist High Tide is abandoned.

October 1956:

Encouraged by deStalinisation, people in Hungary revolt against their own government, prompting Soviet forces to invade the country, crush all opposition and install a new regime with Moscow's backing.

Winter 1956–spring 1957:

Mao, overriding most of his colleagues, encourages a more open political climate with the 'Hundred Flowers' campaign to avoid the social unrest that led to the invasion of Hungary. Students and workers demonstrate, protest and strike across the country.

Summer 1957:

The campaign backfires as a mounting barrage of criticism questions the very right of the party to rule. Mao changes tack and accuses these critical voices of being 'bad elements' bent on destroying the party. He puts Deng Xiaoping in charge of an anti-rightist campaign, which persecutes half a million people – many of them students and intellectuals deported to remote areas to do hard labour. The party finds unity behind its Chairman, who unleashes the 'Great Leap Forward' a few months later.

China, 1957

S O V I E T   U N I O N

M O

Urumqi

Lop Nor

X I N J I A N G

ISLAMABAD

WEST
PAKISTAN

Q I N G H A I

T I B E T

DELHI

NEPAL

Champo

Lhasa

CHANGDU

KATHMANDU

Sikkim   THIMPHU

BHUTAN

I N D I A

EAST PAKISTAN

Mekong

DHAKA

CALCUTTA

Mandalay

Bay of Bengal

BURMA

500 kilometres

300 miles

THAILAND

PART ONE

CONQUEST (1945–49)

1

Siege

When workers in Changchun started digging trenches for a new irrigation system in the summer of 2006, they made a gruesome discovery. The rich black soil was clogged with human remains. Below a metre of earth were thousands of skeletons closely packed together. When they dug deeper, the workers found several more layers of bones, stacked up like firewood. A crowd of local residents, gathered around the excavated area, was taken aback by the sheer size of the burial site. Some thought that the bodies belonged to victims of the Japanese occupation during the Second World War. Nobody except an elderly man realised that they had just stumbled on remnants of the civil war that had resumed after 1945 between Mao Zedong's communists and Chiang Kai-shek's nationalists.

In 1948 the communists had laid siege to Changchun for five months, starving out a nationalist garrison stationed inside the city walls. Victory came at a heavy cost. At least 160,000 civilians died of hunger during the blockade. After liberation the communist troops buried many of the bodies in mass graves without so much as a tombstone, a name plate or even a simple marker. After decades of propaganda about the peaceful liberation of China, few people remember the victims of the communist party's rise to power.[1]

Changchun, in the middle of the vast Manchurian plain north of the Great Wall of China, was a minor trading town before the arrival of the railway in 1898. It developed rapidly as the junction between the South Manchurian Railway, run by the Japanese, and the Chinese Eastern Railway, owned by the Russians. In 1932 Changchun became the capital of Manchukuo, a puppet state of imperial Japan, which installed Henry Puyi,

later known as the last emperor, as its Manchu ruler. The Japanese transformed the city into a modern, wheel-shaped city with broad avenues,
shade trees and public works. Large, cream-coloured buildings for the
imperial bureaucracy appeared beside spacious parks, while elegant villas
were built for local collaborators and their Japanese advisers.

In August 1945, the Soviet army took over the city and, so far as
they could, dismantled the factories, machines and materials, sending
the war booty back by the trainload to the Soviet Union. Industrial
installations were demolished, and many of the formerly handsome
houses were stripped bare. The Soviets stayed until April 1946, when
the nationalist army took over the city. Two months later, the civil war
began, and Manchuria once again became a battlefield. The communist armies had the initiative and moved down from the north, cutting
the railway that connected Changchun with nationalist strongholds
further south.

In April 1948, the communists advanced towards Changchun itself.
Led by Lin Biao, a gaunt man who had trained at the Whampoa Military
Academy, they laid siege to the city. Lin was considered one of the best
battlefield commanders and a brilliant strategist. He was also ruthless.
When he realised that Zheng Dongguo, the defending commander in
Changchun, would not capitulate, he ordered the city to be starved into
surrender. On 30 May 1948 came his command: 'Turn Changchun into a
city of death.'[2]

Inside Changchun were some 500,000 civilians, many of them refugees
who had fled the communist advance and were trapped in their journey
south to Beijing after the railway lines had been cut. A hundred thousand
nationalist troops were also garrisoned inside the city. Curfew was imposed
almost immediately, keeping people indoors from eight at night to five in
the morning. All able-bodied men were made to dig trenches. Nobody was
allowed to leave. People who refused to be searched by sentries were liable
to be shot on the spot. Yet an air of goodwill still prevailed in the first
weeks of the siege, as emergency supplies were dropped by air. Some of the
well-to-do even established a Changchun Mobilisation Committee,
supplying sweets and cigarettes, comforting the wounded and setting up
tea stalls for the men.[3]

But soon the situation deteriorated. Changchun became an isolated island, beleaguered by 200,000 communist troops who dug tunnel defences and cut off the underground water supply to the city. Two dozen anti-aircraft guns and heavy artillery bombarded the city all day long, concentrating their fire on government buildings. The nationalists built three defensive lines of pillboxes around Changchun. Between the nationalists and the communists lay a vast no man's land soon taken over by bandits.[4]

On 12 June 1948 Chiang Kai-shek cabled an order reversing the ban on people leaving the city. Even without enemy fire, his planes could not possibly parachute in enough supplies to meet the needs of an entire city. But the anti-aircraft artillery of the communists forced them to fly at an altitude of 3,000 metres. Many of the airdrops landed outside the area controlled by the nationalists. In order to prevent a famine, the nationalists encouraged the populace to head for the countryside. Once they had left they were not allowed back, as they could not be fed. Every departing refugee was subject to rigorous inspection. Metallic objects such as pots or pans as well as gold and silver and even salt, seen as a vital commodity, were prohibited. Then the refugees had to cross the no man's land, a dark and dangerous terrain dominated by gangs, usually army deserters, who preyed on the defenceless crowds. Many had guns and even horses; some used passwords. The most skilful refugees managed to conceal a piece of jewellery, a watch or a fountain pen, but those found to be hiding an earring or a bracelet in a seam of their clothing risked being shot. Sometimes all their clothes were snatched. A few saved their best belongings by bundling them deep inside a burlap bag filled with dirty rags, including urine-soaked baby clothes, in the hope that the smell would repel robbers.[5]

Few ever made it past the communist lines. Lin Biao had placed a sentry every 50 metres along barbed wire and trenches 4 metres deep. Every exit was blocked. He reported to Mao: 'We don't allow the refugees to leave and exhort them to turn back. This method was very effective in the beginning, but later the famine got worse, and starving civilians would leave the city in droves at all times of day and night, and after we turned them down they started gathering in the area between our troops and the enemy.' Lin described how desperate the refugees were to be allowed through communist lines, explaining that they:

knelt in front of our troops in large groups and begged us to let them through. Some left their babies and small children with us and absconded, others hanged themselves in front of sentry posts. The soldiers who saw this misery lost their resolve, some even falling on their knees to weep with the starving people, saying, 'We are only following orders.' Others covertly allowed some of them through. After we corrected this, another tendency was discovered, namely the beating, tying up and shooting of refugees by soldiers, some to death (we do not as yet have any numbers for those injured or beaten to death).

Half a century later, Wang Junru explained what had happened when he was a soldier: 'We were told they were the enemy and they had to die.' Wang was fifteen when the communists forced him to enrol in the army. During the siege he joined the other soldiers ordered to drive back hungry civilians.[6]

By the end of June, some 30,000 people were caught in the area between the communists, who would not allow them to pass, and the nationalists, who refused to let them back into the city. Hundreds died every day. Two months later, more than 150,000 civilians were pressed inside the death zone, reduced to eating grass and leaves, doomed to slow starvation. Dead bodies were strewn everywhere, their bellies bloated in the scorching sun. 'The pungent stench of decomposition was everywhere,' remembered one survivor.[7]

The situation inside the city was little better. Besides the airdrops for the garrison, some 330 tonnes of grain were required daily to feed the civilians, although at best 84 tonnes were delivered by four or five planes, and often much less. Everything was requisitioned in the defence of Changchun. Chiang Kai-shek even prohibited private trading in August, threatening to shoot any merchant who contravened his order. Soon the nationalist soldiers turned on the civilians, stealing their food at gunpoint. They slaughtered all the army horses, then dogs, cats and birds. Ordinary people ate rotten sorghum and corncobs before stripping the bark from trees. Others ate insects or leather belts. A few turned to human flesh, sold at $1.20 a pound on the black market.[8]

Cases of collective suicide occurred all the time. Entire families killed themselves to escape from the misery. Dozens died by the roadside every day. 'We were just lying in bed starving to death,' said Zhang Yinghua when interviewed about the famine that claimed the lives of her brother, her sister and most of her neighbours. 'We couldn't even crawl.' Song Zhanlin, another survivor, remembered how she passed a small house with the door ajar. 'I entered to have a look and saw a dozen bodies lying all over the place, on the bed and on the floor. Among those on the bed, one was resting his head on a pillow, and a girl was still embracing a baby: it looked as if they were asleep. The clock on the wall was still ticking away.'[9]

Autumn saw temperatures plunge, and the survivors struggled to stay warm. They stripped floorboards, rooftops, sometimes entire buildings in the search for fuel. Trees were chopped down, even signboards were pilfered for wood. Asphalt was ripped from the streets. Like a slow-moving implosion, the gradual destruction of the city started in the suburbs and gradually rippled towards the centre. In the end 40 per cent of the housing went up in smoke. Heavy bombardment by artillery at point-blank range added to the misery, as ordinary people sheltered in shanties strewn with debris and decomposing bodies, while the nationalist top brass took refuge behind the massive concrete walls of the Central Bank of China.[10]

Soldiers absconded throughout the siege. Unlike the civilians who were driven back, they were welcomed by the communists and promised good food and lenient treatment. Day and night loudspeakers beamed propaganda encouraging them to defect or rebel: 'Did you join the Guomindang army? You were dragged into it at a rope's end . . . Come over to us . . . There is no way out of Changchun now . . .' Desertion rates soared after the summer, as the troops received a reduced ration of 300 grams of rice and flour a day.[11]

The siege lasted 150 days. In the end, on 16 October 1948, Chiang ordered General Zheng Dongguo to evacuate the city and cut southwards to Shenyang, the first large city along the railway leading towards Beijing. 'If Changchun falls, do you really think Peiping [the name for Beijing before 1949] will be safe?' Zheng was asked. He gave a sigh: 'No place in China will be safe.'[12]

Zheng had two armies to withdraw: the Sixtieth, composed mostly of dispirited soldiers from the subtropical province of Yunnan, and the New Seventh Army, made up of tough US-trained veterans who had fought on the Burma front. The Seventh stormed out as ordered, but failed to break through the blockade. The Sixtieth refused to leave, and in any event the soldiers were too weak to march all the way to Shenyang. They turned their guns against the Seventh and handed the city over to Lin Biao.

Hailed in China's history books as a decisive victory in the battle of Manchuria, the fall of Changchun came at huge cost, as an estimated 160,000 civilians were starved to death inside the area besieged by the communists. 'Changchun was like Hiroshima,' wrote Zhang Zhenglong, a lieutenant in the People's Liberation Army who documented the siege. 'The casualties were about the same. Hiroshima took nine seconds; Changchun took five months.'[13]

2

War

On 6 August 1945 a B-29 dropped an atomic bomb on Hiroshima. Three days later Nagasaki was erased in a blinding flash of light. Within a week Emperor Hirohito had ordered his armies to lay down their weapons.

The unconditional surrender of Japan was met with jubilation across China, ending one of the bloodiest chapters in the history of the country. In Chongqing, the wartime capital of Chiang Kai-shek, shouts and firecrackers erupted all over the city, 'sporadic at first but growing to a volcanic eruption of sound and happiness within an hour'. Searchlights festively danced across the sky. A flood of cheering, laughing and crying people poured through the streets, overwhelming every US soldier they could find with gifts of cigarettes. After Chiang had read his message of victory over the radio, dressed in a simple khaki uniform without any decorations, he walked out of the broadcasting studio and was engulfed by a joyous crowd. Well-wishers crawled through police lines, others hung from balconies, yelled from rooftops or held their children high above the crowd to see the Generalissimo.[1]

The eight-year war had plumbed the depths of human depravity. After Japanese troops took the capital Nanjing in December 1937, civilians and disarmed soldiers were systematically slaughtered in a six-week orgy of violence. Captives were rounded up and machine-gunned, blown up with landmines or stabbed to death with bayonets. Women, including infants and the elderly, were raped, mutilated and killed by soldiers on the rampage. No accurate death toll has ever been produced, but estimates range from a minimum of 40,000 to an upper limit of 300,000 deaths. During the last years of the war, in retaliation against guerrilla resistance, a pitiless policy of scorched earth devastated parts of north China, as whole villages were burned to the ground. Men between the ages of fifteen and sixty suspected of being enemy were rounded up and killed.

Throughout their occupation, the Japanese had used biological and chemical weapons. Lethal experiments were conducted on prisoners of war in a string of secret laboratories stretching from northern Manchuria to subtropical Guangdong. Victims were subjected to vivisection without anaesthesia after being infected with various germs. Others had their limbs amputated, their stomachs excised or parts of their organs surgically removed. Weapons, including flamethrowers and chemical agents, were tested on prisoners tied to stakes. In Unit 731, a notorious compound near Harbin that came complete with an aerodrome, a railway station, barracks, laboratories, operating rooms, crematoria, a cinema and even a Shinto temple, contaminated fleas and infected clothing were developed to spread plague, anthrax and cholera when dropped on civilians in encased bombs.[2] To escape the Japanese and their collaborators, tens of millions of refugees fled southwards towards Yunnan and Sichuan, where the nationalists had their wartime bases. But even in unoccupied territory people lived in fear, as massive air raids were mounted on civilian targets in the capital Chongqing and other major cities, leaving millions dead, injured and homeless.[3]

With the prospect of peace, the tide of humanity that had flowed from the coast to the interior started to turn. A rickshaw puller spelled out the meaning of Japan's capitulation after reading one of Chongqing's wall newspapers, mumbling, 'Japan is defeated. Can we go home now?' Across China's vast hinterland, millions of involuntary exiles began selling their makeshift furniture, preparing to trek back home and pick up the threads of their former lives, rebuilding families, homes and businesses. Along the banks of the Yangzi River, people searched for boats to float downstream; others pushed carts and trudged on foot in the scorching heat.[4]

The government, too, prepared to return home. The formal surrender ceremony between China and Japan took place on 21 August 1945 at the Zhijiang Airfield in Hunan. In the shade of a cherry tree, Major General Takeo Imai handed over a map showing the positions of his 1,000,000 troops in China. They were allowed to retain their arms and maintain public order until the arrival of nationalist troops, rushed to all the key cities south of the Great Wall in a spectacular sea-transport and airlift operation executed under the command of General Albert Wedemeyer, one of the most senior US military officers in East Asia. In the largest aerial troop movement of the Second World War, some 80,000 soldiers of the Sixth Army were flown to Nanjing to retake their erstwhile capital. In Shanghai, the shabbily clothed soldiers of the Ninety-Fourth Army who stepped out of giant transport aircrafts blinked at the sight of a large crowd waving banners on the runway. 'The peasant soldiers came timidly down the steep ladders, trying to salute, dazed by this overwhelming glimpse of the people they had come to liberate. The liberated wore silken gowns and leather shoes; the liberators' feet were dusty in straw sandals.'[5]

On the streets of Shanghai cheering crowds put up huge portraits of Chiang Kai-shek, decorated with garland flowers and crêpe paper. All along the coast, when troops of the national government entered the cities, 'multitudes of people lined the streets and shouted themselves hoarse to welcome their liberators'. A third army was flown to Beijing, as US air forces landed between 2,000 and 4,000 nationalist regulars daily in a race against the clock. By early November, the last Japanese south of the Great Wall were being rounded up and disarmed.[6]

But Chiang Kai-shek was not the only one making a claim on the territory of China. Two days after Hiroshima had been bombed, the Soviet Union declared war on Japan, keeping to a promise Joseph Stalin had made to Winston Churchill and Franklin D. Roosevelt at Yalta in February 1945. At the Soviet holiday resort on the Black Sea, Stalin had demanded control of the Manchurian seaports of Dalian and Port Arthur as well as joint control with China over Manchuria's railways in exchange for breaking his non-aggression pact with Japan. Roosevelt made these concessions without consulting his wartime ally Chiang Kai-shek. Stalin also requested two months' supply of food and fuel for an army of 1.5 million men. This, too, Roosevelt accepted, as hundreds of shiploads of lend-lease material were sent to Siberia, including 500 Sherman tanks.[7]

As a result, even as they raced to reach Berlin and occupy half of Europe before the Americans, the Soviets still managed to keep almost a million troops in Siberia. On 8 August 1945 they poured across the Amur River into Manchuria with tactical aircraft in support. Armoured trains carrying elite troops moved east along the Chinese Eastern Railway towards Harbin, making gains of up to 70 kilometres a day. A separate drive from Vladivostok was launched southwards into Korea, where the port of Rashin was soon captured. The Japanese had few aircraft and offered little effective opposition. Within days the Russians had won control of all strategic points in Manchuria.[8]

Not far away, a mere hundred kilometres south of the Great Wall, Mao Zedong was counting his troops. After several years of collaboration, a civil war had erupted between the communists and the nationalists in 1927, and in 1934 Mao Zedong and his supporters had been forced to retreat deep inland to evade Chiang Kai-shek's forces. A year later, some 20,000 survivors of the Long March had set up headquarters in land-locked Yan'an, far behind enemy lines, many of the troops living in cave dwellings. After a decade of consolidating his authority, Mao controlled some 900,000 guerrilla fighters in rural pockets across the north of China. He was ready to strike.

But Mao could be overly optimistic in his assessment of the balance of power. He had grandiose plans to incite a rebellion in Shanghai and take over the country's financial powerhouse. Impulsively, he ordered 3,000 undercover troops to enter the city and prepare for a general uprising, which, he hoped, would precipitate a revolution. When reports indicated that his forces were hopelessly outnumbered, with little popular support, he persisted with his strategy. Stalin intervened, telling him to restrain his troops and avoid open confrontations with the nationalists. Mao reluctantly agreed. As the Red Army occupied Manchuria, Mao came up with a new vision: his aim was now to link up with the Russians and claim a belt of territory reaching from Outer Mongolia across all of Manchuria. Four armed groups moved north, including 100,000 troops of the Eighth Route Army under the command of Lin Biao. They soon met up with the Red Army.[9]

But Stalin's immediate concern was to ensure the departure of the American military from China and Korea. The United States, after all, had a monopoly on the atom bomb and Stalin was wary of another world war. In order to achieve this goal, he openly proclaimed his support of the

Chinese National Government and in the Sino-Soviet Treaty recognised Chiang Kai-shek as the leader of a united China. On 20 August 1945, Stalin also sent a message to Mao asking that his troops avoid any open confrontation with the nationalists and consolidate their position in the countryside instead. Mao was obliged to reverse course.[10]

In a weak and divided China, a fearsome prospect unfolded: the Soviet Union could prop up the Chinese Communist Party, leading to the division of the country into a Russian-dominated north and an American-protected south. Negotiations between Stalin and Chiang Kai-shek resumed the day the Red Army invaded Manchuria. In Moscow, T. V. Soong, one of Chiang's most eminent statesmen, had few bargaining chips to put on the negotiating table. In his dealings with Stalin, he had to agree to the concessions Roosevelt had made at Yalta: Port Arthur, a natural harbour on the south tip of Manchuria, would become a Russian naval base, while the Soviets would use the modern port of Dalian on equal terms with China. The Soviet Union and China would co-own the South Manchurian Railway and the Chinese Eastern Railway, both built by imperial Russia. In exchange Stalin recognised the sovereignty of the Chinese National Government over all of China and pledged to turn Manchuria over to Chiang Kai-shek.

With the Sino-Soviet Treaty in his pocket and assured of Moscow's backing for his government, Chiang invited Mao to join peace negotiations and discuss the country's future. At considerable personal risk, Mao flew to Chongqing in the company of Patrick Hurley, the American ambassador. Chiang and Mao had not seen each other for twenty years, and put on contrived smiles at a formal reception held on the first night, toasting each other with millet wine. Mao stayed a full six weeks, wrangling for concessions even as pitched battles between the communists and the nationalists continued on the ground. Eventually, on 18 September, Mao proclaimed: 'We must stop [the] civil war and all parties must unite under the leadership of Chairman Chiang to build a modern China.' A formal statement was made on 10 October, the anniversary of the 1911 revolution that had led to the overthrow of the Qing empire. Back in Yan'an a few days later, Mao explained to his comrades-in-arms that the agreed statement in Chongqing was 'a mere scrap of paper'.[11]

Stalin had publicly given his support to Chiang, but he also wanted to strengthen the Chinese Communist Party as a check on the Chinese National Government – and its American backers. In August he allowed the communists to take over Kalgan. In the nineteenth century, caravans of camels regularly assembled from all over the empire in this key gateway through the Great Wall to carry tea chests to Russia. Kalgan was still called 'Beijing's Northern Door': whoever controlled the old city was in a strategic position to attack Beijing. The Japanese had turned it into an economic and industrial centre, and also left behind an enormous cache of ammunition and weapons, including sixty tanks.[12]

In other cities in Inner Mongolia and Manchuria, Soviet troops were instructed to equip communist units with Japanese arms and vehicles. The exact amount of logistical and military assistance the Soviets gave to the communists is difficult to estimate, but Moscow later claimed that 700,000 rifles, 18,000 machine guns, 860 aircraft and 4,000 artillery pieces were handed over. Behind the scenes, the Soviets recommended that the communists deploy most of their troops in Manchuria. Mao, still in Chongqing, ordered the main force of his guerrilla units to pour across the Great Wall into Manchuria in September. There, with Soviet acquiescence, the communists took in demobilised soldiers, puppet troops and bandit fighters. By the end of the year, Mao had managed to assemble a motley army of 500,000 troops.[13]

Chiang knew full well that the Soviets were co-operating with the communists in Manchuria, but he was in no position to quarrel with Stalin. He also understood the strategic and economic significance of Manchuria, with its steel mills, huge reserves of iron ore and coal, dense forests and rich farmland. He put General Du Yuming in charge of reclaiming the region. His troops were denied permission to land in Port Arthur and Dalian, now under Soviet control following the Sino-Soviet Treaty. When in October 1945 ships from the US Seventh Fleet sailed instead to Yingkou, a minor harbour with rail connections to the interior, they found a communist garrison. Disembarking further south at Qinhuangdao, General Du breached the Great Wall at Shanhaiguan and lunged forward along the railway, meeting little opposition from communist troops. He covered the 300 kilometres from the Great Wall to the industrial base of Shenyang in less than three weeks. Chiang pleaded with Moscow in the hope of being allowed at least to partition Manchuria. Under pressure to fulfil their commitments to the nationalist government, the Soviets relented and allowed nationalist troops to be airlifted into Changchun, further north along the railway from Shenyang.[14]

The reason for Soviet reluctance soon became apparent: cities had been subjected to a wave of looting by the Red Army. James McHugh, one of the first businessmen allowed into Shenyang, reported that the troops had been let loose 'for three days of rape and pillage'. They 'stole everything in sight, broke up bathtubs and toilets with hammers, pulled electric light wiring out of the plaster, built fires on the floor and either burned down the house or at least a big hole in the floor'. Women cut their hair and dressed like men in order to avoid rape. In Shenyang, 'factories lay like raddled skeletons, picked clean of their machinery'. The city, one reporter wrote, 'has been reduced from a great industrial city into a tragic, crowded way station on the Russian-controlled railway to Dairen [Dalian]'. The systematic plundering of Manchuria's industrial infrastructure would later be valued at US$2 billion.[15]

The Soviets delayed the withdrawal of their troops from Manchuria for five months, and the last of their tanks only rumbled across the border in April 1946. They handed the countryside over to the communists, and allowed Lin Biao to deploy his forces on the outskirts of all major cities. His Eighth Route Army, equipped with Japanese weapons, attacked the nationalist garrison in Changchun and killed most of its 7,000 soldiers. Harbin, Manchuria's ice city bordering Russia, was turned over to Mao on 28 April.

President Truman, instead of assisting his wartime ally Chiang Kai-shek, sent George Marshall to broker a coalition government between the nationalists and the communists. Chiang was dependent on continuing American economic and military assistance and had little choice but to acquiesce, even though the prospect of any lasting agreement between both camps seemed more remote than ever. The communists, on the other hand, had nothing to lose: they used the truce to regroup and expand ever further in Manchuria, entrenching themselves in the countryside away from major cities and the railways. The suave and unassuming Zhou Enlai,

Mao's envoy to the peace talks, was a master of deception, cultivating a close relationship with Marshall to present the communists as agrarian reformers keen to learn from democracy. Zhou even persuaded Mao solemnly to declare that 'Chinese democracy must follow the American path.' Mao would agree to almost anything on paper, as long as nobody was checking what he was doing on the ground. When the Red Army pulled out of Manchuria, Marshall came to believe that Stalin had given up on China. His willingness to help Chiang started to waver.[16]

Chiang realised that American support was slipping, but was determined to dislodge the communists from Changchun. His troops met little opposition. In early June 1946, Lin Biao and his army of 100,000 men beat a chaotic retreat towards the north. Chiang's New First and New Sixth Armies went in pursuit, harrying the communists across the Sungari River. Chiang's troops were now within striking distance of Harbin, the only city still in communist hands. Lin Biao's troops were in a state of collapse, as soldiers deserted in large numbers. When interviewed, Zhao Xuzhen, who was a soldier at the time, remembered that even military officers, party members and political instructors absconded in a chaotic retreat: 'some went home, some became bandits, and some surrendered.' But once again Marshall advised Chiang to halt the nationalist advance and proclaim a ceasefire. The American envoy had just visited Yan'an, where Mao had skilfully projected an image of liberal reform and democracy. Marshall even wrote to Truman that the communist forces in Manchuria were 'little more than loosely organised bands'.[17]

The communists used the peace talks to recondition their troops, integrate the 200,000-strong army that had served under the Japanese and recruit more soldiers from the countryside. Other recruits were prisoners of war, criminal elements, Korean units and Manchurian exiles returning from the Soviet Union. All were subjected to harsh training and ruthless discipline, often with the help of hundreds of Soviet technical advisers and military experts. The Russians even opened sixteen military institutions, including air force, artillery and engineering schools. Some Chinese officers went to the Soviet Union for advanced training, others were given refuge in the Russian enclaves of Port Arthur and Dalian. While the Soviets stripped much of Manchuria's wealth, they left the military arsenals of Dalian untouched. With the help of Japanese technicians and local workers, these were put to work, churning out bullets and shells by the million. Logistical support also continued to arrive across the borders, by rail and by air. In North Korea alone, a full 2,000 wagons were allocated to the task. In return, the Chinese communists sent shipments of more than a million tons of grain as well as other products across the border from Manchuria to Russia in 1947.[18]

While the Russians were helping the communists transform their ragtag army of guerrilla fighters into a formidable war machine, the Americans became so disillusioned with the nationalists that they started cutting off deliveries of armaments. As trainloads of equipment moved back and forth across the border between Manchuria and the Soviet Union, the United States began refusing to license military equipment for China, including sales for which the government had already paid. Then, in September 1946, Truman imposed an arms embargo. It lasted until July 1947 – when the nationalists were allowed to purchase a three-week supply of infantry ammunition.[19]

For a while the nationalists battled on, trying to hold on to the cities along the railway that cut through the extensive Manchurian plain, enclosed by heavily forested mountain ranges. In the ebb and flow of warfare, the nationalists lost several cities only to recapture them in bloody battles with retreating communist troops. These were no longer skirmishes in a guerrilla war: hundreds of thousands of troops clashed in giant confrontations that involved artillery and air support, often in temperatures that fell to minus 20 degrees Celsius. Manchuria, by 1947, was turning into a death trap. Chiang kept on pouring his best troops into Manchuria, but Mao never let up, determined to wear down his enemy in a pitiless war of attrition. In Manchuria alone the communists recruited or conscripted approximately 1 million men. In battle after battle, Chiang's best government troops were destroyed. The nationalists also suffered from poor morale, their troops ensconced in cities for months on end, badly paid and without adequate provisions. Supply lines were extended to breaking point, running through the Great Wall along the Beijing–Changchun railway, which was often sabotaged by communist demolition squads. Military equipment was worn out, and in some cases soldiers were so short of ammunition that they could not fire a single practice shot. Lorries were for the most part broken down, but could not be repaired as the sale of spare parts was prohibited under the arms embargo.[20]

———

As Zhang Junmai, a veteran diplomat, campaigner for parliamentary democracy and unsparing critic of the nationalist government, later noted, even if an efficient government had existed it would have been no match for the combined forces of Moscow and Yan'an. But Chiang's government barely functioned. The nationalists faced a mammoth task in taking over a country the size of a continent, and one that had been laid waste by eight years of warfare. Even south of the Great Wall, they endured constant harassment from guerrilla troops: the communists plundered towns, looted villages and left behind millions of homeless people. They controlled large parts of the countryside in Hebei and Shandong, cutting off fuel, energy and food supplies to the cities and feeding inflation. Transport, the key to recovery, had been gravely impaired by the Japanese and was now shattered by the communists, who blew up railways and dynamited bridges. In pitiless partisan warfare, everything that tore society apart operated to the communists' advantage.[21]

Most of all, the nationalists were caught in a vicious cycle that predated their clash with the communists. Ever since Japan had invaded China in 1937, they had been unable to finance the war by selling bonds. Taxation covered only a small portion of the cost of the war. The only way forward was to issue paper currency. This meant that the brunt of the war effort fell on the middle class, undermining the standard of living of people on fixed incomes such as schoolteachers, college professors, government employees and, of course, nationalist soldiers and officers. 'In 1940, 100 yuan bought a pig; in 1943, a chicken; in 1945, a fish; in 1946, an egg; and in 1947, one-third of a box of matches.' By 1947 the cost of living was approximately 30,000 times what it had been in 1936, a year before Japan attacked China. Chiang tried to tame inflation in 1947 by banning the export of foreign currency and gold bullion, imposing a ceiling on interest rates and freezing all wages, but these measures had no lasting effect. By 1949 people could be seen wheeling their money in carts.[22]

For army officers or tax collectors alike, the salaries of government employees were held down to extraordinarily low levels. Soldiers were grossly underpaid, and even officers could not support their wives and children on their regular income. Graft, embezzlement and corruption therefore became rampant in many forms. Tax collectors accepted bribes. The police extorted money by threatening the poor with arrest and imprisonment. In the army, officers withheld salaries, inflated the bills or sold military equipment on the black market. There was no easy solution to the problem. Raising government salaries would have increased inflation, which in turn would have affected the cost of living, leading quickly to the absorption of salary rises and the reappearance of corruption.

The nationalists needed help. They required financial assistance to curb inflation, rebuild the country and buy arms and munitions. Beginning in April 1948, the Marshall Plan, designed by the very man who had tried against all odds to engineer a coalition between Chiang Kai-shek and the communists, provided US$13 billion in economic and technical assistance to help the recovery of Europe. This sum did not include the $12 billion in aid that Europe had received between the end of the war and the start of the Plan. Even after Truman had been obliged to abandon the arms embargo on China, which was no longer consistent with the Truman Doctrine – proclaimed by the president in March 1947 and committing the United States to supporting Greece and Turkey with economic and military aid to prevent their falling under Soviet influence – support for the nationalists was minimal. The United States failed to deliver a paltry $125 million of military help in time even after a Republican majority finally pushed Congress to provide an aid package, which was only passed in April 1948, bringing the total military aid received by China after Victory over Japan Day to something between $225 and $360 million.[23]

The tide turned in 1948. For months on end the communists had launched one assault after another in Manchuria, continually hammering the nationalist-held cities. Chiang, determined to hold on at all costs, kept on pouring more troops into the region to make up for the dead and wounded. The loss of Manchuria, he confided in his private journal, would open all of north China to the communists. He was staking everything he had on one huge gamble rather than retreating and holding the line along the Great Wall.[24]

In December 1947, in more than a metre of snow and a temperature of minus 35 degrees Celsius, Lin Biao launched a massive assault across the frozen Sungari River. The People's Liberation Army, as the communist troops now called themselves, had no air cover, but a thick, icy mist and glacial weather severely limited the nationalists' use of aeroplanes. Pressing their military advantage, most of the 400,000 troops swarmed south and laid siege to the cities along the railway, destroying several government divisions.[25]

Shenyang, just south of Changchun, was Manchuria's stronghold, and one of the country's best arsenals. Lin Biao cut the railway between Beijing and Shenyang and laid siege to the city. Inside this island of dwindling resistance, a civilian population of 1.2 million, swollen to 4 million by people fleeing the communists, was blockaded for ten months. Also trapped were 200,000 nationalist soldiers. Droves of people soon abandoned beleaguered Shenyang. Planes of General Claire Chennault's commercial airline shuttled in and out, evacuating about 1,500 passengers to safety each day, but few could afford to bribe their way on board. Fights broke out at the airfield, as the crack of artillery could be heard in the distance. At night people huddled together in a bomb-blasted hangar. The majority, over 100,000 a month, left by train, rattling west towards the edge of the city's defence perimeter where the line came to an end.[26]

People who were too poor or too sick to leave were soon starving. As early as February, Shenyang was short of food, fuel and ammunition. Vitamin deficiencies caused thousands to go blind, while countless others, many of them children, were wasted by noma, a gangrenous disease that destroyed the face, by pellagra, by scurvy and by other diseases of malnutrition. As a foreign reporter noted: 'I walked down the desolate streets past the emaciated bodies of the dead in the gutters, pursued by unbearably pitiful child beggars and women crying out for help.' Shops along empty streets were boarded up, the red-brick factories standing derelict, many of them bombed during the war and then looted by Soviet troops in 1946. People survived by eating bark and leaves and by pressing soybean cakes, normally used as fertiliser or as cattle fodder. Others picked through the debris on the streets.[27]

A flood of misery poured out of Manchuria – refugees escaping from beleaguered cities, farmers fleeing a bloodied countryside, most of them stumbling forward on foot, a few hobbling on crutches or sticks. In the summer of 1948, some 140,000 pressed their way through the military lines around Shenyang and joined the exodus every month. Then they had to trek across a stretch of wilderness infested with armed gangs who capitalised on the chaos of civil war. But an even greater danger loomed 30 kilometres north of Jinzhou, where the railway crossed the Daling River. The nationalists stood guard on the opposite shore, and fired on anybody who tried to wade, swim or take a boat towards them. The only way across the river was through the twisted girders of the blasted railway bridge. For a fee, local guides would strap the refugees on their backs with rope and pick a passage over the broken bridge, their human burden looking down in terror at the swirling waters far below. From Jinzhou they were packed on refugee trains to Shanhaiguan, where the Great Wall dipped into the Bohai Sea. Here they found a makeshift refugee centre serviced by a single tap with running water. Many people quickly moved on to Beijing and Tianjin, even though few could be housed or adequately fed.[28]

The coup de grâce came in September 1948. Lin Biao staged a frontal attack on Shenyang and deployed close to 300,000 men to encircle Jinzhou, the lifeline to Manchuria. Military engineers blew holes in the city walls. After sustaining 34,000 casualties, Jinzhou fell on 15 October, its remaining 88,000 prisoners being marched off by the People's Liberation Army. A rescue force of 90,000 men, hacking its way through enemy lines outside Shenyang, walked straight into a trap: they were outnumbered and crushed a week later by Lin Biao. In Changchun, the remaining 80,000 troops handed over the city to the communists. Fighting continued in Shenyang for a week, often in bloody hand-to-hand combat inside the city after the walls had been demolished by artillery fire. When the senior remaining officer surrendered on 1 November, the battle for Manchuria was over.[29]

———

Overnight prices in Shanghai rose four- or fivefold. On the international market the gold yuan sank to a tenth of its original value. A wave of defeatism swept nationalist China. The United States began to ship out the wives and children of its military personnel and advised its citizens as far south as Nanjing and Shanghai to evacuate the area. All over the country panic set in, as an army of 750,000 communist fighters, reinforced with tanks, heavy artillery and other weapons captured from the nationalists, marched across the frozen plains of Manchuria through the Great Wall in a southward thrust against Beijing.

General Fu Zuoyi, the nationalist commander in the north, stood little chance as the communists swiftly moved to cut the railway lifelines along the Northern Corridor, which stretched from Kalgan to the port of Dagu. They surrounded Tianjin, China's third largest city, in November 1948, and soon forced Fu Zuoyi to pull his troops back inside the walls of Beijing. Lin Biao drew a siege ring around the city and cut off electricity and water supplies. Within a week the airfields outside the city walls were in communist hands. Soon a strange silence set in over the imperial capital, only occasionally disturbed by shell explosions or machine-gun bursts. At first Fu, one of the most distinguished military leaders in the war against Japan, seemed determined to defend Beijing. Trenches were dug and street barricades hastily erected as soldiers went from house to house commandeering billets. To allow cargo planes to deliver supplies, an airstrip was built on the polo ground of the old legation quarter, in the very heart of the ancient city. In the freezing winter, gangs of padded-gowned forced labour pulled down telephone poles, trees and even buildings on the approach to the runway. Martial rule was imposed. Lorries with teams of policemen and soldiers carrying sub-machine guns and broad swords careened through the streets, reminding the population of their military presence. Outside the city walls, thousands of homes were needlessly levelled, ostensibly to provide a good field of fire for the defending troops.[30]

But everybody in Beijing knew what had happened to Changchun, turned into a 'city of death' by the very general who was now camping outside the city walls. Fu Zuoyi fell into a depression, tormented by the prospect of seeing Beijing, the cultural heart of China, desecrated for no good reason. At first he asked Chiang for permission to resign, but when the Generalissimo refused, he resumed the secret negotiations he had opened with the People's Liberation Army through his daughter, who was a member of the communist party. After a forty-day siege, a surrender document was signed on 22 January 1949. All of the 240,000 troops under Fu were absorbed into the communist army. The treatment that he and his troops received served as an inducement to other nationalist commanders and officers to defect.[31]

For eight days the imperial capital seemed to float in a twilight zone, as the nationalists, some of them still armed, wandered about the city freely as it awaited the communists. Very little changed. In this strange vacuum, Beijing celebrated the Chinese New Year as best it could. Shops were crammed with lanterns traditionally placed outside front doors to welcome the New Year – in the shape of lions, brilliant green rabbits or yellow tigers. But Chiang Kai-shek's portrait on Tiananmen Square was removed.

On 31 January 1949 a vanguard of the People's Liberation Army finally entered the west gates of Beijing. A lorry opened the procession, its loudspeakers blaring the continuous refrain, 'Welcome to the Liberation Army on its Arrival in Beiping! Welcome to the People's Army on its Arrival in Beiping! Congratulations to the People of Beiping on their Liberation!' Then came the soldiers, marching six abreast in full battle regalia, red-cheeked and seemingly in high spirits. Students followed the soldiers, carrying two large portraits, one of Mao Zedong, the other of Zhu De, commander-in-chief of the army. A military band, more soldiers and government employees closed the parade. Most of Beijing was relieved to have survived the siege, but people were cautious with the soldiers, 'watching them from the kerbs along their route [and] expressing no emotion more intense than curiosity'. Scattered nationalist troops looked on in silence. Jia Ke, then a young communist soldier, remembers that 'Everyone crowded around our boys as they sat quietly on the ground. They wanted to get a good look at us. They were very curious. I felt very proud.'[32]

The communists had fervent supporters. Dan Ling, a schoolboy of sixteen, was one of them. All classes were cancelled on liberation day, and Dan was among those selected to carry either a banner flag or a star-shaped paper lantern on a sorghum stem to welcome the People's Liberation Army. He joined the crowd with his fellow students at Xidan, an important shopping area a kilometre west of Tiananmen Square. As the crowd swelled with thousands of curious onlookers, the students were pushed back and forth and soon became separated. Dan tried to elbow his way forward but did not manage to catch even a glimpse of the parade. Abandoning his flag, by now torn to shreds, he spotted a trolley bus and climbed on board, the conductor too distracted by the spectacle to notice that he did not have a ticket. His face pressed against the window, Dan saw the rifles, the bayonets, the bandoliers and the simple but neat uniforms devoid of rank insignia. He witnessed the discipline of the troops and was filled with joy.[33]

On Tiananmen Square, a hastily sketched portrait of Mao Zedong was raised. Mao himself only entered the city several months later, driving to the Summer Palace on the outskirts in a bullet-proof Dodge limousine made in Detroit for Chiang Kai-shek's personal use in the 1930s.[34]

While the Northern Corridor was being annexed by Lin Biao, an even more bloody campaign was in progress near Xuzhou. As in Manchuria and in the north, the war hinged on control of the country's arterial railways. Xuzhou was a vital junction where the trunk line running from Beijing southward to Nanjing intersected with the only east–west railway, meandering from the country's far west to the Yellow Sea. Xuzhou was the key to Nanjing, the nationalist capital, as well as to the prosperous Yangzi Valley.

In November 1948 over a million men surged towards Xuzhou in one of the greatest battles in Chinese history, also known as the Huaihai campaign. On their march out of Manchuria, the communists fielded a force of almost 400,000 men who marched past Beijing in the rush towards Xuzhou. Another 200,000 swept in from the neighbouring province of Shandong, where guerrilla fighters controlled large parts of the countryside. The nationalists deployed 400,000 troops in the flat, rich, water-laced plains around the railway junction. The bald and stocky General Chen Yi, commander of the communist troops, swiftly cut all railway lines and subjected the main airfield to artillery bombardment. Du Yuming, the general who had fought Lin Biao in Manchuria, desperately moved his men over rutted roads and torn-up rail tracks to establish a new line of defence to the east of the city, using the autumn floods to defend the swampy ground to the north and north-west.[35]

Fighting in the countryside was ferocious, as both sides battled for the country's heartland. Nationalists and communists deployed tanks and heavy artillery, while government planes controlled the skies, using cloud-less days and nights to wreak havoc on the enemy. Ancient towns with moats and walls were pounded. Orange flashes of shell explosions came from villages caught in the crossfire, leaving behind nothing but wrecked houses, smouldering amid fields sown with winter wheat. In a village just north of Caolaoji, everything had been set ablaze by mortar shells. Amid the smell of burned thatch and straw, children and women poked forlornly through roofless huts and blackened walls. On a slope in front of the ruins, an old woman bundled up in a black padded jacket rocked in silent grief. All her belongings had been lost. As one communist general later remi-nisced, the People's Liberation Army wiped out village after village with blanket shelling: 'In fighting Du Yuming, we practically flattened the villages, using thousands of shells and countless bombs.' A returning pilot reported that every village in sight was burning: 'the fields were covered with bodies'.[36]

The communists were supported by some 5 million men and women, sometimes even children, conscripted by a tough party leader called Deng Xiaoping: he imposed strict quotas for each village and threatened severe punishment when his orders were not met. These pick-and-shovel crews not only provided logistical support, carrying food and material on their backs to the front, but they were also used as human shields, forced to march in front of the troops. Dense waves of unarmed villagers over-whelmed the nationalists. Lin Jingwu, an ordinary soldier in the trenches, remembered years later that his hands went numb from firing bullets into a sea of civilians. He felt sick at the idea of firing at them and tried to close his eyes, but kept on shooting.[37]

People fled the rust-red plain in droves. Trains packed with refugees rattled past the bodies of men, women and children lying beside the tracks, 'looking like rag dolls'. They had lost their grip and slipped at night from the tops of trains after their hands froze from the cold. The lucky ones – women in ragged tunics with babies on their backs, men clutching bundles of their remaining possessions – had tied themselves to the train roofs. Others were jammed between the carriages.[38]

Xuzhou was a repeat of Shenyang: uncoordinated troop movements, a confused command structure, constant meddling by the Generalissimo, inaccurate field intelligence and low morale among the soldiers created a disaster. Under relentless fire, the nationalists soon retreated inside Xuzhou, becoming entirely dependent on airdrops to stay alive. They quickly ran out of food. Horses were slaughtered, while civilians scoured the streets for bark and roots. Just outside the city walls, women and children in small villages caught between enemy lines froze to death in their mud huts as there was no fuel for fires. Evacuation planes flying back to Shanghai were crammed with soldiers 'dying in their blood and excrement', in the words of one pilot. Panic set in as rumours spread that Chiang had ordered the city to be bombed to prevent any equipment from falling into enemy hands. One by one, the trapped divisions surrendered, as communist loudspeakers boomed out offers of food and shelter. Du Yuming, disguised as an ordinary soldier, was captured as he tried to slip away. By 10 January 1949 the battle was over. The communists had dealt a fatal blow to the nationalists.[39]

———

Once the north had surrendered, the demise of the nationalists was a foregone conclusion. The communists issued a harsh eight-point proposal for peace on 14 January 1949. Two weeks later, a defeated Chiang Kai-shek, for twenty-two years the dominant figure in China, stepped down. Clad in a simple khaki uniform without insignia, from a small drawing room in the Ministry of National Defence in Nanjing he read a formal statement handing over the peace talks to his vice-president.[40]

But it was too little, too late. Everywhere people were apathetic, beaten down by inflation and heavy taxes, sometimes even openly hostile to the nationalists. Despite a muzzled press, the abuses of an increasingly repressive regime were widely reported. The brutal methods used by the police in the hunt for underground agents in particular alienated large sections of the urban population. A powerful propaganda machine presided over by Zhou Enlai mercilessly exploited every failing of the nationalist regime. In this war of images, the communists managed to project a vision of democracy and social reform, largely because nobody besides a few visiting journalists on guided tours ever managed to spend time in their home territory. But, most of all, people were tired of war. After more than a decade of fear and violence, they craved peace at any cost, even under communism.

The communists, meanwhile, used the peace negotiations to rest and regroup. Along the village roads north of the Yangzi River a steady stream of wheelbarrows and donkey carts were building up food reserves. Engines were being dismounted from lorries and installed on river craft. By the end of March close to a million troops swarmed along the north bank of the river that divided the northern and southern halves of China.

As the communists prepared to cross the Yangzi and take all of China, the British government sent a naval sloop from Shanghai to rescue its citizens stranded in Nanjing, the capital on the south bank of the river. The *Amethyst*, with a five-metre Union Jack painted on each side of its grey steel hull, looked like a quaint reminder of a bygone age, when foreign gunboats policed the waters of the Yangzi. Midway between Shanghai and Nanjing, two artillery shells from the north bank hit the sloop. Crippled, it swung helplessly with the current and ran aground on a mud bank. Two white flags were hoisted but the shelling continued for days on end, killing forty-four sailors. The Royal Navy frigate remained trapped for ten weeks before it managed to slip its chain and escape, as the communists demanded that Britain, the United States and France withdraw their armed forces from all of China. Mao saw in the *Amethyst* the perfect symbol of old China and ordered his troops to 'brook no foreign interference'. The attack on the Royal Navy made headlines around the world. Mao was delighted.[41]

The *Amethyst* incident put foreigners in Shanghai on alert. A few days later the communist troops started their final campaign. Nanjing offered only token resistance as the People's Liberation Army crammed junks, sampans and launches to cross the Yangzi to the sound of bugle calls and martial music. The city was already weakened by large-scale defections of soldiers. Looting by civilians was rampant. In the bustling commercial district of Fuzimiao, shabbily dressed men, women and children pillaged in a good-humoured way, laughing and shouting to each other as they hauled sofas, carpets and bedding from the upper floors of the two-storey villas to the lawns below. 'A grinning soldier, who had thrown away his rifle, gingerly carried off a lamp in each hand. An old woman, her grey hair pulled back in a bun, wearing a ragged black tunic and hobbling away on tiny feet, bound in the old custom, happily carried off four elaborately embroidered cushions.' Everything down to the sash windows and plumbing fixtures was stripped from the Ministry of Communications. The floorboards were broken up for firewood. Crowds besieged the airport, trying to force or bribe their way on to planes, while soldiers swung their bayoneted rifles to keep them at bay. A nationalist general barked orders at underlings loading a grand piano aboard an aircraft.[42]

With darkness came fear, as the mood on the streets turned ugly. Shooting could be heard in the distance, and then loud explosions rocked the capital. Fire turned the skies deep red, as departing soldiers set alight ammunition and fuel dumps on the banks of the river. In a dilapidated hotel, members of a Peace Preservation Committee sat around small tables drinking tea and composing slogans to welcome the communists: they were in charge of the city and its million civilians, churning out posters appealing to the population to preserve order.[43]

On 23 April columns of PLA soldiers entered the city, sweating in their padded uniforms. The following day they could be seen sitting in orderly formations on their sleeping bags along the pavements, listening to political instructions from their cadres or singing revolutionary songs. Curious crowds gathered to stare at them or bring them hot water, poured into the mugs the soldiers carried on their belts. Neatly dressed students – earnest young men and women – came out of their dormitories, cheering the arrival of the troops, although most of the soldiers ignored them: they were worlds apart. In the Presidential Palace, Chen Yi and Deng Xiaoping took turns sitting in Chiang Kai-shek's chair.[44]

Once the communists had poured across the Yangzi, China's last great defensive barrier, they moved with great speed. Nanjing was taken in four days. Wuhan, the commercial and industrial centre on the middle Yangzi, soon followed. With a rapid eastward thrust towards the coast, they cut the Shanghai–Guangzhou railway. Shanghai, China's financial powerhouse, was isolated. 'Shanghai will be China's Stalingrad,' vowed the general appointed to defend the city. But most people in the permissive city revered as the 'Paris of the East', dreading the destruction a long siege would bring, hoped that the promise would not be kept.[45]

Shanghai's main defence was a wooden fence, 50 kilometres long, made from stakes cut out of lumber originally delivered by a United Nations relief agency. Inside the city a sense of false calm prevailed, as it continued to pulsate with a boisterous life that seemed to deny the approach of the communists. Gambling proceeded apace in the clubs, cabarets and bars along the Bund. On impeccably manicured lawns, British expatriates continued to play cricket or sip their pink gins in the afternoon sun. At Duke Lear's, the Tango or the Rainbow, hostesses perched on bar stools or slouched in armchairs seemed oblivious of the blockade. And despite inflation, everybody seemed to be trading, whether in dollars, in gold bars or by barter.

In an effort to avoid the looting that had taken place in Nanjing, martial law was declared. Firing squads executed suspected communist agents, black marketeers and other culprits on the outskirts of the city. Before the victims were lined up and shot in the back of the head by the nationalists, they were paraded through Shanghai's busy streets, standing on the back of a lorry with white placards explaining their crimes. Elsewhere, on outlying roads, hundreds of labourers were conscripted to throw up machine-gun emplacements, barbed-wire entanglements and earthworks. At sandbagged sentry posts along main intersections, soldiers poked their bayonets into the bags and bundles of refugees entering the city. A Victory Parade was organised to boost morale, as lorries raced through the streets with workers and students shouting their allegiance to Chiang Kai-shek. From the top floor of Broadway Mansions, Shanghai's tallest apartment building, tenants could see sharp flashes of cannon fire across the Huangpu River. The glow of burning villages appeared further to the north. Here and there tracer shells streaked lines of red across the horizon.[46]

As Chen Yi and his soldiers moved closer into nearby farming areas, fresh vegetables disappeared from the wet markets and sidewalk stands. The siege also forced fishermen to keep their boats idle at the docks. The price of yellow croaker, the city's most popular staple, jumped six times in one day before the fish vanished altogether from the stalls. Crowds thronged around the rice shops, anxious about spiralling inflation and dwindling supplies. The mayor publicly appealed to everyone to plant victory gardens.[47]

After a weary wait of several weeks, Shanghai fell to the communists on 25 May. Barely a shot was fired, as the business community and the triads had quietly switched sides. The nationalists were seen in full retreat, some of the troops marching almost in parade formation, others streaking through the city in terror and confusion, caked with mud from the battle-field. In the red-light district, fleeing soldiers desperately searched the shops for second-hand clothing; the streets were strewn with discarded uniforms. A day later, in the middle of the night, small groups of soldiers under Chen Yi's command began filtering through the French Concession in the south-west. Then they advanced cautiously down the pavements of Avenue Joffre and Great Western Road, hugging buildings closely for protection against the occasional fire from isolated nationalist snipers. By the morning they had reached the Bund.

Shanghai heaved a sigh of relief. There was no looting, raping or requisi-tioning. As in other cities, the soldiers were on their best behaviour, sleeping on the pavement and refusing even offers of water from sympathetic resi-dents. They seemed more like an army of adolescents than the surly, bellicose soldiers portrayed in anti-communist propaganda. Mariano Ezpeleta, the consul-general of the Philippines, was struck by their youth:

> Here they were, the Communist soldiers – mostly teenagers in the first blush of youth, slightly built boys still awkward in gait; others, almost adult country bumpkins trying to steady themselves first on one foot, then on the other. They stood on street crossings, casually held their carbine at rest, looking around open-eyed, obviously bewildered by the ornate and magnificent buildings of the city. One could mistake them for curious cadets from some rural inland town learning their primary lessons in the art of sentinel duty.[48]

Newspapers carried stories on the good behaviour of the soldiers. The *Impartial Daily* in Shanghai trumpeted: 'Public transportation facilities have been restored, and there is not a single soldier of the Liberation Army

who rides the vehicles without buying a ticket, and there are no attempts
to disturb the ordinary queues in order to have prior access to the vehicles.'
Similar stories were widely reported and offered reassurance to apprehensive city dwellers.[49]

The population were relieved. They continued to call the soldiers derogatory names and circulated yokel jokes about them. One anecdote
described a team who found a white porcelain toilet and tried to wash rice
in it. A soldier pulled the rope attached to the cistern, only to look on
aghast as the rice vanished with the bubbles in the bowl. At the opulent
Cathay Hotel, country bumpkins played with the elevators and tied
up their mules in the lobby. Not all such tales were inventions. Feng
Bingxing, a veteran who was twenty-five years old when he marched into
Shanghai, remembered: 'We tried to light cigarettes with light bulbs and
wash rice in toilet bowls. You know, many of our officers and soldiers came
from rural areas and hadn't seen such things when we first arrived in
Shanghai.'[50]

Within a day banners went up near the American Club, proclaiming
'Welcome to the People's Liberation Army'. A huge portrait of Mao
Zedong was hoisted over the Great World Amusement Centre, Shanghai's seething six-floor recreational building. Red flags fluttered over
shop doorways, and lorries decked with red banners carried students and
workers jubilantly waving pennants. Even as machine guns still rattled in
the distance, communist songs blared from loudspeakers in the city
centre. One day after Shanghai's fall, trams and buses started running
again in parts of the city. Their new allegiance indicated by red armbands,
policemen were back on the streets directing traffic. 'On street corners,
hawkers clinked their wares once more, and sidewalk vegetable stands,
bare for almost a week, filled up again quickly with produce from the
countryside.'[51]

———

With Nanjing and Shanghai under communist control, those nationalist
troops who had not yet surrendered continued their withdrawal further
south. Guangzhou, the commercial hub and southern port near colonial
Hong Kong, was the city where Sun Yat-sen had first set up a nationalist

government after the fall of the empire in 1911. Most of the generals fighting each other in the civil war had been trained at the Whampoa Military
Academy, established in 1924. For a few brief weeks, Guangzhou became
a boom town, seat of the provisional capital of the nationalists. Officials of
the Soviet Union, the first foreign legation to flee when communist troops
approached Nanjing, were ensconced on the sixth floor of the Oi Kwan
Hotel, a modern art deco building towering high above the Bund. The
tenth floor housed American diplomats. The nationalists took up most of
the other floors as their headquarters. Further down the Bund, on Shameen
Island, government officials bought up plush Western-style homes shaded
by banyan trees. As new arrivals vied for the few remaining houses and
apartments, cash deposits for a tiny two-room flat shot up to US$4,000.
On the outskirts of the city, the poor lived in shoddy houses thrown up
almost overnight. The city was creaking under the extra load of a mush-
rooming population.[52]

The boom was brief. After a pause of a few weeks the communists
resumed their march. When Guangzhou fell on 14 October 1949, 'with
scarcely more than a quiet sigh', the communists completed a 3,500-kilo-
metre march that had started with the fall of Changchun one year earlier.[53]
After a hasty and chaotic retreat to Chongqing, on 10 December Chiang
Kai-shek flew to Taiwan, never to return.

———

As the communists drove south towards Guangzhou, another army
followed the railway west of Xuzhou. Ahead lay a vast borderland with
frontiers that touched on Tibet, India, Afghanistan, the Soviet Union and
the People's Republic of Mongolia. The region was sparsely populated by
some 13 million people, less than 3 per cent of the estimated total in
China. Deserts, mountains, steppes and lakes formed a harsh but beautiful
landscape, hiding valuable resources in oil, coal, gold, wolfram, uranium
and other rare-earth metals. A Muslim belt ran through the north-west,
with mosques located in all major settlements where Arabic was used in
religious services. One visitor noted in 1948: 'The men's skull caps and the
women's hoods are identifying marks, of course, but their facial features
are quite recognizable also. Their noses are larger and their eyes rounder

than those of the typical Chinese, and the men wear luxuriant beards which are distinctive because of their bushy sideburns.'[54]

Many other groups contributed to an extremely heterogeneous population, nowhere more so than in Xinjiang, the westernmost province bordering on Central Asia. In this grazing land cut up by vast deserts and snow-capped mountains, waves of invasion and migration had left behind Uighurs, Kazaks, Chinese, Taranchis, Kirghiz, Mongols, White Russians, Uzbeks, Tajiks, Tatars and Manchus, among others. The Uighurs, 'with their many-coloured, embroidered skull caps, jackets and leather boots', were by far the most dominant group in Xinjiang, accounting for three-quarters of a population of 4 million. Relations between these different people could be bitter, at times violent, in particular in the nineteenth century when revolts against the Qing empire had flared up and obliged the Manchus to reconquer the entire region. Not until 1884 was Xinjiang fully incorporated into the empire.[55]

The north-west had some of the most efficient provincial regimes in the country, a stark contrast to what happened elsewhere under the nationalists. Ma Bufang, a trim, burly Muslim general, used an authoritarian hand to transform Qinghai, lining the smooth, metalled highways with willow and poplar saplings, cleaning up the cities, irrigating the countryside and building hospitals and medical facilities. In Xining, the capital, one-third of the population went to school; food, clothing and tuition were provided free to all students. Qinghai thrived when most of China was crushed by civil war.[56]

But Ma Bufang was no match for the army that was moving along the railway from Xuzhou. Peng Dehuai, a stout man with a shaven head and the face of a bulldog, led some 150,000 troops against Ma's cavalry of 40,000 armed Muslim horsemen, dashing all nationalist hopes in the region. Lanzhou, the gateway to the north-west on the ancient silk road, fell in August 1949, leading to communist control of the Yumen oilfields.

Xinjiang was soon within reach. It had a troubled history of ethnic strife, made no easier by a significant Soviet presence. In exchange for trading privileges and concessions for oilwells, tin and wolfram mines, Soviet forces had repeatedly helped Sheng Shicai, governor of the province from 1933 to 1944, to repress local rebellions. In November 1940 the Soviet

Union, which needed a buffer state against Japan, took virtual control of the region. Sheng Shicai, who feared that Xinjiang might otherwise share the fate of Poland, invaded and carved up several years earlier by Stalin and Hitler, signed an agreement granting additional concessions for fifty years. At the end of the war, Chiang Kai-shek successfully negotiated an end to the Soviet presence in Xinjiang as part of the Sino-Soviet Treaty. He also compromised with the Kazaks and Uighurs, agreeing to a coalition government in which the nationalists shared power with representatives of the Eastern Turkestan Republic, a political entity established by rebels with Soviet assistance in the northern part of the province.

The communists subdued Xinjiang through a combination of conquest and negotiation. First Mao Zedong invited five of the key leaders of the Eastern Turkestan Republic to Beijing to attend a Political Consultative Conference. On 22 August 1949 Stalin ordered them to co-operate with Mao. Two days later, they boarded a plane in Kazakhstan and headed for Beijing. The plane crashed near Lake Baikal, killing all on board. Speculation was rife, some suspecting that they had been liquidated on Stalin's orders in a secret deal brokered with Mao. The remaining leaders agreed to include their republic within the province of Xinjiang and accepted key positions in the new People's Republic of China. Then, in October, Peng Dehuai surrounded Urumqi, the provincial capital, forcing the nationalists to surrender. Xinjiang was liberated, but by now Peng was running out of steam. On 29 December 1949 he wrote to Mao to explain that he was bankrupt and could no longer feed his troops. 'I reckon that huge help from the Soviet Union is indispensable in solving our present difficulties and in the future building of Xinjiang.' Within weeks Soviet traders, engineers and advisers were swarming all over the region. Convoys of lorries with Russian troops in full winter clothing rumbled through the streets of Urumqi by night.[57]

Tibet had to wait for its liberation. Lhasa expelled a nationalist delegation in July 1949 and a few months later sent a letter to the US State Department indicating that it intended to defend itself by 'all possible means' against communist intrusion. Copies of the letter were sent to London and Beijing. Beijing waited. Negotiations were opened. Offers were made. As Lhasa deliberated, 40,000 communist troops entered Tibet

on 7 October 1950, striking towards the 4,000-metre passes into the bleak
Tibetan plateau. They wiped out all armed opposition at Chamdo, placing
the weak theocratic government under their control. India, independent
since 1947, had just recognised the People's Republic. Prime Minister
Jawaharlal Nehru had championed communist China, assuring the world
that the Tibetan issue would be settled peacefully. Now China controlled
all the major passes through the Himalayas into India and Nepal. Britain
remained neutral, having lost interest in the region as a buffer zone since
India had become independent. The United Nations did not intervene:
they had their hands full with the Korean War.[58]

The communists had now successfully established their borders along
the territory reached by the Qing empire at the end of the nineteenth
century. Just as the Bolsheviks inherited a realm conquered by the tsars, so
the communists could now start building on the empire won by the
Manchus. Only Hong Kong and Taiwan still eluded the reach of the
People's Republic.[59]

PART TWO

TAKEOVER (1949–52)

3

Liberation

Liberation began with fanfare. Communist rule in every important town was inaugurated with a carefully choreographed procession. Soldiers invariably opened the parade, followed by a lorry bearing a huge portrait of Mao Zedong. Dance troupes dressed in blue, red and green dresses and silk scarves, waving red flags and wearing white-towel turbans, performed a traditional harvest dance called 'rice-sprout song' (*yangge*), swaying their bodies to the music played by waist drums, heavy gongs and trumpets. The fluid dance movements were supposed to celebrate peasants in daily activities such as sowing grain or carrying water with shoulder poles. Here, it seemed, was a form of art by the people for the people, to be seen in every procession and at every meeting.

Even in the north, where the rice-sprout song was popular, ordinary farmers would have been puzzled by the way the troupes performed the folk dance. Some of the melodies no longer had anything to do with local folksong but were borrowed instead from the Soviet army. The traditional lyrics, like folk plays everywhere in the world, were often bawdy and downright obscene, telling stories of love and betrayal, but now they celebrated the abolition of the unequal treaties and the victory of the People's Liberation Army. The traditionally complex dance steps had been simplified into three or four basic movements. A cast of traditional characters, from fortune-tellers and henpecked husbands to priests, squires and immortals, were replaced by workers, soldiers and peasants. But in many parts of China traditional rice-sprout songs meant little to ordinary people. In Xi'an, spectators were unable to identify any of the characters in the parade, as they had nothing to do with local opera. 'The only thing that was the same was the ear-splitting banging of the gongs and drums, which reverberated throughout the city so often that most days seemed like New Year's, an audible sign that times had changed.' Many onlookers, nonetheless, enjoyed the festivities, as the celebratory sounds announced the end of war.[1]

In the large cities along the coast, these political rallies were much bigger affairs. On 6 July 1949 tanks and howitzers rumbled up Nanking Road, the heart of the shopping district in Shanghai, followed by armies of workers thrusting their clenched fists into the air in the pouring rain. Some companies sent lorries loaded with workers. One Shell Oil Company lorry had a huge papier-mâché capitalist holding a gigantic $5 bill. Others carried groups of female students in neat white blouses and half-length cotton slacks, chanting to the beat of gongs. A few weeks earlier identical lorries had driven through the streets to celebrate the Victory Parade for Chiang Kai-shek. The same faces shouted themselves hoarse again, but this time they shouted for the communists.[2]

The most important rally of all was held in Beijing on 1 October, as Mao Zedong declared the establishment of the Central People's Government at a founding ceremony attended by 300,000 people. Preparatory work started early. Tiananmen Square, like most of the imperial capital, looked derelict after long years of neglect during the civil war. It was much smaller than today, cluttered with medieval walls, old roads and dilapidated buildings that once served as resting places for officials awaiting an audience with the emperor in the Imperial Palace, also called the Forbidden City. The pitted surface of the square was littered with rubbish. Thistles and errant trees shot up from the cracks in the paving slabs.[3]

Dan Ling was one of those students who eagerly volunteered to help clean up the square. In reward for his hard work, he was allowed to watch the parade. He arrived early on the day of the ceremony, waiting outside the gate in the bitter cold. Drizzle set in after dawn. Once all his fellow students had arrived, they queued up and marched in formation, together with other groups, locating their assigned position on the square. They found it pockmarked with deep pits that had not yet been levelled. Dan and the students sheltered in these pits, huddling closely together to stay warm.[4]

Thousands of banners fluttered in the autumn breeze above a sea of people carefully selected from all walks of life. Li Zhisui, a twenty-nine-year-old doctor who had returned to China from a job in Australia after reading how the communists had taken over Beijing, the city of his birth, without firing a shot, joined the crowds in shouting slogans: 'Long Live the Chinese Communist Party!', 'Long Live the People's Republic of China!', 'Long Live Chairman Mao!' They also sang revolutionary songs.

At ten o'clock sharp, Mao Zedong and the other leaders appeared on a reviewing stand on the great Tiananmen gate, to the south of the Forbidden City. He electrified an already excited crowd. For many, it was their first glimpse of China's messiah. Mao was fifty-six years old, tall, healthy, with a ruddy face. His voice was powerful and clear, and he spoke with decisive gestures. He no longer sported the military uniform in which he had so often appeared in photographs, but instead wore a dark-brown Sun Yat-sen suit, soon to be called the Mao suit. A worker's cap covered his thick black hair, revealing a broad and high forehead. In a message of unity and democracy, he stood together with several non-communist political personalities, including Song Qingling, also known as Madame Sun Yat-sen. Although her sister was married to Chiang Kai-shek, during the civil war she had sided with the communists and was now a figurehead for a united front. But Mao was the centre of attention. To many onlookers he was a truly magnetic force. In a soft, almost lilting voice, he spoke in a strong Hunanese accent, which most Chinese speakers found relatively easy to understand. The effect of his speech was riveting: 'The central government of the People's Republic of China is established!' he proclaimed, as the crowd went wild, shouting more slogans and erupting in thunderous applause. Li almost cried: 'I was so full of joy that my heart nearly burst out of my throat, and tears welled up in my eyes. I was so proud of China, so full of hope, so happy that the exploitation and suffering, the aggression from foreigners, would be gone forever. I had no doubt that Mao was the great leader of the revolution, the maker of a new Chinese history.'[5]

For Dan Ling the most exciting part of the day was the military rally. Troupes danced to the drum and gong beat of the rice-sprout song, and stilt walkers cavorted merrily in colourful costumes above the heads of the crowds. But the army was the centre of the procession, with some 16,400 soldiers in infantry and mounted cavalry, tanks, armoured cars and lorries equipped with machine guns. As the People's Liberation Army paraded across Tiananmen, a few aeroplanes roared overhead in a display of unity and military might. The cadenced tread of soldiers was followed by serried ranks of workers, students and government employees, many carrying coloured paper banners and Mao Zedong portraits, a few of which were torn to tatters by the wind. Dan and his friends stood in the rain for more than ten hours, without food, water or shelter, but nonetheless elated.[6]

———

The following day Dan Ling came down with diarrhoea, which lasted a month and weakened him so badly that it almost took his life. Dan had first encountered the communist party in 1947, when he was fourteen years old. The nationalists referred to the communists as 'bandits', which only enhanced their prestige in the boy's eyes. Outlaws, in folk legends, were often heroes fighting corrupt government officials. Several communist party members were arrested and imprisoned in a courtyard near Dan's home, and sometimes the prisoners were allowed out, singing and putting on plays that impressed Dan and other boys from the neighbourhood. He idolised them, believing that poor people in liberated areas were able to eat their fill and enjoyed equal treatment. One day Dan and two other boys decided to join the communists, who were rumoured to have a stronghold in the mountains to the west of Beijing. Equipped with some food, water and a knife, the boys slipped away in the evening, stumbling across desolate fields and eerie graveyards in the dark. They spent the night in a small village, quickly exhausted their food supply and finally decided to abandon their mission. Dan's escapade only heightened his enthusiasm for the communists. A year later, during the siege of Beijing, wounded nationalist soldiers swarmed all over the city. Some of them bullied people, intimidating even the local police. As the communist troops camping outside the capital cut off the food supply, cargo planes delivered badly needed provisions by parachute. The soldiers fought each other to reach the airdropped packets.

Dan had a vision of communist abundance that a visit to a picture exhibition of Soviet life had only reinforced. He was struck by a painting of a worker's family: beaming parents and rosy-cheeked children sat at a dinner table overflowing with eggs, bread, meat and other kinds of food he could not even name. Dan boasted about the exhibition, posing as an expert on Soviet life and trying to win converts for the cause among family and friends. His parents were lukewarm, maybe because a life of hard work had dulled their imagination, but his two younger brothers drooled over the idea of plenty for all. Dan joined the party aged fifteen, motivated by youthful ignorance and the promise of food.[7]

Li Zhisui, the twenty-nine-year-old doctor, grew up patriotic and proud of his country's culture, literature, art and history. He was enticed by a job as a ship's surgeon in Australia to escape civil war in 1948, but could stay there only temporarily as the country had strict immigration rules that favoured 'whites only'. Living in a small boarding house, his pride crying out against the country's racist policies, he slowly drifted into a state of depression. He rented a house in Hong Kong for his wife, but did not want to live there either, as he was too proud to become the disfranchised subject of an alien king in the crown colony.

Liberation jolted him out of his depression. Li was thrilled when he read about the communist victory, and believed that China would at long last assume its rightful place in the world. When he saw the headlines about the *Amethyst* incident, he immediately interpreted it as a victory against imperialist incursions. After his brother had written to him from Beijing asking him to return, his patriotism was rekindled and he decided to go home. He believed that the united front with non-party intellectuals was real: 'I worshipped the party. It was the hope of new China. I had been like a blind man in Australia, with no idea where I was going. The united front policy had shown me the light.'[8]

Many other Chinese overseas answered the call to serve the motherland. In Hong Kong underground agents took batches of people across the border to Guangzhou. The journey was arduous. The new recruits were asked to dress like farmers and meet in a designated spot near the border. From there they followed their guide on foot across hills and rivers to the liberated areas in Dongjiang. For many, hoisting the red flag was a highlight of the trek. 'My eyes were moist with tears as I saw our flag run up the flag pole.' A group photo was taken to commemorate the occasion. Wong Yee

Sheung, educated at the Diocesan Girls' School in Hong Kong, changed her name to Huang Xing, meaning Yellow Star. Hundreds of others marched with her, stopping at local schools on the way and sleeping on the ground in neat straight rows in the classrooms. After seven days they reached Guangzhou, where they were housed ten to a room in the East Asia Hotel. Across the street, the Oi Kwan Hotel, where the nationalists had set up their headquarters only months before, was decorated with a long banner hanging from the roof: 'The Chinese People Have Stood Up'.[9]

Hong Kong became a great crossroads. Crowds arrived from abroad to join the revolution while refugees poured into the crown colony, clamouring for a haven from the advancing communists. People from all walks of life fled China, taking with them their skills and capital. Dr T. V. Soong, who had negotiated the Sino-Soviet Treaty in 1945, disembarked in Hong Kong, welcomed by a guard of honour. General Long Yun, the former Yunnan warlord, landed with his entourage, but would soon return to China as a leading government official.

Like Soong and Long, most of these refugees were only passing through Hong Kong, soon resettling in South-east Asia, the United States, Latin America or elsewhere. But approximately 1 million people decided to stay. Some were prosperous industrialists who brought entire mills with them and tied their fate to the crown colony. The majority were craftsmen, shopkeepers, farmers and paupers who had crossed the border with little more than the clothes on their backs. Hundreds of thousands begged and roamed the streets, living in huts built of mud, wood, bamboo, sheet-metal, tar-paper and other materials in the hills of Hong Kong and Kowloon. Another 40,000 were street sleepers who managed to claim a space under a veranda or in a basement, living and cooking in the open. Others built squatter huts on rooftops. Those who were slightly better off shared cubicles in tenement houses, each family having just a few square metres. Among the refugees were several thousand soldiers, many crippled and disabled. The regime in Taiwan viewed them as a security risk and refused them entry. After months of surviving in a shanty town clinging to Mount Davis, they were settled at Rennie's Mill by the Social Welfare Office, living in large tents and tin sheds. The place soon became known as Little Taiwan.[10]

Another 1 to 2 million refugees also crossed the Taiwan Straits, following Chiang Kai-shek and the nationalists. Many of them were deeply traumatised. Families were often divided, as soldiers and government officials had left some of the women and children behind in the rush to escape. Ying Meijun, for instance, bade farewell to her one-year-old son at a railway station in September 1949. The boy was crying so much that she left him in the care of his grandmother, fearful of taking him on an overcrowded train. She would not see her first-born child again until 1987, when he was a forty-year-old man broken by years of hard labour on a state farm. As a young child, he used to chase trains along the tracks in front of their home, thinking that his mother was on board. For hundreds of thousands of refugees, all contact with friends and relatives was lost, and for three decades many did not even know who on the mainland was still alive. Their sense of isolation was compounded by the hostility they encountered from the local population. In a massacre known as the 228 Incident in 1947, the nationalists had slaughtered thousands of unarmed demonstrators who protested against the corruption and oppression of the post-war regime. Martial law and a reign of terror followed, creating deep divisions between mainlanders and the Taiwanese for decades to come.[11]

On the mainland the bamboo curtain soon came down, ending one of the largest human migrations in Chinese history. But the vast majority of the population were neither enthusiastic supporters nor diehard opponents of the new regime. Most had little choice but to stay, watching liberation and the fanfare that followed with a mixture of relief, hope and wariness.

After the celebrations came the police. They were less friendly than the soldiers. They did the rounds, inviting themselves into people's homes in their search for forbidden items, from weapons to radios. The policeman who harassed Kang Zhengguo's family in Xi'an had a shabby uniform and a heavy northern Shaanxi accent. 'We always served him tea in the parlour, but he seemed unaccustomed to smooth cedar chairs, and after sitting for a while, he would shift to a squatting position right on his chair, without even taking off his shoes.' He was interested in the family's vacuum-tube radio. The police suspected that the device was used to send wireless telegrams rather than receive broadcasts. The head of the Kang household was repeatedly summoned to the police station for questioning. Exasperated, he eventually surrendered the device.[12]

All over China the police visited people suspected of being sympathetic to the old regime. In big cities like Beijing, Shanghai and Wuhan, special teams trained to take over public security arrived within days of liberation. After briefing by underground members of the communist party, they moved into the precinct stations and police headquarters and ordered everybody to stay at their posts. General Chen Yi, now the new mayor of Shanghai, replaced his peaked cap with a dark beret, exhorting the police force in a three-hour meeting, an unlit cigarette dangling from his mouth: they should 'reform themselves, and at the same time carry on their work without undue anxieties', he explained.[13]

The communists had little choice but to ask former government servants and puppet policemen to stay on. In each department – the post office, the city hall, the police headquarters – some of the top officials of the old regime slipped away while a few new faces appeared. These were the party cadres, charged with overseeing the takeover:

> The typical bureaucrat of the regime in his blue or khaki uniform, like a soldier's, topped by a cloth cap which he often wears even in the office, resembles a Soviet Commissar much more than a Chinese official. He lives frugally . . . He is a poor man and is clothed, fed and housed by the party. His tobacco and his soap are given to him on the official ration, and he hardly earns enough in a month to buy himself a pair of shoddy sandals. He sleeps on the floor, and in requisitioned European buildings he rejects the soft mattresses that would prevent him from sleeping. He is distant with strangers and, apart from those few men who are appointed to deal with 'foreign relations', he is inaccessible. He insists that other Chinese speak to him in the Peking tongue, now more than ever the official language of the whole country, and not in the local dialect of Shanghai or elsewhere.[14]

Former employees of the old government continued to perform most of the daily routines. In 1945 the nationalist police had begun registering households and handing out identity cards in the cities under their control. A household was not just a family: it could include any collective unit like a factory dormitory or a hospital department. The new regime now took over the system of household registration, initially decried by the communists as 'fascist', but gave it a new twist. Food-ration cards were entrusted to the head of each household – a family head, a factory manager or a temple's abbot – and that person was now made responsible for reporting all changes in the constitution of the household. The rationing and distribution of food on the basis of the registration system entailed a staggering amount of paperwork, as each police station had to issue ration coupons several times a month. But it ensured that the state could reach into each and every household as never before.[15]

On top of household registration, every individual was given a class label (*chengfen*), including his or her 'family background', 'occupation' and 'individual status'. There were roughly sixty of these labels, which were further divided into broader class categories. These, in turn, were ranked as 'good', 'middle' and 'bad' on the basis of their presumed loyalty towards the revolution:

Good classes:
Revolutionary cadres
Revolutionary soldiers
Revolutionary martyrs
Industrial workers
Poor and lower-middle peasants

Middle classes:
The petty bourgeoisie
Middle peasants
Intellectuals and professionals

Bad classes:
Landlords
Rich peasants
Capitalists

These class designations would soon be simplified into two opposites: red or black, friend or foe. They would determine a person's fate for decades to come, as children inherited the status of the head of the household.[16]

The police first arrested the regime's most obvious enemies – presumed war criminals, heads of secret societies, prominent leaders of the old regime who had not yet absconded. But soon those belonging to 'bad classes' became suspects, as the communists tried to hunt down hidden enemies of the revolution, undercover agents and enemy spies. China, after all, remained at war. Despite all the victory parades, the last parts of the mainland were not liberated until the end of 1950. The nationalists controlled most of the country's territorial waters, and imposed a blockade on all ports from the summer of 1949 onwards. They used their air force to bomb thousands of junks and sampans assembled along south China's coast for an amphibious invasion of Taiwan, and carried out bombing raids against cities along the coast, from Shanghai all the way to Guangzhou, causing hundreds of casualties even though their targets were supposed to be military and industrial in nature. Arms, ammunition, food and other vital supplies were flown to guerrilla troops operating in Guangxi and other parts of the country. Secret agents seemed to be working ceaselessly, even though they were often captured, while special forces from Taiwan carried out commando raids along the coast, fuelling popular rumours of an impending invasion by Chiang Kai-shek.

A curfew was imposed in the cities. In Shanghai, cars and other vehicles were banned from the streets after 9 p.m. and pedestrians after 11 p.m. Sentinels were stationed at every street corner with rifles and bayonets.[17] Newspapers and radio relentlessly publicised the underground activities of the dreaded enemy, while propaganda posters exhorted the population to vigilance. The enemy seemed to be everywhere. In Tianjin a common slogan was 'Liberate the Entire Country and Capture the People's Enemy Chiang Kai-shek Alive'.[18]

People were encouraged to write to the police or the newspapers. Neighbours and friends denounced each other, often in the hope of reward. Almost overnight half the population seemed to have become communist. 'Everybody claimed to be a guerrilla, a soaking-red partisan,' noted a foreign observer in Shanghai, as people scrambled to prove their allegiance to the new regime.[19] Those belonging to 'bad classes' were visited by the police, interrogated about their past, quizzed about their links with foreigners and sometimes subjected to house searches in the hunt for suspect documents or concealed weapons. Soon even possession of an innocuous radio began to seem suspicious. In Shanghai alone, thousands of sets were confiscated, as well as guns and ammunition.

There were no mass executions: these would come later. But behind the scenes, the new regime's most dangerous enemies were quietly gaoled or executed. Others were registered, interrogated and kept under surveillance. In Shanghai, several hundred so-called 'counter-revolutionaries' – spies, underground agents, criminal bosses – were shot in the months after December 1949. In Hebei province, away from the inquisitive gaze of onlookers, more than 20,000 suspects were executed in the first year of liberation. Soon, the killing rate would rocket everywhere.[20]

Yet for the time being even people with dubious backgrounds, from the regime's point of view, remained largely undisturbed. Most of the professionals – professors, clerks, bankers, lawyers, managers, doctors, engineers – were too vital to a regime trying to establish its authority and build up the economy. But the time for laughter and song was over. All of them were sent to schools to learn the new orthodoxy. Everywhere, in government offices, factories, workshops, schools and universities, people were being 're-educated', poring over official pamphlets, magazines, newspapers and textbooks and learning the new doctrine. 'Everyone is learning the right answers, the right ideas and the right slogans.' It was called 'brainwashing' (*xinao*). From Beijing to Guangzhou, cities became giant adult-education centres. Banks, big shops and commercial offices had their own dedicated libraries. People were asked to transform themselves into what the communists called 'New People'.[21]

Those with a suspect past had to write confessions, admitting all their personal faults and past mistakes. Sometimes a simple admission of wrongdoing could suffice, while more serious public recantations appeared in the newspapers controlled by the party. A few were summoned to appear before large audiences where they were forced to recount their sins and express contrition for them for hours on end. Another weapon was discussion. Recalcitrant individuals were worn down by interminable debates.

Some were locked up in their offices and visited by a steady stream of cadres and political instructors determined to break down all resistance and win the argument. In every case the admission of guilt was added to the person's dossier, which would follow him for the rest of his life.

More vulnerable were classes of people the regime perceived as threats to social order and drains on its resources. They were called 'lumpenproletariat' in Marxist parlance, but 'parasites' and 'trash' by the cadres who had to deal with them: paupers, beggars, pickpockets and prostitutes, but also the millions of refugees and the unemployed who had come to seek shelter in the cities during the civil war. Many urban residents, who craved a return to social order after the chaotic years of civil war, welcomed these measures. Some, however, feared that the cities might be emptied.[22]

In Beijing, the communist troops charged with taking over the prisons found most of them empty. To save food and heat, the municipal authorities had ordered the large-scale release of inmates a few months earlier. On the streets of the capital, some beggars thought that they were quite literally 'liberated': they roved the streets killing dogs, smashing windows and blackmailing shopowners, with some of them managing to make the equivalent of 8 to 10 kilos of grain a day. Rickshaw pullers, on the other hand, took 'liberation' as a licence to flout the traffic regulations, causing mayhem on the streets. Thousands of them were rounded up and confined in makeshift camps on the outskirts of the city. By the end of 1949, some 4,600 vagrants languished in re-education centres and government reformatories.[23]

Like everybody else, they were asked to reflect on their sins, study the new orthodoxy and learn a different trade. Many made the best of their internment, but others sank into depression, despite all the propaganda about their 'liberation'. As one report noted, 'because they feel so miserable and unhappy they feign madness, act crazy and attempt to run away. There are even some small children who cry all the time, begging to be allowed to go home.' A few refused to be re-educated. Liu Guoliao, enrolled in a training course for vagrants, was a proud man, stubbornly proclaiming, 'My head is made of steel, bones and cement. It is beyond reform.'[24]

Conditions in the reformatories were often dreadful. Abuse was rife. In the western suburbs of Beijing, guards stole food and clothing and regularly beat the people they were meant to reform. As a detailed investigation brought to light, some of the children in detention were sodomised. The nurses could be careless, sometimes even brutal, particularly when using syringes. People died every month, the death rate being especially high among the elderly.[25]

In Shanghai too, thousands of thieves, vagrants and rickshaw pullers were arrested and sent to labour camps. Arrests came in waves. In a mere three days in December 1949 more than 5,000 beggars and pickpockets were arrested and deported to custody centres. Many were selected for re-education and sent to training units, but large numbers also ended up in prison. In Tilanqiao, as Ward Road Gaol was now known, by May 1951 over 3,000 undesirable elements had been imprisoned or sent to labour camps in the countryside. Several dozen were executed or died in custody.[26]

People who eked out a living as pedlars and hawkers were also cleared from the streets. In republican China, all manner of goods were delivered to the door, usually carried in baskets, swung from shoulder poles or carted on wheelbarrows, occasionally in donkey panniers. Each hawker had his own peculiar chant or mechanical rattle to advertise his wares. Vendors and itinerant traders also stood on pavement corners, offering every possible item from local fruit and vegetables, cloth, crockery, baskets, coal, meat, toys, sweets and nuts to soap, socks, handkerchiefs and towels.[27]

Within months they were rounded up, questioned and sent back to their home villages. A few were allowed to remain, but prohibited from roaming the streets. Open-air markets were organised where they were assigned stalls to sell their wares. One such market in Tianjin was on a tract of wasteland. A vast marquee built with bamboo went up in two days, and in another day the whole place was walled and roofed with matting. Pitches were marked out and tables and benches appeared. A funfair was organised to attract buyers, as jugglers, tightrope walkers, actors and singers kept the market packed. But the sights and sounds of hawkers trading their goods from door to door largely belonged to the past.[28]

Brothels were closed. In Beijing they were raided by 2,400 police officers on 21 November 1949. Over a thousand women and several hundred owners, procurers and pimps were arrested at a stroke. The re-education camps were already so crowded that the women were locked up in a cluster of decommissioned brothels on Hanjiatan, in the very heart of the city's erstwhile red-light district. They too were put to work and made to attend study sessions examining the evils of feudalism as well as vocational training classes. In order to make a clean break with the past, they were taken to large assembly halls where they had to denounce their former employers, who were often standing on the platform wearing shackles.[29]

Similar scenarios were enacted elsewhere. Between October 1949 and January 1950, Suzhou, Bengbu, Nanjing, Hangzhou and Tianjin, among other cities, stamped out prostitution. In Shanghai a more gradual approach was adopted: the brothels were slowly starved of customers by increasingly stringent regulations. First banquets, gambling, soliciting and rowdy behaviour were prohibited, then all past contracts between the women and the owners were declared void. The police applied relentless pressure, using an inventory compiled by the previous regime listing the address and registration number of each known brothel. Every time one of the 930 or so establishments closed, the address was struck from the list. Several brothel keepers were executed as a warning to others. News of their execution was printed in bold with black borders. Many owners voluntarily handed over the premises, often for lack of customers. Some returned to their home villages, others became tailors, cigarette sellers or even freight hauliers.

Many of the women were sent to a re-education camp. Here, as elsewhere in the country, they were made to follow a strict penal schedule, spending much of their time in study sessions denouncing the mistreatment they had suffered under the old regime. But few conformed to the image of the contrite prostitute projected by propaganda. A fair number were restive and quarrelsome, while a few insulted or physically assaulted the cadres in charge of their re-education. They denounced the manual labour they were forced to perform as a new form of exploitation, apparently unhappy to spend their days locked away, sewing olive-green shirts for the soldiers of the People's Liberation Army. Cao Manzhi, one of the cadres in charge of the whole operation, later admitted that even those inmates who came from low-class brothels did not like being interned and missed their life as prostitutes. But most settled down once they realised that resistance was futile. The majority were sent back to inland areas. Brothels that had managed to survive were finally raided on 25 November 1951. Even at that stage some of the women attacked the cadres in charge of the arrests.[30]

Prostitution was soon proclaimed to be an evil of the past. But in Beijing alone 350 women, some of them only recently released from re-education camps, were soon plying their trade again. Only a handful did so because they could not make a living otherwise. Some pretended to be students or housewives, accompanied by small children and mothers-in-law for cover. A few even wore party uniforms and carried badges. They stood in the doorways openly soliciting customers: 'Come in for a cup of tea!' In other cities too, prostitution went underground. As hundreds of thousands of desperate refugees fled the countryside after liberation, women continued to sell sex in the cities. In Shanghai hundreds of them were arrested in 1952, the women becoming more adept at hiding their activities with every new sweep. In the following years the authorities would adopt much more draconian measures to stamp out vice.[31]

If disposing of vagrants and prostitutes was a challenge, handling the several million refugees, disbanded soldiers and unemployed in the cities represented an even bigger task. In batch after batch, they too were sent back to the countryside, which became the great dumping ground for all undesirable elements. But few wanted to leave the cities where they had rebuilt their lives, however precarious. In Shanghai only one in ten agreed to be repatriated to a village.[32]

In Nanjing an even smaller fraction co-operated. Some steadfastly refused to be resettled, and objected to the military approach used in the dispersal plan. But despite all their objections, a third of a million people – equivalent to a quarter of the population – were sent away from the old regime's capital. The majority were dispatched to Shandong, Anhui and northern Jiangsu, but some ended up working on reclamation projects. More than 14,000 undesirables, mainly beggars, were destined for 'production training camps'.[33]

According to the party line, people were supposed to have a home village, but in reality many had been away for decades and had no relatives or friends left. The idea was that they could till the land, but all too often they were discriminated against as outsiders and given tiny plots of unfertile land that no local farmers wanted. A few missed out on land reform altogether and became local outcasts. Many clandestinely tried to make their way back to the cities.

Hundreds of thousands of demobilised soldiers, petty thieves, beggars, vagrants and prostitutes were also sent to help develop and occupy the resource-rich, politically strategic north-west, a region bordering India, Mongolia and the Soviet Union. From Beijing alone, by the end of 1949, close to 16,000 people were sent to Xinjiang and Gansu. Many objected. One beggar refused to join a work team, arguing that 'Beijing is my hometown. How can I go to the north-west and reclaim wasteland?' In one case a group of disbanded soldiers rebelled before being sent out to the frontier regions. They took control of the re-education camp where they had been confined and ran away in groups. So summary were the decisions made about relocation that in one case eighty-seven individuals, all classified as elderly or invalided, were sent to Ningxia to reclaim wasteland.[34]

Many of those who arrived in the north-west were forced to live in holes in the ground and made to do hard labour all day long, levelling sand dunes, planting trees and digging irrigation ditches. One woman remembered how she was lured to the region with tales of hot water and electricity in every house. After she and other migrants arrived they were told: 'Comrades, you must prepare to bury your bones in Xinjiang.'[35]

On paper the plan was straightforward: empty the cities of undesirables, reform all parasites and create employment. But it was a huge task, made no easier by a deep ideological suspicion of cities overall ('Shanghai is a non-productive city. It is a parasitic city,' complained one newspaper in 1949).[36] The problem was that for every batch of people the authorities shipped away, another group covertly managed to find their way back to the city. In October 1950, up to 2 million refugees were on the road after floods caused havoc in Anhui province. In Nanjing alone 340 people arrived every day from the countryside. Whether young or old, many had to beg and steal to survive. In

Shanghai the refugees slept, cooked and relieved themselves on the streets as every available camp, prison or reformatory built by the authorities since 1949 was already overcrowded.[37]

————

The situation was compounded by steady increases in unemployment in the first couple of years of the takeover, notwithstanding extravagant promises made to workers during the heady days of liberation, when they were heralded as 'masters of the country' ready to 'take charge'.[38] Entrepreneurs and industrialists, on the other hand, were also deceived by the new regime's rhetoric of inclusion in the name of New Democracy, a slogan that promised co-operation with all except the most hardened enemies of the regime. As part of this window-dressing, a small number of non-communist parties like the Democratic League were co-opted and allowed to take part in a Political Consultative Conference, an advisory body that met at the same time as the National People's Congress.

It all started well enough. Years of destruction, inflation and corruption had severely disrupted the economy. Communication networks were badly damaged, and the railway tracks were in disarray. Areas where local power stations had been bombed or coal stocks were low lacked electricity. So the most immediate task in the cities was salvage rather than construction. In Beijing, Tianjin, Wuhan and Shanghai, the barricades erected by the fleeing nationalists were removed from the streets. Shell-damaged sites were cleared, burned-out houses pulled down, concrete fortifications and pillboxes levelled. Building debris was used to fill bomb craters. In Changchun and other besieged cities tens of thousands of bodies were thrown into collective pits. The streets were disinfected. Everywhere telephone lines went up – sometimes a military network running side by side with the restored civil installations. Sunken ships that blocked rivers and harbours were removed. Where generators had been damaged, technicians were helped by the army to repair the machines and mend cables. Railway lines were double-tracked and bridges repaired.[39]

Inflation, though never fully curbed, was at least brought under control. The People's Republic issued its own People's Dollar, called the *renminbi*, and made it the only medium of exchange. Trade in its rivals – greenbacks, silver dollars and gold – was tolerated for a few months, but then the money-changers were forced to close their doors. In Shanghai a massive rally of half a million people denounced gold dealers and other traders as so many speculators. Thousands of students were mobilised to harangue the population against hoarding silver dollars. They kept watch on the bazaars and policed the pavements where foreign coins used to change hands.[40]

Soon the hand of the state started to curb other economic activities. Giant state trading corporations controlled raw materials, severely circum-scribing the scope of private enterprise. Organised on a regional basis, these corporations entered into barter agreements to transfer goods from surplus areas to places of scarcity. In one example, the North China Trad-ing Company exchanged cloth, yarn, kerosene, gasoline, caustic soda and glass for cotton, peanut oil and tobacco from the Central China Trading Company. Many of them also ran state shops and co-operatives, designed to check speculative price increases in a whole range of commodities, from foodstuffs, cloth, farming tools, household equipment, hardware, soap, matches and sugar to stationery.[41]

In many ways the regime merely extended to the rest of the country the way it ran its economy in the regions it controlled before liberation, but this trend was further accelerated by the very effective blockade of the ports imposed by Chiang Kai-shek. Cities such as Tianjin, Shanghai and Guangzhou depended on maritime trade. They could no longer obtain the coal, cotton, steel or oil for their factories or the spare parts for their machines. And as they could not buy from abroad, neither could they sell abroad. All of Shanghai's trade had to be switched from foreign markets to the interior of the country.[42]

But even without the blockade the economy would have been para-lysed. The regime had made no secret of its hostility to foreign governments, with the exception of the Soviet Union and its satellites. Foreign trade was now in the hands of government agencies, and the rate of the *renminbi* was artificially high, meaning that exports were not very attractive on the inter-national market. Even with open ports, the complex and sophisticated industries along the coast were starved of capital. Shanghai's industry, which represented more than half of the country's production, was operat-ing only partially. As one foreign observer noted, 'Cotton spinning mills are working three days a week and have only six months' stock in hand in spite of a big effort to replace American by Chinese cotton transported in junks from the interior. Manchurian industry, which in 1945 was the victim of Russian requisitions, is producing, according to the most reliable sources, 30 per cent of its output under the Japanese.' But the communists were firmly set against all recourse to foreign capital, symbol of imperialist exploitation, and without adequate capital everything soon ground to a halt. They were forced to seek a massive loan from the Soviet Union.[43]

Instead of receiving the material incentives promised by the party, workers were exhorted to produce more. But the workers, ironically, were the most restive group among the population. Hoping to stand at the forefront of the revolution, they demanded increased wages and better working conditions. They became so vocal that the communists introduced a new labour decree making strikes illegal. Their employers, on the other hand, protested that under the slogan of New Democracy they had been promised protection and assured that they could continue to run their enterprises on a private basis. But soon they were compelled to accept wage increases that vastly inflated the costs of labour on their balance sheets.[44]

Heavy, variable and unpredictable taxes on everyone followed, as the regime was desperate for cash. In Beijing, where they were calculated in terms of millet, 31,400 tonnes were raised in 1946, down to 21,000 tons in 1947 and only 10,000 tonnes the following year. Within the first year of liberation the people of Beijing were asked to hand over the equivalent of 53,000 tonnes of millet. Everybody complained, from small shopkeepers driven out of business to ordinary workers unable to feed their families. In Changsha, the once thriving capital of Mao's home province of Hunan, the average tax imposed on all 420,000 residents was 250 kilos of grain per person a year, far above the limit of 80 kilos the regime had mandated for a city of that size. In the case of private enterprise, some of the taxes were retroactive, with little reference to their income during those years. Soon the finance minister Bo Yibo himself admitted that punitive taxes, chaotically and randomly collected by cadres, had damaged commerce. A 120 per cent tax had ruined the tobacco industry.[45]

The cadres themselves were part of the problem. They were attuned to the rigours of guerrilla warfare rather than to the intricacies of international banking and finance that were the daily routine in Shanghai, the greatest commercial centre in Asia. The metropolis was half as big again as Moscow, with a larger foreign population than any other city except New York. Before liberation it had more foreign investment than London or Paris. At first the cadres allowed the city to continue to operate independently as far as possible, but soon the very distance they cultivated from the people became a problem. They checked every bit of advice they were given for fear of error, and in any event lacked the required financial expertise to evaluate the matters brought to their attention.

> They were reticent, reserved, remote. They were unreasonably cautious and suspicious and would not mix with the people. They were not gregarious, neither were they open and communicative. They were coldly correct in their official dealings, but did not want to be enlightened on the problems they were confronted with, even refusing to discuss the problems . . . They would brook no interference and encourage no suggestion. A word of counsel was considered meddling, an offer of help, officiousness. Everybody was under a stigma of doubt, even of guilt.

As Mariano Ezpeleta noted, they insisted on calling everybody 'comrade', but there was nothing comradely about their behaviour.[46]

Distance was maintained not only with foreigners and business leaders, seen as spies in an imperialist lair, but also with other sectors of the population. By the middle of 1949 some 38,000 cadres from the north had entered the region immediately south of the Yangzi River. Many never became accustomed to the food, the climate and the local language. Only a few managed to settle down. In Hangzhou, Ningbo and Wenzhou, the commercial centres of Zhejiang, cadres vented their hatred in consultation meetings with representatives of trade and industry that degenerated into 'struggle sessions' where people were mocked, humiliated and beaten. Soon nobody dared say a word. Shaoxing, a beautiful city of gardens and canals famed for its rice wine, was run as if the party was still fighting a guerrilla war.[47]

Within a matter of months, bustling Shanghai was a dying city. Tianjin slipped into slow decay. Guangzhou almost went bankrupt. Factories were idle, trade ceased. Many firms, small and big alike, were driven into the red. The high end of the luxury market suffered first. In the once thriving jewellery stores on Nanking Road in Shanghai, where gold ornaments competed for attention with finely wrought jade pieces, merchants started selling soap, DDT, medicines, towels and underwear. Where 136 factories had once made cosmetics, only thirty remained in operation, most of them producing toothpaste. In Shanghai's outdoor bazaar at Yuyuan Garden, where curios, crafts and antiques were sold, dispirited merchants sat beside their stalls looking bored or perusing the papers.[48]

Other branches of industry followed. Hundreds of factories making paper, matches, rubber and cotton textiles closed down. Contemporary observers in Hong Kong estimated that about 4,000 concerns in Shanghai, including 2,000 commercial companies and 1,000 factories, went bankrupt. Of some 500 banks in the city, fewer than a hundred were still open, and half of these petitioned the government for permission to wind up their operations. Many of the city's foreign-owned transit and power companies were forced to finance operational deficits by borrowing heavily from the People's Bank, placing them virtually in the hands of the government.

Shopping centres in most big cities now seemed lifeless and deserted. Observed one trader in Shanghai: 'Between the Bund and the Park Hotel the windows of all stores – including the big proud ones like Wing On, Sincere, Sun Sun and the Sun – are plastered with posters which shout: "We Reduce Prices with Pain!", "Shop Closing Down", "Prices Falling Below Cost".' In Wuhan, the inland port once called the Chicago of the East, more than 500 shops went bust, while hundreds of factories closed their doors. In Wuxi, the industrial city north of Shanghai where steam whistles, electric sirens and hooters had once competed for attention, silence prevailed, as hundreds of shops were boarded up. In Songjiang only one of the eighteen cotton mills that had made the reputation of the town managed to remain in business.[49]

Unemployment rocketed. By December 1949 Beijing had 54,000 unemployed people in a population of 2 million. Four years later the population had increased by half, but the number of jobless people had trebled – despite all the successive waves of vagrants, paupers, soldiers, refugees, pedlars and other 'undesirable elements' cleansed from the streets since liberation. Unemployment also increased in Shanghai. In the summer of 1950, a report compiled by the party itself deplored 'incessant' cases of suicide and the sale of children due to joblessness among 150,000 people.[50]

In south China too, many of the unemployed sold their children or killed themselves. Some starved to death. In Fuzhou, the capital of Fujian province just opposite Taiwan, more than 100,000 people were out of work in a city of less than half a million. According to a restricted news bulletin for the leadership, the only help came from the nationalists, who flew over the distressed regions and parachuted down bags of rice. So great was the popular discontent that in Changsha, on six occasions, unemployed workers surrounded the Workers' Union and demonstrated against the communist party. Calls for blood could be heard from the crowd. Similar protests also rocked Guangzhou, the capital of Guangdong, where by the summer of 1950 one in three workers was jobless. In Zhengzhou, one of China's railway hubs, hundreds of porters assaulted the municipal freight office, beat the men in charge and smashed doors, windows and furniture to protest against the low rates they were paid. In Nanjing, where industrial workers had to make do with fewer benefits and less pay than before liberation, complaints were 'ceaseless' and 'reactionary' slogans were scribbled on walls along offices and factories 'everywhere'. In Shanghai, as mayor Chen Yi reported directly to the Chairman, disenchantment was so intense that members left the party in droves while ordinary people petitioned the government and tore down posters of Mao Zedong.[51]

People were told to practise thrift and frugality. Production was extolled, consumption denounced. Ideological purity went hand in hand with economic decline to transform once bustling metropoles into drab zones of conformity. Within months of the revolution, the pursuit of pleasure was frowned upon as a sign of bourgeois frivolity. In Shanghai, as elsewhere, cafés and dance halls were closed down. Clandestine gambling casinos broke up without police intervention. The hotels that had once sealed the city's world-class reputation such as the Cathay (renamed the Peace Hotel), the Palace Hotel and the Park Hotel, had so few guests that some of them offered monthly rates of $25 to $50. The Shanghai Club, reputedly boasting the longest bar in the world, attracted few customers.

Even tea rooms closed their doors. The Race Course at Nanking Road became a military barracks. Nightlife was negligible, as shops were shuttered at six in the evening and clubs a few hours later. Those who ventured out at night were accosted by young communists demanding to see residence certificates and other papers. Fewer rickshaws, buses and pedicabs were seen on the streets. Cars were mostly official, as the cost of petrol became prohibitive. Thousands of vehicles vanished from the streets every month. An unused Buick, less than a year old, was on sale for $500 in June 1950 but found no buyers.[52]

English was no longer the language of international business but a manifestation of imperialist exploitation. No transactions in English were tolerated, and soon foreigners on official business – all channelled through a Foreign Affairs Office – were required to bring along their own translators. 'The talks were formal, carefully uninformative, and recorded by a stenographer,' reported Randall Gould, who worked for the *Shanghai Evening Post and Mercury*. Then the transmission of cables and telegrams in foreign languages was prohibited, except when accompanied by a translation judged to be satisfactory. 'Neon lights and other public advertisements in English were brought down or changed into Chinese. English and French plaques in public parks and gardens were taken down.' The pressure extended to cinemas and eating places, where foreign names became taboo. In the erstwhile French Concession of Shanghai, streets and boulevards were renamed for the most part after local cities and provinces rather than priests, dignitaries, consuls and writers from France. Everywhere the hammer and sickle or the red star went up: they could be seen on trams, buildings, banners and flags, and invariably adorned the badges worn by state employees. Paintings of Chinese and Soviet leaders were hung prominently in public places, in bookshops, in railway stations, in factories, schools and offices, on the gateway to the Forbidden City. And from the very beginning the communists guarded themselves more closely than their predecessors, as sentries kept strict watch at every communist office, even in places where the old regime had none.[53]

The press was brought into line almost immediately. In Beijing, besides the official paper, by February 1949 only one single-sheet newspaper out of twenty-odd daily publications was still in business. In Shanghai two of the four English-language newspapers, both under Chinese ownership, were closed within days. Of the hundreds of different publications several months later only a few remained, all of them printing the same news. There was only one source of foreign information, namely the Soviet TASS Agency. Here too, rather than imposing censorship from above, the authorities relied on self-censorship – which was surprisingly effective once journalists and editors had gone through re-education. As one journalist noted, a party hack nudged them in the right direction: 'The slightest mistake calls down a rebuke, and in each editorial office a few trusty Communists inspect all copy.' The result was absolute conformity. As one student of propaganda noted at the time, 'The Communists' newspaper propaganda technique might be described as the "sledge-hammer type". There is very little subtlety involved. Good and bad, friend and foe, are defined in terms of black and white. Everything is reduced to simple slogans or formulae, and all channels (the radio as well as the press) concentrate simultaneously on pounding them in.'[54]

The way people dressed changed seemingly overnight. Jewellery was seen as bourgeois, as was anything ostentatious. Lipstick and make-up vanished. Young girls cut their curls. Men and women removed their rings. Expensive straps on watches were replaced by a piece of leather or string. 'The fashion was simplicity almost to the point of rags,' noted one woman who had just joined the party. Li Zhisui, arriving from Australia after an absence of seventeen years, was struck by how dreary men and women looked, as most of Beijing was clad in a standard blue or grey cotton that faded almost completely after frequent washing. The same black cotton-cloth shoes were common, and even hairstyles were identical – crewcuts for men and short bobs for women. 'With my Western-style suit and tie, leather shoes, and hair that suddenly seemed long, I felt like a foreigner.' His wife, in her colourful dress and high-heeled shoes, her stylish hair freshly permed, looked completely out of place. Both quickly borrowed more subdued clothes. But they were thrilled nonetheless by the changes taking place. 'When I saw glimmerings that the party was not all I believed it to be, I dismissed them as trivial exceptions to the rule.'[55]

4

The Hurricane

For years Mao Zedong groped to find his way as a young man, first as a scholar, then as a publisher, finally as a labour activist. In the countryside, five years after joining the Chinese Communist Party in 1921, he finally discovered his calling. Still a young man of thirty-three, tall, lean and handsome, he was enthralled by the peasant violence that had erupted in the countryside after the nationalists had launched a military campaign from their base in Guangzhou to seize power from local warlords and unify the country. Russian advisers accompanied the nationalist army, as Chiang Kai-shek, at this stage, was still collaborating closely with Stalin. In Mao's home province of Hunan, the nationalist authorities followed Russian instructions in funding peasant associations and fomenting a Soviet-style revolution. Social order broke down. In Changsha, the provincial capital, victims were paraded in tall conical hats of mockery. Children scampered down the streets singing, 'Down with the [imperialist] powers and eliminate the warlords.' Workers armed with bamboo sticks picketed the offices of foreign companies. Public utilities were wrecked.[1]

In the countryside, the poorest of the villagers took control of the peasant associations and turned the world upside down. They were now the masters, choosing their targets at random, striking down the wealthy and powerful, creating a reign of terror. Some victims were knifed, a few decapitated. Chinese pastors were paraded through the streets as 'running dogs of imperialism', their hands bound behind their backs and a rope around their necks. Churches were looted. Mao admired the audacity and violence of the rebels. He was attracted by the slogans they coined: 'Anyone who has land is a tyrant, and all gentry are bad.' He went to the countryside to investigate the uprisings. 'They strike the gentry to the ground,'

Mao wrote in his report on the peasant movement. 'People swarm into the houses of local tyrants and evil gentry who are against the peasant association, slaughter their pigs and consume their grain. They even loll for a minute or two on the ivory-inlaid beds belonging to the young ladies in the households of the local tyrants and evil gentry. At the slightest provocation they make arrests, crown the arrested with tall paper hats, and parade them through the villages.' Mao was so taken with the violence that he felt 'thrilled as never before'.[2]

Mao predicted that a hurricane would destroy the existing order:

In a very short time, in China's central, southern and northern provinces, several hundred million peasants will rise like a mighty storm, like a hurricane, a force so swift and violent that no power, however great, will be able to hold it back. They will smash all the trammels that bind them and rush forward along the road to liberation. They will sweep all the imperialists, warlords, corrupt officials, local tyrants and evil gentry into their graves.[3]

The violence in the countryside repelled the nationalists, as many of their officers came from prosperous families, and soon they turned away from the Soviet model. A year later, after his troops had entered Shanghai in April 1927, Chiang Kai-shek launched a bloody purge in which 300 communists were dragged through the streets and executed. Many thousands were arrested. The Chinese Communist Party went underground. Mao led a motley army of 1,300 men into the mountains, in search of the peasants who would propel him to power.

———

Twenty years later, in a homage to the Chairman who now controlled vast tracts of the countryside, Zhou Libo published a novel on land reform, *The Hurricane*. The author, an editor of the literary supplement of the *Liberation Daily* in Yan'an, had been transferred in 1946 to Manchuria to join a work team tasked with galvanising the countryside. The team was one of the first to follow a directive Mao had issued in May 1946, as the peace talks between the nationalists and the communists started to unravel.

So far the communists had followed a moderate policy of rent reduction, as they were bound in a popular front with the nationalists in a common war against Japan. Now the May directive called for all-out class struggle in the countryside. All the land, Mao ordered, should be confiscated from traitors, tyrants, bandits and landlords and distributed to the poor peasants. The revolutionary potential of the countryside was to be unleashed, sweeping away the old order and repelling the nationalists.

Zhou Libo's team was sent to Yuanbao, a town near the banks of the Sungari River some 130 kilometres east of Harbin. *The Hurricane* purported to describe what happened next. Under the leadership of the Chinese Communist Party, the peasants of Yuanbao seized power from the local tyrants and abolished thousands of years of feudal land ownership. In public trials where depraved landlords were made to confess their sins, the irate masses raised sticks and beat the villains to death. Soon their revolutionary zeal took them to other villages, sweeping away all remnants of feudalism like a hurricane. The novel, an instant hit, was used as a textbook for other work teams in charge of land reform, and won the much coveted Stalin Prize for Literature in 1951.[4]

But in reality something very different happened in Yuanbao. After the defeat of Japan at the end of the Second World War, most villagers in Manchuria were conservative and regarded the nationalists as their legitimate government. Few knew anything about communism. 'When we went there, at the time the villagers didn't know what we communists were like or what the Eighth Army was. They had no idea,' remembered Han Hui, who was a twenty-two-year-old cadre at the time. In Yuanbao only a few ruffians and vagrants were interested in the communists, and they were the ones who became party activists.

One of the first tasks of the work team was to divide the villagers into five classes, closely mirroring what had been done in the Soviet Union: 'landlords', 'rich peasants', 'middle peasants', 'poor peasants' and 'labourers'.[5] This took place in endless meetings in the evening, as the work teams pored over the life stories of each and every villager with information gathered from newly recruited activists. The challenge was that none of these artificial class distinctions actually corresponded to the social landscape of the village, where most farmers often lived in roughly similar conditions.

In Yuanbao there were no landlords. Han Laoliu, who would become the archetypical villain in Zhou Libo's novel, had been elected head of the local peasant association by the villagers. His wife was a music teacher who sewed clothes in the evening for the schoolchildren. He had no land, but collected rent on behalf of the owner who lived in the county seat or administrative centre. Like the others, he ate coarse grain and had too few clothes to keep him warm in the winter. His greatest claim to wealth was two small windowpanes built into his earth-walled house covered with a layer of straw. 'In reality Han Laoliu had nothing worthwhile,' remembered one villager. 'It's not quite like what's written in that book.'

The next task was to get those identified as 'poor peasants' and 'labourers' to turn hardship into hatred. This, too, took weeks of persistence and persuasion, as the work team had to convince the 'poor' that the 'rich' were behind their every misfortune, having exploited their labour since time immemorial. In so-called 'speak bitterness' meetings, participants were encouraged to tap into a reservoir of grievances. Some vented genuine frustrations that had long been bottled up; others were coerced into inventing accusations against their richer neighbours. Greed became a powerful tool in whipping up class hatred, as members of the work team calculated the monetary equivalent of past misdeeds, urging the poorer villagers to demand compensation.

Weeks of indoctrination also produced true believers who no longer needed prodding along from the work team. Some people were transformed into revolutionary zealots, ready to break the bonds of family and friendship for the cause. Drawn to an ideology that promised liberation, they relished becoming the champions of the exploited, forging a better world full of hope and light. They no longer felt themselves mere farmers plodding along in a forlorn village, at the mercy of the seasons, but instead believed they were part of something new that endowed their lives with meaning. As one missionary caught up in land reform noted, 'They knew their parts well and spoke sharply the proper party phrase at the proper time with the proper emphasis.'[6]

After months of patient work, the communists managed to turn the poor against the village leaders. A once closely knit community was polarised into two extremes. The communists armed the poor, sometimes with guns, more often with pikes, sticks and hoes. The victims were denounced as 'landlords', 'tyrants' and 'traitors', rounded up and held in cowsheds. Armed militia sealed off the village; nobody was allowed to leave. Everybody had to wear a strip of cloth identifying their class background. The landlords had a white strip, rich peasants a pink one while middle peasants wore yellow. The poor proudly displayed red.

One by one the class enemies were dragged out on to a stage where they were denounced by the crowd, assembled in their hundreds, screaming for blood, demanding that accounts be settled in an atmosphere charged with hatred. Victims were mercilessly denounced, mocked, humiliated, beaten and killed in these 'struggle sessions'. Soon an orgy of violence engulfed the village, as people lived in fear of reprisals from private militias led by former village leaders who had managed to escape.

Many of the victims were beaten to death and some shot, but in many cases they were first tortured in order to make them reveal the location of their assets – real or imagined. There was no shortage of volunteers. Liu Fude remembered: 'There were people who only needed to be told to hit somebody and they would do so. For instance Madame Ding, she was that kind of person.' Madame Ding, who worked for Zhou Libo, claimed: 'I did exactly as he told me to do. This is what Zhou Libo would say: "That Sun Liangba can be taken to task," that's what he would say. So I would beat him.' One woman who had been beaten unconscious was about to be buried in a coffin outside the village, when somebody discovered that she was still breathing. A leader ordered that she be dragged out of her coffin and executed. Some of those labelled 'rich peasants' tried to hide in the fields, but they froze to death. In one village alone, out of a population of roughly 700, seventy-three people were killed.

The pact between the party and the poor was sealed in blood as all the land and assets of the victims were distributed to the crowd. The land was paced, measured and distributed to the poor, the name of the beneficiary carved on to a wooden signboard marking the boundary of each plot. Grain was loaded into baskets, furniture lugged off, pigs herded away. Even pots and jars were placed in rattan hampers, making it look like moving day. 'So what did I get?' Liu Yongqing pondered more than fifty years after the looting, his skin leathery and tanned, his hair sparse and grey. 'I got a jar. A water jar.' Lü Kesheng, a man with an open face topped by a dense crop of white hair, got less: 'I got a horse. A horse leg, not a whole horse. We [slaughtered and] divided a horse between four families.' Zhang Xiangling, a young cadre at the time, also got a horse leg. 'My grandfather, grandmother, my great-grandfather, several generations never had a horse's leg. Now we had one! That was just incredible!' Even rags were shared out between the villagers – always according to class divisions, the first choice going to the 'poor peasants' and the 'labourers'.

Once everything in the village had been mopped up, down to the last handful of grain, the poor got into their carts in the middle of the night and visited other villages, hoping that they might find new struggle targets. 'You get what you find' was the motto. Soon hundreds of carts converged on the county seat, each one crammed with farmers armed with banners, pitchforks and red-tasselled spears. 'The rats in the city are even fatter than the pigs in the village.' City people had money. In the county as a whole, 21,000 out of a population of 118,000 were targeted. To ensure that the supporters of the old regime would never come back, many young men joined the army. Their families received extra land and special protection. Soon the soldiers started to besiege Changchun.[7]

China had a hidden asset, one it jealously protected from the prying eyes of strangers in small, family-based villages all across the country. It was the land. Nobody knew exactly how much of it there was, and every government had failed fully to measure, assess and tax it. More often than not the land tax was based on a rough approximation carried out decades if not centuries earlier. Outsiders were often eyed with suspicion, and all the villagers had an incentive to keep some land hidden from the view of the state. No tax, for instance, was generally paid on uncultivated land, such as grave plots, sandy soil, wooded areas or land high up in the hills. As the population expanded and new crops appeared that were suited to soils previously left unploughed (for example the potato and the peanut after the eighteenth century), more and more untaxed land was cultivated without the knowledge of the tax assessors. On top of this, large plots were left unregistered: nobody quite knew the extent of what was called 'black land', and a nationwide survey with vast inputs of manpower would have been needed to uncover it.[8]

Land reform pitted villagers against each other, and as they denounced one another in ferocious meetings, the actual holdings in the countryside finally came to light. Properties of the rich were expropriated and their land parcelled out to the poor. Ground rent was abolished. But now the party knew exactly how much land existed. It determined how much each strip could produce and demanded that each household hand over a designated amount of grain. As one observer noted about Manchuria: 'Heavy grain requisitions to support the Communists' armies of 3 to 4 million men have in many areas not only stripped the countryside of food surpluses but have eaten into subsistence stocks.' On top of tax, foodstuffs including soybeans, corn, rice and vegetable oils were traded with the Soviet Union for industrial equipment, motor vehicles, oil and manufactured supplies, increasing the overall food deficit. Hundreds of thousands of people starved to death in Manchuria as a result.[9]

————————

Village life, on the eve of the communist conquest, was extraordinarily diverse. In the north, where tightly packed villages with houses made from sun-dried mud bricks were strewn across the dry and dusty plains, wheat was the staple. Most farmers owned the land. Further inland along the ancient silk road, set among bare hills and steep ravines on a loess plateau, tens of millions of people lived in caves hewn out of brittle earth. These people of the dust carved out tiny terraces on steep slopes of eroding loess, planting the soil with potatoes, maize and millet. Further south, along the fertile Yangzi valley, rich deposits of silt allowed farmers to produce abundant crops of rice. White plastered houses with black-tiled roofs in closely knit clusters stood among the rice paddies with their raised banks, dykes and embankments.

Even more varied were the communities in the south, from coastal fishing hamlets to aboriginal villages deep in the mountains. Scattered along the coast were whole villages with ostentatious mansions built by returned emigrants. They were directly inspired by foreign architecture, except for the windows, which tended to be narrow and placed high up near the roof as a concession to local geomancy – and as a precaution against theft. The individual character of these houses and their owners stood in contrast to the fortified cities erected by the Hakka, who spoke their own language and built enormous, tower-like, circular edifices which harboured hundreds of halls, storehouses and bedrooms accommodating dozens of families. The villagers often shared the same surname and lived together for support and protection. All over the subtropical south, powerful lineages controlled the land and built extensive villages with ancestral halls, schools, granaries and community temples. The most basic social distinction – as in any other village in the world – was between locals and outsiders.

Nowhere in this profusion of social diversity could anybody called a 'landlord' (*dizhu*) be found. The term was imported from Japan in the late nineteenth century and given its modern formulation by Mao Zedong. It had no meaning for most people in the countryside, who referred to some of their more fortunate neighbours as *caizhu*, an appellation that implied prosperity yet carried no derogatory undertones. There were also plenty of less respectful labels such as 'big belly' (*daduzi*). As S. T. Tung, publisher of the *Chinese Farmer* with a doctoral degree in agriculture from Cornell University, put it at the time, 'China has no "landlord class".' There is little question that absent landowners abused their power, while malpractices were rife in the countryside, but the country did not have a dominant class of junkers or squires, and nothing equivalent to serfdom.[10]

Nor was there anything even vaguely approximating what the communists referred to as 'feudalism' (*fengjian*) in the countryside. For centuries the land had been bought and sold through sophisticated contracts that were upheld in magistrates' courts. In some cases contracts even drew a distinction between the topsoil and the subsoil. The land was freely alienable everywhere. Tenancy rights were also defined contractually, although the vast bulk of the land was in the hands of small owners. Trusts were set up by corporate entities to hold land, for instance temples, schools and, especially in the south, clans sharing a surname and organised around a common ancestor.

The most systematic, reliable and extensive sample survey of farmers was carried out from 1929 to 1933 by a University of Nanking team led by

John L. Buck. They surveyed in detail the entire population of 168 villages distributed over twenty-two provinces, collecting immense amounts of detailed information on the lives of over 16,000 farms. *Land Utilization in China* scrupulously noted the many regional differences and varied forms of employment in the countryside, but the overall image which emerged from the study denied the existence of vast inequalities. Over half of all farmers were owners, many were part-owners, and fewer than 6 per cent were tenants. Most farms were relatively small, and very few were more than twice the average size. Tenants were not generally much poorer than owners, since only fertile land could be rented out. In the south, for instance, tenants on irrigated rice land were better off than owners in the north, even more so since two grain crops could often be grown a year. A majority of farmers supplemented their incomes with handicrafts and other forms of non-agricultural employment which produced roughly a sixth of their incomes. One-third of all farmers surveyed were unaware of any adverse factors in agriculture. None blamed expensive credit, exploitative merchants or land tenure.[11]

But this was before the war. A decade of fighting between nationalists, communists and the Japanese did not substantially change the ownership of the land, but certainly increased violence in the countryside. In Xushui, some hundred kilometres south of Beijing in the dry and dusty countryside of north China, where the fields were covered in sorghum, growing two metres high with purple tassels of grain, the Japanese and the communists were as fierce as each other. Sun Nainai, healthy and talkative when she was interviewed at the age of eighty-nine, explained how the villagers were caught between both camps. The Japanese captured her father-in-law as a guerrilla fighter and gave him a choice: work for the police in his village or be buried alive. He took the second option because he knew that if he agreed to work for the Japanese, the communists would bury his entire family alive in retribution. In the end his family secured his release by paying an enormous ransom. In normal times village life would have been rife with family feuds and personal wrongs, but farmers in war-torn areas were obliged to make even harder choices between resistance, collaboration and survival.[12]

Many people were accused of being traitors. Jack Belden, a journalist

sympathetic to the communists, described how a local leader called Mu
had collaborated with the Japanese and killed dozens of guerrilla fighters.
Just after the war Mu was paraded through the villages where people stood
waiting with kitchen knives to cut out his flesh. He was dragged on to a
stage to face his accusers, and found everyone in the crowd trying to rush
forward at once.

> The cadres did not like the look of things and took Mu out in a field and
> shot him. They handed his body to his family who covered it with straw
> sheets. The crowd found out where he was and grabbed the body away
> from his family, they ripped off the straw sheets and continued to beat
> him with wooden clubs. One boy with a spear stabbed his corpse eight-
> een times in succession. 'You stabbed my father eighteen times,' he
> cried, 'and I will do the same.' In the end, they tore his head from his
> body.[13]

Land reform cut a bloody swathe through the villages under communist
control. Everywhere work teams dug up old grudges, fanned resentment
and turned local grievances into class hatred, and everywhere mobs were
worked into a frenzy of envy as they appropriated the possessions of traditional village leaders. Yuanbao was one of the first towns where land was
traded for blood, but in 1947–8 every village went through a similar ritual:
people were divided into classes, the poor worked up into a fever pitch of
hatred, victims humiliated, beaten and sometimes killed, and the victors
shared the spoils.

One of the most violent regions was Shanxi, where Kang Sheng
presided over a reign of terror. A sinister-looking man with a murky past,
Kang had worked closely with the Soviet secret police in eliminating
hundreds of Chinese in Moscow during the great purges started by Stalin
in 1934. Students disappeared at night, never to be seen again. In 1936
he set up the Office for the Elimination of Counter-Revolutionaries, and
a year later Stalin sent him by special plane to Yan'an. He quickly sided
with Mao, and used the police methods he had learned in the Soviet
Union to oversee security and intelligence. So brutal were his methods
that in 1945 he was replaced.[14]

Sent to Shanxi to oversee land reform in 1947, he fomented all-out class warfare in the countryside by forcing every villager to take a stand. In a hamlet called Haojiapo, he watched approvingly as the farmers forced landlords to kneel on broken bricks. The victims were then beaten, spat upon and had excrement poured over them. Kang Sheng allowed 'the masses' to decide who they did not like, unleashing pent-up frustrations that could target almost anyone. In parts of the region, the search for enemies went so far as to include even farmers classified as 'middle peasants', who were arrested, beaten, tortured and then stripped of their property. In some places one out of five people was branded as a 'landlord'. In Shuo county, nobody dared utter a word when someone was denounced as 'rich', because speaking out might lead to a potentially fatal accusation of 'shielding landlords'. It was enough for one of the poor to point at a farmer and call him a 'landlord' for his fate to be sealed. In Xing county alone, over 2,000 people were killed, including 250 elderly and twenty-five children – the latter were called 'little landlords'.

One of the victims was a man called Niu Youlan. His surname meant 'ox', and he had helped the guerrilla fighters with large gifts of grain, cloth and silver. His collaboration did not save him. In September 1947 the sixty-one-year-old man was dragged on to a stage to face 5,000 villagers. An iron wire was driven through his nostrils. Then his son was forced to pull him like an ox, blood streaming down his face. He was branded with a hot iron and died eight days later, locked up in a cave. As Xi Zhongxun reported to Mao Zedong on 19 January 1948, 'people are drowned in vats of salt water. Some have boiling oil poured over their heads and burn to death.'[15]

Kang Sheng also directed land reform in other parts of the country. Soon his methods were copied everywhere. In Hebei, Liu Shaoqi reported that 'when the masses fight, they beat, torture and kill people, and right now it is out of control'. People were buried alive, dismembered, shot, throttled to death. Sometimes the bodies of the victims were hung from trees and chopped up.[16] Zhang Mingyuan, in charge of land reform in eastern Hebei, witnessed how in one village forty-eight people were beaten to death in less than thirty minutes. But in many cases the violence was carefully orchestrated, as the poor tallied their votes to decide who should die in village assemblies. When names were called out people voted by raising their hands or by casting a soybean.[17]

One reason why the violence spread was that villagers literally got away with murder. After each struggle session the crowd divided up the material possessions of the victims. Greed and lust for power pushed party activists to define the individuals to be targeted in increasingly vague ways. But fear of retribution also fuelled violence. Deng Xiaoping described his experience of land reform in Anhui:

> In one place in western Anhui the masses hated several landlords and demanded that they be killed, so we followed their wishes and killed them. After they had been killed, the masses feared reprisals from the relatives of the victims, so they drew up an even longer list of names, saying that if they could also be killed everything would be fine. So again we followed their wishes and killed those people. After they had been killed, the masses thought that even more people would seek revenge, so again they came up with a list of names. And again we killed according to their wishes. We kept on killing, and the masses kept on feeling more and more insecure, taking fright and fleeing. In the end we killed two hundred people, and all the work we did in twelve villages was ruined.[18]

By the beginning of 1948, when the pressure abated, some 160 million people were under communist control. On paper the party determined that at least 10 per cent of the population were 'landlords' or 'rich peasants', but on the ground as many as 20 and sometimes even 30 per cent of the villagers were persecuted. The statistical evidence is woefully inadequate, but by a rough approximation between 500,000 and a million people were killed or driven to suicide.

———

In March 1951 a letter was published in the *People's Daily*. Several farmers from Hunan had written to ask about land reform. 'Why doesn't Chairman Mao just print some banknotes, buy the land from the landlords and then give us our share?'[19]

It was a good question. That was, after all, what was happening in the island fortress of arch-villain Chiang Kai-shek. Between 1949 and 1953, large landowners in Taiwan were compensated with commodity certificates and stocks in state-owned industries for the land that was redistributed among small farmers. This approach impoverished some wealthy villagers, but others used their compensation to start commercial and industrial enterprises. Not a drop of blood was shed. The experience was based on Korea and Japan, where land reform was successfully carried out under General Douglas MacArthur between 1945 and 1950. Not a drop of blood was shed there either.[20]

Land reform in the north of mainland China had been carried out in the midst of the civil war. But in the south, where the campaign unfolded from June 1950 to October 1952, it could have been peaceful, as the nationalists had fled to Taiwan. Even Stalin advised Mao to pursue a less destructive approach towards the countryside. Having presided over a ruthless war against the kulaks in the Soviet Union at the height of collectivisation in the 1930s, he was in a good position to offer a word of counsel. He had launched a pitiless campaign of dekulakisation in 1928, resulting in thousands of people being executed and close to 2 million being deported to labour colonies in Siberia or Soviet Central Asia. But now Stalin stressed the need to limit the struggle to landlords only and leave the economy of the rich peasants intact in order to speed up China's recovery after years of warfare. His views were wired to Beijing in February 1950. A few months later the Land Reform Law was published, promising a less divisive policy.[21]

It was not to be. Promises on paper were a world apart from the violence on the ground. Mao wanted the traditional village leaders overthrown so that nothing would stand between the people and the party. As a Chinese saying has it, 'The poor depend on the rich, the rich depend on Heaven.' Now all were to become dependent on the party. And unlike the Soviet Union, where the security organs had liquidated the kulaks, Mao wanted the farmers to do the job themselves. The moral values and social bonds of reciprocity that had long regulated village life were to be destroyed by pitting a majority against a minority. Only by implicating the people in murder could they become permanently linked to the party. Nobody was to stand on the sidelines. Everybody was to have blood on their hands through participation in mass rallies and denunciation meetings. Even before the law was published, Mao warned the assembled leaders on 6 June 1950 to prepare for a battle to the death: 'Land reform in a population of over 300 million people is a vicious war. It is more arduous, more complex, more troublesome than crossing the Yangzi, because our troops are 260 million peasant soldiers. This is a war for land reform, this is the most hideous class war between peasants and landlords. It is a battle to the death.'[22]

The need to break traditional village bonds was particularly acute in the south, where a series of popular rebellions directly challenged the communist party. There were many reasons why villagers objected to their new rulers, but the main one had to do with grain requisitions. These were carried out by the military, and often brutally. In parts of Guangdong 22 to 30 per cent of all the grain was requisitioned, sometimes as much as 60 per cent, forcing people to sell everything they had, from their cattle down to the seed necessary to plant the next crop. Throughout the southwest, the region under Deng Xiaoping's purview, ruthless house searches left their owners with just enough food to last for three days. In Sichuan, farmers were beaten, hung up and had smoke blown into their eyes or alcohol forced down their noses when they refused to hand over their crop. A bulletin reserved for the eyes of the top leadership noted that pregnant women were 'frequently' beaten so badly that they miscarried. Whole families swallowed poison in an attempt to find in death an escape from the tax inspectors. In a bizarre incident in Rongxian county, four women and a man were stripped naked and forced to run with kerosene lamps attached between their legs as an incentive to hand over more food. As a result, 2.9 million tonnes of grain were collected in tax from south-west China in 1950, although the state spent 4.3 million tonnes, most of it on an army of 1.7 million troops. Traditionally, the region had produced a grain surplus. Now it was bankrupt.[23]

People rebelled throughout the south. In Hunan, villagers took to the streets to demonstrate against the new regime. In a single incident in Nanxian county, a rice-growing region near Dongting Lake, more than 2,000 farmers clashed with soldiers. Shots were fired and thirteen people were killed or injured. The following day a crowd of 10,000 irate farmers made their way to the county seat. Their demands: 'Stop the Procurements, Oppose the Transportation of Grain'. There were a dozen similar incidents in the province. A secret report described assaults against granaries in Hubei as 'ceaseless'. In Xiaogan a crowd of 2,000 people dragged away 7.5 tonnes of grain from a state warehouse. In Xishui, a county with a long revolutionary history, a crowd forcibly removed food from freight boats. In Enshi, a mass demonstration against procurements resulted in four dead. In Wuli, just outside Wuchang, the local people rebelled against the physical abuse they had to endure from the local cadres as well as 'random beatings and random killings' by members of the peasant association. By March 1950, dozens of 'relatively large rebellions of a mass character' – to use the wooden language of the party – had rocked Hubei. In Guizhou some of the incidents involved over 100,000 insurgents, ready to fight the communist party to the death.[24]

Unrest and rebellion also flared like tiny flash fires in parts of the north where land reform had not yet been carried out. In many parts of Shaanxi, where the dusty, dewless land was cracking from the summer drought, farmers armed with hoes started to hide their wheat for fear of state procurements.[25] Further inland along the ancient silk road, in Yongdeng county, Gansu, people banded together to resist state procurements. In one village, 200 farmers surrounded the grain collectors and beat them. In Minle county they were tied up.[26] In east China, some forty rebellions rocked the countryside in the first three months of 1950 alone. Most occurred in poor regions, and the target was always the same: famished villagers turned against the party and stormed the granaries. The rebels removed 3,000 tonnes of grain, leaving over 120 soldiers and cadres dead. As a report noted, local officials 'are completely unconcerned about the hardships of the masses, and even randomly beat, arrest and kill people in the course of their work, producing antagonisms with the masses'.[27]

The party blamed 'landlords' – as well as spies and saboteurs – for standing behind the rebellions. By expropriating large numbers of them and redistributing their assets, the communists hoped to persuade the villagers to rally behind them.[28]

But as the second round of land reform unfolded, a new problem appeared: the further south the communists went, the less land there was. A world of difference existed between the sparsely populated plains of Manchuria and the crowded villages south of the Yangzi. As there was not enough land to be distributed to the poor, the pledge not to interfere with 'rich peasants' was soon broken. In Sichuan it was enough for a farmer actually to make a profit in order to be classified as a 'landlord'. Families who owned a pot of white sugar or a buffalo to plough the fields were denounced so that their meagre possessions could be confiscated. Even north of the Yangzi, where parts of the countryside had already gone through a gruelling process of land distribution in 1947–8, villagers were subjected to a second round of terror. In Shandong many ordinary farmers were randomly arrested and beaten, regardless of whether or not they met the definition of a 'landlord'. In Pingyi county, where only a quarter of those locked up were landowners, a local party official proclaimed that 'from now on we should kill somebody at every one of our meetings'. Indiscriminate beatings at village rallies were 'common practice': 'some of the cadres drop hints that encourage beatings, others do not interfere when beatings take place'. In Teng county, as one party secretary reported, people were topped with dunce's caps, forced to kneel and then beaten or stripped and exposed to the cold in the winter. Some had their hair pulled out, a few their ears bitten off. In the village of Xigangshan villagers urinated on their victims.[29]

Parts of the countryside descended into a spiral of violence because so many ordinary farmers who were classified as 'landlords' or 'rich peasants' started to retaliate. In a village in Guizhou, seventy-year-old Zhang Baoshan was mistakenly classified as a landlord. Party activists dragged the man to a rally where he was beaten, tortured and drenched in freezing water. Infuriated, two of his sons went on a rampage, hacking several of their enemies to death. Unable to return home, the sons hid deep in the mountains where they were soon hunted down and lynched by a search party. A frenzied mob cut off their tongues and genitals. Their bodies were burned and the ashes thrown into a river. The entire family of Zhang Baoshan, more than twenty people, were beaten before being sent to prison. An investigation later showed that eight people in the village lost their lives as a consequence of random labelling of the poor as 'landlords'.[30]

Sometimes whole villages turned against the communists. In Lanfeng county, Henan, on average one farmer was killed every three days in April

1950. Some of the victims were ordinary people on their way to market. They were set upon by cadres who beat them with the butts of their rifles. After one woman had been shot in the stomach and died amid screaming children and frightened villagers, the crowd turned, overpowering the perpetrators and seizing their weapons.[31]

More subtle forms of resistance appeared everywhere. Despite all the efforts of the work teams in charge of land reform – the painstaking collection of information on the local power structure, the carefully choreographed meetings to 'speak bitterness', the endless propaganda, the village rallies backed up by the power of local militias – ordinary people had qualms about persecuting and stealing from their erstwhile neighbours. Many knew how to keep their emotions in check, locking them away deep inside, to be exhibited only on appropriate occasions. They learned how to perform as a way to survive. Esther Cheo, who joined the People's Liberation Army in 1949, saw how people could switch their emotions on and off during village meetings: 'I noticed one woman shout and scream at the landlord. As soon as her part was played out, she returned to the crowd, took her baby who had been peacefully suckling at another woman's breast, and continued feeding it at her own, while she calmly watched the next participant in the struggle meeting.' Those who shouted the loudest sometimes supported the victims, for instance by furtively returning the spoils that had accrued to them. In Xushui, a young party activist called Sun handed back a bucket of corn to a former employer who had always treated him like a family member. Sun was stripped of his party membership.[32]

As work teams in charge of land reform fanned out south of the Yangzi, they encountered powerful clans that were far more diverse and integrated than the rhetoric of class warfare implied. Entire villages shared the same surname. In Hubei, some of the leaders paraded at denunciation meetings managed to turn the assembled throng against the cadres. In Fang county the farmers unanimously agreed not to dispossess any of those targeted as landlords. In Hunan some wealthy farmers slaughtered their cattle, sold the land and bartered their tools before land reform had even started. In Xiangtan one man pulled down his house to sell the bricks. In two counties some 27,000 fir trees on private land were chopped down before they could be redistributed. In Zhejiang, local leaders harangued the villagers against land reform, warning them that 'year after year the taxes will increase': a few predicted that 'it will be hard to avoid famine in future'.[33]

In Sichuan a few landowners took control of the situation, carefully studying the land-reform law, assembling the villagers and staging fake 'struggle sessions' before the work teams had even arrived. They determined their own class status, ascribing the label of 'landlord' to a mere handful of people. Some voluntarily distributed parts of their land. Others deposited, bartered or gifted their property to other villagers, making sure that people actually sided with them. In some cases entire villages stood firmly behind those denounced as 'landlords'. And when all else failed, some would rather torch their houses than hand them over to the mob. This happened all over Sichuan.[34]

The party interpreted popular resistance as clear evidence that the dark powers of feudalism were still holding sway over the countryside. The less support it found among the villagers, the louder its call for violence. Landlords and counter-revolutionaries, party officials claimed, aided and abetted from abroad, poisoned the minds of the villagers with religion, infiltrated peasant associations with their henchmen and corrupted party cadres with offers of cash and women. Nothing short of terror would overcome the forces of reaction, as ever more murder was mandated. On 21 April 1951, provincial head Li Jingquan ordered that 6,000 landlords, several thousand of them lingering in prison, be paraded and executed in west Sichuan in order to give land reform greater momentum: 'In land reform we should arrest those who lie low, link up with foreign powers and commit counter-revolutionary crimes: we should kill half of them, or about four thousand, in addition to some one or two thousand currently in gaol who still need to be executed. If we follow this plan we will execute five to six thousand of them, which corresponds roughly to the principle of killing a small batch in land reform.' His report was endorsed in Chongqing by his superior Deng Xiaoping, the man in charge of the south-west of China.[35]

Other regions were just as tough, although precise figures are hard to come by. In Luotian, a Hubei county covered in chestnut forests, as many as one out of every 330 villagers was shot. In a mere twenty days in May

1951, over 170 people were executed as 'landlords'. First some of the victims were asked to surrender 500 kilos of grain. Then they were asked for a tonne. Then they were shot. Many of the targets were not wealthy at all, but 'the masses did not dare to speak out' in denunciation rallies.[36]

Mao himself set the tone. In the Pearl River delta in Guangdong, one of the wealthiest and most commercialised regions in China, many landowners had extensive contacts with entrepreneurs from Hong Kong. Large plots of land were also bought by overseas Chinese who planned to come home for retirement. And all along the coast there were villages dominated by wealthy emigrants, their modern houses and foreign manners standing in stark contrast to some of the more traditional hamlets inland. Across the province more than 6 million people were family dependants of overseas Chinese: many women, children and elderly people relied on remittances. In total one-fifth of the land belonged to emigrants living abroad. Fang Fang, the party boss in Guangdong, was aware of their economic importance and tried to protect some of their land from expropriation. In 1952 Mao sent Tao Zhu to take over from Fang Fang. Tao Zhu had made his name in ruthlessly suppressing all opposition in Guangxi, killing tens of thousands of people accused of being 'landlords' or 'counter-revolutionaries'. Some compared him to a tank, crushing all enemies in his path.

Fang was soon summoned by Mao for an audience in Beijing, accused of 'localism', purged and never heard of again. In May 1952 alone, over 6,000 cadres in Guangdong were demoted or persecuted for having followed an 'incorrect party line'. Across the province, ferocious beatings and random killings of landowners and wealthy farmers became the norm. 'Every Village Bleeds, Every Household Fights' was the slogan. People were trussed up, hung from beams, buried up to the neck and torched. In Huiyang county, just across the border from Hong Kong, close to 200 people were killed. Further north in Chaozhou, over 700 committed suicide. In a matter of three months, more than 4,000 people lost their lives, either beaten to death or hounded to their graves by constant persecution.[37]

Poverty became the norm. The relative prosperity that some families had achieved through generations of hard work evaporated overnight. People who had managed to pull themselves up by their bootstraps thanks to a combination of initiative, diligence and perseverance became outcasts. Expertise and experience in the village were derided; success became a mark of the exploiter. Poor peasants and poor workers were extolled instead. They were born red. 'To be Poor is Glorious,' the party proclaimed. But the villagers not only took pride in their poverty, they became fearful of wealth. In Shandong many refused to do more than the strict minimum: 'the party likes the poor, and the poorer the better'. None other than Kang Sheng, put in charge of the province in 1949, reported that productivity in the areas where land distribution had been carried out was in free fall, as villagers believed that it was 'glorious to be poor'. Across the north of China, agricultural output plummeted by a third. Civil war caused massive destruction and population displacement, but as some of the cadres themselves put it rather bluntly, 'land reform has destroyed production'.[38]

A host of different disincentives reinforced each other, creating a vicious circle of impoverishment. The rights to the land were vague, and villagers never felt quite secure in their ownership of confiscated property. Above all, in ferocious campaigns fuelled by fear, greed and jealousy, nobody wanted to rise above the others. The plots themselves were small and often dispersed across the countryside. Many of the beneficiaries lacked the knowledge, utensils, seeds and fertiliser to cultivate the land. The link between the village and the market was disrupted. Shops and enterprises run by landowners were ransacked or went bankrupt. Subsidiary occupations once pursued by villagers were viewed as 'capitalist' activities. In Sichuan, one of the country's wealthiest provinces, about two-thirds of the land distributed to the poor produced less than before.[39]

Another form of impoverishment appeared. Many of the people targeted during the campaign were hardly better off than their neighbours, but across the country there were also families who had accumulated considerable material wealth. Whether scholars, merchants or politicians, many were committed collectors of art objects, sometimes just a few small curios, inkstones, water droppers or figurines to decorate a desk or complement a study, sometimes more extensive collections of rare manuscripts, bronze coins, wooden furniture or ink paintings. In fact, such was the respect for high culture in a country governed for centuries by scholar officials that few households that could afford it lived without some token of the past.

Some of this was distributed during land reform, but much was destroyed, to the point where in June 1951 the Ministry of Culture ordered all antiques and rare books confiscated during land reform to be collected and inventoried. In many cases it was too late. In Shandong, for instance, most of the antiques had already been burned or consigned to the scrap heap, recycled as so many relics of an exploitative past. As an investigation carried out by the party revealed, 'Everywhere old books that were considered to contain feudal ideas were thrown away or used as old paper.' Much larger remnants of feudalism were attacked. In Jining, the Taibai Tower, where the famed Tang-dynasty poet Li Bai was rumoured to have lived, was torn down (a replica was erected in 1952). In Liaocheng the grave of the eighteenth-century poet and painter Gao Fenghan was excavated. In Jimo the labouring masses helped themselves to six graves dating back to the Han dynasty. In Zibo several Buddhist statues and temples, seen as so many marks of superstition, were mutilated. In Laoshan, a coastal mountain near Qingdao considered to be one of the birthplaces of Taoism, a large collection of more than a hundred Ming and Qing scriptures from the Huayan Temple were used as scrap. Some of the classics of Buddhism were used to roll cigarettes. There were many other examples, 'too many to enumerate', according to one report, as many cadres treated historical relics as 'rubbish' or 'superstition'.[40]

By all accounts, by the end of 1951 over 10 million landlords had been expropriated and more than 40 per cent of the land had changed hands. The exact number of victims killed in the land reform will never be known, but it is unlikely to have been fewer than 1.5 to 2 million people from 1947 to 1952. Millions more had their lives destroyed by being stigmatised as exploiters and class enemies.[41]

5

The Great Terror

By the summer of 1950 the communists had few friends left. The party, Mao explained to his colleagues, was 'hitting out in all directions', making nothing but enemies. Capitalists disliked the communist party, the jobless were restless and most workers were disgruntled thanks to the economic slump. In the countryside villagers were taxed to the hilt, while in the cities intellectuals feared losing their jobs. Those working in the arts resented political interference. Opposition to the new regime was rife in religious circles. 'The entire country is tense,' Mao noted, and 'we are rather lonely'. The party had to make friends and isolate its enemies one by one. Ease up the pressure on the ethnic minorities, he advocated. Appease private merchants, create a united front with democrats and take a long view in reforming intellectuals. 'Advance slowly.'[1]

Who were the real enemies who should be tackled? 'Our general policy', Mao continued, 'is to eliminate the remnant Nationalist forces, the secret agents and the bandits, overthrow the landlord class, liberate Taiwan and Tibet and fight imperialism to the end.'[2]

Less than three weeks after Chairman Mao's speech, the North Korean People's Army crossed the 38th-parallel border and invaded South Korea. On 25 June 1950, the United Nations Security Council unanimously condemned the invasion, and a few days later President Truman rallied to the defence of his South Korean ally. A UN counter-offensive under General Douglas MacArthur drove the North Koreans back past the 38th parallel on 1 October 1950, the first anniversary of the founding of the People's Republic of China. Two hundred thousand Chinese troops secretly entered North Korea on 18 October. A week later they attacked the UN troops near the Sino-Korean border.

The war provided a pretext to rally popular support for the regime and strike hard against the enemies Mao had described only months earlier. On 10 October, traditionally celebrated as National Day by the nationalists, Mao issued a directive to liquidate 'remnant nationalist forces', 'secret agents', 'bandits' and other 'counter-revolutionaries' who stood in the path of revolution. For a full year a Great Terror would run alongside land reform, shaking the country to its very roots and forcing people from all walks of life to take sides.

How many 'bandits' and 'secret agents' were still threatening to overthrow the communist regime in October 1950? Quite a few according to the propaganda machine, relentlessly pumping out dark warnings of sabotage and subversion by hidden spies and fifth columnists. Paranoia was intrinsic to the regime, which lived in fear of its own shadow. The party had long developed a habit of blaming every setback on real or imagined enemies. Behind every poisoned well or granary that went up in flames lurked a spy or landlord. Every act of resistance by ordinary farmers – and there were many – was seen as proof of counter-revolution. Tension was also deliberately cultivated to keep people on edge and justify ever more intrusive forms of policing.

On the other hand there was a real threat to the new regime in much of the south. As we have seen, dozens of armed rebellions and popular insurrections endangered the regime in provinces such as Hubei, Sichuan and Guizhou. In Guangxi, a subtropical province covered in karst mountains and lush forests on the border of Vietnam, over 1,400 cadres and 700 troops had been ambushed and killed by opposition elements by the summer of 1950. The communists had eliminated 170,000 nationalist troops from the province in the first months of liberation, but soon violence flared up again, as villagers joined the opposition. In Yulin county over 200 villages took part in armed rebellions. In a single village in Yining county a third of all men vanished into the forest to join the rebel forces. For decades the communists had waged a highly mobile war on the nationalist government in scattered raids and ambushes, striking vulnerable targets only to withdraw immediately into the countryside. 'The enemy advances, we retreat; the enemy camps, we harass; the enemy tires, we attack; the enemy retreats, we pursue.' So Mao had written in 1930. Now his own party faced the threat of guerrilla warfare in the south.[3]

Mao singled out Guangxi for special blame, lambasting its leaders for 'shocking leniency' towards the insurgents. The province acted quickly, killing 3,000 guerrilla fighters in the first couple of months following the 10 October 1950 directive. Then Mao sent Tao Zhu, the man popularly characterised as a 'tank', to crush all opposition, killing 15,000 people by March 1951. Over 100,000 were sent to prison, where many died of starvation and sickness. In parts of Yulin a fifth of the entire population was put behind bars. Others were labelled as landlords, their wives and children persecuted in their absence. By the summer of 1951, Tao Zhu wired a message to Mao: 'Guangxi: 450,000 bandits pacified; 40,000 killed; one-third may or may not have deserved death.'[4]

By the time the campaign ended in October 1951, a total of 46,200 had been killed, or 2.56 per thousand of the total population in the province. In other words, more than one person out of every 400 had been executed.[5]

But the terror was just as relentless elsewhere. The man Mao entrusted with overseeing the operation was Luo Ruiqing. He was born into a landlord family in Nanchong, a region rich in rice, oranges and silkworms in mountainous Sichuan. He never smiled, having suffered a facial injury while fighting against the nationalists. His mouth was frozen in a permanent rictus. Like Lin Biao, Luo was trained in the famed Whampoa Military Academy under Chiang Kai-shek, but joined the communist party in 1928. He was one of the first to be sent to the Soviet Union, where he worked with the secret police. In Yan'an, he was put in charge of cleaning up an anti-Mao faction in the rival Fourth Front Army. This he apparently did with such 'crudeness, savagery and maliciousness', according to one high-profile refugee, that he earned the gratitude of the Chairman. Once he became head of the security machine in Beijing, he hung a huge portrait of Felix Dzerzhinsky in his office. The founder of the Cheka, the infamous state security organisation in the Soviet Union, was his model and mentor.[6]

Luo was an essential cog in the machinery of repression, transmitting the Chairman's orders directly to the provincial leaders. When Li

Xiannian, the leader of Hubei, went to see him in Beijing in January 1951, a mere 220 counter-revolutionaries had been liquidated in his province. The killings accelerated. By February 8,000 suspects had been executed, followed by a further 7,000 in the spring. Soon 37,000 people had been eliminated, as parts of the countryside descended into a reign of terror where cadres ruled by the gun. So habitual became reliance on terror that Li Xiannian could no longer restrain the campaign he had started. Some local officials refused to stop the killings, using terror as a routine tool of control. They blackmailed their superiors when told to curb the executions: 'If I am not allowed to kill people, I won't help out with production and I won't mobilise the masses. I'll just wait till you issue me with your permission and then I'll work on the masses.' In the end, more than 45,000 people were killed, or 1.75 per thousand of the population in Hubei.[7]

Like steel production or grain output, death came with a quota mandated from above. Luo Ruiqing could not possibly oversee the arrest, trial and disposal of the many millions who became the targets of terror, so instead Mao handed down a killing quota as a rough guide for action. The norm, he felt, was one per thousand, a ratio he was willing to adjust to the particular circumstances of each region. His subordinates kept track of local killing rates like bean counters, occasionally negotiating for a higher quota. In May 1951 Guangxi province, for instance, was told to kill more, even though a rate of 1.63 per thousand had already been achieved. Guizhou province, destabilised by popular uprisings, requested permission to kill three per thousand, and the Liuzhou region five per thousand. 'The provincial party committee of Guizhou requests a target of three per thousand, that too is too much, I feel. This is how I look at it: we can go over one per thousand, but not by too much.' Once a death rate of two per thousand had been achieved, the Chairman opined, people should be sentenced to life imprisonment and sent to work in labour camps.[8]

Mao adjudicated the numbers, posing as a voice of moderation. He lashed out at 'rightists' who fell behind their target but reined in the zeal of 'leftists'. Words of praise were handed out in directives circulated among the top leadership. In March 1951 the Chairman lauded Henan for having killed 12,000 counter-revolutionaries, as the province steeled itself for liquidating another batch of 20,000 in the spring, bringing the total to about 32,000. 'In a province of 30 million that is a good number.' But figures were merely a guide, he warned, as more might have to be killed. Mao emphasised that the terror should be 'stable' (*wen*), 'precise' (*zhun*) and 'ruthless' (*hen*): the campaign should be carried out with surgical precision, without any slippage into random slaughter, which would undermine the standing of the party. 'But before anything else, the term "ruthless" has to be emphasised.' Perusing the reports he was handed by Luo Ruiqing, he nudged the country further: 'In provinces where few have been killed a large batch should be killed; the killings can absolutely not be allowed to stop too early.'[9]

Mao was deliberately vague, forcing his underlings to pore over every one of his numerous remarks, speeches and directives for guidance on how to carry out the terror. He allowed his subordinates to compete with each other in presenting new ideas and policies. Mao casually picked and chose from among their proposals. This form of government allowed ambitious elements to push for a more radical implementation of what they thought were the Chairman's true intentions, although it left them open to criticism later if their initiatives backfired. It also meant that everybody in the top leadership became implicated in the terror. Nobody merely acted under orders, as leaders created their own guidelines, trying to guess what was required of them. Deng Zihui, the regional boss of south China, and Deng Xiaoping, for instance, suggested in February 1951 that between half and two-thirds of all counter-revolutionaries be executed. Mao approved, on condition that the killings be 'secretly controlled, without disorder or mistakes'.[10]

Another proposal came from Rao Shushi, the man in control of the east of the country. On 29 March 1951, Rao proposed that the campaign be moved from the 'outer circle' to the 'inner circle', meaning that the fight should be taken to traitors and spies within the party. Mao approved, sweeping aside the idea that the party was 'killing too much'. A central directive on a purge of enemies within the ranks was issued on 21 May 1951.[11]

By April 1951 three out of every five provinces had reached or surpassed the target of one per thousand. In Guizhou three per thousand had been eliminated, despite the words of admonition from the Chairman.[12] Over a million people lingered in prison, and Luo Ruiqing ordered all arrests to cease for several months so that the backlog could be cleared. But by the summer the lull in the slaughter came to an end, as Luo expressed regret for the kindness shown to enemies of the regime and announced that 'we must kill and resolutely eliminate the remnant forces of counter-revolution'.[13]

———————

Mao oversaw the campaign from his headquarters next to the Forbidden City, casually adjudicating the death rate according to each case. In a few places the terror barely lived up to its name, petering out in the hands of highly selective cadres. But many of Mao's underlings were willing executioners. In an increasingly fractured society, the terror was also driven from below by people seeking retribution, settling old grudges or righting personal wrongs in the name of revolution.

The party archives are full of cases of blatant abuse driven by cadres eager to show their determination to stamp out counter-revolution. In Yanxing county, a wealthy region in Yunnan covered in salt flats, over a hundred middle-school students were arrested and tortured in April 1951 after an anonymous denunciation reached the local party headquarters. Wu Liening, ten years old, was hung from a beam and beaten. Ma Silie, aged eight, was tied up on a cross in a kneeling position. A wooden pole was placed across his thighs and pressed down by two of his tormentors, crushing his legs and knees on the concrete floor. Even Liu Wendi, aged six, was accused of being the head of a spying squad. Two of the children were tortured to death. This was not an isolated example. A team of militia in Sichuan also tried to uncover counter-revoultionaries among schoolchildren. Some had both hands and feet tied up while being suspended upside down, others were made to go through mock executions. Three were tortured to death, another five of the children committed suicide. About fifty of the victims survived the abuse, although many were crippled or maimed for life.[14]

In Guangdong a full third of all the victims were wrongly accused – by the standards of the party itself. In Luoding county, a single case of suspected theft by a student led to the arrest and interrogation of 340 young people aged thirteen to twenty-five. Only after hundreds of letters of complaint were sent to the provincial inspectorate was one leading official dispatched a year later to investigate the case.[15]

In the fight against counter-revolutionaries entire hamlets were mistakenly eradicated. In one notorious incident in Bigu, Jiangxi, a squad leader discovered smoke coming from a cluster of homes suspected of harbouring enemies. He opened fire without asking any questions. Then all the houses were torched. Twenty-one people were killed, another twenty-six victims later dying of their wounds. All except one were women and small children.[16]

As cadres rushed to achieve their killing quota, false arrests were common. They reached over 50 per cent in parts of Guizhou. In Congjiang county, fewer than a third of all arrests were based on any kind of concrete proof. In Chang'an village, Xie Chaoxiang aroused suspicion by merely knocking on the door of a landlord. He was locked up and beaten till he denounced forty-eight other farmers, most of them poor. Eight of these were arrested and beaten unconscious, doused with water, revived and beaten again. Six committed suicide. In another case a man killed himself after he was accused of having murdered eight people in 1929 – when he was a baby aged one.[17]

Merely looking suspicious could determine a person's fate. In Qujing county, Yunnan, 150 'bandit spies' lingered in prison without any supporting evidence. As the cadre in charge explained, 'if they look like bandits, and they look like spies, we call them bandit spies'. A mere link with the old regime, no matter how tenuous, could lead to death. In Fushun, a county in Sichuan, 4,000 government employees were arrested for having had contact with the nationalists at one point or another in their careers. Often the local cadres had to second-guess what their superiors expected from them, in much the same way that party leaders tried to divine what their Chairman really wanted. Both Yunnan and Sichuan were under the firm grip of Deng Xiaoping, who wrote to Mao to announce that counter-revolutionaries were rife in the local government, while up to 90 per cent of the local cadres in some villages in Yunnan were spies, landlords or other bad elements.[18]

As with land reform, leaders everywhere were afraid of falling behind, comparing their performance with that of others. Villages, counties and provinces emulated each other, preferring to kill too many rather than too few – and risk being purged as 'rightists'. In Yunnan some cadres killed at random: 'Some places simply look at how many have been arrested and how many have been killed elsewhere and then hurriedly proceed to arrest and kill within a few days.' Some party members were so afraid of appearing to be lacklustre that they had to steel themselves. As a party official enjoined: 'You must hate even if you feel no hatred, you must kill even if you do not wish to kill.' Thousands were silently executed in order to fulfil and surpass the quota.[19]

As the gaols – from formal prisons to schools, temples and clan halls commandeered by the military – were overflowing, the authorities sometimes thought it more convenient to execute the inmates rather than go through all the formalities of an investigation. In west Sichuan, as Hu Yaobang reported, 'there are extremely few people sentenced to a term of five or more years, as some comrades feel that if a prisoner is given a long sentence, he might as well be killed to save time'.[20]

Sometimes party members used the terror to pursue their own vendettas against the local population, trying to conceal their activities from their superiors. All over Sichuan local cadres killed secretly, eradicating their enemies without any of the public rallies mandated by Beijing. In Maogong, a town where the communists had regrouped under Mao Zedong after crossing the rugged Great Snow Mountain during the Long March in June 1935, only ten victims of a four-month reign of terror were announced in a public notice. A further 170 were covertly assassinated. Twenty were stabbed to death with bayonets. A few of their heads were cut off and displayed outside the city gates. Some of those killed were farmers who had never participated in any opposition to the party. Maogong was an area inhabited by ethnic groups, and only stark violence, the local cadres reasoned, would bring them to heel.[21]

By May 1951 the situation was slipping out of control in those regions of south China controlled by Deng Zihui and Deng Xiaoping. The Chairman intervened, ordering that authority to kill must be transferred one level up, removing the initiative from the counties.[22] A frenzy of killing ensued, as party officials hurried to eliminate their targets as fast as possible before the impending deadline. In the Fuling region, made up of some ten counties with terraced fields along the Yangzi River in Sichuan, they disposed of 2,676 suspects in ten days. A further 500 were executed in the two days following the deadline, by which time 8,500 people had been

killed in little more than two months. Fuling was not exceptional, although
the full scope of what happened will never be known. When underlings
asked the party secretary in Wenjiang county to approve further killings
from a batch of 127 prisoners, he simply said, 'Just have a look and pick a
few.' Fifty-seven were shot within three days after the moratorium had been
imposed. In west Sichuan, a thousand victims were systematically slaughtered every day for a gruesome week before the authority to kill was lost.[23]

Across the country people were tortured or beaten to death. A few were
bayoneted and decapitated. But for the most part they were shot. This was
not always as straightforward as it might seem. In the ancient city of Kaifeng,
dotted with temples and pagodas, the executioners first tried to shoot their
targets in the head, but this turned out to be so messy that after a while they
aimed for the heart instead. This too proved difficult. Some shots missed,
leaving the victims writhing on the floor in agony so that they had to be shot
again. Killing demanded skills that came only with practice.[24]

Occasionally a victim had to kneel and bow, as a long machete-like
knife came swinging down to sever the head from the body. In Guangxi
the heads were sometimes suspended by ropes on wooden frames, resembling football goalposts, at the entrance to the market place. The crimes of
the victims were written beside the posts.[25]

The countryside echoed to the crack of the executioner's bullet, as real
and imaginary enemies were forced to kneel on makeshift platforms and
executed from behind before the assembled villagers. Usually only a few of
the targets were shot. This is how Zhang Yingrong, who was carried on a
wooden plank on to the stage after being beaten, remembers the occasion:

> There were ten others on the stage for denunciation, all tied with ropes.
> My eldest brother was there beside me, his arms held behind him by
> two militiamen, his body bent to 90 degrees. I lay on the wooden plank,
> looking up. The rain had stopped. Amid the loud shouting, I could hear
> the river nearby. The clouds had dispersed and the sky was clear blue. I
> thought: People lived harmoniously under the same sky in the same
> village for many years. Why did they act like this now? Why did they

hate each other and torture each other like that? Was that what the Communist revolution was all about? All the 'class enemies' had been beaten; their faces were swollen and their heads scarred. Beatings couldn't quench the Communists' thirst. They started killing. After that meeting, all the former officials under the old regime were executed, including my brother; their children were sentenced to ten or twenty years in jail, where some lost their minds, or died.[26]

After public executions, family members were often allowed to collect the bodies. In the countryside silent figures would move stealthily towards the corpses at dusk, clutching some straw with which to wrap the bodies and improvised stretchers to carry them back home. But sometimes the killers blew up the bodies of their victims with dynamite, a practice so common that some provinces had to issue a formal ban against it.

Some victims were executed away from the public eye, in forests, near ravines and riverbanks, alone or in batches. The bodies were thrown into pits or shallow mass graves, but a few were left to rot. Relatives often spent weeks trying to find the corpses of their loved ones. Those who were fortunate collected what remains they could gather and gave them a discreet burial. Zhang Mao'en had to wait ten months before receiving permission to collect the body of his brother, who had been shot by the roadside and dumped into a ravine in Yunnan. 'My brother's rotting corpse looked like a fallen tree stuck in a stream. My second oldest brother and my mother went down into the water to drag it out, and it fell to pieces. We collected the bones, washed them, and put them in a box we had brought with us.'[27]

Sometimes the bodies were eaten by wild animals. In Hebei some of the mass graves were so shallow that feral dogs dug up the remains and devoured them. In Sichuan one woman suspected of having hidden a gun was dragged away and so badly tortured that she hung herself from a tree. Her body was dumped in the forest and eaten by wild boars.[28]

———

The terror initially claimed fewer lives in the cities. Party leaders were concerned about the adverse publicity that too many executions might generate. They also had to compromise with the professionals, businessmen, entrepreneurs and industrialists on whom the economy still depended. But the conciliatory tone soon changed.

On 13 March 1951 some 200 military leaders assembled in Jinan, the provincial capital of Shandong, to attend a concert organised in their honour. As applause erupted at the end of a folk performance, a young man stood up at one of the tables, walked towards Huang Zuyan, a top-ranking military leader, and fired a gun. The bullet entered his neck and exited through the jawbone. Huang collapsed on his chair before slumping to the ground, covered in blood. As the guests panicked and hid under the tables, the aggressor fired one more shot before killing himself. Huang later died on his way to hospital. Wang Jumin, the assassin, was thirty-four years old and had joined the communist party in 1943. He had turned against the cause after his family was attacked during land reform.

Mao put the party on high alert. Here was a case that showed how devious the enemy could be: penetrating the party, lying low for years before suddenly striking out against leaders at the highest level. 'We absolutely cannot be irresolute. To tolerate evil is to abet it. This is critical.'[29]

Within days of the assassination, Mao demanded 'several batches of big killings' in the cities. When writing to Huang Jing, the party secretary of Tianjin, he invoked the will of the people to justify more shootings: 'The people say that killing counter-revolutionaries is even more joyful than a good downpour.'[30]

Raids were organised across the country. In Shandong, where the assassination had taken place only weeks earlier, the police rounded up over 4,000 suspects overnight on 1 April. In Jinan, where 1,200 were arrested, people spent the night peering fearfully through the windows, trying to find out who was being dragged away. Within days several dozen had been executed in public, attracting words of praise from the Chairman. Shandong, he pronounced, was a model for those 'faint-hearted comrades' who failed to carry out the campaign resolutely.[31]

Three weeks later, on 28 April, the police swept through Shanghai, Nanjing and fourteen other cities in one co-ordinated raid, targeting 16,855 individuals. It was a Saturday, and Robert Loh, a returned student who had joined a Shanghai university two years earlier, spent the evening marking student essays. 'For hours I heard the screaming of sirens and the roar of lorries speeding through the streets. I was uneasily aware that some-thing momentous was happening, but I was not alarmed. The next morning, however, the servants reported in consternation that thousands of people had been arrested. They said that all those who had held posi-tions in the Nationalist Party under the previous regime were taken by the security police.'[32]

The doors of those who had been arrested were sealed with a large red paper X, meaning that the belongings of the occupant were not to be disturbed until the police had investigated them. So many red crosses appeared on doors that the Shanghai police took over public buildings as prisons. The raid had been well prepared. For weeks before the night of the arrests the Public Security Bureau had requested all those who had worked for the nationalists to register. The stated purpose was to give those who had made 'political mistakes' a chance to 'start life anew'. Autobiographies had to be submitted and details of every known person had to be provided, whether family, friend or associate. With every full confession came the promise of lenient treatment.

Public executions followed. 'One of the execution grounds was near the university. Every day we would see truckloads of prisoners. While we were in our classes we would hear the terrible shooting. The lorries carrying away the corpses dripped blood onto the road that ran past the university buildings.' Robert Loh, like others across the country, was forced to attend more than one shooting. The stated purpose was to educate the people, although he left more terrorised and sickened than enlightened.

> I remember especially the trial of a factory foreman who had extorted money from his employees and had seduced women workers under him. When found guilty, he was shoved off the platform. He rolled grotesquely because of his tied hands. While he was still on the ground, a policeman shot him through the head. I was about ten paces away. I saw the splatter of the victim's brains, and the obscene twitching of his body.[33]

With the executions came a wave of suicides, as desperate people threw themselves from tall buildings along the Bund. The police soon erected nets which jutted out from windows on the first floor. Instead of leaping from windows, candidates for death now took running jumps from the roof. One man landed on a rickshaw, killing himself, the puller and his passenger. After the police and the military had started guarding all tall buildings, corpses appeared daily in the rivers of Shanghai.[34]

Mass executions were held in every city. In Beijing they were chaired by the mayor. Peng Zhen shouted at a mass meeting in Beijing: 'How should we deal with this herd of beastly tyrants, bandits, traitors and spies who are guilty of the most heinous crimes?'

Answered a crowd of followers: 'Execute them by firing squad!'

Peng: 'We have already disposed of a number of counter-revolutionaries, but there are still some in prison. Besides, there are still spies and special agents hiding in Beijing. What shall we do with them?'

The crowd: 'Suppress the counter-revolutionaries resolutely!'

Peng: 'Among the accused today there are despots in the markets, among fishmongers, real-estate brokers, water carriers and nightsoil scavengers. How should we cope with these feudal remnants?'

The crowd: 'Execute them by firing squad!'[35]

The large gatherings in stadiums in Shanghai, Tianjin and Beijing were carefully orchestrated, from speeches scripted in advance to ritual denunciations of victims on stage. But smaller batches were executed in front of party activists as a way of testing their resolve, determination and loyalty to the cause. Esther Cheo, who was being groomed for promotion to cadre, had to attend a mass execution in Beijing: 'We were taken in a lorry to the place of execution, near the famous tourist spot, the Temple of Heaven. The victims were kneeling down beside cheap coffins, their hands tied behind their backs with wire. About six security police moved nonchalantly along shooting them in the back of the head. As they fell, some of their heads split open, some just fell with a neat little hole, while others had their brains splattered all over the dusty ground and on to the clothes of the next victims.' As she turned away in revulsion, a cadre grabbed her by the shoulders. 'Take a good look!' he shouted. 'This is what the revolution is all about!' She screamed and wanted to hide her face, but he held her tight and forced her head around to make her look. She saw her companions running over the bodies, cheering.[36]

Few victims ever spoke out. The cadres in charge had honed their skills in mass rallies during land reform, and they knew how to prevent a last-ditch attempt by the condemned to proclaim their innocence or shout anti-communist slogans. Threats of retaliation against family members were very effective. Other measures were used. As one organiser explained: 'We put a wire ring around every accused person. If he tries to struggle or resist, the soldiers have only to pull the wire back against his windpipe and choke him.' Sometimes local authorities mandated a rope instead of wire.[37]

There were fewer slippages in the cities, where it is unlikely that more than one per thousand of the population was killed. Mao thought that fewer would be acceptable in order not to antagonise the public. He calculated in April 1951: 'So in Beijing, with its population of about 2 million, over 10,000 have already been arrested and 700 of these have been killed, while another batch of 700 is scheduled for execution. Killing roughly 1,400 should be enough.'[38]

––––––––

The campaign of terror was over by the end of 1951, but the killings never really stopped. With each new wave, ever larger sections of the population were brought into the fold. In Zhejiang, one of the smallest and most densely populated provinces, with valleys and plains along its coastline and mountain ranges covering most of its interior, a quarter of a million militia mounted guard along all the major roads at the peak of the campaign. Few enemies of the regime managed to escape from this tight network, and many died of hunger and cold in the mountains.[39]

But along Zhejiang's ragged coast were several thousand islands where the hand of the state barely reached. A huge waterland covered south China, veined with canals, guttered and bankless meandering rivers, fields flooded in terraces and lakes both natural and artificial. Even as most cities built asphalt, concrete and macadam roads for modern transportation, water travel continued to be popular. All along China's busy coast, freighters, tankers and ferries plied their trade next to fishing trawlers and traditional junks. The navigable rivers also swarmed with traffic, ranging from lorchas with batten lug sails to modern motor ships.

The inhabitants of this water world engaged in fishing and marine farming. Some were sea nomads, traditionally treated like outcasts and long barred from living on shore or marrying land people. Living in the Pearl River delta in south China, the Tanka viewed water as the safe element, land being fraught with danger. They spoke their own dialect, mooring their sailing junks and shrimping vessels side by side to form vast flotillas which even had their own floating temples and religious boats. Many fled after liberation, taking their boats and families to Hong Kong, where they joined immense floating cities of up to 60,000 people near Aberdeen and Yaumatei.

Other groups thrived on the water. Generations of boatmen worked and lived on board large cargo-carrying vessels along the Grand Canal, an ancient waterway completed in the seventh century to haul the grain tribute from the south to the imperial capital in the north. Flower boats, often decorated in a riot of colours, carried the nightsoil that fertilised the fields in the provinces along the coast. Coal barges and grain boats cruised on the many waterways of Shandong, where the Yellow River intersected with the Grand Canal. On the Yangzi, the riverfront of Shashi was crowded with junks anchored side by side. Further upriver, a floating population of trackers waited to be hired to haul ships through the shoals and gorges of the Yangzi.

This watery world had always attracted smugglers, drifters and outcasts. The party saw it as the last refuge of counter-revolutionaries. In the ports along the Guangdong coast, the authorities believed, up to half of the population smuggled contraband goods and harboured enemy agents. Further north, on the islands along Fujian and Zhejiang, some were secretly in touch with the nationalists in Taiwan. The vice-minister of communications Wang Shoudao described the water population as a troublesome shadow world of 4 million people, steeped in feudal customs and riddled with gangsters who controlled the ports along the coast. One out of every fifty was a counter-revolutionary, he calculated.[40]

Luo Ruiqing agreed. In December 1952 he set a killing quota for people living on the water of one per thousand. Nine times as many were to be deported to labour camps. Thousands were executed in the following year.

Many more were taken from their boats and sent away to do hard labour, as the revolution finally moved from the land to the water.[41]

———

No one will ever know how many people were killed at the height of the Great Terror. The way statistics were gathered varied widely from one place to another and, more importantly, almost everywhere secret killings took place which were rarely reported. The most complete set of available figures are for the provinces under the leadership of Deng Zihui from October 1950 to November 1951. The total reached over 300,000 victims, or 1.7 per thousand of the local population (see Table 1, p. 100). And as Luo Ruiqing cautioned in his report on these provinces, a further 51,800 executions were earmarked to take place over the following months, most in Guangdong.[42]

The provinces under Deng Xiaoping, namely Guizhou, Sichuan and Yunnan, are unlikely to have had killing rates below two per thousand. In the entire region of Fuling, composed of ten counties, the rate was 3.1 per thousand. Elsewhere in Sichuan the rate was as high as four per thousand. In the entire province of Guizhou, as we have seen, the rate was three per thousand. In an oral report to Deng Xiaoping the figure of 150,000 executions for all three provinces was mentioned in November 1951.[43]

In east China, as early as April 1951 the reported killing rates already stood at more than two per thousand in Fujian and Zhejiang. They were lower in Shandong, but even before the summer began the region as a whole claimed over 109,000 executions.[44]

In the north, the situation was more complex because so many killings had already taken place before the campaign was launched on 10 October 1950. In Hebei, for instance, 12,700 victims were executed in 1951, but in the year leading up to October 1950 more than 20,000 had already been killed.[45] All of the north-west, from Gansu to Xinjiang and Tibet, remains difficult to assess in the absence of reliable archival material. On the other hand, in Manchuria, already bloodied by the civil war, the killing rate was lowered to 0.5 per thousand in May 1951.[46]

Table 1: Total Executions Reported in Six Provinces, October 1950–
November 1951

Province	Total killed	Death rate (per thousand)
Henan	56,700	1.67
Hubei	45,500	1.75
Hunan	61,400	1.92
Jiangxi	24,500	1.35
Guangxi	46,200	2.56
Guangdong	39,900	1.24
Total	301,800	1.69

Source: Report by Luo Ruiqing, Shaanxi, 23 Aug. 1952, 123-25-2, p. 357

The only total aggregate from the archives to date is Liu Shaoqi's figure of 710,000 provided at a top party convention in 1954, a figure Mao repeated two years later.[47] In a total population of approximately 550 million at the time, this can only have represented the lowest possible estimate, equivalent to a national killing rate of 1.2 per thousand. Liu was, no doubt, willing to present the party only with a politically acceptable figure, one far removed from the evidence contained in the reports filed at the time. A more plausible estimate comes from Bo Yibo, who in the autumn of 1952 mentioned more than 2 million victims. Although this figure cannot be verified, on balance it is the most likely estimate if both reported and secret killings of counter-revolutionaries from 1950 to the end of 1952 are taken into account.[48]

Several million people were sent to labour camps or subjected to surveillance by the local militia. Countless more became outcasts. As the politics of hatred tore apart the social fabric of community life, tens of millions of people were permanently branded as 'landlords', 'rich farmers', 'counter-revolutionaries' and 'criminals'. These were the black classes, who stood in opposition to the vanguard of the revolution, called red classes. But the label was inherited, meaning that the offspring of outcasts were also subjected to constant persecution and discrimination, all sanctioned by the party. These children would be singled out by teachers and bullied at school, sometimes attacked by followers of the Youth League on their way back home. The adults became the targets of every subsequent political campaign, some of them paraded, shouted at and spat upon in denunciation meetings no fewer than 300 times – before the Cultural Revolution even started in 1966. They were the scapegoats of revolution, maintained alive in a permanent class struggle as a reminder to all of the fate awaiting those found to be on the wrong side of the party.[49]

But even those who survived the terror with their reputations intact now lived in fear. The party had no compunction in executing innocents, so innocence was no guarantee of survival. The unpredictable nature of the campaign was of course the very basis of terror, as nobody could be quite secure in thinking that they were beyond reproach. Formerly close communities drifted apart, leaving people isolated and fearful of each other. By the time the campaign was over, a breakdown in normal human relationships was noticeable. As Robert Loh observed: 'During the persecution, friend had been made to betray friend; family members had been forced to denounce each other. The traditional warm hospitality of the Chinese, therefore, disappeared. We learned that the more friends we had, the more insecure our position. We began to know the fear of being isolated from our own group and of standing helplessly alone before the power of the State.'[50]

Society became more regimented, even for party members. In the months following the assassination of Huang Zuyan, sentinels started appearing at major government offices. Searches became more common. Li Changyu, who became a party member in January 1951, remembers: 'In those days there were ad hoc guards at the office doors of high-level leaders, and a guard had to be posted at the gate whenever a large-scale meeting was to be held. Anyone entering the meeting place was searched, and if a weapon was found the high alert went up all around.'[51]

In the first year of liberation people could wander at will into different government organisations, or drop in to visit friends. But much tighter security regulations soon appeared everywhere. Esther Cheo noted:

Almost overnight each government organisation took on its own autonomy. We had to sign a paper at the gate and be questioned what our business was. The insistence on secrecy grew to ludicrous lengths. It was impressed upon all of us that there were spies everywhere. We were issued with identity cards, badges and more identity cards together with photographs. I still have them now, a little faded but clear enough to see my name, my place of birth and my rank. We became suspicious of strangers and each other, so that it was no longer comfortable to see each other, because it would mean a long report back on what we talked about and why. One became insular and only stayed within one's own place of work, lived among one's own fellow workers, shared the same dormitories, ate in the same canteens.

Erstwhile friendships faded away. Visitors stopped coming. People turned inward, leading increasingly blinkered lives. A mass exodus of all foreigners further deepened the country's insularity.[52]

6

The Bamboo Curtain

The Festival of the Dead, according to the lunar calendar, falls on the fifteenth day of the seventh month. A ceremony is traditionally held for those wandering ghosts who have not yet found their way to the next world. In 1951 the occasion came on 17 August, but instead of celebrating the festival with lanterns, songs and plays, in Beijing groups of people loitered on the streets, waiting for something to happen. They were unsure quite what to expect. There were obvious preparations for an execution, as groups of vehicles made their way towards the Bridge of Heaven, where most killings usually took place. When the formal procession finally arrived, onlookers were taken aback by what they saw. The first carriage, filled with armed soldiers, was followed by a jeep with a foreigner standing in the back. Tall and erect, with a long white beard, his hair brushed back, he peered into the distance with his hands bound together. Another jeep carried a Japanese man, also tied up and forced to stand. Several more vehicles followed, full of police officers who were laughing and apparently enjoying themselves. According to Radio Peking, the streets were thronged with people who shouted 'Down with imperialism! Suppress counter-revolutionaries! Long live Chairman Mao!' According to the sister-in-law of one of the condemned as well as the British embassy, the crowds were uncomfortably silent.[1]

Antonio Riva and Ruichi Yamaguchi were the first foreigners to be sentenced to death in communist China. Riva, an Italian pilot who had relocated to Beijing in the 1920s to train the nationalists, and Yamaguchi, a Japanese bookseller, were convicted in a one-hour trial of a plot to murder the Chairman. The conspirators, so the state media trumpeted, had planned to fire mortar shells at a reviewing stand outside Tiananmen

Gate during National Day celebrations. Several other foreigners received long prison sentences as part of the conspiracy. The Italian bishop Tarcisio Martina, aged sixty-four, head of the Roman Catholic diocese of Yixian in Hebei province, was imprisoned for life (he was expelled in 1955 and died a few years later).

The evidence hinged on a mortar seized from Riva's house and a drawing from Yamaguchi's notebook. The Stokes mortar was a non-functional part of an antique from the 1930s which Riva had found in a pile of junk outside the Holy See legation. The drawing was a map of Tiananmen Square commissioned by the Beijing Fire Department, to whom Yamaguchi was selling firefighting equipment. The ringleader of the imperialist plot was an American serviceman named David Barrett, who had simply been a neighbour to both men but had moved out a year earlier. 'I never at any time . . . attempted to assassinate or contrive the assassination of anyone,' he protested from Taiwan at the time of the trial. Twenty years later Zhou Enlai, the premier from 1949 onwards, apologised to him and invited him back to China. The whole affair was a fabrication designed to frighten the foreign community and scare local people away from any association with outsiders.[2]

After they had been executed in the capital, Riva and Yamaguchi were quietly buried in the outskirts of the city, on a farm that looked no different from any other, except for wooden markers and a few headstones scattered among broad fields of melons and vegetable marrows. Most of the graves were overgrown with vegetation, but here and there the markers were newer and could still be spotted. This was one of the burial sites for counter-revolutionaries executed at the Bridge of Heaven. Riva's wife, determined that her husband should be buried in a Catholic cemetery, eventually managed to wrestle his body back from the Public Security Bureau. His improvised coffin of thin wood was exhumed and the body placed in a proper coffin. On a clear day with a stark blue sky, the coffin was loaded from the field on to a mule cart and covered with a black cloth marked with a white cross. After a five-hour trek along rutted roads covered in dust, the cart reached the Zhalan Cemetery, shaded by the green foliage of cypresses, pines and poplars. The premises had been given to the Jesuits in 1610 by the Ming emperor Wan Li to receive the body of Matteo Ricci. Here Antonio Riva was finally laid to rest. In the following years the

Jesuits would be denounced and expelled. In 1954 the grounds of the cemetery were taken over by the Beijing Communist Party School. For good measure, most of the graves were vandalised during the Cultural Revolution. Only a few remain today, hidden from view.[3]

———————

Matteo Ricci was an Italian Jesuit who arrived in China in 1583 and adopted the language and culture of the country in order to spread the Catholic faith. The first foreigner to receive permission to remain in the imperial capital in 1601, he spent the rest of his life teaching, translating and befriending leading scholars in Beijing. Other missionaries soon followed, but few were allowed to stay in the empire. Foreign traders – Portuguese, Spanish, Dutch, British – were confined to a small area outside the city walls of Guangzhou after 1757. Only in the wake of the Opium Wars of 1839–42 and 1858–60 did more substantial foreign communities gain a foothold in the empire, living in concessions under foreign administration in treaty ports such as Shanghai and Tianjin. Foreign residents were subject to the extraterritorial jurisdiction of their own courts. They could buy land and houses in the treaty ports and travel in the interior for business purposes. After the Treaty of Shimonoseki concluded in 1895 they could also build factories and manage workshops.

Some of these ports were transformed into beacons of modernity. In Shanghai, a quiet weaving and fishing town before 1842, a massive urban infrastructure appeared that rivalled the very best internationally, ranging from sewerage systems, port installations, communication networks and insurance facilities to hospitals, banks and schools. First the Russians and later the Japanese developed Dalian, changing it from a small fishing town into a major deep-water port in Manchuria.

Many of the best local enterprises were also established in the concessions, often with foreign partners in order to obtain security of persons and property. The historian Hao Yen-p'ing has written about a 'commercial revolution' at the end of the nineteenth century, as local compradors and foreign entrepreneurs joined forces to pursue new opportunities created by free trade. Bills of exchange eased credit, the money supply grew with Mexican dollars and Chinese paper notes, the volume of trade

expanded on international markets and global communications under-
went a revolution. Local merchants often dominated these new synergies,
financing as much as 70 per cent of all foreign shipping.[4]

But the real boom came after the fall of the Qing empire in 1911. Within
less than a decade the number of foreign residents in the Republic of China
trebled to well over 350,000. Even as the concessions were retroceded to
China – some in 1918, the last few in 1943 – the foreign influx continued.
Many lived insular lives, their existence revolving around the expatriate
community. But just as many settled and laid down roots in the country.
Whether British, French, American or Japanese, entire families could be
established in the country for generations: in many cases treaty-port life was
home, regardless of whether or not much contact was established with local
people. Many settler families had children, and not all of these were sent to
boarding school, as English, American, French, German and Japanese
schools in China maintained their own national curricula. Many children
born of missionary parents or business people grew up in China, some
becoming bilingual and profoundly attached to their adopted country. As
the historian John K. Fairbank noted, 'treaty-port cemeteries are filled with
foreigners who understood China well enough to live and die there'.[5]

The government itself was fully aware of the role of foreigners as
conduits of cultural and technological transfer. Leaders like Yuan Shikai
and Chiang Kai-shek used a stream of experts, including League of Nations
technicians, Japanese legal advisers, German army officers, British
construction engineers, French postal personnel and American transportation experts. In the first few years of the republic alone, among the most
prominent advisers were Ariga Nagao, prominent international jurist;
George Padoux, expert on public administration; Henry Carter Adams,
standardiser of railway accounts; Henri de Codt, writer on extraterritorial
jurisdiction; William Franklin Willoughby, noted political scientist; Frank
J. Goodnow, legal adviser; and Banzai Rihachiro, military expert. At less
eminent levels, many foreign employees contributed to the country's
modernisation, ranging from engineers, clerks, accountants and lawyers to
teachers and translators.[6]

There were also many thousands of missionaries in republican China
who were active in religion, medicine and education. Christianity was the

country's third most important faith with close to 4 million followers. Missions were behind several hundred middle schools and thirteen colleges and universities, including Hangchow Christian University, Lingnan University, the University of Nanking, St John's University, Shanghai University, Shantung Christian University, Soochow University and Yenching University. One reason why missionary activities increased dramatically in the early twentieth century is that so many links were forged with domestic forces of reform, whether in educational reform or public health: '"Young China" of the 1910s and 1920s was frequently the product of missionary schools,' writes the historian Albert Feuerwerker, whether they were urban reformers, leading journalists or professional sociologists. Missionaries were also present, as early as 1919, in all but a hundred of the 1,704 counties in China and Manchuria, many speaking the local dialect and living in close contact with the local population.

Over 100,000 European refugees also ended up in China, starting with more than 80,000 White Russians after 1917, followed in the 1930s by some 20,000 Jews from Germany, Austria, Czechoslovakia, Poland, Lithuania, Estonia and Latvia. They brought with them knowledge, experience and expertise, further enriching the social fabric of republican China. They ran a whole range of businesses, from beauty parlours to pastry shops and kosher restaurants. Some acquired Chinese citizenship.

The cumulative effect of these waves of immigration was that some of the cities along the coast of China, from Beijing in the north to Guangzhou in the south, were as cosmopolitan as their counterparts in Europe or the United States. Shanghai had a bigger foreign population than any other city except New York.

The first sign that not all foreigners would be welcome under the new regime came from Shenyang, taken over by the People's Liberation Army in October 1948. From the roof of the American consulate, Elden Erickson watched the soldiers marching down the streets. 'I remember there was an old lady that they just shot and went right on. They saw us looking over the top of the building and they started shooting at us.' Acting on advice from Stalin, a few weeks later the communists threw a cordon around the consulate building. The American consul Angus Ward and his staff were held under house arrest for a year, accused of using the consulate as headquarters for espionage. All communications were cut off. 'Passers-by were even arrested for waving greetings,' Ward remembered. Water, light, heating and medicine were denied. Buckets of water had to be carried in as temperatures dropped to 40 below zero. Every day anti-American demonstrators paraded around the building shouting slogans and waving placards. In November 1949, Ward and four other members of his staff were finally arrested and put on trial for 'inciting a riot'. A day after the United States had appealed to thirty nations, including Russia, their sentences were commuted to immediate deportation. By the end of December 1949, after forty hours in an ice-cold carriage with all windows stuck wide open, they reached Tianjin, where they were handed over to American diplomats.[7]

This was far from an isolated incident. As the communists swept through China in 1948–9 they harassed foreigners in general and Americans in particular. In April 1949 soldiers entered the residence of the American ambassador John Leighton Stuart, barging into his bedroom on the second floor where he lay ill. 'Who are you?' the envoy asked. Stuart was one of the few foreigners to have stayed behind in Nanjing, hopeful of reaching an understanding with the communist party. Born in Hangzhou in 1876 to Presbyterian missionary parents, he was more fluent in Mandarin than in English. He had spent his entire career in China, in 1919 becoming the first president of Yenching University. A few months later Mao Zedong published a sarcastic editorial, 'Farewell, John Leighton Stuart', denouncing him as a 'loyal agent of US cultural aggression in China'.[8]

But for most foreigners the exodus started even before liberation. Many read the signs and packed their bags before it was too late. Israel evacuated several ships of Jewish refugees from Shanghai as early as 1948. Yet even as the People's Liberation Army was massed outside Beijing and Tianjin, most governments advised only those without major commitments to leave while adequate transportation was still available. 'It's all most people talked about, whether at work, at home or at parties – to leave or not to leave,' a former British resident of Shanghai recalled. The United States was the first country to order the wholesale evacuation of all its nationals. On 13 November 1948, half a year before the communists had even reached Nanjing, Ambassador Leighton Stuart advised his secretary of state that 'emergency evacuation procedures for practically all of China' had become imperative. US naval forces in the western Pacific helped to transport thousands of Americans and other foreign nationals.[9]

The decision sent shockwaves through the foreign community. Other countries followed suit. The Philippines, for instance, sent a converted tank-landing ship to evacuate a motley crowd of itinerant musicians and their families. Manila also generously accepted 6,000 White Russians who had come to China to escape the Soviet state and had few illusions about the nature of communism. But the British continued to play down the risks of social disorder and advocated 'standing fast for the time being'. They were jolted in April 1949, when the *Amethyst* was shelled and trapped for ten weeks. 'One by one people are making up their minds to leave,' wrote Eleanor Beck, a United Nations employee, a week after the Royal Navy frigate ran aground.[10]

But many decided to wait and see, reluctant to abandon their homes, jobs and personal possessions. The longer they wavered, the more they stood to lose in a rapidly falling market, as newspapers filled up with advertisements for houses, cars, refrigerators and other household goods.[11]

At first all had seemed well. Many foreigners heaved a sigh of relief as they emerged from liberation with barely a scratch. The communists repeatedly guaranteed the protection of foreign nationals and their property, and they seemed equal to their word during the takeover of the country. There were no riots or looting. Some foreigners wrote enthusiastically about how courteous groups of soldiers occasionally borrowed household goods only promptly to return them, in stark contrast to the thuggish behaviour of nationalist soldiers.[12]

But the official hostility was unmistakable, as was the vitriolic propaganda in the press endlessly attacking every perceived slight and injustice of the past. Every reminder of imperialism, whether real or imagined, seemed to rankle, with the result that every trace of foreign involvement in the economy, religion, education and culture was considered incompatible with the goals of a new China – from missionary schools, democratic institutions, international banks and foreign films down to legal language and street signs in English. Soon even the continued use of English on electricity bills in Shanghai was stridently denounced as betraying 'a strong sense of colonial influence'. When one foreigner turned up at the Telegraph Office with a query about sending a radiogram, an official thrust a cardboard sign stating 'Speak Chinese Only' in his face. His colleagues laughed loudly and puffed out their chests.[13]

'Those who had long been humiliated now took every opportunity to humiliate,' writes the historian Beverley Hooper. Foreigners became vulnerable, as even minor transgressions were blown up in the media as perennial symbols of imperialist aggression. One of the most notorious cases involved the vice-consul William Olive, a slight, unassuming young man who was detained for three days on rations of bread and water in Shanghai for driving along a street that had been closed for a victory parade on 6 July 1949. He was brutally beaten, denied medical treatment and forced to sign several confessions. The local press widely exploited the case to portray the communists as liberators of Shanghai from imperialist oppression. 'All is not well with imperialism,' trumpeted an evening newspaper on 12 July 1949 in short poetic verses:

> When the tables are turned,
> We Chinese have no further need for you knaves.
> Imperialists beware,
> All is not well with you any more.[14]

There were countless incidents involving foreigners, some petty and niggling, others sparking international condemnation. Foreign consulates were officially ignored and subjected to minor indignities and annoyances. Foreign correspondents were banned or censored. Various restrictions were placed on the movements of foreigners. Soon the entire foreign population was required to register with a local Bureau for Public Security. As one foreign student reported from Beijing in July 1949: 'The procedure is long and onerous. It involves several visits, the writing of quadruplicate answers in Chinese to a fairly detailed questionnaire (rejected if answers are incomplete or wrong), and submission of six photos. The climax is a personal interview, lasting anywhere from fifteen minutes to an hour, at which all answers are recorded.' Some of the interviewers were former government employees from the nationalist regime, but in the corner, taking no part in the procedures, sat a cadre. Then came house calls by security personnel. 'It wasn't unusual to find party officials sitting in the living room,' recalled an employee of Jardine Matheson. 'They'd want to know your whole life history.'[15]

Less than two months after liberation, many foreigners decided that they had seen enough. In September 1949 a relief ship was allowed into Shanghai and evacuated 1,220 passengers of thirty-four nationalities. Each had to apply for an exit visa, a cumbersome process which took several days. 'I have never been so thankful for anything in my life as I am to be here,' wrote Eleanor Beck in her diary as the *General Gordon* sailed down the Whampoa River. 'Don't let anyone fool you about communism.' 'Fare thee well, passengers of the *Gordon*,' declared one newspaper triumphantly.[16]

And still some foreigners gritted their teeth and resolved to carry on. In 1950 extortionate taxes ruined the foreign community's cultural and charitable organisations. Hospitals, schools and churches were taxed out of existence, while once prosperous social clubs went bankrupt. Foreign enterprises were squeezed to the limit. Assertive employees, their class hatred fired up by labour unions, exacerbated the situation by demanding massive pay rises and shorter working hours. When the foreign owners could no longer bear the costs, their enterprises were acquired without expropriation and resultant compensation claims. Again the *General Gordon* went to pick up hundreds of dispirited foreigners, this time in Tianjin.[17]

The campaign of mistreatment reached its highest pitch in the months following China's entry into the Korean War in October 1950. A few months later, on 16 December 1950, the US Department of State ordered a freeze on all the tangible and intangible assets in the United States of residents of China. The People's Republic reciprocated by freezing all American assets, taken over by Military Control Commissions. In the following months foreigners, Americans in particular, were denounced as so many spies and agents gathering information for the imperialist camp, whether they were students, missionaries, entrepreneurs or diplomats. By March 1951, dozens of American nationals lingered in prison on baseless charges, held incommunicado, sometimes without any charges being brought at all. Funds deposited by the remaining churches, schools, hospitals and charitable organisations were frozen. Before long all American enterprises throughout China were under government control. Workers, according to the Chinese press, celebrated the occasion 'with the discharge of fireworks and the display of flags and bunting'.[18]

Other nationals were also persecuted. Exit visas were withheld for months on end until every asset had been voluntarily surrendered. Bill Sewell, a university lecturer in Chengdu, Sichuan, explained:

> Intent to leave the country had also to be advertised in the local press: and from old servants and others arose endless claims which had to be investigated and settled, increasing the delay. The cadres had to make sure that no university property was mixed with private possessions, so that all baggage had to be listed and every item repeatedly checked. Some thought that bloody-mindedness was carefully cultivated by many officials. Further to add to the difficulties many foreigners were finding ready money hard to obtain. Anxiety, mixed now with anger, now with depression, haunted those who helplessly waited for the signal to depart.[19]

Once they were allowed to leave, stringent regulations limited the amount of personal belongings that could be taken abroad: no automobiles, no bicycles, nothing made of bronze, silver or gold and a very limited number of carpets, scrolls, shades and other objects. Only one piece of jewellery or one watch per person was permitted. Personal papers looked suspicious and were prone to be confiscated – if they were not interpreted as classified information. Many left the clutter of a lifetime behind, departing with a mere suitcase of clothes. Liliane Willens, born in Shanghai to Russian Jewish parents who had fled the Bolshevik Revolution, had to present her photo and stamp albums for inspection. The examiner meticulously removed a photo of her and her sister, still children, sitting on each side of their amah, who was wearing a white jacket and black trousers. Apparently her clothing was an unacceptable sign of imperialist exploitation.[20]

Some were stopped even with an exit permit. When Godfrey Moyle, who had worked at the insurance department of Jardines, turned up at the border in Tianjin in June 1951, an official took his passport, slowly read it, looked at him again, and then without a word tore the document into shreds. The official shouted one word: 'Cancelled!' Moyle was speechless. 'I couldn't get one word out, not a word would come.' He was never told why his permission to leave had been revoked, and had to wait a further two years for a new document.[21]

But departure could be a much more protracted affair for many business owners. The communists rejected the principle of limited liability and held whoever appeared to be in charge personally responsible for the discharge of a company's obligations – shareholders, office managers, accountants, sometimes even custodians. Leading entrepreneurs and industrialists who could no longer meet the extravagant claims from tax collectors and labour unions were routinely sent to prison until the appropriate sum of money had been secured or wired from abroad. H. H. Lennox, the manager of the Shanghai and Hongkew Wharf Company, which became insolvent in 1950 as a result of the blockade and shortage of shipping, was put behind bars for his inability to pay the workers their annual bonus. 'Here he found himself with some 40-odd Chinese also under temporary detention. Apart from some sandwiches he had with him and a narrow bench around the room there were no amenities whatever in this place.'[22]

Fiscal policy was made retroactive, meaning that it applied not only to current assets and profits of foreign businesses but also to past activities. Employing close scrutiny of account books and forcibly obtained testimonies, local cadres invariably found some reason to recover what they believed the regime was entitled to. Much of this was achieved through tight control of all banks. The Bank of China was taken over by the regime and started acting like a chief comptroller, it alone being authorised to provide credits for foreign trade. Banking operations were reduced to a minimum along the once famous Bund of Shanghai.

The law offered little recourse, since it was vigorously suppressed as an instrument of imperialist exploitation. Lawyers were prohibited from even setting foot in the courts, where judicial proceedings were determined by a presiding judge loyal to the party. Many prominent members of the bar in Shanghai who had acted as legal advisers to foreign firms were never heard of again. All existing codes, including civil and criminal, were suspended.[23]

Foreigners were also persuaded to part with their homes. The technique was always the same: predatory land and house property taxes and very heavy cumulative fines for failure to pay on due dates, combined with the fact that property could no longer be sold on reasonable terms, meant that most people preferred tacitly to let the ownership interest lapse. And once foreigners faced the threat of an exit visa being deferred for ever, they were often keen to hand over their assets to the People's Government.[24]

For instance, in Beidaihe, a luxury resort with rocky headlands and sandy beaches, hundreds of foreign organisations such as embassies and missions owned beautifully designed houses overlooking the Bohai Gulf. After English railway engineers had linked the fishing village to Tianjin and Beijing in the late nineteenth century, Beidaihe rapidly became a popular destination for wealthy elites and foreign diplomats seeking shelter from the summer heat. The Second World War and the civil war forced many to leave China without being able to sell. By September 1952 the only foreigner left was a certain Mr Baldwin, who led 'a tranquil but rather melancholy life', fishing for bass and cultivating his fruit trees. Most of the properties had been converted into Rest and Recuperation Centres for party officials. After Mao had written a poem about the resort in 1954 it became a favourite retreat for the party leadership.[25]

On 25 July 1951 came a sweep of all foreigners, part of the build-up towards the public execution of Antonio Riva and Ruichi Yamaguchi. In Beijing the police handcuffed and hauled away dozens of priests, nuns, students, professors, merchants and doctors of different nationalities. Many vanished without trace, as foreigners by now led isolated lives cut off from the outside world. Harriet Mills, the daughter of Presbyterian parents who was researching the essayist and writer Lu Xun on a Fulbright Fellowship, spent nearly two years in chains for possessing an ex-army wireless set and for having been in touch with Yamaguchi. Allyn and Adele Rickett, also Fulbright Fellows, were arrested the same evening as they were having dinner with Harriet Mills. They too spent several years in prison, subjected so often to thought-reform sessions that they themselves ended up believing that they were spies.[26]

On 2 August 1951, Beijing secretly passed a new resolution ordering the expulsion of all foreigners except for those under arrest. By the end of the summer the foreign community had no illusions left. The only place where foreigners could still be seen in significant numbers was Tianjin. The once thriving port of northern China had become the only official exit for foreigners leaving the country. Even residents of Shanghai now first had to take a train to Tianjin before boarding a ship. The city was crowded with people waiting for transportation. Once glamorous hotels stood as forlorn remnants of decayed glory, their rooms occupied by a few anxious foreigners. In one of these, an abandoned red-and-gold ballroom led to a smaller dining room with dying flowers on the tables. Strips of paper that had been glued on the windows as a precaution against air raids during the civil war had not yet been removed.[27]

Shanghai had been emptied of its foreign population by the end of 1951. In Beijing too, a once thriving foreign community was broken and destroyed. When thirty-six people convened for Christmas dinner at the British embassy, the gathering included not only all diplomatic staff, but the entire British community in the region.[28]

Two years later came the turn of other foreign population groups. First some 25,000 Japanese held since the end of the war were repatriated. Then came 12,000 White Russians. Many were reduced to complete destitution and 'died as a result of the bitter cold, hunger and sickness'. Their mass expulsion started at the end of the year.[29]

In 1926 an ominous shadow was cast over the Christian churches during the unrest in the Hunanese countryside. Thrilled by the revolutionary violence, a young Mao Zedong reported how local pastors were paraded through the streets, churches looted and foreign missionaries silenced. Although the unrest soon abated, foreign missionaries continued to be targets in communist-controlled areas in the 1930s and early 1940s. During the civil war, advancing communist troops confiscated church property, closed down mission schools and persecuted or killed dozens of local and foreign believers.

In July 1947 guerrilla fighters seized a Trappist monastery in Yangjia-ping, a remote valley north of Beijing, burning down the cloister and interrogating, torturing and sequestering its resident monks. In January

1948, in the middle of the winter, six of the monks were handcuffed, chained and escorted on to a makeshift platform, their white habits infested with lice and encrusted with blood. A frenzied crowd surged forward as the victims were jostled to their knees. A local cadre read out the verdict: death, to be carried out immediately. One by one, as the shots rang out, they collapsed next to each other. 'Their lifeless bodies were dragged to a nearby sewage ditch and dumped into a heap, one on top of the other.' A few months later twenty-seven other monks, most but not all local, had died of maltreatment. Nobody knows how many Protestant and Catholic missionaries were killed in China between 1946 and 1948, but estimates range up to a hundred.[30]

Half of the more than 4,000 Protestant missionaries evacuated their stations before liberation. Some had spent years of internment in Japanese concentration camps and were wary of the communists. Others left due to poor health and old age. But well over 3,000 Roman Catholic missionaries were ordered to stay at their posts. Missionaries held extremely diverse views, from the austere and solitary Trappists who eschewed material possessions and avoided all idle talk to the more reform-minded members of the YMCA, involved in welfare activities in the cities. Hopes of working alongside the communists sustained a few. Others viewed any such co-operation as 'compromising with the Devil'.[31]

For about a year the decision to remain in China seemed justified. Foreigners were registered, schools infiltrated, hospitals inspected, religion denounced and Christians interrogated, although many missionaries remained optimistic. Nevertheless the signs were not good, even though the pressures were far from uniform. 'The coils are tightening daily,' noted Bishop John O'Shea half a year after the communists entered his diocese in south Jiangxi. Like other foreigners, missionaries were subjected to all sorts of restrictions. Some became virtual prisoners in their own missions, forbidden to leave the compound. And increasingly the communists took over these buildings for quartering military troops, storing grain or holding public meetings, step by step squeezing many missionaries out of their premises.[32]

Economic pressures were also applied in the form of rent, taxes and fines, an experience missionaries shared with other foreigners. The government was 'taxing them on a ruinous scale', wrote the Vatican of its missions in mid-1950. One by one they had to close their doors.[33]

Then came the Korean War. A month after China had entered the conflict in October 1950, arrests of foreign missionaries began. In mass trials and frenzied demonstrations they were accused of espionage and subversive activity. Protestant missionaries left in droves. By the end of 1951 no more than a hundred remained in China.[34]

But the Roman Catholics, who received their orders from the Vatican, were enjoined by the apostolic delegate, Antonio Riberi, to resist at all costs. Despite the trials, parades and denunciations, over 2,000 missionaries kept their ranks closed to any form of official infiltration. The arrest of the Italian bishop Tarcisio Martina in September 1950 for involvement in the plot to kill Mao Zedong was used as a pretext to banish the Holy See from China. Even before Martina had been thrown in gaol for life, Riberi was placed under house arrest, subjected to nightly visits and frequent interrogations by the police for several months. In September 1951 he was expelled for 'espionage activities'. Communist soldiers escorted him from Nanjing to the Hong Kong border. Throughout the journey vociferous campaigns were organised, with loudspeakers placed at street corners and railway stations, in hotels and restaurants – all blaring out propaganda denouncing the papal delegate as a 'lackey of foreign imperialism'.[35]

Mao himself was intrigued by the Vatican, especially its ability to command allegiance across national boundaries. The tenacity of the Catholics perturbed him. But even more suspect was the Legion of Mary, known in Chinese as the 'Army of Mary' (*Shengmujun*), prompting the communists to fear that it might be a military formation. Many of their members, threatened with imprisonment, steadfastly refused to sign confessions renouncing alleged 'counter-revolutionary' activities. On 14 August 1951 the Public Security Bureau ordered the organisation to be destroyed 'within a year'.[36]

Two days after Riberi had been paraded in Shanghai on his way to Hong Kong, a squad of eleven police officers with sub-machine guns arrested Aedan McGrath, the envoy of the Legion of Mary. Before McGrath was locked up, his watch, rosary beads and religious medals were confiscated. The laces of his shoes and the buttons on his trousers were removed.

He was forced to stand naked for hours on end. Several months later he was transferred to Ward Road Prison, a solid gaol built by the British in 1901 where his cell had no bed, no chair, no window, nothing at all except a bucket. Food was slopped into a filthy square tin and passed through the bars twice a day. He endured countless interrogations, accompanied by sleep deprivation and naked exposure to the biting cold of winter. After thirty-two months he was finally brought before a tribunal where his crimes were read out to him. Two days later he was released, escorted on to a train and expelled from China.[37]

Others were not so lucky. In December 1951 the sixty-year-old Francis Xavier Ford of the Maryknoll Society, an American Roman Catholic bishop, was accused of 'espionage' and 'possession of weapons'. He was never brought to trial. He was paraded in some of the villages where he had done mission work since 1918, his neck bound with a wet rope that almost choked him as it dried and shrank. The mob beat him with sticks and stones till he was knocked to the ground. He died in prison and was buried on the outskirts of Guangzhou.[38]

In many cases entire groups of missionaries were arrested in carefully targeted raids. In Qingdao, Shandong, twenty-seven brothers of the Society of the Divine Word were rounded up on 3 August 1951, sent to gaol and expelled two years later. While the missionaries were under investigation, the police carried off their chalices, vestments and other sacred objects. Cemeteries were desecrated, graves opened, altars removed, floors dug up and pillars demolished in the search for hidden weapons and radio transmitters. When nothing was found, pieces of junk, from bits of wire to old rosaries, were collected and presented as evidence of radio equipment. Medicine was called poison. The paranoia was contagious, as some missionaries began losing their bearings after months of harsh imprisonment, ceaseless interrogations and outlandish accusations. In Lanzhou, Father Paul Mueller refused to eat, thinking his food was poisoned, and claimed the guards used death rays against him. He died of an untreated infection in prison.[39]

Even those who left of their own accord were harassed. When Adolph Buch, a French priest who began his career as a Vincentian missionary in China in 1906, decided to pack his bags and leave in October 1952, he took with him a collection of butterflies he had gathered in his spare time over the years. They were confiscated by customs officials. 'They accused me of wanting to send my collection to the States, to be sent back laden with germs.' When the eighty-seven-year-old man shuffled across the Lowu Bridge into Hong Kong, he also came without his hearing aid, as it was illegal to take any mechanical devices out of the country.[40]

But many allegations were far more sinister. As the regime liquidated hundreds of mission hospitals, some of the foreigners in charge were accused of mistreatment and arrested on trumped-up charges. After a dying woman had been brought to the Luoyang Catholic Hospital, her husband begged the doctor to operate, despite repeated warnings that the operation had little chance of success. Weeks later local cadres pressured the man to bring charges against Father Zotti, the director of the hospital, who was sentenced to one year in prison and a further year under house arrest. Many similar cases followed.[41]

Wild accusations of wilful murder also accompanied the seizure of over 250 missionary orphanages. After liberation, relatives or strangers brought severely ill children to these homes. The sisters in charge could not save all of them. In December 1951 five nuns were paraded through jeering crowds in the streets of Guangzhou, accused of having murdered over 2,116 children in their care. The court proceedings, held in the red-walled Sun Yat-sen Memorial Hall, were broadcast for hours on end in five languages. Then the shrill, emotional voice of the prosecutor read the indictment, including charges of inhuman treatment and illegal sale of children. In between inflammatory speeches, several witnesses were brought forward, including children sobbing into the microphones, their words lost in tears and shouts from the crowd. At the climax of the show trial, two of the nuns were condemned to prison, the others to immediate expulsion from China.[42]

A week later two French nuns and a priest were beaten with sticks as they were forced to dig up the decomposing bodies of babies they were alleged to have killed in another orphanage. The excavation went on for twelve hours a day for twelve days, armed guards making sure that they worked without respite. Further up north, in Nanjing, the Sacred Heart Home for Children had earlier been labelled a 'Little Buchenwald', its sisters also accused of deliberately neglecting, starving, torturing children and selling them into slavery. Similar incidents, all carefully orchestrated, also occurred in Beijing, Tianjin and Fuzhou.[43]

By the end of 1952 dozens of foreign missionaries languished in prison, many with their hands and feet in chains. Close to 400 were officially expelled that year, while various forms of pressure forced over 1,000 more to leave. A further purge of any remaining church influence came in the summer of 1953. A year later all but one Protestant missionary had left the country. A further fifteen were detained and about to be expelled. Three hundred Catholic missionaries were still in China. Seventeen of these were in prison, sixty were under interrogation and thirty-four were on their way out of China. The others would soon follow.[44]

Even before the People's Republic had been formally established, the Soviet Union was everywhere. 'Pictures of Soviet leaders are almost as prominent in public places in Peiping [Beijing] as those of Chinese communist leaders,' reported Doak Barnett in September 1949. Russian and Chinese flags flew side by side on landmark buildings. Sino-Soviet Friendship Associations opened with great fanfare in all major cities. Streets were named after the Soviet Union. The main road in Harbin was called Red Army Street, while people walked through Stalin Avenue in the middle of Changchun. In Shenyang visitors were greeted with the view of an enormous granite-mounted Red Army tank in honour of the Russians who had liberated Manchuria from Japanese imperialism. Translated Soviet literature appeared in bookshops, railway stations, schools and factories. Some were textbooks for the Chinese Communist Party. Newspapers and radio went to great lengths to pledge allegiance to the Soviet Union, follow Moscow on foreign policy and praise Stalin as the leader of the socialist camp. In Beijing a gigantic Soviet exhibition was staged 'to introduce systematically the great socialist construction of the USSR'.[45]

The Soviet presence expanded dramatically after Mao's statement on 30 June 1949, the anniversary of the Chinese Communist Party, that China should 'lean to one side'. 'The twenty-eight years' experience of the Communist Party', he declared, 'have taught us to lean to one side, and we are firmly convinced that in order to win victory and consolidate it we must lean to one side.' Between the side of imperialism and the side of socialism there was no third road. Neutrality was camouflage. Mao had a word for those who believed that China should approach Washington and London in search of foreign loans: his word was 'naive'. 'The Communist Party of the Soviet Union is our best teacher and we must learn from it.' As *Time* commented a few weeks later, 'In this statement was just about all the world needed to know about the past, present and future attitudes of the Chinese Communist Party.' That same month Liu Shaoqi, Mao's dour second-in-command, was sent to the Soviet Union to hold meetings with top ministers and visit a whole range of institutions. He saw Stalin on six occasions. After two months he returned to China with hundreds of advisers, some of them travelling on his train.[46]

For the previous twenty-eight years the Chinese Communist Party had depended on Moscow for financial support and ideological guidance. From the age of twenty-seven, when a Comintern agent handed him his first cash payment of 200 yuan to cover the cost of travelling to the founding meeting of the Chinese Communist Party in Shanghai, Russian funds transformed Mao's life. He had no qualms about taking the money, and used Moscow's support to lead a ragged band of guerrilla fighters to ultimate power. The relationship had its ups and downs. There were endless reprimands from Moscow, expulsions from office and battles over party policy with Soviet advisers. Stalin constantly forced Mao back into the arms of his sworn enemy Chiang Kai-shek. Moscow openly favoured Nanjing, even after the nationalists had presided over a bloody massacre of communists in Shanghai in 1927. For the best part of a decade, Chiang's troops relentlessly hounded an embattled Mao, forcing the communists to find refuge in a mountain base and then to traverse some 12,500 kilometres towards the north in a retreat later known as the Long March. But even the Long March was funded by Moscow, as the Comintern contributed millions of Mexican silver dollars. Without these funds the communists would not have got very far.[47]

At the end of the Second World War, Stalin, always the hard pragmatist, signed a treaty of alliance with the nationalists. But he also secretly helped Mao, handing over Manchuria to the communists in 1946. During the civil war Stalin stayed on the sidelines, warning Mao to beware the United States, which supported Chiang Kai-shek, now recognised as a world leader in the fight against Japan.

Even when victory seemed inevitable in 1949, Stalin remained suspicious of Mao. Prone to discerning enemies everywhere, Stalin wondered whether Mao might emulate Tito, the Yugoslav leader who had been cast out of the communist camp for his opposition to Moscow. Stalin trusted no one, least of all a potential rival who in all probability harboured a long list of grievances. Aware of the need to earn his master's recognition, Mao spared no effort vociferously to condemn Tito. 'Stalin suspected that ours was a victory of the Tito type, and in 1949 and 1950 the pressure on us was very strong indeed,' Mao later recollected. In a show of adulation, he tried to present himself and his party as true communists and sincere students of the Soviet Union, worthy of its assistance.[48]

Despite his allegiance to Stalin, Mao resented the way he had been treated by Moscow in the past. But he had nowhere else to turn to for support. In 1949 his regime desperately needed international recognition as well as economic help to rebuild the war-torn country. Mao first declared the policy of 'leaning to one side' and then sought an audience with Stalin. Several requests were rebuffed. Then, in December 1949, Mao was finally asked to come to Moscow.

Fearful of enemy attacks, Mao travelled in an armoured car with sentries posted every hundred metres along the railway lines. Even before he crossed the border he was irked by Gao Gang, the man in charge of Manchuria. Rumours had it that portraits of Stalin were more common in the region than those of the Chairman himself. Months earlier Gao had visited Moscow and signed a trade agreement with Stalin. When Mao realised that Gao was sending gifts to Stalin in a carriage attached to the Moscow-bound train, he had it uncoupled and returned the tribute.[49]

This was Mao's first trip abroad, and he was visibly nervous, pouring with sweat as he stalked up and down the platform in Sverdlovsk during the long train journey. In Moscow the Chairman was given the cold shoulder. Mao expected to be welcomed as the leader of a great revolution that had brought a quarter of humanity into the communist orbit, but within the Soviet sphere for several months now a shroud of silence had been placed over the victory of the Chinese Communist Party. Vyacheslav Molotov and Nikolai Bulganin, two of Stalin's henchmen, greeted Mao at Yaroslavsky Station but did not accompany him to his residence. The Chairman gave a speech at the railway terminal, reminding his audience how the unequal treaties between Tsarist Russia and China had been abolished after the Bolshevik Revolution in October 1917, a broad hint referring to the treaty signed between the nationalists and the Soviet Union five years earlier as a result of the Yalta accords. Stalin granted Mao a brief interview that day, flattering and praising him for his success in Asia, but also teasing him by feigning ignorance of the real reason for his visit. Five days later, Mao was treated as a guest of honour among many other delegates who had travelled to Moscow to celebrate Stalin's seventieth birthday.[50]

But then Mao was whisked off to a dacha outside the capital and made to wait several weeks for a formal audience. Meetings were cancelled, phone calls never returned. Mao lost patience, ranting about how he was in Moscow to do more than 'eat and shit'. Stalin was wearing down his guest, insisting that the Yalta accords were binding – including Soviet control over the ports of Port Arthur and Dalian as well as the Chinese Eastern Railway in Manchuria.

Zhou Enlai came to the rescue, but even with his diplomatic skills it took another six weeks to reach an agreement. Russia insisted on keeping all the concessions that the nationalists had been forced to make at the end of the Second World War. Anastas Mikoyan and Andrey Vyshinsky were brutal negotiators, laying down their conditions in blunt terms. While they agreed to return the ports and the railway by the end of 1952, they insisted that their troops and equipment be allowed to move freely between the Soviet Union and Manchuria as well as Xinjiang. Mao was also quickly disabused about Mongolia, which he viewed as just another part of the Qing empire to be reclaimed by the People's Republic of China. The independence of Mongolia, arranged by Stalin and accepted by Chiang Kai-shek in 1945, was beyond debate. Zhou also had to concede exclusive rights on economic activity in Xinjiang and Manchuria. Rights to mineral deposits in Xinjiang were granted for fourteen years. Mikoyan repeatedly badgered Zhou for ever higher quantities of tin, lead, wolfram and antimony, all to be delivered by the hundreds of tonnes a year to the Soviet

Union. When Zhou meekly countered that China did not have the means to extract such large amounts of special metals, Mikoyan cut him off by offering help: 'Just say what and when.'[51]

On 14 February the Treaty of Friendship, Alliance and Mutual Assistance was finally signed, but all Mao obtained was $300 million in military aid over five years. For this modest sum Mao had to throw in major territorial concessions, so heavily reminiscent of the unequal treaties concluded with foreign powers in the nineteenth century that they were contained in secret annexes. China also agreed to pay thousands of Soviet advisers and technicians high salaries in gold, dollars or pounds. As the historian Paul Wingrove notes, 'Mao's victorious, independent, revolutionary state was being treated in much the same way as the captive territories of Eastern Europe, from which the Soviet Union also extracted the standard tariff in exchange for services of "experts".' And in an echo of the extraterritorial rights that had been abolished under Chiang Kai-shek in 1943, none of the Russians would be subject to Chinese law. Mao's hands were tied. China was weak and needed a strong protector as international positions were hardening in an unfolding Cold War. The treaty provided just that, extending the Soviet Union's protection in the event of aggression by Japan or its allies, in particular the United States. But despite all the fanfare around the treaty, Mao and Zhou must have left Moscow feeling aggrieved at how they had been treated.[52]

New foreigners started arriving in 1950, flocking to Beijing, Shanghai and other cities by the hundreds, some with their families, others on their own. These were the Russian advisers and technicians. At first they formed new communities in the old concessions, but soon they dominated the foreign scene. In Shanghai they were concentrated in a special compound in the city's most luxurious suburb, several kilometres west of town. A beautiful, unspoilt area with landscaped parks and opulent villas where foreigners shot duck, played golf and strolled along the creeks, the garden city of Hongqiao was soon requisitioned by the military. Foreigners were expelled, Russians moved in. Residents in the area were given twenty-four hours' notice of the requisitioning of their property and ordered to move out.

'Those who objected were forcibly evicted, and their furniture was carried out and placed in trucks.' Technicians, pilots, fitters and others working at the airport, built in the area in 1907, occupied the vacant properties. Sentinels guarded the compound day and night. A bamboo fence went up, tall and solid. Locals soon referred to the area as the Russian Concession.[53]

In every major city Russian advisers were isolated from the local population and quartered in closely guarded compounds. In Guangzhou the island of Shameen, where foreign companies and consulates had built stone mansions along the waterfront, became the centre of official life. Russian advisers were billeted in the Canton Club, once an exclusive domain for British members with private gardens, tennis courts and a football field. In Tianjin some took up quarters in the Jubilee Villas on London Road, where armed guards with tommy guns patrolled the entrance. Others stayed in the old Soviet consulate, where the facilities were updated with a three-metre brick wall topped by electrified barbed wire.[54]

Russians were rarely seen, except when they came out on shopping expeditions, sullen-looking, wearing long leather coats, wide-bottomed trousers, leather boots and large-brimmed felt hats. 'When they enter a shop all other customers are asked to leave.' Their very high rate of pay, combined with restrictions on the export of currency, meant that they tended to buy luxury goods that were too expensive for the general population. 'The Soviet experts were seen everywhere in the Shanghai shopping area; they avidly bought up all the American and European watches, pens, cameras and other luxury imports which were still available but which no Chinese could afford,' noted Robert Loh. Soon they were spotted snapping up antique furniture, Oriental carpets, Limoges porcelain and other objets d'art, loaded by the crateful at the airport to be sent back to the Soviet Union.[55]

By October 1950, as China was about to enter the Korean War, the Soviet presence included some 150,000 soldiers and civilians. In Port Arthur, where Stalin had a naval base and port privileges, the Russians had an army numbering 60,000. Along the railways linking the port to Vladivostok were another 50,000 troops, most of them railway guards. There were air force units in the north of Manchuria. Everywhere in China batches of uniformed men arrived as army and air force instructors.

But the Soviet reach went well beyond the military. Thousands of civilian technicians helped build roads, bridges, factories and industry all over the country. In the ministries in Beijing, hundreds of them shadowed their local counterparts, coaching them in Soviet ways. The largest group – 127 specialists – was in the Ministry of Higher Education.[56]

The flow went both ways, as one delegation after another visited the Soviet Union. A few were trade missions, but most went to learn the techniques of running a one-party state. Wang Yaoshan and Zhang Xiushan, for instance, spent four months touring the Soviet Union with a large delegation to study political organisation, from the training of urban cadres to the composition of the Central Committee in Beijing. Zhou Yang, vice-minister of culture, headed a team of fifty that inspected every aspect of propaganda, filing no fewer than 1,300 formal questions during their three-month stay, which included six visits to the newspaper *Pravda*. In every domain – from state security, city infrastructure, cadre training, economic construction and ideological work to heavy industry – China was copying the Soviet Union.[57]

Trade with the Soviet Union shot up, a trend accelerated by the Western blockade during the Korean War. As China had limited foreign currency and gold reserves, it also paid for loans through exports. The basic trade pattern was the exchange of credit, capital goods and raw materials for special metals, manufactured goods and foodstuffs. Pork was bartered for cables, soybeans for aluminium, grain for steel rolls. Since the supply of such metals as antimony, tin and tungsten was limited, most Chinese exports to the Soviet Union consisted of agricultural commodities, ranging from fibres, tobacco, grain, soybeans, fresh fruit and edible oils to tinned meat. Soon the vast majority of exports were destined for Moscow.[58]

As 'Learn from the Soviet Union' became the motto, cadres and intellectuals studied Stalin's *The History of the All-Union Communist Party: A Short Course*. It was read like the Bible. Russian became compulsory in schools. One British woman living with her Chinese husband at Xiamen University noted: 'Training camps and training centres were established and Russian became the first foreign language (actually the only foreign language) in all schools at various levels. On the education front every minute detail was copied from the Russians without discrimination, even the lunch hour was pushed back to three in the afternoon in order to ensure the practice of having six classes in succession in the morning.'[59]

The Sino-Soviet Friendship Association – with its 120,000 branches – distributed books, magazines, films, lantern slides and plays, as well as generators, radios, microphones and gramophones to spread the message. Dozens of exhibitions were organised on themes from 'Soviet Women' and 'Soviet Children' to 'Construction in the Soviet Union'. Even news in Chinese originated from the Soviet Union, as TASS, the official Soviet news agency, rapidly became the main source of information. As everybody was told again and again, 'The Soviet Union's Today is our Tomorrow'.[60]

7

War Again

Liberation had come with the promise of peace. In 1949 most of the population had welcomed the People's Liberation Army with a mixture of relief and wariness, hoping that they would be allowed to go about rebuilding their lives, families and businesses after more than a decade of warfare. Mao instead threw his people into a prolonged war in Korea in October 1950.

───────

At the Yalta conference in February 1945, Stalin not only wrangled secret concessions on Manchuria from Roosevelt, but also negotiated over the joint occupation of Korea, which had become a Japanese colony in 1910. The Korean peninsula extends for about 1,000 kilometres southwards of Manchuria, from which it is divided, for the greatest part, by a natural border formed by the Yalu River. In the extreme north-east, not far from Vladivostok, is a border of less than 20 kilometres with the Soviet Union. The Red Army marched into the northern half of the Korean peninsula in August 1945 with almost no resistance, halting at the 38th parallel for the American troops to arrive from the south. The Russians installed Kim Il-sung as the head of their provisional government.

Born in 1912, Kim could barely speak Korean. His family had settled in Manchuria when he was still a young boy. He joined the Chinese Communist Party in 1931, carrying out guerrilla raids against the Japanese north of Yan'an. In 1940 he was forced to flee across the border into the Soviet Union, where he was retrained by the Red Army, rising through the ranks to become a major by the end of the Second World War.

When he arrived in Pyongyang on 22 August 1945, Kim had been in exile for twenty-six years. He immediately supported Mao, sending tens of thousands of Korean volunteers and wagonloads of military supplies across the border to help the communists fight Chiang Kai-shek in Manchuria. Kim also used Soviet advisers to build up the Korean People's Army. Stalin equipped it with tanks, lorries, artillery and small weapons. But Kim was bound by his protector, unable to send his troops south to attack the American-backed Syngman Rhee without the permission of the Soviet Union. Kim had to watch in frustration as Mao took over China, bringing a quarter of humanity into the socialist camp while Korea remained partitioned.[1]

Kim pushed repeatedly for an assault on the south, but Stalin was in no rush for an open conflict involving the United States. Yet by the end of 1949 Stalin started to waver. The Americans had not intervened in the Chinese civil war and had all but abandoned Chiang Kai-shek on Taiwan. In discussions with Mao, who was in Moscow in late 1949, Stalin suggested moving some of the Korean troops in the People's Liberation Army back across the Yalu River. Mao agreed, and sent over 50,000 veterans back to North Korea. Then, in January 1950, the United States indicated that Korea no longer fell within its defence perimeter in the Pacific. Kim badgered Moscow again on a number of secret trips to Moscow. Stalin now went along with the idea of an assault on the south, but was wary of becoming entangled in a costly adventure. He refused to commit any troops: 'If you should get kicked in the teeth, I shall not lift a finger. You have to ask Mao for all the help.' In April Kim went to see Mao.[2]

Mao, in turn, needed Stalin. He could not invade Taiwan without the requisite sea and air power, which had to come from Moscow. And he could hardly deny the Koreans the opportunity to unify their own country now that most of China stood under one flag. Mao pledged to support Kim with troops if the Americans entered the war.[3]

Military deliveries to North Korea from the Soviet Union jumped dramatically, including tanks and planes. Russian generals took over planning for the attack, setting the date for 25 June 1950. Under the pretext of a border skirmish, a comprehensive air and land invasion with a massive force of North Korean troops was launched. The south was ill prepared, with fewer than 100,000 soldiers. Alarmed at calls for a march north to overthrow the communists, the Americans had deliberately denied Syngman Rhee armour, anti-tank weapons and artillery heavier than 105 mm. His troops crumbled within weeks.[4]

President Truman acted rapidly, warning that appeasement would be a mistake and vowing to repel the North Koreans. On the day of the invasion, the United Nations passed a resolution committing troops to support South Korea. The Soviet Union's ambassador to the United Nations, who had been boycotting proceedings since January over Taiwan, was expected to return to the Security Council and vote against the resolution, but Stalin told him to stay away. Two days later tacit agreement was received from the Soviet Union that American intervention would not lead to an escalation. Stalin did nothing to prevent Western involvement in the conflict. He alone knew that Mao had made a commitment to sending troops to Korea. Perhaps he hoped that China would destroy large numbers of Americans in the conflict.[5]

Truman ordered US troops based in Japan to assist South Korea. Determined to fight global communism, the president obtained $12 billion from Congress for military expenditure. Soon American soldiers were joined by troops from fifteen UN member nations, including Great Britain and France. In August the tide turned, as the United Nations counter-offensive retaliated with tactical superiority in tanks, artillery and air power. General Douglas MacArthur reached the 38th parallel in October 1950. He could have stopped there, but so confident was he that Mao would never dare to enter the conflict that he decided instead to push all the way to the Yalu River, ignoring the most basic security concerns of the People's Republic.

On 1 October Stalin wired Mao a message asking him for five or six divisions to assist the North Koreans. He suggested that they be called 'volunteers' to maintain the pretence that China was not formally involved in the war. Mao had already moved some of his troops up to the border and the next day he asked them to 'stand by for the order to go into [Korea] at any moment'.[6]

The Chairman spent the following days convincing his senior colleagues to back him. Only Zhou Enlai offered cautious support. Lin Biao, who had won the day in Manchuria during the civil war, feigned illness to turn down command of the troops. The other leaders, including Liu Shaoqi, strongly opposed entering the war, fearing that the United States might bomb the country's cities, destroy its industrial base in Manchuria and even drop atomic bombs on China. Marshal Nie Rongzhen recalled that those who opposed the decision felt that after years of warfare 'it would be better not to fight this war as long as it was not absolutely necessary'. Peng Dehuai only reluctantly agreed to assume command of the offensive after a sleepless night tossing and turning on the floor of his hotel room in Beijing, as the bed was too soft for comfort. 'The tiger always eats people,' he explained, 'and the time when it wants to eat depends on its appetite. It is impossible to make any concessions to a tiger.'[7]

Mao took a huge gamble. He hoped that America would not expand the war to China for fear of provoking the Soviets. He was also convinced that the Americans had no stomach for a prolonged war and would be no match for the millions of soldiers he was prepared to throw into the conflict. He believed that he would have to fight the Americans at some point, all the more so since Truman had sent the Seventh Fleet to protect Taiwan at the start of the Korean War. Fighting the imperialists in Korea would be easier than launching an amphibious assault on fortress Taiwan. Most of all, a hostile Korea on the Manchurian frontier would represent a serious security threat to the People's Republic.

There was also quiet rivalry with Stalin. Korea was the arena where Russia and China were competing for dominance over Asia. Stalin was ahead of the game, having so far gone to great lengths to keep the Chinese communists out of North Korea. But once Russia's satellite forces started to disintegrate, Mao was ready to march in from Manchuria, reverse the rout and assume the leadership of the communist camp in Asia.

But Mao sought to extract a price from the Kremlin, and on 10 October 1950 sent Zhou Enlai and Lin Biao to negotiate with Stalin in his Black Sea dacha. Stalin committed ammunition, artillery and tanks, but reneged on an earlier promise to provide air cover, as the planes would not be ready for another two months. Stalin even wired Mao to let him know that China did not have to join the war. But Mao persisted: 'With or without air cover from the Soviet Union,' he replied, 'we go in.' Zhou Enlai buried his head in his hands after he read the cable. On 19 October, hundreds of thousands of Chinese troops surreptitiously began entering North Korea.[8]

———

The Chinese troops took the United Nations forces by complete surprise. The United States had very little information about what was going on inside China, and most of its covert military presence in the country had collapsed by September 1949. But a report cabled to Washington on 19 October by the military attaché in Hong Kong, based on information provided by Chen Tou-ling, the former general manager of the China Air Transport Corporation, warned that 400,000 troops were massed on the border and primed to cross into Korea. The Dutch Foreign Ministry, using information gathered by its embassy in Beijing, also provided the Americans with detailed intelligence on an imminent invasion of Korea. These warnings were ignored.[9]

So convinced was General MacArthur that China would never enter the fray that when reports came in of PLA troops crossing into Korea, he flew his Douglas C-54 Skymaster over the Yalu River – at considerable risk to his own safety. He saw nothing. The 130,000 troops under Peng Dehuai's command were hard to detect, marching under cover of night without any of the usual mechanised activity or wireless traffic that could have revealed their presence.

They attacked out of the blue on 25 October, wiping out several South Korean regiments, but retreated into the mountains as suddenly as they had appeared. General MacArthur brushed the incident aside, interpreting these early probes as evidence that the Chinese were few in number and reluctant to fight. On Thanksgiving Day, in bleak and blustery weather, he began a final push to end the war and bring American soldiers 'Home by Christmas'.

The Americans fell into what one historian has called 'the largest ambush in the era of modern warfare'.[10] On 25 November, MacArthur's men were struck by massive numbers of hidden soldiers. Their bugles blaring, drums, rattles and whistles adding to the din, screaming Chinese troops appeared in the middle of the night, shooting and throwing grenades. They instilled sheer terror in the United Nations forces. Wave after wave of ferocious assault groups hurled themselves on to gun positions, trench lines and rear areas. The onslaught almost instantly changed the course of the war, forcing the Americans into a headlong retreat southwards. The communists recovered Kim Il-sung's capital Pyongyang on 7 December.

Without air cover, his supply lines dangerously extended and without adequate provisions of food and ammunition, Peng Dehuai pleaded for a halt along the 38th parallel, but Mao was determined to press on. Seoul, capital of South Korea, was taken during the Chinese New Year in January 1951. By now a devastating blow had been dealt to the United States. Truman declared a State of National Emergency, telling the American public that their homes and nation were 'in great danger'.

Mao's prestige was greatly enhanced, but the cost to his own soldiers was enormous. The fighting took place in extreme weather, with temperatures plummeting to minus 30 degrees Celsius, made worse by freezing winds and deep snow. Most troops had no padded shoes. Some wore thin cotton sandals and a few even went barefoot, wrapping rags around their feet before going into battle. Blankets and jackets were burned out by napalm. Whole units froze to death, while frostbite attacked the hands and feet of many troops. Up to two-thirds of all soldiers also suffered from trench foot, which sometimes resulted in gangrene. Starvation was widespread, as the supply lines were hopelessly stretched and under constant fire from prowling enemy aircraft. In some companies one in six men suffered from night blindness caused by malnutrition. Dysentery, among other diseases, was common, and was treated with opium. After the exhilaration of the first few weeks, morale was low, as the men were physically exhausted by the work they were made to do. Some were so worn out that they committed suicide.[11]

Soon the troops ran out of steam. They were able to sustain themselves into the early months of 1951 by capturing arms and supplies from the retreating enemy. Soldiers learned to eat C rations. Li Xiu, a propaganda officer, remembered that the soldiers quickly took to American biscuits. 'Without the American sleeping bags and overcoats we captured, I am not sure we could have gone on.'[12]

The tide soon turned. On 26 December 1950, General Matthew Ridgway arrived in Korea to take command of the American forces as MacArthur's subordinate. In the first weeks of 1951 he regrouped the United Nations forces and counter-attacked, first cautiously probing his opponent's determination before launching more robust offensives, creating fields of fire with carefully deployed men and firepower that mauled the Chinese troops. He called his strategy the 'meat grinder', slowly pressing forward with devastating artillery and tanks, shattering the enemy again and again. Mao refused to retreat, wiring orders that his troops counter-attack instead. In the first two weeks of February alone, Ridgway inflicted an estimated 80,000 casualties.[13]

Peng Dehuai rushed back to Beijing in February, confronting Mao in his bunker at Jade Spring Hills over the massive losses caused by reckless warfare. The Chairman listened, but was too enthralled by his own fantasies of victory over the capitalist camp. Peng was told to hold the line and to expect a long war. On 1 March Mao cabled Stalin, proclaiming his determination to wear down the enemy in a protracted war: 'In the last four offensives, we have sustained 100,000 casualties among combatants and non-combatants of the People's Volunteer Army, and we are about to replenish the troops with 120,000 soldiers. We are prepared for another 300,000 casualties in the next two years, and we will furnish another 300,000 troops.'[14]

On the American side, General MacArthur toyed with the idea of using nuclear weapons. He even briefly contemplated invading China, but was sacked by President Truman in April 1951. Ridgway, who replaced him, now assuming overall command of all United Nations forces in Korea, refused to go further than the 38th parallel.

A stalemate emerged in the summer of 1951. Armistice talks began in mid-July, but were broken off by the communists. Stalin slowed down negotiations to bring the war to an end, as he had little to gain from peace. He was keen to see more American troops destroyed in Korea, and probably not unhappy to have a potential rival locked into a costly conflict. But Mao also repeatedly rejected peace proposals. As he had indicated to Stalin even before a stalemate was reached, he was prepared for the long term. The longer the war lasted the more ammunition, tanks and planes he could badger out of the Soviet Union. The Chairman used the war to expand his army and build up a first-class arms industry, all with Soviet help.[15]

The pretext Mao used to justify dragging his feet at the negotiating table was that the Americans held some 21,000 Chinese prisoners of war, most of whom refused to return to China. Held in camps in South Korea, they tattooed their bodies with anti-communist slogans to prevent forced repatriation. Some wrote letters with their own blood. 'The POWs cut open the tips of their fingers and use them as fountain pens,' a Red Cross delegate reported. 'I saw a number of these letters in question. It is an awesome sight.' Mao demanded the return of every single prisoner of war, and Stalin encouraged him in his hardline position.[16]

So the war lasted another two years. The battle lines barely changed, but the casualties were enormous. Trench warfare forced many soldiers to spend weeks buried inside foxholes, tunnels and shelters from which they could emerge only at night. Bodies, shells and garbage were everywhere, but there was hardly any food or water. Soldiers sometimes drank the moisture that dripped from rocks. Captain Zheng Yanman remembered an attack in October 1952: 'There were about one hundred soldiers inside the tunnels, remnants of six different companies and ranging in age from sixteen to fifty-two. About fifty of the men were wounded, and they had received no medicine or medical assistance. They were lying around, some of them dying, and nobody seemed to care. In one of the shelter holes there was a pile of more than twenty bodies.' Soldiers who deserted were executed on the spot.[17]

Many of the soldiers were former nationalist troops who had surrendered during the civil war. Mao had few qualms in consigning them to their deaths in Korea. In fighting the communists in Xuzhou three years earlier, some of them had been obliged to shoot unarmed villagers, used as human shields by the communists. Now they were made to exhaust the enemy's bullets in one wave after another, as flesh and blood was hurled against modern armament. An American machine-gunner described what happened as he countered headlong night attacks by massed Chinese infantry: 'We could see them tumbling down like bowling pins,' he wrote. 'As long as the flares were up we never had trouble finding a target.'[18]

Stalin's death in March 1953 brought about a quick armistice, but the cost of the stalemate had been prodigious. From July 1951 to the ceasefire on 27 July 1953 millions of soldiers and civilians died. China sent some 3 million men to the front, of whom an estimated 400,000 died. Despite the terrible human cost, Korea was Mao's personal victory. He had pushed for war when his colleagues had wavered. His gamble paid off. China had brought the world's most powerful nation on earth to a standstill. China had stood up.[19]

The war had lasting domestic consequences. The official line on how the conflict had started in June 1950 was that the South Koreans, incited by American imperialists, had attacked the peaceful North Koreans in an act of flagrant aggression. People from all walks of life in China met this explanation with a mixture of disbelief, incomprehension, fear and outright panic. Many could not help but wonder how the campaign launched into the south had proceeded with such efficient military planning and dispatch. In Shanghai students and professors openly asked what the North Koreans were doing in the south. Fears were rife about an impending cataclysm with the United States. Rumours spread like wildfire. In Shenyang, close to the Korean border, talk of the start of a Third World War did the rounds: 'The United States have entered the war, the Third World War has started!' In Nanjing some people were so anxious that they phoned the *People's Daily* to ask if a new world war had begun. Anxiety over war went in tandem with hopes for a return to the old order. 'The Soviet Union has already surrendered unconditionally, now the war criminal Mao Zedong will be arrested!' it was whispered in Manchuria, while others announced the impending collapse of the regime: 'The Americans and Chiang Kai-shek have already recaptured Hainan Island, Lin Biao has been sacrificed!'[20]

The threat of a nuclear conflagration created deep anxiety, which official propaganda on imperialism's impending collapse scarcely dented. In October 1950, as the United Nations troops approached the Yalu River, Mao's grandiose description of American imperialism as nothing more than a paper tiger was quietly mocked in Shanghai. Some opined that if the United States was a paper tiger, China was not even a pussycat.[21]

Fear of an impending invasion reached fever pitch. People worried about bombs being dropped on cities and the enemy entering Manchuria. In Shenyang thousands took to the roads in panic. Over 1,200 workers abandoned their posts at the First of May Factory, while one in five absconded from the Municipal Tool Factory. Teachers, doctors, students, even party members scrambled on to trains to escape south, convinced that the end was nigh. Those who stayed behind hoarded food, clothes and water. Messages of opposition to the party appeared in schools, factories, offices, hospitals and dormitories, scribbled on walls, etched into the furniture, scrawled even on to kettles in canteens. Some were concise: 'Beat the Soviet Union'. Others were long diatribes against communism.[22]

The party responded with a campaign of terror. But in November 1950 it also tried persuasion through a campaign called 'Resist America, Aid Korea, Preserve our Homes, Defend the Nation'. Mass meetings were held in every school and factory, while propaganda in newspapers, magazines and the radio tried to whip up the population in a furore against the enemy. Not a day went by without some stirring denunciation against the United States in the *People's Daily* or other state-controlled publications. The *South China Daily*, for example, trumpeted its utter contempt for America:

> This is a country which is thoroughly reactionary, thoroughly dark, thoroughly corrupt, thoroughly cruel. This is the Eden of a few millionaires, the hell of countless millions of poor people. This is the paradise of gangsters, swindlers, rascals, special agents, fascist germs, speculators, debauchers, and all the dregs of mankind. This is the world's source of all such crimes as reaction, darkness, cruelty, decadence, corruption, debauchery, oppression of man by man, and cannibalism. This is the exhibition ground of all the crimes which can possibly be committed by mankind. This is a living hell ten times, one hundred times, one thousand times worse than any hell that can possibly be depicted by the most gory of writers.[23]

Zhou Enlai himself set the tone, becoming an eloquent spokesman for the Hate America Campaign, and never tiring of denouncing the imperialist plot to enslave the world. Mao Dun, minister of cultural affairs and prominent novelist, announced that 'Americans are veritable devils and cannibals.' Returned students from America were made to publish recantations, including denunciations of bestialism and depravity. Cartoons and posters portrayed President Truman and General MacArthur as serial rapists, bloodthirsty murderers or savage animals. Loudspeakers persistently blared forth the same slogans and speeches. 'Even inside the house with all the windows closed,' noted a Beijing resident, 'you hear the constant, unchanging music and the speeches, and if you open the windows you are nearly deafened by the noise.' Calculated vituperation and genuine outrage were hard to disentangle in these endless tirades, but the message was clear enough: people had to hate, curse and despise the imperialists.[24]

Everything was carefully orchestrated from above. A central directive dated 19 December 1950 specifically ordered that feelings of admiration and respect towards the United States should be changed into 'Hate America, Despise America and Look Down on America'.[25]

This goal was to be accomplished not just by relentless propaganda, but also through renewed study sessions and mass rallies. Many were disorganised. In one Shanghai university, the faculty and the entire student body were given ten minutes to dress and assemble at the campus square one wintry day in 1950. Printed banners were thrust into their hands with messages such as 'Down with the Soft-Worded, Cloak-and-Dagger Lies of the American Imperialists' and 'Protest against Austin's Shameless Lies'. 'Everyone was asking what it was all about, but no one seemed to know,' explained Robert Loh. 'We were told to shout the slogans printed on the banners. Thereupon we were marched for five hours all through Shanghai.' Back at the university they were made to listen to a fiery speech from the party secretary. Only then did they understand that they had just participated in a spontaneous demonstration against a speech by Warren Austin, the American representative on the United Nations Security Council. Thereafter they were called out at regular intervals to protest against imperialist lies. 'We rarely knew what the issue was until we read the story of our "voluntary demonstration" in the papers.'[26]

These were university students, but ordinary people who tried to pursue their own lives in the midst of ferocious campaigns against 'counter-revolutionaries', 'tyrants', 'evil gentry' and 'landlords' found the Hate America Campaign even more confusing. In Lanzhou, the provincial capital of Gansu, rallies in support of the war took place almost every week in the early spring of 1951, although some of those who marched against America still had no idea what the campaign was all about – despite countless leaflets, speeches and propaganda films. Those who refused to participate were fined or labelled as members of a secret society. Despite these threats, people were apprehensive, as rumours circulated that women who turned up might be sent to Korea to cook meals for the soldiers. In Guangzhou, where patriotic parades of half a million people were held, ignorance was widespread. In one power plant where the local Propaganda Department tested more than a hundred workers on their knowledge, one in six did not know where their ally was and more than a quarter had never heard of Kim Il-sung. Propaganda seemed barely to penetrate parts of the countryside. In one village in Shixing county, sixty women enrolled in a literacy class did not know whether 'Korea' was the name of a place or a person.[27]

After the voluntary rallies came the voluntary donations. Money was needed to buy war materials once stalemate was reached in Korea in the summer of 1951. Stalin had finally begun delivering the long-promised planes, but he demanded payment from China for all the military equipment he sent to Korea. More uniforms, more medicine, more guns, more tanks and more planes were needed, the government explained. Detailed directives with charts outlined the contributions that everyone was expected to make. 'Wealthy individuals' were called upon to donate gold, jewellery, dollars or other foreign currency. Robert Loh soon discovered how much was required. 'The first time I was approached, I voluntarily agreed to contribute the amount of a half month's salary. I learned quickly that this was regarded as insufficient; the collector kept after me until I had pledged three months' salary. I found that the other professors pledged the same amount, but the collectors never once dropped the fiction that our contributions were voluntary.'[28]

Workers were urged to increase production or work overtime without compensation. But the bulk of popular subscriptions fell on the farmers. Here too leaders at every level set the tone, keen to outdo each other in collecting ever larger amounts to demonstrate how determined they were. North-east China proudly announced that 9.3 million yuan had been collected by October 1951. Unwilling to lag behind, Deng Xiaoping, who was responsible for the entire south-west, announced in November 1951 that contributions for the war in Korea were a revolutionary task of great ideological import in which 'no slacking' would be tolerated. Gifts of artillery, tanks and aeroplanes were essential to victory and each man and woman was to donate the equivalent of 2.5 to 4 kilos of grain.[29]

The pressure to collect colossal sums of money from people already heavily taxed was difficult to resist. In parts of Sichuan some government employees were forced to pledge a third of their salary each and every month until the end of the war. Elsewhere three months' salary seemed to be the norm, although some were taxed half a year's pay. But that was not the end of it. In many places schoolchildren were enrolled in the campaign, and they pilfered from their parents. Some bartered away shoes and clothes for a mere fraction of their value, while others rummaged through their homes and pinched scissors, knives, pots and pans, all sold as scrap iron.[30]

Those least able to resist the pressure were farmers, in particular in regions where they were entirely dependent on the party after land reform had been carried out. Just as city people contributed a third of their pay, farmers were sometimes bullied into parting with a third of their crop. In a village in Huarong county, a third of the millet was taken after the harvest as a contribution to the war effort and another third as tax. But many of the poor could not afford donations. In one Sichuan village alone, dozens of farmers stripped naked in a meeting convened to meet the required target in donations. They were so poor that all they could give were the clothes they were wearing. In other parts of the province, women were forced to shave off their hair as a gift to the party.[31]

Some people were driven to an early grave. In Wangcheng, Hunan, a poor farmer called Dai Fengji was forced to give 14 kilos of millet. 'I am the only one working in my family and eight people depend on me. My wife is sick and needs medicine. Nobody can look after my children. How can I possibly afford that much?' The head of the Peasant Association had a simple answer: 'Dead or alive you will donate.' The farmer jumped into a pond and drowned. Nobody knows how many people were bullied to death, but in Sui county, Hubei, five people committed suicide, unable to cope with the pressure.[32]

Despite the hysteria of the campaign, conducted at a time of terror when a mere hint of disapproval might attract the potentially fatal label of 'counter-revolutionary', some people refused to contribute. When they still persisted after several visits from the authorities, they were sometimes fined the equivalent of what had been expected in the first place. But some forms of pressure were less benign. In parts of Xinjiang people were forced to strip and stand in the glaring sun for hours on end. Some activists went around Nanjing putting up notices on people's doors stating the amounts they were expected to contribute. One man who showed insufficient enthusiasm was dragged on to a platform and taken to task from eight o'clock in the morning until the middle of the night. After he had agreed to contribute 10 yuan for six months, he was bullied again the following day until he increased the total to 300 yuan.[33]

But donations alone could not win a war. The army needed men. At each rally a wave of enthusiastic volunteers signed up, most of them idealistic students from the cities. In Guangzhou alone 13,000 people, many of them still in high school, wanted to go to the front and fight the enemy. Some, like Robert Loh, were suspicious of all the propaganda, but others like Li Zhisui followed the war closely. Then working in a clinic for the country's leaders, Li was thrilled that China was defeating the United States: 'Even as the Korean War dragged on inconclusively, I was proud to be Chinese.' After all, this was 'the first time in more than a century that China had engaged in a war with a foreign power without losing face', as the doctor put it, a view shared by many other intellectuals who were responsive to patriotic propaganda. Li tried to join the army but his superiors told him to stay put.[34]

People in the countryside were less keen, especially in regions where years of forced conscription had left the population war-weary. In Manchuria, right next to Korea, uncounted numbers of young men tried to escape conscription. In Dehui county alone, several thousand went undercover in the cities, even refusing to return home to help their families with the harvest for fear of being caught and sent to the front. When people in Wendeng county, Shandong, heard about conscription, their faces 'changed expression as if hearing about a tiger'. Young men took to the hills, a few even cutting off some of their fingers in order to avoid the draft. In Daixian, Shanxi, young men were on the run in a third of all the villages.[35]

But, like everyone else, army recruiters had quotas to fill. In Gaoping county, also in Shanxi, they pounced on their targets during fake village meetings, held to lure men out of their homes. The conscripts were locked up at night, although over a hundred still managed to escape. When the county leaders finally decided to keep only those who had genuinely volunteered, of 500 detainees all but a dozen absconded. Sometimes family members were ransomed or locked up to entice the men to enlist. In Yueyang, Hunan, a woman who insisted that conscription should be voluntary was tied up and hung from a beam in front of the assembled villagers as a warning to others.[36]

In the region straddling Henan, Hebei and Shandong, ten counties reported cases of young men leaping into wells in attempts to escape from recruitment. Several hung themselves, two jumped in front of a train. Such acts of desperation seem rather extreme but made sense in the context of the campaign of terror that was unfolding at the same time. As Zhou Changwu, a farmer from Hunan, put it, 'Under the nationalists we would hide in the mountains during conscription, but now we will be denounced as spies if we go up there and hide: there really is no way out.'[37]

The economic cost of the war was enormous. In 1951 military expenses swallowed up 55 per cent of total government spending. Thanks to the Korean War, the annual budget that year was 75 per cent higher than in 1950.[38]

The mainstay of the regime's budget was public grain taken from the farmers. Manchuria became the rear base and staging area for the war, with hundreds of thousands of troops moving along the South Manchurian Railway and the Chinese Eastern Railway under Soviet control. Manchuria was China's breadbasket, producing an agricultural surplus even when the rest of the country suffered from famine. Its industrial heart was a small triangle formed by Shenyang, Anshan and Fushun, churning out about half of all coal and most of the country's pig iron, steel products and electrical power. Manchuria had arsenals and supply depots for the troops in Korea. Soon it became a haven for the hundreds of planes supplied by Stalin, hovering over the stalemate across the Yalu River.

Villagers in Manchuria came under relentless pressure to contribute grain, cotton and meat for the war effort. The People's Congress noted that at the end of 1950 in many parts of the region the insatiable demands from the army had swept aside the restrictions on procurements designed to protect ordinary people from hunger. By the end of the year, a third of the region had sunk into poverty, as villagers lacked cattle, food, fodder and tools. Some even had too little seed to plant the next crop.[39]

The pressure did not abate over the following two years, as coercion on the ground became the norm. Cadres locked villagers into meetings until they agreed to deliver more grain. They sealed off the mills and entered homes, moving furniture, probing cupboards and lifting floorboards in search of hidden grain. The militia blockaded entire villages, allowing no foodstuffs to enter or leave until the quota had been fulfilled. One in three villagers was starving. In Huaide county people ate wild herbs and soybean cakes, normally used to feed poultry and cattle. Horses were starved until they fell over, and were then eaten, which was considered a sign of extreme deprivation unknown since the civil war. Near Changchun villagers bartered all their belongings, including their clothes, to meet their tax obligations. Some families sold their children. The provincial party committee in Jilin decided that widespread starvation in the province had nothing to do with natural disasters: it was the direct result of the coercion that came with orders to supply more grain.[40]

Further south Sichuan was known as the country's rice basket. As Deng Xiaoping proudly proclaimed his determination that every man and woman should contribute up to 4 kilos of grain in war donations, tens of thousands of people in the county of Ya'an alone were reduced to foraging for roots to eat. In Yunnan, also under Deng's purview, more than a million people were starving, many of the victims stripping the bark off trees or eating mud that filled the stomach but often caused excruciatingly painful death as the soil dried up the colon. But the pressure did not abate. In November 1951, despite ruthless requisitions, Deng Xiaoping announced that farmers in south-west China would be asked to contribute an extra 400,000 tonnes of grain beyond the usual procurements. Six months later 2 million people were starving in the region, with reports of cannibalism reaching the higher echelons of the leadership.[41]

The war did nothing, either, to help the urban economy. Chapter 3 showed how a recession in the spring of 1950 crippled such once bustling hubs of trade and industry as Shanghai, Wuhan and Guangzhou. Tianjin, the commercial centre in the north, managed to keep afloat. With Shanghai blockaded by the nationalists, much of the export trade was routed through Tianjin, which was beyond Taiwan's reach. But the Korean War brought about trade restrictions imposed by the United States on more than 1,100 commodities, badly hitting private importers and exporters. A full embargo followed in October 1950, leading to a 30 per cent decline in foreign trade in the first half of 1951. The city port was allocated government contracts for war materials, and some of the new state trading companies thrived on the back of the war, but the private sector soon entered a terminal decline.[42]

Beijing put the country on red alert in April 1952, charging that the Americans had secretly been waging germ warfare since the end of January. The enemy had allegedly dropped infected flies, mosquitoes, spiders, ants, bedbugs, lice, fleas, dragonflies and centipedes over parts of North Korea and Manchuria, spreading every variety of contagious diseases. The Americans had also purportedly released contaminated rats, frogs, dead foxes, pork and fish. Even cotton, Beijing warned, could spread plague and cholera. Enemy planes, it was claimed, had deployed these biological weapons in about a thousand sorties, most of them over Manchuria but a few reaching as far south as Qingdao, the port of Shandong province.[43]

Beijing first alleged that the United States was waging germ warfare in February 1952, claims that rapidly made headlines around the world. The charges gained credibility after several captured American pilots confessed to dropping the disease-carrying insects on Korea and China. Even more damaging was an international commission chaired by Joseph Needham, a Cambridge University biochemist, who published a lengthy report corroborating these allegations – after visiting Manchuria and finding one diseased vole.[44]

The regime's propaganda machine went into overdrive, giving renewed impetus to the Hate America Campaign. Endless articles on anthrax-laden chickens or brittle bombs filled with tarantulas appeared in the newspapers, with photos showing clumps of dead flies, close-ups of diseased insects, microscopic images of bacteria and smudges identified as germs. In Beijing there were reports of germ-laden joints of pork, as well as dead fish (forty-seven of these found on a hilltop), corn stalks, medical goods and confectionery.[45]

A revolving exhibition toured all major cities. In Beijing it filled three large halls, with exhibits of parachuted cylinders allegedly full of germ-carrying insects, and maps indicating where the Americans had dropped biological weapons 804 times at seventy points. In the corner of one room, a loudspeaker broadcast the recorded confessions of two captured enemy pilots over and over again. Their written statements were displayed in a glass case. A series of microscopes revealed bacteria cultures claimed to have been developed from infected insects. One photograph showed three victims of plague who had been infected by flies dropped by enemy planes.[46]

The campaign strongly resonated in China, where the Japanese had conducted experiments in germ warfare during the Second World War. Now that Japan was an ally of the United States, it was easy to imagine that those tests had carried over into the Korean War. Beijing highlighted how scientists from the notorious Unit 731 had been granted immunity after the Second World War in exchange for their expertise – even though the United States denied this at the time and would only reveal the extent of their collaboration with the Japanese scientists decades later. After General MacArthur had openly toyed with the idea of using the atom bomb, the threat of mass destruction seemed all too plausible, lending credibility to the idea of secret biological weapons. In Asia more generally, as Frank Moraes, the editor of the *Times of India*, noted, public opinion was sensitive to the idea that the Americans were using Asians as guinea pigs for another weapon of mass destruction. Li Zhisui, the doctor working for the party leaders, was only one among many intellectuals appalled by the news that the United States was using bacteriological warfare in Korea.[47]

But some observers were less convinced. On 6 April the *New York Times* published an article demonstrating that the photos presented as proof by the *People's Daily* were fraudulent. One scientist who had pored over the evidence pointed out that infected lice and fleas could not survive the freezing temperatures of North Korea in winter. Weeks earlier people in Tianjin had already expressed similar doubts: 'The weather in Korea is very cold, how come the flies have not frozen to death?' one of them wondered. Others were openly sceptical of the danger from the alleged germs, suspecting they were fake. Li Shantang, identified by the regime as a 'counter-revolutionary' who had worked for the nationalists, boldly proclaimed that 'This is all communist propaganda in an attempt to get the world to hate America, don't listen to all that rubbish!' In Manchuria farmers shrugged their shoulders, pointing out that insects always appeared at the end of winter.[48]

Others panicked. The outbreak of the Korean War had unleashed fears of a Third World War. Now, two years later, some people lived in terror of an invisible enemy seemingly lurking in almost any kind of organic matter. In Shenyang several people who had been bitten by insects rushed to the hospital pleading for treatment. The premises were already crowded with those suffering seizures, pains or partial paralysis, all induced by the mere sight of a bug. A few hoarded food in anticipation of an apocalypse. Others, believing that the end was nigh, squandered what was left of their savings on wine and meat for one final feast. In places as far away as Chongqing, children were locked up inside their homes for fear of contamination. Entire villages in Henan shut down, as rumours spread of secret agents poisoning the wells. More worrying to the regime was the popular habit of interpreting natural catastrophes as harbingers of dynastic change. It was whispered that the regime was about to collapse and the nationalists would return. 'Heaven, the old regime is coming back!' proclaimed someone in Dalian. In Linying, Henan, farmers desecrated images of Mao, burning out his eyes, tearing down the posters or even attacking them with choppers.[49]

Everywhere, it seemed, poor villagers turned to miracle cures, drinking holy water thought to have magical powers. In Xuchang, surrounded by tobacco plants on the northern plain of Henan, thousands of farmers turned up at various sacred locations to drink the water, said to confer protection against germ warfare. In a village in Dehui, a region in Manchuria where brutal levies had brought famine, up to 1,000 believers gathered daily around an ancient well. Some were demobilised soldiers from the Korean War who came by bus from neighbouring provinces. The authorities decried these practices as superstition, but the local cadres were just as jittery. In Wuyang county the entire leadership locked themselves up in the government's health bureau to drink realgar, traditionally used in alchemy to ward off disease. They also covered themselves in a miracle balm.[50]

Whatever their reactions to the allegations, around the country people were mobilised to detect germ-warfare attacks. In Manchuria suspected victims were doused in a liquid solution of DDT. In Andong, close to the border, a team of 5,000 equipped with gauze masks, cotton sacks and gloves were on the hunt, scouring the surrounding mountains around the clock for suspicious insects. In Shenyang 20,000 people were deployed to mop floors, sweep streets, remove trash and disinfect the city down to every last pavement slab. Here is how Tianjin fought back against biological infection:

Case #4: June 9, 1952. Insects were first discovered at 12 noon near the pier at the Tanggu Workers Union Hall. At 12:40 p.m., insects were discovered at the New Harbour Works Department, and at 1:30, in Beitang town. Insects were spread over an area of 2,002,400 square metres in New Harbour, and for over twenty Chinese miles [approximately 10 kilometres] along the shore at Beitang. Insect elimination was carried out under the direction of the Tianjin Municipal Disinfection Team. Masses organized to assist in catching insects included 1,586 townspeople, 300 soldiers and 3,150 workers. Individual insects were collected and then burned, boiled or buried. Insect species included inchworms, snout moths, wasps, aphids, butterflies . . . giant mosquitoes, etc. Samples of the insects were sent to the Central Laboratory in Beijing, where they were found to be infected with typhoid bacilli, dysentery bacilli and paratyphoid.[51]

Carried out like a military campaign, the drive to cleanse the country soon alienated large sections of the population. In Beijing everybody was inoculated against plague, typhus, typhoid and just about every other disease for which there was a vaccine, whether they wanted it or not. In the countryside compulsion assumed a wholly different dimension. In parts of Shandong the militia would arrive and block off both sides of the market, locking villagers in until they had been injected. In a village in Qihe the military locked all the houses and injected the assembled villagers themselves. Some young men, already worried about conscription, clambered over walls to escape. Women carrying their children tried to hide in a ditch and were too frightened to return home. Everywhere threats were common, and some of those who refused an injection were portrayed as spies on the imperialists' payroll. In Shaanxi, too, the campaign treated ordinary villagers as so many potential enemies to be brought to heel. In some places local cadres commanded that 'he who does not kill flies is guilty of germ warfare'. Households that failed to comply with the instructions had a black flag pinned on their front door. Under the pretext of germ warfare, a few women were forced to undergo a humiliating physical examination before a wedding certificate was granted.[52]

One commendable result of this phobia was that some of the most important cities were cleaned up. In Beijing the pavements were scrubbed, holes in the road were filled and households ordered to paint the walls of their houses up to a height of a metre with white disinfectant. Trees were ringed with disinfectant to keep them free from crawling insects. In a swampy city like Tianjin, where mosquitoes could easily breed, local residents were organised in brigades and supplied with picks, shovels and poles to fill in hundreds of cesspools, one bucketful of soil at a time.[53]

But the drive to clean up cities also had adverse effects on the natural environment. Shrubs, bushes and plants were removed to deprive pests of hiding places. Large bushfires were started to fumigate flies and mosquitoes. Lime whitewash appeared everywhere, on buildings, trees, bushes and even grass, killing vegetation and turning villages and cities into a grey mass streaked with white and dotted, here and there, with red. DDT and other harmful pesticides became a permanent feature in the attack on nature, helping to turn cities into stark concrete landscapes devoid of greenery.[54]

The campaign also had another visible effect. Many residents, from traffic police and food handlers to street sweepers, started wearing cotton masks, which always surprised foreign visitors. This habit would last for decades. In the words of William Kinmond, it gave 'even young girls and boys the appearance of being fugitives from operating rooms'.[55]

From north to south, people were also required to kill the 'five pests', namely flies, mosquitoes, fleas, bedbugs and rats. In Beijing every person had to produce the tail of one rat every week. Those who greatly exceeded the quota were allowed to fly a red flag over the gate of their house, while those who failed had to raise a black flag. An underground market in tails rapidly developed. In Guangdong, the campaign for rodent prevention also came with strict quotas. In July 1952 each district was ordered to kill at least 50,000 rats, the tails to be severed and delivered to the authorities preserved in ethanol. As in Beijing, the pressure was such that many people turned to a thriving black market to meet their share of the quota. In some cities even 0.20 yuan was insufficient to secure a tail. In Shanghai the issue was not so much rat tails as insect larvae, which had to be collected by the tonne. The penalty for delivering too few buckets was deprivation of all material benefits. As a result, people even took trains to the countryside to collect the stuff, or else tried to bribe their way through the entire process.[56]

Although the campaign did much to spread awareness of the causes of some diseases, it did little to improve basic health care. In January 1953 a report presented at a nationwide conference on hygiene revealed that the incidence of gastrointestinal diseases had actually increased the previous year. In Shanxi hundreds of tonnes of sugar products contained flies and bees. In Shanghai dead rats were found in moon cakes, while in Jinan maggots wriggled their way through bean-paste cakes. Entire groups of people suffered from appalling disease rates, ranging from tuberculosis to hepatitis. In parts of the country half of all miners were sick, as the relentless drive for higher output had led to the neglect of even the most basic facilities. Nine months later the Ministry of Health, in a self-criticism addressed to Mao Zedong, accepted that much of the campaign in 1952 had been based on coercion and had proved wasteful, 'to the point where it prevented the masses from engaging in production and gave rise to their discontent'. More detailed investigations showed the extent of waste caused by the campaign. In Shaanxi, for instance, a full year's supply of medicine had been squandered in just six months, as local officials had pursued showcase projects for the campaign rather than using their scarce resources to improve the health of the people they represented.[57]

―――――

Dogs never appeared on the list of 'five pests' but were also targeted for elimination. All over China one could find them, many of them crippled and mangy, wandering the streets and rubbish dumps in packs, fighting with each other for a scrap of food. In the cities some families kept them as pets, while in the countryside they were popular for guard duty, herding and food. They were routinely put down in communist-held areas during the civil war. Like everything else, the cull came in stages after liberation. In Beijing, a swoop cleared thousands of wild dogs from the streets, often with the support of local residents, as policemen armed with wire nooses on bamboo poles rounded them up. Then, by September 1949, dog owners were required to register their pets and keep the animals indoors. A year later the destruction of registered dogs started. Some of the animals were voluntarily turned in, but a few owners refused to surrender them. In a few cases the police were even confronted by angry dog keepers, who sometimes had the crowd on their side. The police then started breaking into houses. Owners came back home to find their doors broken down and their pets gone.[58]

But the campaign really took off during the fight against germ warfare, when teams of dog chasers appeared on the streets, carrying out house-to-house searches. Most of the animals were removed to an enormous compound outside the city wall. As one resident in Beijing noted, 'They were taken away in small carts like garbage cars, closed tight and packed solid, and if you passed one you could hear them thrashing inside and see blood on the sides of the cart.' In the compound hundreds of dogs were kept in cages. As the dogs were not fed, they attacked each other, the stronger eating the weaker. Occasionally a policeman would put a wire noose over the head of a healthier specimen and swing it around till it choked to death. Then the animal would be flung to the ground and skinned. The hide, still steaming from the body heat, was put over a cage to dry as the other dogs cowered underneath.[59]

Even though her roommates objected to the animal, Esther Cheo kept a small female dog in her dormitory, which she had taken in as a puppy. She shared all her food with it, and the dog was named Hsiao Mee, after the millet they ate. During the cull one of her colleagues who disliked dogs opened the door and let her out. The dog was soon caught and carried away, but, with the help of a high-ranking cadre, Esther managed to locate the compound where the animals were kept. 'I walked up and down stumbling over dead and dying dogs, shouting out Hsiao Mee's name, trying to drown out the barks and whines of hundreds of dogs. Eventually I found her. She was in a cage with several others. She jumped up and tried to lick my face, trembling with fear and perhaps excited, hoping that I had come to take her home. I could only sit there and stroke her.' Esther came back to the compound regularly, even taking a pair of scissors to the dog's coat in the hope that she would not be slaughtered for her skin. But in the end all she was allowed to do was to feed her pet some scraps of pork from the canteen and look on as the animal shivered and ate from the bowl in her mangled coat. Finally, with the help of a sympathetic cadre, Esther was given a pistol. She took off the safety catch, pressed the barrel against the dog's ear and blew her head off.[60]

Dogs were denounced as a threat to public hygiene and a symbol of bourgeois decadence at a time of food shortages. Except for those owned by a few privileged diplomats and top officials, they were soon cleared from the cities. But parts of the countryside continued to resist for several years. In Guangdong, efforts to impose a cull backfired in 1952, as angry villagers openly defied the authorities. Killing a landlord was one thing, but taking away a man's dog was another matter altogether, as they protected homesteads, crops and livestock. In Shandong, where almost every family kept a dog, repeated culls also failed. In the end, however, even the countryside fell into line.[61]

Stalin died in March 1953. Within months the new leadership in Moscow moved rapidly towards an agreement over Korea with the Americans and signed a ceasefire on 27 July 1953. Allegations of germ warfare also ended abruptly as the extent of the deception came to light in Moscow. The claims, apparently, had first come from commanders in the field. Mao Zedong and Zhou Enlai ordered a laboratory investigation of the evidence and dispatched epidemic-prevention teams to Korea, but even before the tests were completed they had begun condemning the United States for engaging in bacteriological warfare. Once the reports had turned out to be inaccurate, Mao was unwilling to abandon the propaganda benefits of his crusade against the United States. A report to Lavrenti Beria, head of Soviet intelligence, outlined what had happened: 'False plague regions were created, burials of bodies of those who died and their disclosure were organized, measures were taken to receive [sic] the plague and cholera bacillus.' On 2 May 1953 a secret resolution of the presidium of the USSR Council of Ministers dismissed all allegations: 'The Soviet Government and the Central Committee of the Communist Party of the Soviet Union were misled. The spread in the press of information about the use by the United States of bacteriological weapons in Korea was based on false information. The accusations against the Americans were fictitious.' A top-ranking emissary was sent to Beijing with a harsh message: cease all allegations at once. They stopped as suddenly as they had started.[62]

PART THREE

REGIMENTATION (1952–56)

8

The Purge

On a cold, wintry day in February 1952, a crowd of 21,000 filled the stadium in Baoding, the provincial seat of Hebei. On the stage sat several judges. Facing the people stood two victims, their hands tied behind their backs, eyes fixed on the ground, two armed guards in thick padded jackets right behind them. Long banners, reaching from shoulders to waist, denounced them as criminals and traitors. Zhang Qingchun, head of the Hebei Austerity Inspection Committee, detailed the heinous crimes each of them had committed. A stony silence followed his long speech, as the judge finally stood up to pronounce the death sentence. Heads bowed in submission, the accused never lifted their faces to look at the crowd or their accusers. They were immediately marched off to the execution grounds of Baoding. As a sign of mercy, they were shot in the heart rather than in the head.[1]

Had it not been for the identity of the victims, the trial might have looked like any other public execution carried out in the name of the people. But this one was different. Liu Qingshan and Zhang Zishan were key players in the local party hierarchy. One was the former secretary of the Tianjin Prefectural Committee, the other the head of the Tianjin Commissioner's Office. Arrested in November 1951, they were accused of abusing their power, diverting funds and conducting illegal economic activities. Each had used his position to build a small empire, amassing exorbitant profits, embezzling large sums of money and squandering most of it.

The trial caused ripples throughout the ranks of the party. Mao himself had approved the executions, despite pleas for pardon from Huang Jing, the head of Tianjin. 'Only if we execute the two of them can we prevent twenty, two hundred, two thousand or twenty thousand corrupt officials from committing various crimes,' the Chairman opined. Even their record of past service to the cause did not save them from the firing squad. Their deaths were meant to serve as a warning to others in the party.[2]

Three years earlier a nervous Mao had entered Beijing, joking that he was going to sit the imperial examination. 'We should be able to pass it,' Zhou Enlai reassured him. 'We cannot step back.' 'If we retreat we fail,' Mao chimed in. 'Under no circumstances can we be like Li Zicheng, all of us have to make the grade.'[3]

Li Zicheng was a folk hero who had formed a rebel army to fight the Ming dynasty in the seventeenth century. He won popular support by promising a new era of peace and prosperity. Hundreds of thousands of villagers rallied behind his calls for land distribution and the abolition of exorbitant grain taxes. In 1644 his victorious rebels sacked the capital, Beijing. The Chongzhen emperor, in a fit of drunken despair, tried to kill his daughters and concubines, hoping to save them from the hands of the rebels. Then he stumbled to the imperial gardens on a hill behind the Forbidden City, loosened his long hair to cover his face, and hanged himself from the rafters of a pavilion. Li Zicheng proclaimed himself the emperor of a new Shun dynasty, but it was not to last. Within months the Manchus crushed his army at Shanhaiguan and founded the Qing.

In a long essay commemorating the fall of the Ming 300 years before, the poet Guo Moruo warned in 1944 that Li Zicheng had been able to hold the capital only for a matter of weeks, as his rapacious troops terrorised the population and succumbed to widespread corruption. Guo's essay spelled out the analogies between the Ming bandits and the communist rebels, warning that strict ideological discipline would be required in the civil war to control China. Mao liked the essay and wrote to Guo: 'Small victories lead to arrogance, big victories even more so. They result in repeated failures. We must be careful not to make the same mistake.' The essay was published in Yan'an, the remote and isolated mountain area in Shaanxi where the communist party had established its headquarters during the Second World War.[4]

Far behind enemy lines, Mao used his political skills in Yan'an to consolidate his own role within the party, making sure that the constitution endorsed Marxism-Leninism and Mao Zedong Thought, the political theories developed in his official publications. In 1942 he launched a major purge of his enemies, eliminating his rivals one by one, a drive he called a 'Rectification Campaign'. As Gao Hua, a leading historian of the purge, has noted, its goal was 'to intimidate the whole party with violence and terror, to uproot any individual independent thought, to make the whole party subject to the single utmost authority of Mao'. Mao orchestrated the entire campaign, supervising everything down to the last detail, but he let his henchman Kang Sheng take centre stage. Other close allies of the Central General Study Committee, set up to investigate the dossier of every party member, were Peng Zhen, Li Fuchun, Gao Gang and later Liu Shaoqi. The Study Committee ran everything, unhindered by any constitutional constraints, in effect converting the party into Mao's personal dictatorship. Leading officials such as Zhou Enlai, Peng Dehuai, Chen Yi and Liu Bocheng were forced to produce self-criticisms, write confessions and apologise for past mistakes. Everybody went through the wringer, as accusations of spying spiralled out of control. Party members at every level were forced to denounce others, trying to save themselves from false allegations. Endless witch-hunts took place, as thousands of suspects were locked up, investigated, tortured, purged and occasionally executed. At night the ghostly howls of people imprisoned in caves could be heard. These were the ones who had lost their minds during the inquisition.

By 1944 over 15,000 alleged agents and spies had been unmasked. Mao allowed the terror to run amok, assuming the role of a self-effacing, distant yet benevolent leader. Then he stepped in to curb the violence, letting Kang take the fall. Those who had managed to survive the horror turned to him as a saviour. The Rectification Campaign was the prototype of many movements to come.[5]

Guo Moruo's essay on the fall of the Ming came at the height of the Yan'an terror. Mao had it reprinted and widely distributed, warning that weak-willed cadres who had survived the guns of the enemy would be defeated by the 'sugar-coated bullets' of the bourgeoisie, a metaphor for corruption. By the end of 1951, almost three years after the conquest of the country, it seemed indeed that the underhanded ways of capitalism were vanquishing the party. The sudden expansion of power and the intake of new members had weakened ideological purity and bred complacency. A taste for the good life extended from the top leaders all the way down to local cadres, who felt that, after fighting hard for the revolution, they should sit back and enjoy the material perks to which their struggle entitled them. 'Extravagance, waste and much feasting' flourished among the lower ranks, tarnishing the image of the party.

Bureaucracy crippled the economy, threatening China's ability to conduct the war in Korea. The budget ballooned out of all proportion. Even worse, many cadres were corrupt, pocketing large sums of money they should have contributed to the war effort. Zhang Zishan and Liu Qingshan had just been arrested. The Chairman imagined that their case was merely the tip of the iceberg, as a plethora of greedy hands dipped into the state coffers. Mao warned his colleagues: '[We] must pay serious attention to the fact that our cadres have been corrupted by the bourgeoisie and are guilty of severe embezzlement. [We should] pay attention and detect, expose and punish them. We also need a big struggle to deal with them.'[6]

It was time to clean out the party. Bo Yibo, minister of finance, was put in charge of the campaign, but Mao presided over the entire operation, issuing dozens of directives to other top leaders. The Chairman barely consulted his senior colleagues. All had to report to him directly. Zhou Enlai was treated like a secretary at his master's beck and call. By the end of December, the Chairman demanded that monthly reports from the county level upwards be sent directly to Beijing so that the performance of their officials could be monitored.[7]

Mao used his control of the central apparatus to set the tone and whip up the pressure. As usual, his instructions were vague, leaving his subordinates to guess what his real intentions were. Seemingly everyone was a target, from powerful ministers down to local officials. No legal definitions existed of what precisely constituted 'corruption', not to mention 'waste', which was so broad a category as to include virtually everything from deliberate stripping of state assets to minor acts of negligence. Mao was adamant: 'Although waste and corruption are different in nature, the losses caused by waste are bigger than those caused by corruption, and are similar to embezzlement, theft, fraud or bribery. So we should severely punish waste at the same time as we severely punish corruption.' The only guideline was the distinction between trivial suspects, described as mere 'flies', and larger cases labelled 'tigers'. Big tigers were those who had embezzled over 10,000 yuan, and small tigers were guilty of fraud involving more than 1,000 yuan.[8]

Tiger-Hunting Teams tried to outdo each other in trapping their targets, encouraged from above by Mao. Units were set against units, counties competed with counties, provinces vied with provinces. On 9 January 1952 the Chairman praised Gansu for resolutely fighting tigers. He worried that other provinces, where corruption was even worse, had set much lower targets: 'this is not realistic', he pronounced. On 2 February 1952 Zhejiang reported that there might be up to a thousand tigers inside its borders. Mao scoffed, pointing out that in a province of that size at least 3,000 cases could be discovered. Five days later came the announcement that Zhejiang harboured 3,700 tigers. Mao circulated the report, urging other provinces to adjust their targets upwards. Soon Bo Yibo enthusiastically reported a new record of 100,000 tigers for all of east China.[9]

On the ground people scrambled to fulfil their quotas. Some took advantage of the winter holidays, enrolling students in Tiger-Hunting Teams. Tommy Wu, a student aged twenty-four, was sent with six other students to the Art Supply Service attached to the Zhejiang Institute of Fine Arts, located on the shore of the West Lake in Hangzhou.

> I worked there under the office of the Campaign Against the Three Evils. The entire staff and all the workers were organized to study party policies attached to this campaign. The staff was then called upon to make a clean breast of their crimes and accuse others they knew to be criminals as well. These crimes included embezzling, forgery, theft, bribery and other forms of corruption. Some suspects were already being locked up in isolated rooms within the offices. Most of those locked up were directors on various levels. Some were even old party members from the early Yan'an days. We had no mercy on those we saw to be 'criminals'.

In the end, despite all the pressure, Tommy Wu's team only found a man who had appropriated a camera and a little more than a hundred yuan. They spent three months on the entire campaign.[10]

Up in Beijing, Dan Ling, the schoolboy who had come down with diarrhoea after standing on Tiananmen Square for ten hours to watch the parade in October 1949, was now a member of the Communist Youth League. He worked for the Number One Automobile Factory and was also asked to join a Tiger-Hunting Team. They soon identified a manager suspected of having stolen an expensive piece of equipment. A former member of the nationalist party, his services had been retained because of his technical expertise. Dan was given a list of the man's alleged crimes, and put in charge of a meeting to question him. Assembled workers at the factory screamed at the victim, 'Confess!', but an admission of guilt was not good enough. He was pressed for more confessions and forced to denounce others.

Mass rallies were held. The Ministry of Heavy Industry organised a huge parade in Zhongshan Park, dragging out every major suspect and forcing them to confront the masses in denunciation meetings. Extensive publicity surrounded the most notorious cases. In Beijing the biggest tiger was Song Degui, an officer in the Public Security Bureau who seemed to embody every kind of depravity. He was accused of siphoning off a gigantic sum of money. He had had an affair with the wife of a former capitalist, and then slept with the woman's daughter. He was even a drug addict. Song was wonderful material for Dan's team, who studied the case as a guide for their own investigations.[11]

'Every organization became a battlefield where ruthless struggles were fought.' First major culprits like Song Degui were forced to admit their own corruption, then they were made to inform on the corruption of others below them in an effort to save themselves. Suspects were also unleashed on other suspects in mutual-denunciation sessions: this was called 'using a tiger to bite a tiger'. Lesser offenders were suspended from their duties and put under house arrest so that they could 'reflect on their past behaviour'. Even those who were not suspect had to make reports on their past activities and proffer self-criticisms, only to risk being denounced and ostracised.[12]

Soon 'confessions' began to pour out of every government office. Corruption seemed to be everywhere. Another 133 cadres besides Song Degui were found to be corrupt in the Ministry of Public Security. In the Ministry of Finance, government officials had connived with the private sector to defraud the state of goods worth millions of yuan. Overall, in the upper echelons of power, an astounding 10,000 people were corrupt, according to Bo Yibo, including eighteen big tigers who had taken more than 10,000 yuan.[13]

Even more serious was the situation among the rank and file, as local cadres socialised with businessmen and entrepreneurs, accepting bribes as if they were fringe benefits. In the entire north-west, 340,000 cases of corruption were uncovered, although Xi Zhongxun suggested that in reality there might well be three times as many culprits. In Tianshui, Gansu, one out of every three officials working in tax collection lined his own pockets. Other regions were just as bad. In Jinan, the capital of Shandong, the leading officials of virtually every department wined and dined private entrepreneurs. In the police, bribes extended from the ordinary patrolman all the way up to the head of a police station. One deputy mayor was guilty of having lavished 3,000 yuan – or sixty times the monthly salary of a skilled worker – on entertaining guests in less than a year. The local Bureau for Industry was accused of taking 70,000 yuan in kickbacks. Everywhere, it seemed, the sugar-coated bullets of the enemy had created a class of corrupt, depraved government officials just as bad as their predecessors.[14]

Many people applauded the campaign. Here was a party so determined to stamp out corruption that it even shot some of its own leaders. 'The general belief was that the regime really was going to clean up its ranks. I also believed this, and I approved of it,' noted Robert Loh, who now worked for a cotton mill in Shanghai. Others, such as Chow Ching-wen, a leader of the Democratic League co-opted by the communist party, had seen the extravagance and corruption from the inside and also believed that the movement was necessary to correct the situation. But others had their doubts. Dr Li Zhisui, who was such a supporter of the cause that he became frustrated when he was not allowed to join the war effort in Korea, felt a deep anguish that would stay with him for the rest of his life. His brother and cousin, the very men who had introduced him to the communist party three years earlier, were now being attacked, although Li knew they were innocent. But he was too afraid to speak out. 'Had I defended them, I too would have been attacked.'[15]

Underneath the veneer of a well-orchestrated campaign, the pressure to find targets produced abuse at every level. In Hebei some suspects were insulted, beaten or forced to stand in the cold without clothes. The sessions could last for days on end, as the victims were 'ceaselessly interrogated until they uttered a figure [of embezzled funds] that corresponded to the one demanded of them'. In Wu'an county, hair was pulled and heads were plunged into toilets. Over a hundred tigers were discovered using these methods, although not one single case was based on hard evidence. In Shijiazhuang suspects were buried in snow, forced to kneel on hot ashes or threatened with execution. A few were paraded through the streets with tall conical hats, to the delight of the children who had joined Tiger-Hunting Teams.[16]

When no tigers could be identified, the cadres turned against the workers instead. In the Shijiazhuang Railway Factory, several hundred of them were subjected to struggle sessions that were so gruelling that one man drank petrol to put an end to the misery. In the North-west Normal University in Lanzhou, Gansu, official support for violence was such that:

> everyone, whether or not there is any proof of corruption, is beaten at denunciation meetings, and even their wives are beaten and denounced. Some of the merchants outside the campus are dragged into the school and beaten. Once the suspects have been beaten, they are tortured. For instance, they are forced to sit on their haunches with a kettle of boiling water on their heads, they are stripped of their clothes, beaten with ropes, sometimes until they pass out, a few almost to death.[17]

But under cover of popular approval and high-power publicity for outstanding cases, something even more sinister was taking place. The authorities were quietly liquidating many government officials without trial. 'Disappearances' became common, and they pointed towards another purpose of the campaign: the liquidation of a whole group of people. When the communists had first come to power in 1949, they had urged all the civil service employees to remain at their posts, repeatedly assuring them of the regime's protection and even gratitude. They helped by maintaining the continued operation of essential services; they ensured a smooth transfer of power. By late 1951, however, sufficient communist cadres had been trained to take over the administration. The former employees were no longer needed, and many were purged.[18]

Close to 4 million government employees were hounded throughout the campaign, some of them tortured so badly that they chose to commit suicide. In a summary made in October 1952, at the end of the campaign, a secret report by An Ziwen concluded that 1.2 million corrupt individuals had been discovered to have embezzled a total of 600 million yuan. Fewer than 200,000 of these culprits were party members, demonstrating the extent of the purge against civil servants who had been retained from the previous regime. The report also admitted that at least 10 per cent of all cases were based on false accusations and forced confessions. But in the end it mattered very little that so many victims had been wronged, as long as the government was cleansed of its most unreliable elements. Tens of thousands of people were sent to labour camps.[19]

A few high-ranking leaders were executed in public, but it is doubtful that the real corruption at the top of the party was tackled. Chow Ching-wen, who welcomed the campaign at first, quickly became disabused. He noted that 'those who were corrupt, but loyal to Mao, escaped with only their money confiscated and light punishment, while those who were found to be wavering in their support of Mao were killed'. After Zhang Zishan and Liu Qingshan had been arrested, a team of investigators pored over the dossiers of the top leadership in Tianjin, finding a web of deceit involving scores of senior party members, most of whom escaped with a mere slap on the wrist. As Chow noted, 'to punish all the offenders would give a bad name to the regime and even threaten its stability'.[20]

———

Soon the campaign moved beyond the ranks of the government. Dark hints that malevolent outside forces were undermining public morality were everywhere. On 30 November 1951, as he was about to launch the campaign against corruption, Mao told the leadership that 'our cadres have been corrupted by the bourgeoisie'. Over the following weeks reports came in from cities all over the country, linking government officials to cases of bribery, theft and tax evasion by businessmen and entrepreneurs. On 5 January 1952 Mao reached the conclusion that the bourgeoisie had been waging a 'savage offensive' against the party that was 'more serious and dangerous than a war'. A resolute counter-offensive was needed to deliver a fatal blow within a matter of months. In the words of historian Michael Sheng, 'Mao now declared war on the bourgeoisie.'[21]

The war came in the guise of a campaign against the five alleged sins of the bourgeoisie: bribery, tax evasion, pilfering government property, cheating on contracts and stealing state secrets. These terms were broad enough to encompass virtually anything. Cadres jumped at the opportunity to deflect accusations of corruption against themselves, and turned on private trade with a vengeance.

The business community was already reeling from three years of communism. Not all of its members had tied their fates to the new regime by deciding to stay behind in 1949. Many entrepreneurs and industrialists had fled the country even before Manchuria fell to the communists. For a brief period after the Second World War, trade and commerce seemed to be booming again. Factories went back into production after the devastation of the war, and some businessmen had ambitious plans for expansion. But the nationalists soon started interfering with the market, adopting policies that subjected private enterprise to the heavy hand of the state, heralding what would happen after 1949. In the banking sector, for instance, over 200 banks were competing for customers in 1945, but by 1948 the Bank of China had imposed a virtual monopoly, as its competitors had been driven out of business or taken over by the government. The central bank, in turn, started controlling the import and export of foreign currency, limiting what individuals could take with them while travelling abroad to just US$200. Chiang Kai-shek's son, Chiang Ching-kuo, was put in charge of fighting inflation: he gaoled several thousand entrepreneurs in Shanghai for corruption before abandoning state control in October 1948.[22]

Squeezed out of business by the nationalists, entrepreneurs and their families started leaving in droves in the years following the Second World War. Many went to South America. Paraguay, where a visa could be obtained on arrival, was an attractive destination. Brazil also loomed large, all the more since Soong May-ling, the wife of the Generalissimo, had visited the country in June 1944. Some industrialists shipped whole factories to South America, while others bought properties, acquired stakes in banks, oil and shipping or invested in coffee and cocoa plantations from São Paulo to Caracas and Buenos Aires.

A few had exceptional foresight, others were just lucky in deciding to relocate abroad well before 1949. Another popular destination was Hong Kong. The Japanese occupation of China from 1937 onwards had already prepared many industrialists to emigrate to the crown colony, as they sought a safe haven away from the mainland. Many thought that their exile would be temporary and took only the bare essentials with them. Others went back and forth, hoping to be able to resettle after the end of the war. Alex Woo's family came to Hong Kong in 1948, stayed for a while and then decided to go back: 'The first time we came was by boat, but after three months we went back to Shanghai. Things there were getting really bad so my father came out with my younger brother and myself. I was just eight years old. There were no longer any commercial flights so we took a military plane. It was just before the Communists marched in,' he remembered. Many families tried to hedge their bets, moving some members to South America, keeping a foothold in Hong Kong while packing off a few of the younger ones to study in the United States.[23]

In some cases one or more members stayed in China in order to protect the family assets. In the case of the Rong (also known as the Yung family), one of the wealthiest in the country, most of their assets were liquidated or mortgaged to the hilt before 1949. They left behind one of their seven sons as an informal hostage to the bank. Aged thirty-three, a graduate of St John's University in Shanghai, Rong Yiren looked after some twenty textile factories and flour mills with 80,000 employees.

The communists welcomed him – as well as the many shopkeepers, bankers, traders and entrepreneurs who had no choice but to remain in China in 1949. The official slogan was the New Democracy, and the party assured those now labelled as the 'national bourgeoisie' that they could continue to run their enterprises on a private basis. In reality, as in the satellite states of the Soviet Union, the New Democracy was part of a bogus coalition between different forces that the party was simply unable to control at this early stage. When they took the country in 1949, the communists suffered from an acute shortage of manpower, leaving them little choice but to use the commercial and industrial skills of the business community. Like the retained government employees, they were told to stay in their jobs and work for the new regime.[24]

Privately Mao had no illusions about the need to eliminate capitalism. In May 1949, as the leadership camped on the outskirts of Beijing, preparing themselves to take over the country, Mao shared a meal with Huang Kecheng, then a commander in the army. The Chairman asked him what the communist party's first priority should be, now that victory was close. Having seen the devastation caused by years of warfare, Huang opined that economic reconstruction would rank highest. Mao sternly shook his head: 'No! The most important task is class struggle. We have to resolve the question of the capitalist class.' Months earlier he had lambasted as 'muddle-headed' those who thought that the party should rely on the bourgeoisie.[25]

Whatever the long-term strategy of the party, private business was soon in dire straits. In the first year after liberation many enterprises were compelled to accept wage increases that vastly inflated the costs of production. Punitive taxes followed, some of them applied retroactively, bearing little relationship to the actual income of private enterprises. Their remaining assets were further drained through the enforced purchase of Victory Bonds. The cadres appointed to supervise commerce and industry compounded the problem. Many lacked basic knowledge of the world of trade and business and were reticent and suspicious, checking and rechecking every transaction. The trade embargo imposed by the nationalists also crippled international commerce, while the communists began redirecting all foreign trade towards the Soviet Union after Mao returned from Moscow in early 1950. Once bustling commercial districts had slipped into decay by the summer of 1950, as described in Chapter 3.

Aware that taxation was killing the proverbial goose that lays the golden eggs, finance minister Bo Yibo reformed the tax system in June 1950. Labour activism was curbed, while the state started ordering products in massive quantities from some of the larger industrial concerns, saving them from bankruptcy. The People's Bank of China selectively used 'encouragement loans' to rescue other private concerns, increasing their dependence on government credit.

Tariff and exchange controls brought the business community closer to its knees. Gradually everything standing between the entrepreneur and the state was eliminated. The rule of law was suspended. People's tribunals replaced independent courts. In June 1950, branches of the party-controlled

All-China Federation of Trade Unions were substituted for independent trade unions. From 1951 onwards, local branches of the party-controlled All-China Federation of Industry and Commerce likewise took over from independent chambers of commerce. To maintain the appearance of the New Democracy, industrial leaders like Rong Yiren were invited to join their boards. The party also set up compulsory Management Committees to negotiate conflicts between workers and their bosses, in effect controlling both labour and capital.[26]

The Korean War brought a further clampdown on the private sector. A Donations Drive replaced the Victory Bonds Campaign, as massive contributions in gold, jewellery, dollars or other foreign currencies were extracted from manufacturers, entrepreneurs and traders to finance the war. But, most of all, the campaign of terror that unfolded after October 1950 silenced all opposition to the regime. As hundreds of thousands of real or imagined enemies were executed before large crowds, entrepreneurs feared being dragged away to the police station to face accusations of being 'a person of the compradore class who built up his fortune by means of depriving the legal livelihood of the working class' or 'an agent working for the nationalist government'. As most foreigners were hounded out of the country, they left behind a vulnerable, fearful and isolated bourgeoisie cut off from all their contacts with the rest of the world.

The campaign against the bourgeoisie unleashed by Mao in January 1952 followed well-established techniques which had been fine-tuned during land reform. At denunciation meetings the workers were encouraged to turn against their managers. The trade unions established work brigades, each member taking an oath of loyalty and promising to 'stand firm' and prosecute the campaign thoroughly. Traditional links with employers were severed as employees 'spoke bitterness', urged by local cadres to dig out every past slight they could think of. The workers were now the masters. Party activists took the lead, searching for evidence of criminal activity. 'Clerks and workers, on instructions from their labour unions, pried into account books, opened safes, and eavesdropped on telephone calls in a feverish search for something incriminating.' Entire cities were placed on a war footing, as lorries trundled through business districts, stopping before shops with their loudspeakers blaring: 'Hey, proprietor!

Evidence of all your misdeeds is now in our hands. Confess!' The windows of suspected businesses were plastered with bills and placards, while gangs of demonstrators blocked their entrances. Denunciation boxes, bright red with a small slit at the top, were provided to make it more convenient for people to denounce others. Big banners fluttered over busy streets: 'Sternly Punish Corruption Culprits'.[27]

Terrified merchants, traders and bankers crowded into confession meetings to confront their accusers. Before he was locked up in his office to write a confession on his work in the cotton mills operated by Rong Yiren, employee Robert Loh found that posters had been put up on the wall in front of his desk. They contained slogans such as 'Crush the Vicious Attack of the Capitalist Class', 'Surrender, You Vile Capitalist', 'A Complete Confession is the Road to Survival, Anything Less Will Lead to Death'. A loudspeaker was installed in one of the office windows. It sputtered briefly and then burst into an ear-splitting racket, broadcasting the mass meeting under way in the main dining hall. Most of it was an harangue against capitalism, as party activists worked the crowd into a frenzy. Then cadres took over the microphone to address Loh directly. They shouted abuse, insults and threats, admonishing him to make a full confession. This went on for a full afternoon. In the evening a cook dropped a blanket on the floor and reluctantly placed a bowl of noodles on the edge of his desk. Guards made sure he could not leave, even accompanying him to the toilet. Later, when he tried to sleep on the floor of his office, they sat grimly in front of him, refusing to turn off the lights at night.

This went on for two days. On the morning of the third day, as he was escorted to the party secretary's office, the employees jeered and called him a 'capitalist swine' and 'unscrupulous dog'. Some spat at him, a few tried to hit him. The most vehement were those with whom Loh had been most friendly. 'At first, this cut me deeply, but then I realized that precisely because they had been friendly to me, they would be the ones threatened the most and for their own safety they would strain to show that they no longer had anything but hatred and contempt for a capitalist criminal like me. Oddly enough, this thought made me feel better.'

After more admonitions from the leading cadre, Loh spent another two days of torment under the constant scrutiny of his guards, listening to the accusations broadcast over the loudspeaker and trying to come up with a plausible crime for which he could atone. He submitted one confession after another. His seventh attempt was accepted. Then came the day of reckoning, as he had to 'face the masses'.

> My entrance was the signal for a tremendous uproar. The screams of rage, the shouted slogans and insults, were deafening. I was made to stand with humbly bowed head before the small stage on which the communist officials sat at tables. I had lost 13 pounds. I was filthy, unshaven and exhausted. My knees trembled with both weakness and fear. The shouting behind me was turned off suddenly. The party secretary rose and read off the list of the people's charges against me.

When he had finished, Loh had to bow to the crowd. One by one, representatives from every group of employees came to the stage to denounce him.[28]

Robert Loh escaped relatively lightly. Many others did not. Some were terrorised with threats of the death penalty, and then told that their fate depended on their own contributions to the campaign. In order to save themselves, they turned on others. Terror sometimes drove them to become even more ferocious than the cadres. Since they had exclusive knowledge of their own particular branch of business, they were also in the best position to pinpoint crimes to which others were pressed to confess. Even wives and children were used in the denunciations. In Changsha an accountant named Li Shengzhen provided information on dozens of cases, denouncing his own father. 'Relatives are not as close as the state and members of the same class,' he proclaimed, according to security boss Luo Ruiqing, who proudly reported the case to the Chairman. The communist press reported that children were instructed to expose the crimes of their parents. One told his father, 'If you don't confess your own corruption, other people will expose you just the same; if you remain obstinate, I won't recognize you as my father.'[29]

Denunciations took place under intense pressure in closed meetings. But sometimes they were made in public, as victims turned up in their warmest clothes, expecting to be sent to a labour camp in Manchuria.

Some captains of industry – Rong Yiren, Liu Hongsheng, Hu Juewu – shook with fear as they stood on the stage, desperately hurling accusations at each other, Bo Yibo explained with satisfaction when writing to Mao Zedong. Breaking down in tears, Rong Yiren openly proclaimed his shame when confronted with his family's exploitative past, confessing to 20 million yuan in ill-gotten gains, an amount he had arrived at by spending weeks going through mountains of ledgers.[30]

Techniques acquired during land reform were widely used to inflict pain and humiliation. In the cities some victims were tied up, ordered to kneel on a small bench or bend down for hours on end. Sleep deprivation was common. Tactics became rougher in the countryside. Throughout Sichuan people accused of being 'capitalists' were cursed, stripped, beaten, hanged and flogged. Work teams often served as judge, jury and executioner, deciding, for example, to double a fine when a payment was made immediately and to shoot those who failed to pay up on more than four occasions. In some cities in Guangdong, tax inspectors took factory owners to witness public executions, pointing out that they would meet the same fate if they failed to comply. Some workers in Jiangmen, on the other hand, presented a 'bill for exploitation' to the factory owners, who were beaten, forced to kneel in accusation meetings and locked up in the toilets. Other forms of physical torture were 'very common'. In Shenyang merchants were stripped by the workers and forced to stand in the cold for hours on end.[31]

Few victims died, but many committed suicide. 'The sight of people jumping out of windows became commonplace,' reported Robert Loh, who saw it happen twice, even though he seldom left his house during this period. 'The coffin makers were sold out weeks ahead. The funeral homes doubled up so that several funerals were held simultaneously in one room. The parks were patrolled to prevent people from hanging themselves from the trees.' In Beijing, when the frozen West Lake began to melt in spring, more than ten bodies were found in one corner alone.[32]

Suicide was not easily accomplished, as suspects were under constant supervision. But nothing bred ingenuity quite like despair. Some entrepreneurs who had links to the pharmaceutical industry managed to obtain cyanide pills and swallowed them when dragged away to attend struggle

General Chiang Kai-shek (left) and Communist Party leader Mao Zedong, Chongqing 27 September 1945.

Chinese nationalist troops retreat to the Yangzi River, 31 December 1948.

Soldiers of the People's Liberation
Army, Nanjing, April 1949.

Crowds of onlookers
observe the first soldiers
of the People's Liberation
Army, April 1949.

Lin Biao, the commander who oversaw the siege of Changchun and conquered Manchuria.

J. Leighton Stuart standing in front of a poster of General George C. Marshall.

Zhou Enlai in Moscow, heading a delegation of government and military leaders in 1952.

Victory parade, Shanghai, June 1949, shortly after the communists had taken the city.

Shanghai, June 1949, as the communists take control.

Refugees of the civil war, April 1949.

An evacuation ship transporting refugees.

Mao Zedong proclaims the founding of the People's Republic of China in Beijing.

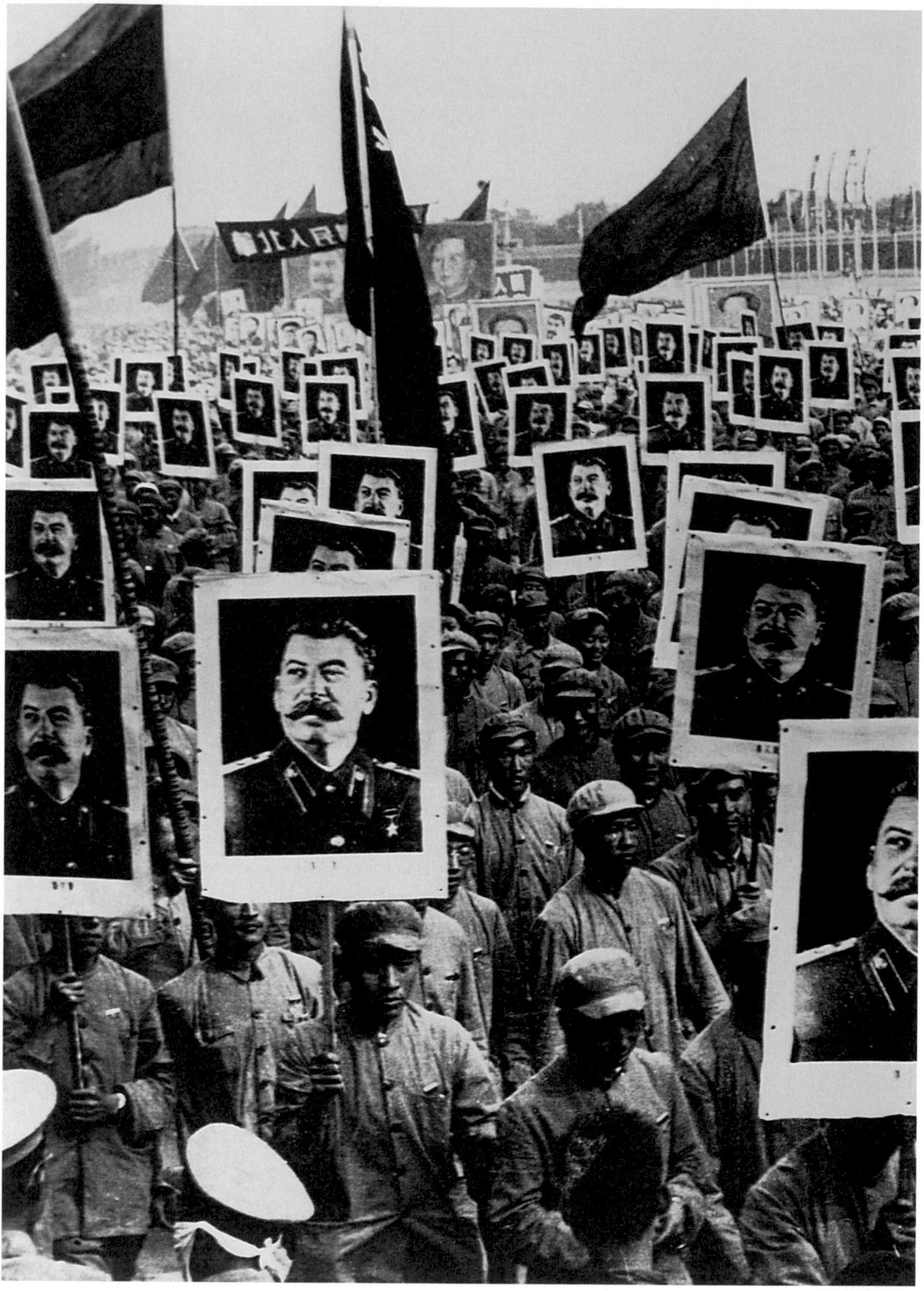

Chinese communists carry placards bearing pictures of Joseph Stalin, as they celebrate the first anniversary of the new regime in China.

An alleged 'landlord' facing a People's Tribunal minutes before being executed by a shot to the back in a village in Guangdong, July 1952.

A grief-stricken woman stands amid the ruins of a village just north of Caolaoji, destroyed by fighting during the civil war.

Yue Songsheng, a representative of industry and commerce, presents a red envelope to Zhou Enlai and Mao Zedong during the official celebration of the 'Successful Socialist Transformation', at Tian'anmen Square, 15 January 1956.

Queue outside a food shop, 1957.

Maintenance of a statue of Mao.

Mao Zedong in 1957.

meetings. Others would hide a piece of rope and hang themselves in a closet. A few slashed their wrists with a watch crystal while wrapped in a blanket, pretending to sleep on the office floor. The majority jumped from windows. Accurate statistics are impossible to come by, but in Shanghai, the city that bore the brunt of the attack, 644 people killed themselves in two months, or more than ten daily – if one can trust the statistics the party compiled.[33]

In an orgy of false accusations and arbitrary denunciations, few escaped with their reputations intact. By February no more than 10,000 of a total 50,000 'capitalists' in Beijing were considered honest. Similar figures came from other parts of the country. To punish all would wreck the economy. Mao had a solution to this conundrum. He came up with a quota, ordering that a few should be killed to set the tone, while exemplary punishment should focus on 5 per cent of the most 'reactionary' suspects. Across most cities, by a rough rule of thumb, about 1 per cent of the accused were shot, a further 1 per cent sent to labour camps for life, and 2 to 3 per cent imprisoned for terms of ten years or more.[34]

The vast majority – classified as 'basically law-abiding' and 'semi law-abiding' – were given fines, as the campaign was used to finance the Korean War. Outside the People's Bank in Shanghai, a queue 1.5 kilometres long could be seen, as small shopkeepers eagerly sought to sell their few gold possessions to pay the heavy fines imposed on them. The queue was restive, as some had to wait their turn for several days. Eventually the government agreed to accept their gold as a deposit against their debts. The payment was registered on the day of the deposit and no return was allowed. Before long, all the savings of the business and merchant community were appropriated, reducing many to poverty and further undermining the financial structures of the country.[35]

In the spring of 1952 the government quietly attempted to bring the campaign against the bourgeoisie to a close. After May Day, tax burdens were gradually eased, property evaluations reconsidered, fines imposed during the campaign reduced and crippled firms offered low-interest loans. Help was neither unconditional nor universal, as the state could now pick and choose which firms to keep afloat, strengthening its grip on the private sector. The loans came with new conditions, including a 75 per cent share of the profits for the state, while dividends, bonuses and managerial salaries had to come out of the remaining 25 per cent.[36]

It was too little, too late. By March 1952 the entire state system was at a standstill, reeling from months of self-purification. Few cadres were willing to take any decisions – when they were not busy pursuing ideological backsliders and corrupt elements. Everything was referred to the next level up the chain of command in the party hierarchy. Delays became common, apathy was widespread.

Combined with the attack on the bourgeoisie, this resulted in the paralysis of commerce and industry. From managers down to workers, everyone was apparently tied up in denunciation meetings. Industrial output plummeted, trade ground to a halt. In Shanghai goods accumulated uncollected in temporary sheds pitched out in the open. Imported cotton had to be kept on board ships as the millhands were too busy denouncing their owners. In Tianjin, the Number One Cotton Mill worked at only a third of its capacity. Stoppages were everywhere: knitwear production fell by half, and freight transportation plummeted by 40 per cent compared to the months prior to the campaign. In some sectors workers saw their earnings slashed by two-thirds. Banks in the city stopped making loans. Tax income collapsed.[37]

The situation was similar elsewhere. In Zhejiang province, traditionally dominated by trade, the business community lost a third of its capital, with ruinous consequences for the local economy. In the capital Hangzhou, half the profits made in the previous year had to be withdrawn from banks to meet back taxes, refunds and fines imposed for 'corruption' – not including a standard tax at 23 per cent as well as other contributions, donations and incentives. Further south, across Guangdong the volume of trade was down by 7 per cent in 1952 compared with the previous year. In some cities, for instance Foshan, famed for its ceramic art, it was down by 28 per cent, in large part due to punitive measures imposed on private business.[38]

Small enterprises could no longer pay their employees. Unemployment rocketed. The number of workers who lost their jobs as a direct consequence of the campaign against the bourgeoisie amounted to 80,000 in Shanghai, 10,000 in Jinan and 10,000 in the region around Suzhou, an old commercial city along the Yangzi where the wealth of its former merchants was displayed in whitewashed houses with dark-grey tiles, stone bridges, ancient pagodas and secluded gardens. In Yangzhou, enriched by centuries of trade in salt, rice and silk, the turmoil caused by the campaign was so great that workers started turning on each other. Further inland, in the city of Wuhan, once described as the Chicago of the East, 24,000 workers lost their jobs as trade dwindled to a mere 30 per cent of its level the previous quarter. Railway transportation and tax collection came to a standstill. The whole city was a scene of desolation. In Chongqing, Sichuan, 20,000 people were without work thanks to the campaign, and many families had to survive on less than half a kilo of grain a day. Some ate the husks of corn or hunted wild dogs to stave off hunger. Discontent was brewing, with slogans such as 'rebel against the campaign' doing the rounds among disgruntled employees.[39]

The countryside, still linked to the cities through a network of traders, merchants and suppliers, also suffered. In the south, basic items of trade such as oil, tea and tobacco leaves remained uncollected, hurting the farmers who depended on them for their livelihoods. In the region around Shanghai, prices of agricultural goods imploded, robbing the farmers of the capital necessary for spring ploughing. And even if they had enough seeds to plant the next crop, cadres from north to south refused to give any lead, awaiting an official end to the purge inside the ranks. This was true of Jilin, up in Manchuria, where the campaign under Gao Gang was so severe that village leaders spent all their time in meetings, fearful of denunciation as rightists. The fields lay bare. In the south, agriculture also came to a halt in large parts of the countryside. In Jiangshan county, Zhejiang, a mere quarter of all villagers were at work. Most of them just sat back, waiting for orders. And all this occurred, of course, in the middle of the Korean War, when crushing requisitions to feed the soldiers at the front had already reduced large parts of the countryside in Manchuria and Sichuan to man-made starvation.[40]

9

Thought Reform

Like pilgrims visiting a holy site, busloads of tourists regularly wander over the yellow loess hills of Yan'an, the heart of the communist revolution. In groups wearing identical tour caps or colour-coded shirts, they file into the cave where Mao once lived and worked, respectfully admiring his spartan, whitewashed bedroom furnished with a bed, a deckchair and a wooden bath. A family portrait hangs on one wall, showing the Chairman with his fourth wife and one of his children. Outside the cave, carved out of the brittle hillside, tourists pose for group photographs.[1]

More than seventy years earlier, tens of thousands of young volunteers had poured into Yan'an to join the communist party. Students, teachers, artists, writers and journalists, they were disenchanted with the nationalists and eager to dedicate their lives to the revolution. Many were so excited after days on the road that they wept when they saw the heights of Yan'an in the distance. Others cheered from the backs of their lorries, singing the 'Internationale' and the Soviet Union's 'Motherland March'. They were full of idealism, embracing liberty, equality, democracy and other liberal values that had become popular in China after the fall of the empire in 1911.

They were quickly disillusioned. Instead of equality, they found a rigid hierarchy. Every organisation had three different kitchens, the best food being reserved for the senior leaders. From the amount of grain, sugar, cooking oil, meat and fruit to the quality of health care and access to information, one's position in the party hierarchy determined everything. Even the quality of tobacco and writing paper varied according to rank. Medicine was scarce for those on the lower rungs of the ladder, although leading cadres had personal doctors and sent their children to Moscow. At the apex of the party stood Mao, who was driven around in the only car in Yan'an and lived in a large mansion with heating especially installed for his comfort.[2]

In February 1942, Mao asked the young volunteers to attack 'dogmatism' and its alleged practitioners, namely his rival Wang Ming and other Soviet-trained leaders. Soon the criticisms that he unleashed went too far. Instead of following the Chairman's cue, several critics expressed discontent with the way the red capital was run. A young writer called Wang Shiwei, who worked for the *Liberation Daily*, wrote an essay denouncing the arrogance of the 'big shots' who were 'indulging in extremely unnecessary and unjustified perks', while the sick could not even 'have a sip of noodle soup'.[3]

After two months, Mao changed tack and angrily condemned Wang Shiwei as a 'Trotskyist' (Wang had translated Engels and Trotsky). He also turned against Wang's supporters, determined to stamp out any lingering influence of free thinking among the young volunteers. Just as the rank and file were investigated in a witch-hunt for spies and undercover agents, they were interrogated in front of large crowds shouting slogans, made to confess in endless indoctrination meetings and forced to denounce each other in a bid to save themselves. Some were locked up in caves, others taken to mock executions. For month after month, life in Yan'an was nothing but a relentless succession of interrogations and rallies, feeding fear, suspicion and betrayal. All communications with areas under nationalist control were cut off, and any attempt to contact the outside world was viewed as evidence of espionage. The pressure was too much for some, as they broke down, lost their minds or committed suicide. Mao demanded absolute loyalty from intellectuals, who had to reform themselves ideologically by continuously studying and discussing essays by him, Stalin and others. When Mao brought the Rectification Campaign to an end in 1945, he apologised for their maltreatment and pointed the finger at his underlings. The victims saw him as their saviour and accepted their own sacrifices during the campaign as an exercise in purification necessary to enter the inner circle. They embraced their mission, ready to save China by serving the party. Wang Shiwei was killed in 1947, reportedly chopped to pieces and thrown into a well.[4]

In August 1949, two months before the People's Republic was founded, Mao published an editorial entitled 'Cast Away Illusions, Prepare for Struggle'. He denounced Hu Shi, Qian Mu and Fu Sinian, three leading university professors who had fled south with the nationalists, as 'running dogs' of imperialism. He put the educated elite on notice. 'Part of the intellectuals still want to wait and see,' he observed. They were 'middle-of-the-roaders' who still harboured illusions about 'democratic individualism'. The Chairman urged them to unite with progressive revolutionary forces.[5]

With liberation, millions of students, teachers, professors, scientists and writers – in communist jargon termed 'intellectuals' – found themselves forced to prove their allegiance to the new regime. They were joined by compatriots who had returned from overseas to answer the call to serve the motherland. Like everybody else, they attended endless indoctrination classes to learn the new orthodoxy, studying official pamphlets, newspapers and textbooks. And like everyone else, they soon had to write their own confessions, making a clean breast of the past by 'laying their hearts on the table'. They were asked to re-educate themselves, becoming New People willing to serve the New China.

Many did so with relish. For years they had seen the decay and corruption of the nationalist regime, helpless to remedy these, while underground propaganda had done much to portray the party as the only true force for change. 'You know, for honest young people, the ideals propagated by the communist party were really attractive. Democracy, equality, everybody enjoying the fullest freedom: is there anything more meaningful for a young man than to allow this world to change for the better?' remembered Cheng Yuan, then a quiet but determined student from a respected family of scholars in Chongqing. His two elder brothers were highly placed officials in the nationalist party, but Cheng had already been won over by an underground cell in high school. A student of physics at Peking University during liberation, he embraced the new learning, plunging into the classics of Marxism to seek self-improvement.[6]

Some viewed the party almost as a surrogate family. Liu Xiaoyu, born in an impoverished and broken home, abused and beaten by her foster parents, was a student at the Ginling Women's College, a Christian university in Nanjing, when she joined the underground movement. She was never so happy as in the first year of liberation, taking classes in a military school: 'Many students joined, as we got up together and studied historical materialism and the history of social development. It was a tough life, but in my heart I was happy: this was the new life.'[7]

She was not the only one. Within months the new regime made the study of Marxism-Leninism and Mao Zedong Thought compulsory at all levels, but even senior academics did not wait for the call to set up study groups. Jin Yuelin, a philosopher and logician born in 1895, took the lead by teaching Marxist philosophy at Tsinghua University and taking classes in Russian. He published an article denouncing his own work as the product of a bourgeois mind. Feng Youlan, a leading philosopher trained at Columbia University, boarded a ship back to the motherland in 1948, full of anticipation. So confident was he that the new regime would be a resounding success that on leaving the United States he surrendered his visa, which was valid for life. Back in Beijing he repeatedly distanced himself from his own landlord background, taking up the study of Marxism with the zeal of a new convert. In July 1949 he opened a conference in Beijing to 'propagate Marxism-Leninism and Mao Zedong Thought'. He corresponded with Mao, announcing his determination to reform himself and selflessly serve the new society. 'It is very good for someone like yourself, who has committed errors in the past,' answered the Chairman, 'to be prepared to correct them now, if this can indeed be carried out in practice.' A month later Feng publicly repudiated his earlier philosophical musings, which spanned several decades. He would spend the next thirty years rewriting his work, constantly trying to conform with the latest dogma.[8]

But Mao was deeply suspicious of educated people, and wanted them to demonstrate their mettle. Book learning was out, practical experience was in ('only social practice can be the criterion of truth', the Chairman opined). Already in 1927, when he had compared the peasants to a hurricane, he had hinted that everybody would be put to the test: 'There are three alternatives. To march at their head and lead them? To trail behind them, gesticulating and criticising? Or to stand in their way and oppose them?'[9]

To prove their commitment to the new order, hundreds of thousands of intellectuals were sent to the countryside as part of the work teams tasked with carrying out land reform. They had to dirty their hands, living and working alongside poor farmers for several months, helping the cadres to make a class analysis of each village. Then they had to bloody their hands, participating in the denunciation meetings during which some of the traditional leaders were accused of being landlords, traitors or tyrants.

For many it was a baptism of fire. Some had never set foot in the countryside, and few had ever spent much time working with their hands – traditionally taboo in a society run by scholars. Liu Yufen, who had just turned twenty at the time and was freshly graduated from a party school, remembered: 'I visited the poorest home in the village, it had no bed, no sheets or blankets, just an old man wearing old cotton clothes made of rags held together by a few threads. I was completely shaken by seeing such conditions.' Cut off from all modern amenities, living in rough, cramped huts where whole families huddled together with their livestock, then rising at the crack of dawn to haul manure or dig earth all day long, many experienced culture shock. They overcame it quickly, often through a combination of necessity, fear and conviction, assisted by daily study sessions in which their peers assessed and criticised their performance.[10]

But an even greater challenge was to see revolution in action. Few were prepared for the sheer violence of land distribution, as victims were beaten, tortured, hanged and sometimes shot. All had to reconcile the huge gap that existed between the propaganda on the one hand and the reality of revolution on the other. They had to steel themselves, silencing the doubts that welled up when they witnessed physical abuse, constantly reciting the vocabulary of class struggle to justify the violence. A vision of communist plenty for all had to be conjured up to see past the squalor of denunciation rallies and organised plunder. They had to convince themselves that they had seen the New World. Some even had to will their hands to stop shaking when they were asked to pull the trigger. A friend of Liu Yufen trembled so violently when ordered to execute a man condemned as a counter-revolutionary that every one of his shots missed its target: the regular soldiers in the execution squad finished the job for him.[11]

By no means all passed the test. Some were courageous enough to criticise the violence of land reform. Several members of the Democratic League, co-opted by the communist party as part of the New Democracy, denounced the random torture and killing that was taking place in the countryside, demanding instead that a court of law should deal with landowners who had committed genuine crimes in the past. Others stressed the need to treat everyone humanely, even victims of land reform. A few queried the notion that every landlord was bad to the bone: 'There are bad farmers too, who like to eat but shirk work, while some landlords work hard and practise thrift their entire lives.' But few persisted in such views, which were derided as 'bourgeois' and 'humanist'. When Yue Daiyun, a young woman who had joined the underground movement in Beijing before liberation, tried to protect an old and impoverished tailor from the execution squad, her leader denounced her as a bourgeois sentimentalist who could not take a firm class stance. Unlike others, she failed in her attempt to preserve her own fate through self-deception: 'I tried to use "class" in order to force myself to look past all sorts of inhuman acts of violence. But I saw how so-called class designations were entirely artificial.' After the tailor had been shot, she felt pain resembling 'one half of my body being torn from the other'.[12]

But most decided to 'march at the head and lead', in the Chairman's words. If they wanted a job under the new regime, they had little choice but to become willing accomplices – whether through opportunism, idealism or sheer pragmatism. Many did so with relish. Feng Youlan used the experience to distance himself from his own landlord background and prove his revolutionary credentials. He took a lead in helping farmers outside Beijing confiscate the property of landowners and hailed revolution as a transformative experience. For Wu Jingchao, a sociology professor at Tsinghua University, the most memorable moment of his time in the countryside came when a pauper jumped up from the crowd at a rally, ripped off his shirt and started beating his chest before grabbing a landlord by the collar, angrily waving a finger in his face. Wu enthused about land reform in the *Guangming Daily*: 'After liberation, we also studied the class viewpoint and the mass viewpoint, but what we learned is nowhere near as profound as a month's practice.' Mao approved and wrote to Hu Qiaomu, the head of the propaganda department: 'This is very well written, please order the *People's Daily* to reprint it and have the New China News Agency circulate it.' Wu Jingchao's career seemed assured.[13]

Many were genuinely filled with anger towards the old order. Zhu Guangqian, already in his fifties and a founding figure in the study of aesthetics in China, could feel hatred flow through his entire body. 'When

I heard a peasant air his grievances against a landlord, the tears streaming down his cheeks, it seemed as if I myself was transformed into that angry peasant, and I really regretted not being able to step forward and give that landlord a good thrashing.'[14]

Some went further. Lin Zhao, a headstrong, idealistic young woman who wrote searing denunciations of government corruption before joining the underground movement in 1948, told her classmate that 'my hatred for the landlords is the same as my love of the country'. This she demonstrated by ordering a landowner to be placed in a vat of freezing water overnight. She felt 'cruel happiness' on hearing the man scream in pain, as this meant that the villagers would no longer be afraid of him. After a dozen victims were executed in the wake of a rally she had helped organise, she looked at each of the corpses, one by one. 'Seeing them die this way, I felt as proud and happy as the people who had directly suffered under them.' She was barely twenty.[15]

'You do not need to be overly anxious about seeing results in haste; you can come around gradually,' Mao told Feng Youlan in October 1949 after the philosopher had announced his intention to reform himself. But two years later his time was up. As the previous chapter showed, Mao launched a purge of the government and assaulted the business community in the autumn of 1951. He was also ready to expand the model of thought reform, first developed in Yan'an, to the entire country. Willingly or involuntarily, the educated elite were to be regimented and absorbed into the state bureaucracy and have their creative freedom or independent livelihood rooted out.

In October 1951 Mao announced that 'Thought reform, especially thought reform of the intellectuals, is one of the most important prerequisites for the realisation of democratic reform and industrialisation.' Shortly afterwards, Zhou Enlai, dressed in a grey woollen Mao suit, lectured 3,000 eminent teachers in the Huairen Hall in the party headquarters at Zhongnanhai. The premier warned them that they were imbued with the 'mistaken thoughts of the bourgeois class and the petty bourgeoisie' and must work hard to 'establish the correct stand, viewpoint and method of the working class'. The lecture lasted a full seven hours. Wu Ningkun, a scientist educated in America who had only just returned to China, against the advice of his brother in Taiwan and his elder sister in Hong Kong, gave up his perfunctory attempt to take notes after a mere hour. 'Little did I know that the seven-hour report was nothing less than a declaration of war on the mind and integrity of the intelligentsia for the next forty years!'[16]

Before boarding the USS *President Cleveland* for his homebound voyage six weeks earlier, Wu Ningkun asked T. D. Lee, a fellow graduate student who later won the Nobel Prize in physics, why he was not coming home to help the new China. His friend answered with a knowing smile that he did not want to have his brain washed. For Wu and countless others, ideological education now became the norm, as sessions of self-criticism, self-condemnation and self-exposure followed one another, day in, day out, until all resistance was crushed and the individual was broken, ready to serve the collective. As in Yan'an a decade earlier, everyone had to name their relatives and friends, and provide details of their political background, their past activities, their every belief, including their innermost thoughts. Even transitory, fleeting impressions were to be captured and scrutinised, as they often revealed the hidden bourgeois underneath a mask of socialist conformity. All this took place under formidable social pressure, before assembled crowds or in study sessions under strict supervision, as other participants tried to find a chink in the armour of every suspect, grinding him down with a barrage of probing queries.[17]

'One day we found that the university's party organization had been suddenly strengthened. A new ruling specified that a member of the party or the Youth League should sit at every table in the dining hall and should occupy a place in every dormitory room. These Communists took notes on the day and night behaviour of every student. Even the words of a student talking in his sleep were recorded and considered for political significance.' So observed Robert Loh, still working at a university in Shanghai at this time. In Shanghai, in addition to endless group meetings, a lorry was sometimes parked in front of the house of an accused, a loudspeaker pouring out a shrill stream of invective.[18]

Few of those denounced managed to withstand the pressure for more than a few days, frantically writing confession after confession in a desperate search for something the leading cadre would accept. Stubborn teachers who insisted on their innocence were usually locked up in a room and harassed by relays of cadres until a confession was obtained. In Nanjing, teachers and professors were hauled on to a stage, hung up and beaten. Several committed suicide. 'We will crush those who resist,' announced the party secretary of Nanjing, whose report was praised and circulated by Mao. In Chengde, the vast imperial garden city formerly used as the summer residence of the Manchu emperors, some teachers were arrested and killed.[19]

Many tried to atone for their past misdeeds, whether real or imaginary. Jin Yuelin, the logician who took classes in Russian, wrote twelve confessions before he was considered reformed. Feng Youlan, despite all his best efforts, failed to pass the test. Chen Xujing, a leading sociologist with a degree from the University of Illinois, stood in front of the assembled students and staff of Lingnan University and atoned for a full four hours, reduced to tears: he too failed to appease the authorities.[20]

In some cases extremely loyal intellectuals were hounded so fiercely that they became alienated from the party. This too served a purpose, as Loh noted in the case of a colleague called Long:

> At first, I considered the Communists stupid for alienating Long. After the betrayal, persecution and humiliation he had received from the Communists, he undoubtedly hated them, and they therefore had turned a valuable pro-Communist into an anti-Communist. Only later did I perceive that the Communists had been fully aware of Long's loyalty to their cause and were equally conscious that after the 'reform' he was disaffected. They had succeeded, however, in terrorizing him so thoroughly that henceforth, regardless of what he thought, he spoke and acted during every waking moment exactly as the Communists wanted. In this state, the Communists felt safer and more secure about him.[21]

Another true believer was Liu Xiaoyu, the young woman who had embraced the communist party as her own family. 'We all felt fear. We stopped speaking even to those with whom we were normally very close. You did not dare speak with others about what was on your mind, even with those close to you, because it was very likely that they would denounce you. Everybody was denouncing others and was denounced by others. Everybody was living in fear.' But what ultimately caused her to lose faith in the party was the unprecedented intrusion into her own private life. She had just married, but was now accused of spending too much time with her husband instead of devoting herself to revolution. 'There were people who lingered around our home, peeping through the windows and the gap in the front door, trying to find out if we were behaving in an intimate manner. They were supervising us around the clock, and if they saw anything suspect they would report it at a public meeting, making you feel really embarrassed.' She was soon denounced as a servant of imperialism who harboured ulterior motives.[22]

But not everybody was willing to go along. Gao Chongxi, an expert in the chemical industry at Tsinghua University, committed suicide. At the East China Normal University in Shanghai, Li Pingxin was so viciously denounced that he took an axe and tried to chop off his own head. He bled to death. Eileen Chang, on the other hand, was one of the few who would not even buy into the patriotic rhetoric of the new regime. One of the most talented writers in China, she quietly slipped across the border to Hong Kong under a false name in 1952.[23]

Thought reform was by no means confined to elite universities. In Zhejiang the campaign extended to students from middle schools, some aged only twelve: they were ordered to cleanse themselves not only of 'reactionary' views, but also of 'extreme selfishness'. In Guangdong too, middle-school students were mobilised to fight counter-revolutionaries hidden in their ranks. In the Luoding Number One Secondary School, for instance, eighty students were arrested. Up in the north-western provinces, sometimes even children in primary schools were berated for harbouring bourgeois thoughts. Soon any form of insubordination was interpreted as a dangerous sign of individual restiveness to be nipped in the bud. In schools throughout Jiangxi province bullying was so intense that 'student suicides happen incessantly'. In one case a boy suspected of having stolen 15 yuan was put in leg irons and lashed with bamboo whips till he made a full confession. Others were locked up in solitary confinement, a few driven to insanity. Hu Chunfang refused to collect firewood: 'I came to study technology, not to chop wood.' For this impertinence he was dragged off to a denunciation meeting. As his school authorities put it: 'we beat one to scare the many'.[24]

By the end of 1952 virtually every student or teacher was a loyal servant of the state. The food they received depended on their performance. And like all other government employees, they were required to accept any form of employment to which the party directed them. The state needed millions of young people to help build up the border areas such as Inner Mongolia, Xinjiang and Manchuria. It also wanted experts to provide technological advice in the countryside. Thought reform thoroughly crushed any resistance to assignment to a job in a distant and often unappealing place. Socialism lauded the collective, meaning that the government's needs now took precedence over individual preference. On the other hand, young assistants with more reliable political qualifications replaced foreign-trained professors in the cities. Others with degrees from some of the world's best universities were sent to such posts as assistant clerk in a village library or cashier in a district bank. 'None of them received assignments of any real dignity or service,' to quote Robert Loh.[25]

The campaign had the desired result of destroying the unity among intellectuals, removing them from positions of authority and debasing them before the people. It also served another purpose. In early 1952, the higher educational system needed 'readjustment', according to the authorities, which meant that the colleges of various universities were reshuffled and merged. This was intended to disguise the elimination of all Christian universities throughout China. Ginling Women's College, which Liu Xiaoyu had attended years earlier, was merged with University of Nanking. Yenching University, established under the leadership of John Leighton Stuart in Beijing in 1919, was closed. Lingnan University, where Chen Xujing had listed his faults in a mass rally lasting four hours, was incorporated into Sun Yat-sen University in Guangzhou. Years later some of its staff would flee to Hong Kong to establish a liberal arts college with the same name. The whole higher-education system was altered beyond recognition. 'No trace of intellectual prestige remained, nor any of the spirit and tradition which had distinguished one institution from another.'[26]

The pressure did not abate. Almost every year the regime identified a high-profile scholar as a counter-revolutionary, making him the target of vociferous denunciations by the propaganda machine. After Mao had denounced Hu Shi in August 1949, students and teachers were compelled to distance themselves from the liberal essayist, philosopher and diplomat. As a young student in Hunan, Mao had written enthusiastically about him. In 1919, when Mao had worked as an assistant librarian at Peking University, he tried to audit his classes, but Hu Shi would have none of it: 'you are not a student, so get out of here!' Now the Chairman ensured that his work was banned. Hu Shi's own son stepped forward to repudiate his father as a 'reactionary' who had paved the road for capitalism: 'until he returns to the embrace of the people he will always be the people's enemy and also my own enemy'. 'We know, of course, that there is no freedom of speech,' Hu Shi responded from New York. 'But few persons realise that there is no freedom of silence, either. Residents of a communist state are required to make positive statements of belief and loyalty.'[27]

Liang Shuming was another *bête noire* of the Chairman. Both were born in 1893, but Liang was a brilliant thinker hired at the age of twenty-four by the philosophy department in Peking University when Mao was still an obscure primary-school teacher. A year later, in 1918, the two met briefly at the home of Mao's teacher in Beijing, although Liang paid the Hunanese student little attention. But in 1938, as the philosopher travelled to Yan'an, a composed and polite Mao instantly recalled the meeting: 'A long time ago, we met in 1918 at Peking University where you were the big professor and I was part of the lowly library staff. You probably don't remember that during your frequent visits to Professor Yang's house, it was I who greeted you at the door.' Liang left Yan'an highly impressed, although he did not believe that class theory applied to Chinese society or could solve the country's problems. He maintained an intellectual relationship with Mao, presenting him with copies of his own work. Like others, in 1949 he openly praised the Chairman and embraced the new China. Flattered by the relationship, a year later an amiable Chairman invited him to become a committee member of the Political Consultative Conference. More courtesy visits and pleasantries on the national situation followed, the Chairman on occasion sending his own car to ferry the professor to

Zhongnanhai. In September 1950 Mao saw to it that Liang was moved to a private residence near the famous Marble Boat built by the Empress Dowager Cixi in the Summer Palace.

But Liang was no pushover. In 1952, at the height of the attack against private business, he wrote to the Chairman to explain that 'merchants by no means are all dishonest', somehow doubting that they were organised enough to launch a concerted attack on the communist party. In a letter widely circulated to the top leadership, Mao denounced these views as 'absurd'. The relationship cooled. A year later, at a meeting of the Political Consultative Conference, Zhou Enlai encouraged Liang Shuming to speak freely and at length, which he did, deploring the impoverishment of the countryside. Urban workers, Liang argued, 'live in the ninth level of heaven while the peasants dwell in the ninth level of hell'. A few days later, in a long speech occasionally punctuated with biting interjections from Mao himself, an angry Zhou berated Liang for being a reactionary. Liang was stunned into silence. But the following day, as the meeting resumed, he stubbornly tried to defend his position, even threatening to withhold his respect from the Chairman were he denied time to explain himself. A stern Mao remonstrated with him from the rostrum, but Liang persisted, even asking point-blank if the Chairman himself had the magnanimity to engage in self-criticism. By now people in the audience were screaming for the philosopher's blood. 'Liang, step down from the podium! Stop him from uttering this nonsense!' Still he did not budge. Mao, cool and collected, granted him ten minutes, which Liang thought insufficient. To further uproar from the audience, a vote was somehow decided. The philosopher lost, ending an extraordinary stand-off. A lengthy 'Criticism of Liang Shuming's Reactionary Ideas' appeared later, comprehensively demolishing him as a 'hypocrite' and a 'schemer' – among other things. Mao used a sledgehammer: 'There are two ways of killing people: one is to kill with the gun and the other with the pen. The way which is most artfully disguised and draws no blood is to kill with the pen. That is the kind of murderer you are.' Chiang Kai-shek was the murderer with the gun, standing behind Liang Shuming. The philosopher's career was over. He moved out of his residence in the Summer Palace.[28]

None of these attacks was confined to high politics. Every one of them fuelled a new hunt for real or imagined enemies throughout the education system. In July 1954, for instance, Hu Feng, writer and art theorist, sent a long letter to the party comparing their stultifying theories to knives thrust into the brains of writers. Hu himself, though a Marxist, had never joined the communist party. He had earned the grudging respect of his literary peers in the 1930s for his understanding of the complexities of Marxism, but had also made enemies by acrimonious squabbles over highly abstract and sometimes trivial points of theory. More than once he had unleashed his sharp pen against orthodox followers of the party line like Zhou Yang and Guo Moruo. Even more damaging had been his attack on cultural policy in Yan'an in 1942. The party, he had written, 'wants to strangle literature. It wants literature to take leave of real life and it wants writers to tell lies.'[29]

Twenty years later, some of his enemies had become the powerful enforcers of literary dogma. At a meeting of the Political Consultative Conference in Beijing, the same venue where Liang Shuming had been shouted down a year earlier, Guo Moruo launched a veiled attack on writers who praised 'bourgeois idealism'. Hu picked up the hint and quickly backtracked, writing a self-confession a month later in January 1955. But he was already a man marked for destruction, as the party machine advanced inexorably. Zhou Yang, the high priest of the Propaganda Ministry who had toured the Soviet Union with a large delegation in 1950, personally supervised the campaign against him. In April the *People's Daily* denounced Hu Feng, dismissing his self-confession as 'insincere' and 'treacherous'. In the following months a further 2,131 articles taking the writer to task appeared in the press. Incriminatory extracts from private letters Hu had written to some of his friends were published to discredit him further. Mao personally assisted his persecution, not hesitating to stoop so low as to write damning commentaries on the published extracts. In June 1955 Hu was condemned as the head of a counter-revolutionary clique, deprived of all his posts, tried in secret and sentenced to fourteen years' imprisonment (although he would not be released till 1979).[30]

The hunt was on. A campaign of terror unfolded to root out all his supporters, real or imaginary. Red banners appeared in the cities, declaring: 'Resolutely, Thoroughly, Completely and Exhaustively Uproot All Hidden Counter-Revolutionaries!' Wu Ningkun, who had arrived from the United States a mere six weeks before the thought-reform campaign opened in October 1951, by now knew the drill and joined a chorus of denunciation. He despised himself for doing so. 'I knew the bell was not tolling for Hu Feng and other innocents alone.' Sure enough, he too was soon confronted at a meeting of more than a hundred faculty and staff members at Nankai University in Tianjin, accused of being the ringleader of a counter-revolutionary gang of four. His house was ransacked, as drawers, suitcases and trunks were turned upside down in the search for weapons and radio transmitters. His letters, notebooks, manuscripts and sundry papers were taken away. One accusation meeting followed another, as his inquisitors took turns to shout abuse and fire questions at him on every aspect of his past, trying to wear him down. His ordeal would last until the summer of 1956.[31]

Encouraged by the publication of letters that Hu Feng and his followers had exchanged, some of the country's most eminent writers started digging up dirt on each other. Ding Ling had set literary China on fire with iconoclastic short stories in the late 1920s. After she joined the communists in Yan'an, she found herself in hot water for exposing the leadership's cavalier treatment of women. Mao, for one, had set the tone by abandoning his third wife for younger company. For her impertinence, Ding Ling was sent to labour in the countryside. She had avoided the execution squad by viciously denouncing Wang Shiwei, whom she accused of having stooped to the level of a 'latrine'. Later she worked hard to atone for her errors, and in 1951 her novel *The Sun Shines over the Sungari River*, a celebration of land reform and its revolutionary violence, won the Stalin Prize for Literature. But the Hu Feng affair cast a shadow over her career, as she had maintained a friendship with the writer since her days in Yan'an. Unavailingly, she denounced him, but soon she herself with her former colleague Chen Qixia was attacked for heading a counter-revolutionary clique. Unable to withstand the pressure, Chen confessed to all sorts of imaginary crimes in the hope of shortening his ordeal. Then he handed over all the correspondence he and Ding Ling had exchanged in the previous years, accusing her of attempting 'to seize the leadership of literary circles'.[32]

These were heady confrontations, as leading members of the intelligentsia vied to cast dirt on each other to preserve themselves, but similar incidents occurred among ordinary people across the country. Dan Ling, the young student who had joined a Tiger-Hunting Team in 1952, was now working as a technician in a tank factory in Baotou, a new city being built near the Mongolian Desert. He too participated in meetings denouncing Hu Feng. Like other workers, he was encouraged to expose anyone suspected of sharing Hu's 'bourgeois idealism'. Zhang Ruisheng, one of Dan's close friends and a graduate from Tsinghua University, was among them. One day three plain-clothes policemen turned up at the factory and searched his room. They found nothing incriminating, but a cloud of suspicion continued to hang over him, as he was the son of a wealthy Tianjin capitalist. Soon the factory managers ganged up on him, calling meeting after meeting to denounce him and force him to reveal his 'counter-revolutionary secrets'. In the end, his vehement insistence that he was innocent paid off, and he was cleared after a long investigation.[33]

There were countless similar cases all over the country, as teachers, doctors, engineers and scientists suspected of possessing 'counter-revolutionary' links with 'foreign powers' were persecuted. Luo Ruiqing, who now pitched in as head of security, brought the inquisition to bear upon 85,000 teachers in middle schools. One in ten was purged as a deviant element who sabotaged socialism, plotted against the party or encouraged student unrest. In primary schools the number was double. In total, across the country, over a million people were forced to confront accusations of plotting against the state in 1955, leading to the discovery of 45,000 bad elements. This did not include the arrest of more than 13,500 'counter-revolutionaries' within the ranks of the party. In Hebei alone over 1,000 cliques were uncovered, more than 300 of a counter-revolutionary nature, including an Underground Anti-Communist Alliance, a Free China Team and a Reform Party. In the Hu Feng case, forty-eight 'core members' and 116 'ordinary members' were targets for the secret police across the country.[34]

Thousands committed suicide. Wu Ningkun, arriving at the scene of his daily interrogation one summer morning, discovered his inquisitors chattering excitedly among themselves. A senior member of the English Faculty had just been found drowned in the decorative pond in front of the library. In Shanghai, Yu Hongmo, the manager of a publishing company, swallowed a large needle in an attempt to kill himself. He lived.

Many others became unemployed, tramping about looking for jobs or turning to theft, some of the women even selling their bodies to eke out a living. In the capital alone there were more than 4,000 such cases, including Wang Zhaozheng. A student expelled from Wuhan University, he petitioned the State Council and the Chairman on ten occasions for the right to emigrate to Hong Kong. Then he approached the British embassy, directly threatening to tarnish the reputation of the country. Luo Ruiqing instructed his underlings to crack down on people like Wang and lock them away in the gulag.[35]

With the literary inquisition came a great burning of books. In Shanghai, a total of 237 tonnes of books were destroyed or sold as scrap paper between January and December 1951. The Commercial Press, one of the largest in the country, had roughly 8,000 titles in print in the summer of 1950. A year later a mere 1,234 of these were considered acceptable for circulation. Lectures were given on 'How We Should Dispose of Bad Books'. Sometimes entire collections were consigned to the flames, as with 17,000 cases of books from the famous anthology of literary masterpieces belonging to Wang Renqiu. In Shantou, one of the treaty ports opened to foreign trade in the nineteenth century, in May 1953 a giant bonfire lasting three days swallowed up 300,000 volumes representing 'vestiges of the feudal past'. So eager were some cadres in charge of policing culture that they pulped anything they could lay their hands on, including books that were not even included in the black list – which, admittedly, was confusing as the list was endlessly amended. Thus in Beijing even the work of Sun Yat-sen, hailed as the father of the nation by the communist party, was taken off the shelves, while in 1954 the equivalent of a tonne of copies of a French tourist guide to Beijing was recycled. The going rate paid to dealers in second-hand books, a rapidly dwindling trade, was 4 or 5 yuan a kilo. Sometimes students themselves collected suspicious volumes and handed them over to their teachers for destruction, while concerned citizens delivered banned items to their local party office. Pedlars on pavements who continued to sell martial-arts novels or popular love stories were arrested by the dozen in police raids and dispatched to the gulag.[36]

After September 1952, editors and publishers were required to register with the government and submit regular reports. Few classics of the country's great literary heritage remained in print. The *Book of Odes* was the only one of the thirteen classics of literature that could be obtained, because it was deemed to contain popular chants of ancient times. A few poets, for instance Qu Yuan, who lived in the third century BCE, also escaped destruction because they were said to have written 'for the masses'. The central government, which won complete control over the press and publishing houses within a few years of liberation, supervised all such censorship.[37]

Instead readers received a dreary diet of Russian textbooks, translated by the thousand from the end of 1952 onwards, as well as the theoretical productions of the communist leaders, the works of Mao Zedong taking pride of place (severe restrictions on the use of gold were decreed in 1954, but among the exceptions, besides dental fillings, was the use of gilded foils on selected works of the Chairman). The bulk of published material, however, consisted of propaganda work, designed for every conceivable group and every conceivable subject. This included pocket-sized comic books churned out in their tens of millions for children, telling stories of class heroes, imperialist spies, war victories, production records and the building of a new socialist society. Writers working for the party produced a small number of approved works, but their output was minimal. Even those leftist writers who had flocked to the side of the communists – Lao She, Ding Ling, Mao Dun – were no longer in a position to produce the literature of protest that had made their fame before liberation. As one farsighted observer put it, 'The failure of the hundreds of literary lights gathered in Beijing and Shanghai to produce a single work of distinction in the course of five years of communist rule may be an early indication not only that they misunderstood the nature of the communist cause they helped but also that they have been unable to adjust themselves to Mao's rule.'[38]

But most of all, thanks to relentless campaigns of thought reform, people themselves were careful to select reading material that was politically correct. Nobody wanted to run the risk of being infected with bourgeois poison when dreaded struggle sessions were bound to follow. Maria Yen, a student at Peking University, wrote:

Translations of the modern Soviet novelists were safe, of course; we could buy the works of such popular writers as Fadeyev and Simonov. Older masters who had influenced a whole generation of Chinese writers – Turgenev and Dostoevsky and even translations of Gorki – were dismissed as obsolete. In Chinese literature it was all right to read the works of Zhao Shuli, Ding Ling's *The Sun Shines over the Sungari River* and the so-called 'collective productions' of young writers, which were hailed as being rich in 'party traits'. Virtually everything else, including books the Communists had previously praised as 'progressive', was suspect.

This was in 1951, before censorship tightened up.[39]

Still, truly voracious readers managed to survive, often on private collections kept away from prying eyes. Kang Zhengguo, then still a young boy in the ancient capital of Xi'an, had a rebellious streak and was sent to live with his grandparents. The old house, with its whitewashed walls, hardwood floor and delightful jumble of old furnishings, was a treasure trove of all sorts of books, stuffed away in dusty piles in the attic. Kang devoured everything he could get his hands on, from Buddhist sutras and swashbuckling novels to old newspaper clippings pressed between the pages of an oversized edition of *The Thirteen Annotated Classics*. The collection would survive until the advent of the Red Guards in 1966.[40]

The beat of folk drums and the chant of revolutionary song displaced classical music. Records of Beethoven, Chopin, Schubert, Mozart and other foreign composers seen as bourgeois were quietly put away. To celebrate the tenth anniversary of Mao Zedong's Yan'an talks on literature and art, the entire staff of the Central Conservatory of Music in Beijing decided in 1952 to debate how best to apply the Chairman's theories to their work, and concluded that musicians must be 'in harmony with concrete reality'. The same year the president of the Shanghai Conservatory – one of the most renowned in Asia before 1949, and a leader in modern music – wrote to the *Liberation Daily* to attack blind worshippers of Western music who thought that 'music need not have ideological content'.[41]

Jazz was so much in demand before liberation that Shanghai was considered the music capital of Asia. Budding players from all over the world, as well as experienced musicians from the United States, performed in the many venues for popular music right up to 1949, but within weeks after the fall of Shanghai nightclubs were boarded up or converted into factories. The regime banned jazz outright, decrying it as degenerate, decadent and bourgeois. Even more in demand, in the decades before liberation, were female singers who incorporated Hollywood songs, jazz orchestration and local folk music into popular tunes. Music by stars such as Zhou Xuan was widely broadcast over the radio and played on the gramophone, only to be denounced as pornographic after 1949. The destruction went further: the great majority of the 80,000 records produced in the era before communism were deposited in a state archive where they deteriorated beyond repair.[42]

Soon ears became attuned to the new music introduced by Soviet cultural delegations. Radios started broadcasting such tunes as 'The Favours of the Communist Party are Too Many to be Told', 'Hymn to Chairman Mao', 'Song of the New Woman' and 'Brother and Sister Plough the Wasteland'. Singing became popular. Unlike solos, which were intolerable expressions of bourgeois individuality, group singing was safe. And it helped spread propaganda, with songs composed for every type of activity. Farmers sang of land reform, workers of labour rights. 'Soldiers sing while marching or when they stop to rest. Schoolchildren sing a great part of their day. Prisoners sing four hours a day. In all the indoctrination courses for the candidates for government positions, singing takes up three to four hours daily.' Students gathered in parks on special occasions, singing a strident 'Song of the New Peasant' or its equivalent to the accompaniment of drums and gongs. Girls in choirs belted out such catchy tunes as 'Ten Women Praise their Husbands'. The singing was taught with the same demanding discipline as everything else, with the result that it was often very impressive. Some may not have sung from the heart, but everybody knew the words, as they echoed through city streets and mountain valleys. Children were soon seen singing on their way home, swinging an arm to beat the cadence.[43]

Loudspeakers helped. They seemed to be everywhere, placed at street corners and railway stations, in dormitories, canteens and all major institutions. They often blasted the same tune, as people assembled in the morning for their fifteen minutes of calisthenics. They broke up the day, alternating between political speeches and revolutionary songs as people had their lunch break or made their way back home at the end of their shift. They played more songs in the evening. So widespread and intrusive were loudspeakers that regulations curbing their use after midnight had to be introduced in Beijing, with little effect.[44]

With new songs came new plays, welcomed at least initially by many viewers. Young people in particular did not always care for old-style Chinese opera with its classical plots and extravagant costumes. Maria Yen, like many other students who supported the revolution, rushed to see *The White-Haired Girl*. When the curtain went up she saw the interior of an ordinary farmer's hut, with realistic, rough furniture, a dab of snow against the papered window. 'And no lords and ladies with falsetto voices minced out on the stage; instead we found a simple peasant, bent with work and with age, speaking to his young daughter.' The old father was forced to surrender his daughter into the hands of his rapacious creditor, but was so heartbroken that he hanged himself. 'Some of us were close to tears as we watched the landlord and his hired bully pull the girl away from the father's body to carry her back to the landlord's household. All over the audience we could feel the indignation rise as we watched the girl being beaten and abused like a slave by the haughty women of the household.' The plot was simple. The daughter becomes pregnant, and the landlord promises marriage, but sells her to a brothel instead. She escapes and hides in a cave with her baby for two years, her hair growing long and white. The communists liberate the village from the Japanese, and the young girl is finally reunited with one of the guerrilla fighters, a childhood friend she always loved. The landlord stands trial as the peasants shout their verdict: the death penalty. It was a gripping story. The dialogue, singing and acting flowed naturally, creating a spectacle that touched the emotions of many who watched it. The audience burst out in applause as the villainous landlord was dragged off for execution and the curtain came down.[45]

The White-Haired Girl was produced as an opera, as a film and also as a ballet. It was performed by professional theatre societies, travelling drama groups, military acting troupes and amateur actors organised in factories, offices, schools, universities and youth clubs. Other plays, for instance Cao Yu's *Thunderstorm*, were endorsed, all following the precise rules and regulations of the Drama Reform Committee, set up by the Ministry of Culture in July 1950. And conversely, anything that smacked even remotely of bourgeois individualism was proscribed. A few foreign playwrights managed to survive – largely thanks to the fact that they were allowed in the Soviet Union. In the case of Shakespeare, for instance, two leading critics from Moscow had concluded that the English bard had exposed the evils of the capitalist system, which paved the way for a performance of *Romeo and Juliet* by a theatre school in Beijing in 1956 – something so exceptional in the People's Republic that it warranted a full review in the *Illustrated London News*.[46]

Theatre was propaganda, and it spread even further thanks to short, simple and very topical plays. Like the rice-sprout songs performed by the dance troupes of the People's Liberation Army, military actors helped propagate the message by mounting popular plays almost anywhere, in squares, gardens, parks and other public spaces where pedestrians could be corralled to watch and applaud. The plays always addressed the latest government campaign in simple terms easily comprehensible to illiterate farmers, but they became rather predictable. There was always a scene of a soldier placing his foot on the protruding belly of an enemy lying on the ground with legs in the air, whether he was an evil landlord, undercover spy or imperialist exploiter.[47]

———

Shanghai had been second only to Hollywood in terms of the film industry. But much of it was destroyed in the Second World War, and whatever vestiges remained the new regime swept away. The most popular genres had happily mixed pulp fiction, swashbuckling adventure and comedy with avant-garde techniques to create a celluloid language which was popular all over China. Classical-costume, knight-errant, martial-arts and magic-spirit films attracted even larger audiences, capturing not only millions in China, but many more abroad, since South-east Asia was their biggest market. Hollywood itself was popular. When the communists marched into Shanghai, the Cathay was advertising *I Wonder Who's Kissing Her Now*, a musical film in Technicolor featuring June Haver. None of this was exclusive to the great cities along the coast, since already in the 1930s cinema had penetrated deep into the hinterland. Even in Kunming, a medium-sized city in the subtropical south, half a million people went to see the 166 films shown in 1935.[48]

A campaign against foreign cinema followed within months of liberation. Foreign films were deemed reactionary and decadent, and were ousted by Russian ones – for instance *Lenin in October, The Virgin Land* and *The Great Citizens*. Within a year or so hundreds of employees were working at several dubbing centres. Some of the films were well done and inspiring, especially those made before the war (for example *The Battleship Potemkin*), but many were dull, even in the eyes of leftist students. So few people wanted to see them that they were never profitable. In Beijing prices had to be cut several times to attract a crowd. Still the masses stayed away, until the authorities granted the theatre operators permission to show foreign pictures from outside the Soviet Union for five days a month. But the contrast between a full house for reactionary films and the rows of empty seats on days when healthy productions were shown was an embarrassment. A prompt ban resolved the issue. The Korean War brought an end to Hollywood everywhere in the country. In cinema, as in other art forms, the tremendous burst of creativity that was supposed inevitably to follow revolution, as artists were freed from the fetters of feudalism and imperialism, never materialised.[49]

———

Like every other social group, religious leaders were lured into the embrace of the party by promises of freedom. They were quickly disabused. The pretence of religious freedom was upheld for a year or two after liberation, but the leadership were secretly determined to extirpate all rival belief systems. In February 1951, Hu Qiaomu, who headed the propaganda department, upheld the Soviet attack on the church as an example for emulation. But as he spoke to his underlings, he warned that it would take time to ferret out all diehard believers.[50]

Buddhism was only loosely organised and therefore made an easy target. Monasteries were destroyed, monks were beaten or killed, copies of the Buddhist canon were burned and sacred images were melted down for their metal. Land was confiscated and Buddhist properties broken up. In some places the clergy was reduced to 'a state of terror', in the words of a contemporary. Some became targets in the vast persecution designed to break the power of traditional elites during land reform. 'In most cases they would strip the clothing from the upper half of a man's body and bind his hands behind his back and his feet too, and then he would kneel facing the masses and confess his crimes,' remembered one monk from a monastery near Nanjing. In the Lingyin Temple, the largest in Hangzhou, a crowd of 4,000 assembled in front of a makeshift platform made of tables piled on to each other. Five monks were forced to face the crowd. The verdict was always the same: 'You see how fat and pretty he is. Why is he so fat? He has been eating the blood and sweat of the people. He is an exploiter, an evil person. Everyone says he should be killed. But the People's Government is magnanimous. It will send him to labour reform.' In the large cities the tone was more subdued, and some of the most devout followers among the elderly were allowed to keep their faith. But no new converts were accepted. In Shanghai, for instance, a quarter of all 2,000 monks and nuns were dispersed by February 1950.[51]

Particularly vulnerable were the country's minorities. The ancient town of Lijiang in Yunnan, crisscrossed by bridges and canals, was dominated by the Nakhi, who had their own language, literature and customs. They built houses that looked deceptively simple, but had delicate patterns on the interiors of casements and doors. Their temples, too, seemed rather plain from the outside, but were richly decorated with carvings on poles, arches and statues of gods. Revolution, in Lijiang, followed the same pattern as elsewhere. 'All the scamps and the village bullies, who had not done a stroke of honest work in their life, suddenly blossomed forth as the accredited members of the Communist Party, and swaggered with special red armbands and badges and the peculiar caps with duckbill visors which seemed to be the hallmark of a Chinese Red,' noted one long-term resident. Old Nakhi dances were prohibited and replaced by the rice-sprout songs which nobody recognised. Learning them after work became compulsory, as did attendance at interminable indoctrination talks at daily meetings. There were continual arrests, often in the dead of night, and secret executions. Local priests were banned. The lamaseries were desecrated, priceless tankas burned or smashed, sutras destroyed and lamas either arrested or scattered. The lamasery halls were converted into popular schools, 'as if there were not enough buildings elsewhere for this purpose'.[52]

Similar scenes occurred all over Yunnan, an ethnically diverse province in the far south-west bordering Burma, Laos and Vietnam. In Kangding county the army occupied several lamaseries. One monastery in Mao county was converted into a prison. Sometimes the local monks and nuns were treated as counter-revolutionaries; some were killed in denunciation meetings. The entire family of a woman selling herbal medicine was put to death. In another case a nun was forced to cut out her tongue. She choked to death on her own blood.[53]

A more inclusive approach was tried after the Great Terror. A Chinese Buddhist Association was formed in Beijing in November 1952. It was a servant of the state. Instead of exhorting its followers to practise quiet contemplation and introspective meditation, it demanded that Buddhists participate in land reform, struggle against counter-revolutionaries and take a lead in the 'Resist America, Aid Korea' campaign. Thought reform was mandatory. Monks, like teachers, professors, engineers or entrepreneurs, had to reform themselves, denounce each other, abandon their 'feudal ideology' and demonstrate their hatred towards class enemies. Gone was the idea of compassion and kindness extended to all living beings without discrimination. And once the monks, too, were civil servants, the Buddhist Association, in 1954, worked hard at discouraging the burning of paper money, celebration of festivals and sacrifices to the spirits. Accepting pious donations was denounced as 'cheating the masses'. Heads of monasteries had to pledge that they would not provide hospitality to travelling monks, who should be engaged in production instead. Deprived of all their traditional sources of income, monks were forced to work, often on plots of poor land. Already in 1951 the monks of Baohua Shan, the most famous ordination centre in central China, 'were suffering virtual starvation – there was not even diluted congee to eat'. In Yunmen Shan the monks had to manage on one meal of thin gruel a day.[54]

Many took the path of least resistance and disrobed. Some became farmers, others joined the army. Sometimes the former monks and nuns continued living at their monasteries, but let their hair grow. A few of them abandoned their vows, married and raised livestock. But the regime kept the decimation of the Buddhist clergy carefully hidden from public view. The official policy was to claim the same monastic population year after year – half a million in 1950 and still half a million in 1958. But the pressure never abated, and already in 1955 a party official in a secret meeting commended the fact that the number of monks had declined to a mere 100,000.[55]

The same duplicitous approach was adopted towards the buildings themselves. As tens of thousands of monasteries were converted into barracks, prisons, schools, offices or factories, in Beijing vast amounts of money were lavished on the Yonghegong Temple. It stood bright and spotless, its joss sticks smouldering away in their jars of sand, leaving no ash. The conservation work was carried out to support the government's policy towards the border areas. There were 6 million Buddhists in China and another 7 million in Xinjiang, Inner Mongolia and Tibet. And at the heart of Tibet was religion, tightly organised and pervasive. Mao cautioned his colleagues to proceed slowly, as the loyalty of the lamas must first be won over. In total, about a hundred monasteries and pagodas were repaired between 1951 and 1958 – out of the 230,000 places of worship that had monks and nuns in residence before liberation. Some were part of a conservation programme, a few were even protected by law, but most served as showcases for foreign dignitaries. The United States supported Buddhism in South-east Asia, forcing the People's Republic into quiet competition for the allegiance of its religious neighbours. The ever suave Zhou Enlai regularly invited Buddhists from Burma, Ceylon, Japan and India to visit the country's beautifully repaired temples, occasionally offering a relic bone or a tooth of the Buddha in religious ceremonies that would have been decried as the height of superstition under different circumstances.[56]

Despite the atmosphere of regimentation, the party never managed to stamp out popular Buddhism. Villagers continued to turn towards religion in times of hardship. In 1953, following widespread disease and famine in Henan, thousands of pilgrims flocked towards the White Horse Temple in Luoyang, one of the cradles of Buddhism in China. On 25 March 1953 alone, some 20,000 people converged on the temple, queuing quietly to benefit from the healing touch provided by monks. Two years later, Wang Feng, in charge of the Ethnic Affairs Committee, expressed his surprise at the fact that in some cities 'crowds of over 100,000 ceaselessly assemble to worship, pray for rain, burn incense or bow to Buddha'. Much of it was tolerated, as the days of brutal suppression still lay ahead.[57]

No such patience was shown towards Taoism, which had no fellow believers outside China. Taoist belief in magic and divination was decried as superstition. And because of its association with secret societies in past rebellions, it was also identified as a political threat. Priests, monks and nuns were sent to orientation centres to train as carpenters and seamstresses, while shrines to ancestors and local deities were destroyed. In a village south of Guangzhou, temples were indiscriminately smashed immediately after liberation. Community festivals ceased and sacrificial ceremonies were curtailed; what religious activity was tolerated was driven from public view back into the homes of the villagers. The power of religion to unite and strengthen community bonds was broken.[58]

But the amorphous, scattered and independent nature of many of these millenarian societies continued to bother the regime, as they reappeared under different guises after their dispersal by the authorities. During the Great Terror of 1951 their leaders were ruthlessly persecuted. They seemed to be everywhere. In Hebei the provincial boss estimated that 8 per cent of the population belonged to some cult or another, amounting to some 2 million people. He arrested 3,500 ringleaders within the first few months of 1951. Followers were given a chance to withdraw. In Beijing, according to one observer, more than 100,000 members of the Yiguandao, the Way of Pervading Unity, had apostatised by June 1951. Huanxingdao, Shengxiandao, Baguadao, Xiantiandao, Jiugongdao – there were dozens of popular religious sects and societies that were ruthlessly persecuted. And the pall of superstition seemed to hang with particular weight on people in the south. In the ports along the coastline of Guangdong, up to half the residents apparently followed one cult or another. In Shenzhen, a small fishing village just across the Hong Kong border, nineteen secret societies were counted, the most powerful one being the Yellow Ox Party, whose members were accused of smuggling, robbing and carrying out intelligence work for the enemy. Many were rounded up and executed. But despite all the killings, in

1953 head of security Luo Ruiqing could still list hundreds of leaders in counties from Yunnan, Sichuan and Zhejiang to Anhui.[59]

In the face of repression, people either dropped all visible signs of allegiance or went underground – quite literally. In north China underground chambers were built with tunnels long enough to connect strategic places throughout entire villages. In Shaanxi alone, in 1955 the police uncovered over a hundred subterranean hiding places. In Hebei province, some sectarian leaders took refuge in tunnels for more than four years. In Sichuan the hated Yiguandao did not even have to hide: it flourished to the extent that in 1955 it was recruiting local cadres and members of the militia. In Gansu province, Taoist sects appeared to rule entire regions. And folk religious practices also had great staying power in other ways. There were endless reports of secret stones, holy water, sacred tombs, magic trees or ancient temples around which village people crowded in times of need, often in the hundreds if not thousands.[60]

———

Before liberation there were approximately 3 million Catholics and 1 million Protestants. Their faith was singled out for slow strangulation. Brutal persecution, at least in the first years of the new regime, was not compatible with a policy of toleration. But in September 1950, a National Christian Council set up by the communist party issued a *Christian Manifesto* requiring all believers to sever foreign connections. Some termed this a 'Manifesto of Betrayal', but those who refused had to face accusations of aiding and abetting imperialism. Gradually the pressure increased. Cadres and activists questioned believers, at home, in church, at the market place or in the police station, day and night. They were cajoled, threatened, pressed, nagged and prodded, sometimes for days on end. Like all other people in China they were called upon to reform themselves and provide accusations against others. They had to join daily study sessions, examine their links with foreign imperialists and renounce their faith at public meetings. Everywhere religious networks crumbled, as people left the church in droves.[61]

Protestants were further isolated by the rise of a 'Patriotic Church' in 1951. It received funds from the state, preached according to the state and followed every command from the state. Those who refused to join were put under house arrest and sent to labour camps. In parts of the country Christians were forbidden to have rosaries, patron-saint medals or cruci-fixes. Homes were searched and prayer books, catechisms and holy pictures destroyed. Churches were stripped of sacred objects. Troops carried away altars and benches. Seminaries for training clergy were banned. Zhang Yinxian, a nun in Yunnan, remembers how her church was left empty. 'It used to be so glorious. Overnight, everything was gone. Rats took over the place. We used to have four hundred people working at the church. Only three were left – me, my aunt, and Bishop Liu Hanchen.' All three were ordered out but refused to leave. They were allowed to stay for a few months, but were then taken away by the militia, paraded through the village and put on public trial.

> We faced hundreds of villagers with raised fists shouting revolutionary slogans. Some spat at us. Such hatred. As the leader worked up the crowd, a peasant activist came up and slapped Bishop Liu in the face. My aunt stepped forward. 'How dare you slap him.' The activist used to be a poor farmer, and when the Communists confiscated the prop-erty of landlords, he was one of the beneficiaries. He pointed at my aunt and yelled back, 'You are a counter-revolutionary and we have defeated you. You are the lackey of the imperialists who exploited us.' My aunt said, 'We are not. We came from poor families and we've never exploited anybody.' The activists shouted again, 'You are still stubborn and won't admit your defeat. You need to be punished.' Fists were raised and the crowd began chanting, 'Down with the counter-revolutionary nun!' My aunt wouldn't back down. She said to her abuser, 'Slap me if you want. If you slap me on the left side of my face, I will give you the right side too.'

They were compelled to perform hard labour under the supervision of local cadres for many years.[62]

Congregations that had no foreign ties fared just as badly. Mazhuang, a quiet, sleepy Shandong town surrounded by fields of corn and hemp, was the centre of a unique Pentecostal communitarian church called the Jesus Family. Founded in 1927, it consisted of dozens of small communities in which several hundred believers worked and lived together under a family head. Private property was banned, all goods were shared and economically self-sufficient communities followed an egalitarian lifestyle. None of this spared them from persecution. In 1952 their land was confiscated and their followers were dispersed as a 'secret society' with close links to imperialism. Their leader was attacked and thrown into prison. He died in 1957.[63]

Reformed churches, on the other hand, fared better. In Beijing, St Michael's Church had red flags draping the main altar, communion rail, vestibule and the path to the gate. Streamers hanging from the church columns proclaimed 'Long Live Mao Zedong' and 'Long Live Communism'. Portraits of Mao and other leading communists replaced pictures of the Sacred Heart, the Virgin Mary and various saints. Attendance dwindled. Not far away, on Wangfujing, previously known as Morrison Street, the Roman Catholic church had a red star above the cross on its tower. Like the restored Yonghegong Temple, it was a showcase for foreign dignitaries.[64]

By 1954 the number of Catholic believers had been almost halved from 3 million to just over 1.7 million. Where up to 16,000 churches had dotted the religious landscape of China in 1949, a mere 3,252 remained standing. Protestants also proved difficult to crush. Their numbers went down to 638,000, with over 6,700 places of worship still in operation. But despite the denunciations, arrests and deportations, Christianity was hard to stamp out. In some places it even experienced a revival. In Huzhuang, Shandong, over a thousand pilgrims gathered to pray on Easter Sunday in 1955. In Wucheng county, where the church had been converted into a school, some 800 followers erected a tent to celebrate the resurrection of Jesus. In the Roman Catholic Diocese of Caozhou, also in Shandong, the faithful had increased by 80 per cent in a year. Some priests addressed their flock in their own homes. Wang Shiguang, sent out to the countryside, was able to recruit 700 followers. Priests came from places as far away as Beijing and Shaanxi to preach to the poor. Throughout the province, by contrast, believers deserted the Patriotic churches. Some of them stood empty. It was the same story in Sichuan. In Xichang county, priests set out to tend to congregations in distant Chongqing and Chengdu. In Kangding, the church was one of the few buildings spared by an earthquake in 1955. The locals saw this as a sign from God and flocked to mass from all over the county.[65]

The turning point came at the end of 1955, as the party tried to clamp down on all religious activities still outside the fold of the Patriotic Church. As thousands of counter-revolutionary cliques were uncovered in the wake of the Hu Feng affair, a fatal blow was dealt to an already weakened church in Shanghai, described as the 'Catholic fortress' of China. On the night of 7 September, the bishop, a mild-mannered but determined man called Ignatius Gong Pinmei, was rounded up along with more than twenty priests and nuns and hundreds of lay Catholics. By the end of November, 1,500 believers had been incarcerated, accused of counter-revolutionary crimes, collusion with imperialism, spreading rumours, poisoning the minds of youth and organising acts of violence – among other crimes. Further arrests took place in Shandong, Zhejiang, Fujian, Guangdong, Hubei and Sichuan, where counter-revolutionary cliques also operated 'under the cloak of religion'. Newspaper editorials, cartoons and articles featured attacks on the bishop, as headlines proclaimed that the police had 'Smashed the Gong Pinmei Counter-Revolutionary Clique'. The bishop was sentenced to life imprisonment.[66]

Muslims too were subject to constant humiliation. In Jiangyou, Sichuan, they were lynched and beaten. 'There is no such thing as a good Muslim,' proclaimed a party official. In Xindu county, every mosque was confiscated and handed over to the poor. Party secretary Zhu Xijiu organised a team to dig up several thousand Muslim graves and headstones marked with Quranic inscriptions. The stone tablets were used to build granaries and repair dykes. A few ended up as building blocks for pig sheds. In mosques taken over by peasant associations, the mihrab, indicating the direction worshippers should face when praying, was destroyed. The raised platform, normally used by the imam to address his congregation, was turned into a stage for mass meetings. Some of the areas reserved for ritual ablutions were used as female toilets.[67]

Similar abuse was also common across the Muslim belt running through the north-west, and soon open rebellion rocked the region. In parts of Gansu, Qinghai and Xinjiang shots continued to be heard every night in 1950 despite a strict curfew. Armed rebellions broke out regularly, some of them involving thousands of people and leading to heavy losses in the months following liberation. 'The principal reason for these incidents is the failure to carry out strictly our policy on minorities,' concluded a report on several uprisings in Gansu. In one case more than 2,000 Muslims assaulted the town of Pingliang, where abuse and beatings were described as 'common' and Muslim schools were used to raise pigs.[68]

But few lessons were learned. In another incident a year later a crowd of 8,000 surrounded the county head of Ningding, also in Gansu. Over a thousand people were killed in a bloody showdown, prompted by anger at Chinese domination over a largely Muslim region. The local population was particularly enraged when eight corpses were dumped in the wilderness without proper burial. The bodies belonged to Muslims who had frozen to death in prison. The whole area was terrorised by Chinese militia, who used their power to loot and pillage the Muslims.[69]

Again and again, the government had to bring in government troops to reinforce the local militia, putting to death insurgent leaders responsible for murder, arson, robbery and organised rebellions. A more conciliatory approach towards Islam appeared in 1952. Communist cadres were cautioned to respect Muslim customs. Soldiers were enjoined to refrain from saying the word 'pig' before a Muslim or from washing at Muslim bathing places. Special provisions were designed to leave the land owned by the mosques intact. Muslim leaders who co-operated with the government were used as figureheads for new associations promoting 'patriotic ideological education' – for instance the Chinese Islamic Association organised in Beijing in May 1953.

But, most of all, in 1953 the Muslims living along China's strategic border areas received an empty gift called 'autonomy'. All over China autonomous districts, autonomous counties, autonomous prefectures and autonomous regions appeared for 'minority' people. Xinjiang, where Muslims had long dreamed of a Uighur Republic, was carved up into different portions, for instance the Sibo people near Gulja, the Kazakhs in the north and the Tajik in the Sarikol area of the Pamir mountains. In October 1955 the Uighur presence was formally recognised by naming Xinjiang a Uighur Autonomous Region. But the borders of the 'autonomous' parts of the province were drawn in such a way that no ethnic group could control an area they dominated numerically. Territories with a relatively homogeneous minority were divided up, while cities and prefectures with large Uighur populations were denied any autonomous status. The Ili Kazakh autonomous prefecture was set up in a region dominated by Uighurs, while Korla was the capital of a Mongol autonomous prefecture mostly populated by Uighurs. It was a predictable strategy of divide and rule, or, to borrow from ancient Chinese tactics, a case of 'using barbarians to deal with barbarians'. And from top to bottom the party controlled every important decision in these government structures.[70]

Thought reform was less pronounced in these restive borderlands, but nonetheless indoctrination went hand in hand with autonomy. Before liberation the mosques were in charge of education, teaching the Koran and at least enough Arabic for the faithful to understand the religious services. The new regime made great efforts to bring all Muslim children into government schools, where science was taught in Chinese. Special schools were set up in the capital for Muslims, including the Central Institute for Nationalities in 1951, while the Islamic Theological Institute oversaw training for religious leaders. In the Muslim belt, indoctrination of the imams was introduced by 1951, supplemented by reform through labour for obstinate religious leaders. Those who went along, using the pulpit to help propagate the new ideology, became clergymen. They were paid a stipend by the state after the lands, mills, shops, orchards and other belongings of the mosques and madrasas were redistributed, stripping Islamic institutions of their economic independence.[71]

Gradually, as hundreds of thousands of settlers arrived by lorry from the coastal areas to develop the region, Islam receded into the background. The white skullcaps and long jackets, so ubiquitous before 1949, were seen only at times of worship at the mosque, as men and women alike wore the blue and black uniform of the revolution. Visitors from Pakistan noted in 1956 that there were no free newspapers, while most of the libraries contained books devoted largely to communism. All radio sets were tuned to Beijing. It was gradual assimilation. But the real assault on Islam would come only with the Red Guards in 1966.[72]

10

The Road to Serfdom

On 30 June 1949, as victory in the civil war seemed assured, Mao announced that China would 'lean to one side'. Under the leadership of Lenin and Stalin, the Chairman explained, the Communist Party of the Soviet Union had built 'a great and splendid socialist state'. 'The Communist Party of the Soviet Union is our best teacher and we must learn from it,' he continued. And in the Soviet Union, farming had been collectivised to serve the needs of industry. China would be no different. 'Without socialisation of agriculture, there can be no complete, consolidated socialism.' Judging by the Soviet Union's experience, Mao added, this would require 'a long time and painstaking work'.[1]

The work would be painstaking indeed, but the road to collectivisation took much less time than anybody could have anticipated.[2] This road was taken out of necessity as much as by choice as soon as land reform came to an end. Once the villagers all had a roughly equal share of the land, there were not enough animals and tools to go around. Before land distribution, farming was a full-time occupation for some people, but only an avocation for others. And even then, a fully occupied farmer seldom had more than one working animal and a small set of farming equipment. The further one went south, the more acute the problem became, as population density increased. The archives offer examples of stark warnings of the consequences of land reform. From Yichang, a transportation hub along the Yangzi River in Hubei, came a message from the party headquarters explaining that the land was no good to the poor, as they lacked cows, tools, seed, fertiliser and even sufficient food simply to survive the spring season. The problem was 'widespread', but it was particularly pressing in areas where land had just been redistributed. 'This year the outlook for poor peasants and farm labourers truly bears no reason for optimism. Their productivity cannot be increased, their lives cannot be changed.' Collectivisation seemed the only way forward.[3]

In many places villagers started sharing ploughing animals and tools among several families after they had received a plot of land. The owners were rarely enthusiastic about their common use, since no one but themselves would take good care of them. So at village meetings local cadres nudged them along the path to collectivisation. A platform would be hastily erected, decorated for the occasion with red flags and pictures of Chinese and Soviet leaders. In one case an agricultural expert rambled on for hours. The key message was somewhere towards the end, catching the attention of the villagers. 'Since there is a shortage of ploughing animals and tools,' the man shouted, 'it has been decreed that you may borrow your neighbours' animals and tools. The local government will see to it that nobody refuses to share these things with his neighbours.'[4]

This was the first stage of collectivisation. Families who shared tools, working animals and labour were called 'mutual-aid teams'. Not much of the aid was mutual. While in the past it had been common to pool together during busy seasons, the farmers had done so voluntarily, not under threat of denunciation by local cadres. Villagers who refused to go along with collectivisation ran the risk of being called 'unpatriotic', 'Chiang Kai-shek roaders' or 'backward elements'. In some cases cultivators who preferred to remain independent had strips of paper pinned on their backs, denouncing them as 'capitalists' or 'go-it-aloners'. In Yuechi county, Sichuan, a local cadre forced a villager to hang a board around his neck reading 'lazybones'. Another was humiliated with a sign of the tortoise, a graphic metaphor for the penis. Not far away, in Guang'an, another villager who preferred to cultivate the land on his own was forced to walk the streets beating a gong, warning onlookers: 'Do not follow my example, you should not refuse to join the mutual-aid teams!' At least in one village in the same region villagers were given a choice. The local leader displayed two posters, one pledging allegiance to Mao Zedong, the other to Chiang Kai-shek: each villager was asked to sign up for the leader of his choice. But most of all, those who refused to share were deprived of the loans they needed to tide them over.[5]

New conflicts appeared, even though all grudges were supposed to have been settled with the revolutionary righteousness of land reform. The working animals that had not been killed during land distribution were now borrowed, and many of them were badly neglected. When they were returned to their owners they were often miserable, sick and filthy. Some were worked to death. When, on the subtropical island of Hainan, water buffaloes were passed around the village instead of being returned at the agreed date, the owner had to plant his rice without first ploughing the land, resulting in stems with pale ears that bore no rice. When boats were borrowed for two weeks they were never returned, prompting others in turn to be more cautious with property. Some pretended that their vessels were not seaworthy, others preferred to fill them with river mud rather than to lend them out. Farming tools, to be shared by mutual-aid teams, were often broken, due either to neglect or to sheer spite. Conflicts between those who lent and those who borrowed soon undermined the very notion of private property. The poor proclaimed that 'it is glorious to be poor', pushing for the equal distribution of all assets: 'if there is food all should eat it, if there is money all should use it'. Fear and jealousy meant that poverty became the norm.[6]

The very term 'rich' inspired dread. In some cases the poor pushed for much more radical sharing, anticipating the People's Communes that would come with the Great Leap Forward in the summer of 1958: everything was pooled together, no matter what each person contributed. In some places in Hainan as many as 6 per cent of all teams practised this form of radical egalitarianism. In one extreme example a team of five families even shared the cost of weddings. But in a fateful anticipation of the famine that followed the Great Leap Forward, those who could not contribute as much as others were soon marginalised. Pregnant women were cursed for eating from the common pot without working in the fields. Farmers were reluctant to go to market for fear of being denounced as slackers. With the blurring of private property, theft also became more common. As one report noted, 'social order is abnormal', as entire villages sank into a form of open anarchy where every bit of property became fair game.[7]

Hainan had been the last place to be liberated, Manchuria the first. In Manchuria too the introduction of mutual-aid teams impoverished the countryside – often before the rest of the country. Farmers slaughtered their cattle before they had to share them. Good horses were traded for old nags, carts with rubber tyres bartered for antiquated ones with wooden wheels. The trend started in the spring of 1950. Less than a year later, a third of the countryside was in dire poverty, lacking working animals, food, fodder and tools. Sometimes there was not enough seed to plant the next crop. And even with sufficient seed, the job was badly carried out with sprouts distributed unevenly over the fields. As a report to the People's Congress noted, 'the masses lack enthusiasm'.[8]

Other problems appeared. Land distribution was supposed to have confined the most glaring inequities to the past, freeing the productive potential of the masses from the dead hand of feudalism. But all over the country transactions in land appeared as soon as it had been redistributed. In 1952 poor farmers sold or exchanged parts of their share in Zhejiang province. In one village in Jiande county alone, half the land passed through different hands, sometimes sold to rich farmers and city merchants. In the Jinhua region up to 7 per cent of the redistributed land was rented out at an average rate of 20 per cent of the estimated yearly yield.[9]

The situation was similar elsewhere. In Langzhong county, Sichuan, up to one in six of all farmers were driven by sheer destitution to sell their parcel, reversing the land reform that had taken place a year or so earlier. Some could not even afford the land tax. Land distribution was also supposed to bring to light all the holdings previously hidden from tax inspectors. But in large parts of Jiangsu and Anhui – among other provinces – many plots remained untaxed. Called 'black land', it reached an extraordinary 70 per cent of the overall surface in one district of Qiao-cheng, Anhui. Sometimes farmers and cadres colluded in hiding the best plots or turning prime ground into wasteland in the land register. As one village head boldly proclaimed while pacing the fields with a measuring tape in Suxian county, Anhui, 'measuring the land is all about deceiving those above us and helping those below us'. But more often than not, the beneficiaries of 'black land' were the local cadres, who now lorded it over the commoners – as was the case in Jilin province. By one rough estimate, produced by the highest echelon of power in charge of several provinces, roughly half of all local cadres were corrupt. In some regions a new elite had emerged, as one in ten families headed by party officials lived like rich farmers, hiring labour, charging high interest rates and speculating in land.[10]

Everybody had received a plot of land, so everyone had to pay tax – in the form of grain. But before liberation not every villager was a farmer, and even those who tilled the fields often had sideline occupations, making handicrafts in their spare time to supplement the family's income. In some regions entire villages specialised in producing paper umbrellas, cloth shoes, silk hats, rattan chairs, wicker creels or twig baskets for the market. Much of this handicraft wealth was squeezed out by the new regime or forced into mutual-aid teams. Before the revolution, blacksmiths would camp near the hot-water shops or public mills of a village, their furnaces resounding with the blows of the hammer on the anvil as they worked with recycled iron to provide cultivators with agricultural tools. Now many of them worked in teams under the watchful eye of the state. In Huili, Sichuan, the weight of hoes and rakes doubled under collectivisation. The quality was so poor that in some cases the tools had to be discarded after a day or two of use in the fields.[11]

Entire industries in the countryside were wiped out. A good example is what happened in Xiaoshan, an affluent county in Zhejiang where over half the local people relied on the craft of paper-making for an income. The profession demanded special skills, passed on from generation to generation, as hemp, ramie, mulberry and bamboo had to be soaked, pounded and washed to retrieve the long fibres, which were then cleaned in a lime solution and pressed into sheets. Within a year of liberation the industry was taxed out of existence, as fewer than a quarter of 200 small factories managed to remain in business. A once thriving population was reduced to digging up bamboo shoots, cutting grass and stealing wood to eke out a living. Xiaoshan was by no means exceptional, as private enterprise was denounced as a bourgeois pursuit throughout the country. In all of Hubei province, by 1951, the income that most people in the countryside obtained from secondary occupations was cut in half compared to earlier years. More than ever before, the villagers relied on agriculture. In many provinces the output of sideline occupations in the countryside would not match pre-war levels until the 1980s.[12]

But as an ever greater proportion of villagers were funnelled into agriculture, the actual amount produced per person declined after the redistribution of land. Work teams dispatched by the Committee on Land Reform reported that entire counties in Hubei plunged into starvation. There were numerous reasons for widespread hunger, but most were manmade. Cadres who hailed from the north issued orders while ignoring the conditions of the local economy. Villagers were locked up in meetings all night long. Animals starved to death. Tools were lacking. In some villages four out of five residents had no food to eat. Lending had come to a complete halt, as everybody feared being stigmatised as an 'exploiter'. The poor had nowhere to go, as charitable institutions from the old regime had been disbanded.[13]

Famine stalked large swathes of the countryside in 1953. In the spring, 3 million people in Shandong went hungry. Five million people were destitute in Henan, close to 7 million in Hubei and another 7 million in Anhui. In Guangdong over a quarter of a million people went without food. In Shaanxi and Gansu over 1.5 million people went hungry. In Guizhou and Sichuan desperate farmers sold the seeds on which their next crop depended: this was the case with a quarter of the people in some villages in Nanchong county. The practice was also common in Hunan, Hubei and Jiangsu. In Shaoyang county, Hunan, starvation compelled even farmers who used to be well off in the past to sell everything they had. In many of these provinces desperate parents even bartered their children. Villagers were reduced to eating bark, leaves, roots and mud. Famine was a familiar challenge in traditional China, and natural disasters were responsible for a good deal of this hunger. The year of Stalin's death saw floods, typhoons, frosts and blights on an unprecedented scale.[14]

But many reports also pointed the finger at brutal grain levies as well as incompetence, if not callous indifference, on the part of local cadres. In Shandong, each villager had to subsist on roughly 20 kilos of grain a month in 1952. In terms of calories, 23 to 26 kilos of unhusked grain are required each month to provide 1,700 to 1,900 calories per day, an amount international aid organisations consider to be the bare minimum for subsistence. Fodder, seed and other necessities had to be taken out of this amount, meaning that farmers had to live on a mere 163 kilos per year, or less than 14 kilos a month. The state reduced this amount to 122 kilos in 1953, the equivalent of a starvation diet at just over 10 kilos a month. And Shandong was hardly an isolated example. In Jilin, as Chapter 7 showed, brutal grain levies during the Korean War caused widespread famine in 1952. That year, the farmers were left with an average of 194 kilos a year. But the rate of procurement went up from 42.5 per cent to 43.8 per cent in 1953, further reducing the share for each village to a mere 175 kilos, equivalent to less than 15 kilos a month: that, too, was a starvation diet, barely supplemented by a few occasional greens. These are telling figures, even if they do not always capture the human dimensions of hunger. In Nanhe, a dust-swept county on the barren plain of Hebei, the number of children sold out of sheer destitution increased inexorably after 1950: eight children in 1951, fifteen the following year and twenty-nine by 1953. The party archives are silent about the heart-wrenching decisions that impoverished families must have reached in trading their offspring for a handful of grain, but they do mention the local cadres: they stood by as lenders exacted extortionate rates of up to 13 per cent per month. And sometimes they joined the fray, throwing their weight around to impose even higher rates.[15]

The party had an answer to all these problems, and it was to travel further down the road to collectivisation. Speculators, hoarders, kulaks and capitalists were blamed for all the trouble – despite years of organised terror against counter-revolutionaries and other enemies of the socialist order. More rather than less state power was seen as the solution. Starting in 1953, the mutual-aid teams were turned into co-operatives. Tools, working animals and labour were now shared on a permanent basis. Villagers retained nominal ownership of their plot but secured a share in the co-operative by staking it along with those of other members in a common land pool. The co-operatives soon overshadowed the entire lives of the villagers, selling seed, salt and fertiliser, lending money, fixing the prices, determining the time of the harvest and buying up the crops.

This second stage of collectivisation was also supposed to be voluntary, although by now the grip of cadres and the militia on the countryside was such that no realistic alternatives existed. This time around many villagers went even further in trying to withhold their possessions from the communes. As one report noted, it was 'very common' for villagers to abandon years of frugality and slaughter their animals. One couple managed to devour a 50-kilo hog all on their own, not saving any of the meat. Up in Jilin – to take a different example – Sun Fengshan killed his pig in the hope of keeping it from the state's reach, but lacked any facilities to freeze and store the meat. Much of it was eaten at night by dogs, leaving his family crying at the loss. Instead of borrowing from each other, people now turned to the state – with no intention of repayment. The poor were often at the vanguard of collectivisation. In Yangjiang, they accepted state grain while openly declaring that none of it would ever be returned. One man who carted away 1,500 kilos of rice was asked how he would ever be able to reimburse his loan. 'In a year or two we will have socialism and I won't pay back shit' was his answer.[16]

Traditional village rights and customs were neglected or destroyed. There was a scramble over common resources that had not been confiscated and redistributed with land reform, for instance pastures, moorlands or salt marshes where animals were allowed to graze, or riverbanks and woodlands where children collected firewood. People tried to grab what they could before the state collectivised everything. In Huaxian county, Guangdong, a crowd of 200 fought over the forest, resulting in many injuries. In Maoming a village organised a team of 300 to cut down the trees belonging to a neighbouring hamlet. Disputes also flared up over rivers and ponds, creating 'a tense and insecure situation in the countryside'.[17]

The amount of land under cultivation decreased with the introduction of co-operatives. People pooled their plots, but large tracts were abandoned because their owners were compensated with so few shares that it was not worth the trouble. In Jilin province 40,000–50,000 hectares of farmland were cast aside during the first phase of co-operativisation. Even carefully cultivated fields fell into neglect. Explained Wang Zixiang, a farmer in Sichuan, who allowed his terraced field to collapse to the ground: 'Why repair it when it will soon revert to the collective?'[18]

Despite popular resistance, expressed by slaughtering cattle, hiding or destroying assets and slacking at work, the speed with which villages were transformed into co-operatives was stunning. It was driven by political imperatives, as party officials of all levels were keen to take a lead, hoping to be rewarded by a good word from the Chairman. In Jilin province, for instance, fewer than 6 per cent of all farmers belonged to a co-operative in 1953. A year later a third had been enrolled, causing what one report referred to as 'chaos'. Everywhere cadres forced farmers into co-operatives. In 1953 there were only about 100,000 of them. By 1955 more than 600,000 were spread across the country, locking in 40 per cent of all villagers.[19]

The most damaging change to the countryside was the introduction of a monopoly on grain by the end of 1953. The state decreed that cultivators must sell all surplus grain to the state at prices determined by the state and in co-operatives run by the state. This was the third stage of collectivisation.

The aim behind this momentous shift was to stabilise the price of grain across the country, eliminate speculation and guarantee the grain needed to feed the urban population and fuel industrial expansion. As famine spread in 1953, the state discovered that private merchants spiked the price of food. They hoarded rice and wheat in the hope of making a higher profit. It was a phenomenon common in all agrarian societies in times of crisis, but in this case the situation was made worse by the existence of co-operatives. Not only did farmers slaughter their cattle in defiance of collectivisation, but they also hid their grain. And when they went to market to sell their crop, they often preferred to turn to private merchants rather than to the state co-operatives charged with collecting the crop. The co-operatives adhered rigidly to a set of opening hours which took no account of farmers' working schedules, whereas private shops welcomed customers at any time of day. The co-operatives themselves did such a poor job that many preferred to delegate the task to independent grain traders. Everywhere, it seemed to the leadership, capitalist practices were subverting the socialisation of the countryside.[20]

Private merchants, of course, were a convenient scapegoat for the famine. There was another, more pressing reason why the state introduced a monopoly on grain. The reality was that the economy was a disaster.

Land reform had failed to usher the country into an era of prosperity. Trade was in dire straits. The state was running a huge deficit, with its expenditure twice as big as its income. When the leaders convened in July 1953 to scrutinise the finances, they were staring at a black hole of 2.4 billion yuan.[21]

One cause of the deficit was foreign trade. Since Beijing dramatically oriented its exports away from the West towards the Soviet Union, it had become dependent on Stalin to earn foreign currency. China tried relentlessly to sell more goods to its reluctant partner. By the admission of the leaders responsible for foreign trade, they constantly pestered and harassed their Soviet counterparts. But in 1953 the Soviet Union only took 81 per cent of a proposed list of items for export, falling far short of expectations.[22]

To add insult to injury, Stalin sharply reduced the amount of aid he was willing to commit to China's first Five-Year Plan, due to begin in 1953. When Zhou Enlai met the Soviet boss in September 1952, he asked for a loan of 4 billion rubles. Stalin replied that the Soviet Union 'will have to give something, although the exact amount must be calculated. We cannot give 4 billion.' And Stalin made numerous demands in return, asking, for instance, for large amounts of natural rubber – 'at least 15,000 to 20,000 tonnes each year'. When Zhou demurred, Stalin threatened to cut the number of lorries that China had requested. He wanted more rare-earth metals, including lead, tungsten, tin and antimony. And he insisted on foreign currency to cover the costs of the trade imbalance between China and the Soviet Union.[23]

This meeting was followed by endless others, as Li Fuchun, a bookish man with a self-effacing air who was in charge of the negotiations, spent ten months in Moscow bickering and wrangling for more concessions. Stalin died in March 1953, but he and his successors forced Beijing to accept deep cuts. The rate of growth that China wanted to pursue, Stalin said, was 'rash': he cut it from 20 per cent down to 15 per cent. He reduced the number of industrial complexes built with Soviet assistance from 150 to 91. He vetoed several projects related to military defence. As Li put it, 'We just asked for everything we wanted, and we wanted too much, too fast.' Mao and his colleagues had little choice but to accept a watered-down deal in June 1953.[24]

A few weeks later, Mao asked the Financial Committee to come up with ways of requisitioning more grain. Chen Yun, Bo Yibo and others had already proposed a state monopoly on grain in 1951, but abandoned it after local cadres warned that any attempt to curtail the freedom of farmers to sell their crop in local markets would provoke a backlash. But now the time seemed right. A few leaders still voiced reservations. Deng Zihui, the regional boss of south China who was now in charge of a powerful committee on agriculture, queried the wisdom of taking food without any exemption from those interior provinces where the soil was poor, saline or infertile. Even Chen Yun, one of the architects of the earlier plan, warned of rebellions. But he too sided with Mao.[25]

The grain monopoly was imposed in November 1953. The system worked as follows. The government estimated what the yield per hectare of any given field would be. This figure was often much higher than the actual yield, and it was sometimes raised again under pressure to produce more. The government also determined the quantity of grain that each person should eat. This was set at roughly 13 to 16 kilos per head each month – a little more than half the required amount of unhusked grain to provide 1,700 to 1,900 calories per day. It was a starvation diet imposed equally on all villagers. This amount, as well as the land tax and the seeds required for the next sowing, was deducted from the estimated yield. What remained was considered surplus. It had to be sold to the state at a price fixed by the state. Extra grain above the basic ration could be bought back from the state by the farmers – if they could afford it, and if there was any grain left after it had been used to feed the cities, fuel industrialisation and pay off foreign debts.

The leadership knew full well that taking control of the harvest was tantamount to declaring war on the countryside. It was so reminiscent of what the Japanese had done in north China during the Second World War that the party leaders agreed to avoid the term 'procurement'. They used a euphemism instead, calling the monopoly a 'unified sale and purchase system' (*tonggou tongxiao*). Among themselves they talked of a 'yellow bomb', knowing that villagers would resist and fight the system. But they preferred it to the only other alternative they could envisage, namely a 'black bomb', as grain merchants would continue to exploit the market to their own advantage as long as no monopoly was imposed.[26]

The yellow bomb destroyed the very foundations of village life in China, turning a great proportion of the cultivators into bonded servants of the state. Everywhere there was resistance fuelled by rage against the party, most of it covert, but some of it public. Even some local leaders preferred to side with the villagers, whether out of strategic calculation or genuine concern over their welfare. In parts of Guangdong up to a third of the cadres helped farmers to hide their grain. Public village meetings were held in Zijin to devise ways of holding back some of the food from the grain inspectors. Open resistance was common. In Zhongshan county, not far from Macau, eighteen villages protested for four consecutive days against the grain monopoly. Arson and murder were rife.[27]

In Jiangxi province some villagers invited themselves into the homes of the cadres, searched the premises and then heartily tucked into the food, leaving behind a token payment in exchange for the meal: 'In the past, when you were working, you came to my house for a meal and you gave me 0.10 yuan, so now I too give you 0.10 yuan.' Others took seats and refused to budge, occupying the homes of party officials they disliked. Leaflets appeared seemingly out of nowhere, calling on people to resist state procurements. Bemused grain inspectors came upon teams of children roaming the countryside, loudly cursing Chairman Mao and the government.[28]

Harking back to a form of resistance that had appeared in 1950, groups of villagers blocked cargo boats in Hubei, adamant that grain should be used to feed the people who had actually produced it. In one village the women took a lead, as a hundred of them blocked access to the local granary. Elsewhere, 300 women armed with sticks and stones cut off access to the cargo boats. A few hurled pots filled with urine towards the agents of the state. In Sichuan, banners and tracts denouncing grain requisitions were unfurled. 'Down with Mao Zedong!' or 'Resolutely Eliminate the People's Liberation Army' appeared by roadsides in Hanyuan and Xichang, while elsewhere popular ditties mocked the party.[29]

The state responded with more violence. As the militia dragged away the grain, some of the poor would break down in tears, crying for fear of hunger. Those who resisted, or failed to meet their quota, were beaten. It was 'common', the state Bureau for Grain reported from Guangdong, for recalcitrant elements to be stripped and left standing in the cold for hours on end. All over the province thousands of people were locked up for refusing to sell their grain. Up in the north, in Baoding, Hebei, there were scenes of chaos when the procurement teams entered the village. People hid in the toilets, others pretended to be sick, a few coming out to hurl abuse at the cadres, only to be beaten, some of the elderly women wailing in despair and fear. In the Handan region, cadres were blunt: 'if you don't report your excess grain, we will stop sales [of edible oil, salt and other basic items] for ten days'. In twenty-four villages in Yuanshi county, just south of Shijiazhuang, villagers were spat upon, pushed around, tied up and beaten in order to force them to produce the grain. A subsequent investigation revealed that in Yuanshi, violence was used in over half of all the 208 villages. The cadres used torture techniques learned during earlier campaigns. A few openly dismissed the villagers as mere 'slaves'. Mock executions were held, while one pregnant woman was beaten unconscious. Even children were forced to stand upright for hours on end, a form of punishment that was apparently 'very common'. Suicides were described as 'ceaseless'.[30]

Sometimes pitched battles occurred between the people and the security forces. Luo Ruiqing, the head of security, counted dozens of cases of unrest and open rebellion in the countryside. In Zhongshan county, Guangdong, thousands of villagers rebelled in early 1955 and demanded an end to the grain monopoly. Four companies of public security forces were sent in to quell the unrest. People were killed on both sides of a bloody battle that lasted several days. In the end 300 farmers were dragged away to prison. In Luding, Sichuan, a sacred place in revolutionary mythology where the communists had battled the nationalists over the only suspension bridge spanning the torrential Dadu River in 1935, six riots were reported in a single month. In Miyi, also in Sichuan, people from ten villages seized weapons from the militia and converged on the party headquarters. Until the archives fully open, there is no way of knowing how many people were crushed by the state machinery during these uneven confrontations.[31]

On a few occasions the state had to give in. In parts of Gansu dominated by the Tibetans – Xiahe, Zhuoni and other counties – procurements came to a complete halt after several regional leaders were shot dead in an ambush. The region was rife with rumours of rebellion. 'Better rebel than wait for death through starvation' was one slogan that made the rounds. The party was compelled to fall back, ordering that a steady supply of grain be guaranteed to Tibetans throughout the provinces of Gansu, Qinghai and Sichuan.[32]

But outside politically sensitive areas the pressure was relentless. Rather predictably, even the basic survival ration that the system was supposed to leave untouched sometimes vanished, leaving villagers with nothing to eat. In Qingyuan, Guangdong, all but two members of an entire co-operative were forced to sell all their food. Sometimes party secretaries took a lead in allowing the state to seize every last kernel of grain. Qiu Sen, a member of a public security committee, sold almost 500 kilos, leaving him and his family of five a mere 110 kilos, barely enough to feed them for two months. And as the situation slipped out of control, some local authorities started reducing the amount of grain that could be sold back to the villagers. They often discriminated against the black classes, those outcasts labelled during land reform as 'landlords', 'rich farmers' and 'counter-revolutionaries'. In Yangjiang nobody classified as a landlord was sold any grain at all, whether they had enough to eat or not (they often did not, because their land had been redistributed and their assets confiscated). In Deqing even farmers classified as 'middle peasants' were barred from buying grain, regardless of their actual circumstances. In Hainan grain was sold only if a village had suffered from 'shortages' for a period of at least three months. In Fengcheng, Jiangxi province, cadres pledged to sell grain only to those households who fulfilled their procurement quota.[33]

––––––––––

It was not sufficient to collect the grain. It had to be sieved, winnowed, cleaned, milled, stored, transported and sold. Common enemies were birds, rats, weevil or mildew, which had to be kept at bay. Grain had to be dry or it would rot. The most simple containers were wicker baskets, and they were made in a great variety of shapes and sizes. Earthenware jars were used for hulled grain. Granaries also existed, although before liberation most of the grain was consumed where it was produced, meaning that few large storage facilities were needed. The grain could be stored in round bins built of straw and clay, often on a cement or sandrock floor to keep out rodents and ground moisture. More common were burlap sacks, stacked up in a granary or in a simple tarpaulin shed. In Shaanxi caves were sometimes used, while on the loess plateau in the north the grain was sunk into pits lined with wooden boards, dug up to 12 metres deep with a floor of tamped earth. Whatever means had been devised to store the crop, there was one constant: people looked after it because their livelihoods depended on it.[34]

Now the state took over, and at great expense. The farmers, pedlars, handlers, traders, millers and others who had made a profession out of looking after the grain were pushed aside as so many speculators and capitalists. And not only did state employees increasingly look after the grain, but they also had to expand the volume of storage dramatically. Even when grain was kept for local consumption, the monopoly mandated that farmers sell it first to the state, which could sell it back to them later if they could afford it. Not surprisingly, the state suffered from a shortage of storage facilities that would last for decades. The cost was prohibitive. In 1956, according to one expert, 'the costs to the state of storing grain for more than three years were equal to the value of the grain itself'.[35]

As larger state-controlled concerns replaced small, individual or family-run facilities, many of the perennial problems that had plagued grain storage spiralled out of control. In January 1954, for instance, every province in east China reported a large increase in food that was overheating and becoming damp. In Shanghai alone 40,000 tonnes developed mildew. The problem was compounded by local cadres, who cared more about quantity than quality: their job was to demonstrate to their superiors how much they had procured, not how well they performed this task. In some cases they deliberately allowed high humidity to increase the overall weight. A few even bulked up the volume by adding water. Here is the scene that met one visitor when the doors of a warehouse opened in south China:

Moths and beetles swarmed out, and I saw several rats as big as young rabbits scurrying across the floor. Different kinds of containers were haphazardly stacked on the slab-stone floor. There were also torn sacks of various sizes, along with earthenware jars and wooden casks. In one corner were huge reed-mat bins into which flour was dumped. I recoiled at the sight of insects buzzing and flitting around, not to mention the worms in the bins. The flour in one bin was covered with a blue mould that smelled awful.[36]

Thanks to its monopoly on grain, in 1954 the state took in more than ever before, in absolute numbers and as a proportion of the overall crop. In Shandong the amount procured jumped from 2 million tonnes in 1953 to just under 3 million in 1954. Even when the increase was relatively modest it could be devastating: in Hebei it went from 1.9 million tonnes to 2.08 million, which represented a shift from 23.5 per cent up to 25.9 per cent of the harvest. In Shaanxi the overall proportion of food taken away increased from 19.5 per cent to 25.5 per cent in 1954. One of the highest proportions of all was in Jilin, where 50.7 per cent of all the grain was hauled away, even though the crop that year shrank to 5.31 million tonnes. It left the villagers with an average of 145 kilos a year.[37]

Deng Zihui, the man who oversaw work in the countryside from Beijing, put it in a nutshell. In July 1954, ten months after the monopoly had come into effect, he admitted that before liberation on average a villager had about 300 kilos set aside for food each year. Now that amount was reduced for every one of them, from north to south, to just about half a kilo a day, or a third less. And other foodstuffs were also lacking. Most people outside the cities never received more than 3 kilos of edible oil a year. Deng called the monopoly on grain 'the only way when there is no way', and that way was to 'spread the pain evenly'. He would soon pay the price for his frankness.[38]

Evenly spread pain meant starvation, which was widespread in 1954, coming right on the heels of the famine in 1953. Already on 2 January 1954 the Central Committee warned that farmers were being driven to their deaths due to the state monopoly. In Henan and in Jiangxi, 4.5 million people were in dire straits. In Hunan up to one in every six villagers went hungry. Three million lacked food in Shandong. In Guizhou and Sichuan, where up to a quarter of the population in mountainous areas did not have enough to eat, people sold their clothes, their land and their homes. Across the country people sold their children. In the single county of Ji'an, Jiangxi, thirty-two were sold within two months. This happened even in subtropical Guangdong. In a village in Puning county, Zhang Delai sold his offspring for 50 yuan. It was enough to buy rice and see him through the famine. In Anhui hordes of up to 200 beggars roamed the countryside. Some froze to death. In Linxia, Gansu, some of the victims were too weak even to walk down the road to the next village. 'The main reason', explained the inspectors dispatched by the provincial government, 'is that local cadres have not paid sufficient attention to the conditions of the crop last year and have committed serious errors in carrying out the unified sale and purchase system.'[39]

Most of these reports pointed out how much of the starvation was man-made. But in August the Central Committee decided to ascribe the worst famine since 1949 to 'natural disasters'. Instead of helping people in the countryside, it stressed how vital it was to procure the state-mandated amounts of grain, oil and cotton, all of which were essential to 'industrial production in the cities and the socialist reform of industry and commerce in the countryside'. A year later, as the telltale signs of famine appeared again in the spring of 1955, Liu Shaoqi and Zhou Enlai approved a directive explaining that 'among those who shout loudly about grain shortages, the absolute majority in fact do not lack grain at all'. Zhou Enlai, as head of the State Council, merely tinkered with the numbers, concluding that the monopoly worked rather well. It worked so well that already in November 1953 and September 1954 it had been extended to oil crops and cotton respectively. Soon it covered all major foodstuffs and agricultural raw materials.[40]

————

One response to collectivisation was to leave the countryside. Villagers had always supplemented their income by going to the city in the slack season, working in factories or peddling goods. Sometimes they would stay away for years on end, sending remittances back home to support their families. In Raoyang county, Hubei, a quarter of all men from the countryside worked in the cities during the winter months in the early 1950s. But the state did not encourage rural mobility. Soon after liberation it sent millions of refugees, unemployed, demobilised soldiers and other undesirable elements to the countryside. They kept on coming back. Despite state efforts to reverse the flow, there were close to 20 million rural migrants, often relegated to dirty, arduous and sometimes dangerous jobs on the margins of the urban landscape. As in the old days, they came in search of new opportunities and a better life, but other motivations also drove migration. As the state curtailed private commerce, pedlars, traders and merchants left the countryside in droves, seeking better pastures.

But most of all, people took to the roads because they wanted to escape from famine. After the state imposed a monopoly on grain, many villagers voted with their feet and joined a massive exodus from the countryside. In March 1954, over 50,000 villagers poured into Jinan, the capital of Shandong. In Port Arthur, more than 19,000 of them overwhelmed the small city in the autumn of 1953. They begged the Soviet troops for help. Eight thousand farmers were looking for work in Anshan, the site of a sprawling steel and iron complex in Manchuria. In the streets of Wuhan, the industrial city on the Yangzi, hundreds of impoverished villagers could be seen, many of them begging for food. Some had sold all their clothes; a few tried to commit suicide, possibly disappointed by the reality of the city that had been a beacon of hope. Some protested in front of government offices, screaming, crying, a few waiting to die. But the biggest magnet was Shanghai. In the summer of 1954, around 2,000 refugees came by train every single day. Hundreds also arrived by boat, some of them too poor to buy a ticket.[41]

In April 1953 the State Council had already passed a directive seeking to persuade hundreds of thousands of farmers in search of work to return to their villages. The attempt failed to stem the flow. In March 1954 even more stringent regulations were put on the books, curtailing the recruitment of workers from the countryside. In the following months the public security organs were beefed up, and substations were established everywhere to control the movement of people and guard the cities against a rural influx. Then, on 22 June 1955, Zhou Enlai signed a directive introducing the household-registration system, used in the cities since 1951, to the countryside.

It was the rough equivalent of the internal passport instituted decades earlier in the Soviet Union. Food was rationed from August 1955 onwards, and its distribution closely tied to the number of people registered in each household. The ration cards had to be presented at local grain stores, thus preventing the large-scale movement of people. But while the subsistence of urban residents was guaranteed by the state, rural residents had to feed themselves. From retirement benefits to health care, education and subsidised housing, the state looked after many of its employees in the cities, while letting people registered as 'peasants' (*nongmin*) fend for themselves. This status was inherited through the mother, meaning that even if a village girl married a man from the city, she and her children remained 'peasants', deprived of the same entitlements accorded urban residents.

The household-registration system also carefully monitored the movements of people, even within the countryside, as a migration certificate was required for anybody thinking of changing residence. No government in China had ever restricted freedom of residence or prevented migration, except in contested zones during wartime. But in 1955 the freedom of domicile and freedom of movement came to an end for people in the countryside. Those who moved in search of a better life were now called *mangliu*, or 'blind migrants'. It was a reverse homophone of *liumang*, meaning hooligan.[42]

The household-registration system tied the cultivator to the land, making sure that cheap labour was available in the co-operatives. This was the fourth stage of collectivisation. A mere step now separated villagers from serfdom, namely the ownership of the land.

11

High Tide

A solar eclipse was always a bad omen in traditional China, but New Year's Day was the worst time for one to occur. On 14 February 1953, the first day of the lunar calendar, the moon partially blocked the sun, casting a dark shadow over the earth. Less than three weeks later Stalin died. In China flags stood at half-mast, with strips of black cloth flying on top. Public buildings in the capital were draped with black. At the Soviet embassy, the queue of mourners was four deep and so long that some streets had to be temporarily closed to traffic. People wore black armbands distributed by party activists standing on street corners. Further towards Tiananmen Square, in front of the entrance of the Forbidden City, a huge red platform was piled high with artificial wreaths and paper flowers. A portrait of Stalin towered above it. Loudspeakers alternated between funeral music and instructions to the crowd on how to behave. 'Don't sing – don't laugh – don't walk aimlessly – don't shout – keep order – behave as you were instructed in the newspaper.' The crowd was silent.[1]

The Chairman bowed before the portrait and laid a wreath. But he did not give a speech. For the previous thirty years he had followed Stalin's advice, sometimes willingly, sometimes grudgingly. Even in the midst of civil war, as his troops were gaining the upper hand, he continued to look to Moscow for advice and guidance. He was a faithful follower of Stalin and took pains to prove his loyalty by declaring that China would 'lean to one side' in 1949. After liberation the flow of telegrams between Beijing and Moscow increased even further, as the Chairman requested Stalin's advice on seemingly every matter.

Mao was a loyal student of Stalin, but even so the relationship had never been an easy one. Mao held many grudges against his mentor, who had humiliated him in Moscow only three years earlier. And he deeply resented the presence of Soviet troops in Manchuria. But most of all Mao wanted to be more Stalinist than Stalin would allow. In November 1947 the Chairman had written to Moscow to explain that he intended to eliminate all rival political parties: 'In the period of the final victory of the Chinese revolution – as was the case in the USSR and Yugoslavia – all political parties except the CCP will have to withdraw from the political scene.' But Stalin disagreed, telling him that the opposition parties in China would have to be included as part of a New Democracy for many years to come. 'After the victory,' Stalin explained, 'the Chinese government will be a national revolutionary and democratic government, rather than a Communist one.' Mao demurred, maintaining the pretence of democracy even as he set out to build a totalitarian state. Then, in February 1950, Stalin urged the Chairman to pursue a milder approach to land distribution, sparing the rich peasants who could help the country recover after years of warfare. A few months later Mao published a Land Reform Law which promised a less divisive policy even as violence tore the countryside apart. And in 1952, only months before he was felled by a stroke, Stalin had whittled down funding for China's first Five-Year Plan, warning the Chinese leadership that they were requesting too much, too soon.[2]

Stalin's death was Mao's liberation. The Chairman was at last free from the restraining influence of Moscow. No longer were there any major constraints on his political vision. Of course, he continued to submit his views to the Kremlin, as telegraph wires continued to hum between the two red capitals, but no Soviet leader commanded as much respect as Mao, who had brought a second October Revolution to a quarter of the world, and fought the United States to a standstill during the Korean War. Soon the Chairman began to distance himself from the Soviet leadership.

He also drifted away from his colleagues. Mao had led his men to victory in 1949. Korea, too, was his personal glory, as he had pushed for intervention when other leaders in the party had wavered. He stood head and shoulders above his peers.

Even before Stalin died, Mao had started to undermine Liu Shaoqi and Zhou Enlai, who were in charge of the day-to-day handling of the economy, and were becoming too influential for Mao's comfort. Zhou, the soft-spoken, slightly effeminate premier, had learned a decade earlier never to challenge the Chairman. In 1932 rivals of Mao had handed command over the battlefront to Zhou. The result had been a disaster, as Chiang Kai-shek mauled the communist troops and forced them on a Long March away from their bases in the south. After Mao had gained the upper hand in Yan'an, Zhou's loyalty was tested in a series of ferocious self-criticism sessions from September to November 1943. He was accused of having led a faction that had sided with one of Mao's rivals. Zhou grovelled and admitted that he had been a 'political swindler' who lacked principles, something he blamed on his pampered upbringing in a 'feudal aristocratic family'. It was a gruelling experience, but Zhou managed to emerge from the ordeal as Mao's faithful assistant, putting his organisational skills entirely at the service of the Chairman in order to redeem himself.[3]

Liu Shaoqi had gone to Moscow as a student in 1921. He was a frugal, taciturn man, best known as a zealous apparatchik who would regularly toil away through the night. Two decades later, in Yan'an, he and Zhou had sat at opposite ends of the table, as Liu was neck-deep in the campaign to flush out spies and saboteurs from the party. Although he left the dirty work of extracting confessions from suspects to Kang Sheng, the grim man who had worked with the Soviet secret police, Liu was the main architect of a theoretical framework justifying the witch-hunt. He excelled at his task and became Mao's second-in-command in 1943.[4]

Mao lacked interest in matters of daily routine and organisational detail, and he needed first-rate administrators he could trust to carry out his vision. Zhou and Liu were his able servants, always at his beck and call, come day or night. The Chairman's schedule was erratic, as he suffered from severe insomnia, anxiety attacks and depression, often caused by his constant fear that other high-ranking leaders were disloyal to him. Trust was of the essence. Mao relied on heavy doses of barbiturates, chloral hydrate and sodium seconal to sleep, and he often dozed off during the day and worked throughout the night, not hesitating to summon his staff and colleagues at all hours. He expected them to turn up immediately. So, in turn, top officials like Liu and Zhou relied on sleeping pills to get some rest, as they could never quite synchronise their working schedules with the routines of the Chairman.

Lack of sleep was only a minor inconvenience. They had to cope with Mao's unpredictable mood swings, tiptoe around him, flatter his ego and avoid any comments that might provoke suspicion or misunderstanding. They had to decipher his often obscure remarks, used to keep them guessing about his intentions. But the Chairman also deliberately employed vague terms to conceal his own ignorance, particularly in the realm of economics, of which he understood very little. He rarely voiced an opinion on concrete financial issues; when he did so, he sounded uninformed. This too was a delicate issue for Zhou and Liu, all the more so since they had to assume responsibility for running an increasingly complex state bureaucracy encompassing millions of employees. It was tempting for them to leave aside some of the more technical details of the economy in order to avoid embarrassing their master. But this was also fraught with danger, as Mao had a habit of switching unpredictably from complete aloofness in government affairs to obsessive attention to detail. During the purge of government ranks in 1952, for instance, he issued directives on the number of culprits to be arrested almost daily, only to abandon interest suddenly as the campaign tapered off, leaving Liu to cope with the mess.[5]

By 1952 Zhou and Liu had assembled a powerful team of economic managers, including Bo Yibo, Chen Yun, Li Fuchun and Deng Zihui. Mao began to feel that he was being sidestepped, losing his grip over his subordinates as the debate over the economy became ever more complex. He was also impatient with slow economic growth, and realised that some of his colleagues had doubts about the pace of collectivisation. Liu, in particular, took the view that a transition to socialism would take a great deal of time. He even envisaged a business community that would contribute to the national economy for years to come. This jarred with Mao, but while Stalin was still alive he had to be prudent in taking Liu to task. Liu had studied in Moscow. In the summer of 1949 he had been the party's envoy to the Soviet Union, and Stalin had showered attention on him in six separate meetings. Mao, on the other hand, had been given the cold shoulder. In late February 1953, as Mao learned that Stalin was on his deathbed, he tried to stop Liu, who was in hospital for an appendectomy, from finding out. Liu was excluded from the memorial ceremony in honour of Stalin a few weeks later.[6]

In early 1953 Mao confronted Bo Yibo, the minister of finance who was part of Zhou and Liu's team of economic managers. Bo was responsible for a new tax system that alleviated some of the pressure on the private sector. In a note circulated to Bo and copied to several other top leaders, the Chairman complained bitterly: 'I did not know about this until I read about it in the newspapers, and I still don't understand it!' Zhou immediately realised that the Chairman was angry, and wrote a letter that very evening to try to defuse the situation. But a few days later the Chairman confronted Bo Yibo during a top leadership meeting: 'The revision of the tax system was not reported to the Centre in advance, but it was discussed with the bourgeoisie. The bourgeoisie is seen to be more important even than the Party Centre! This new system is welcomed by the bourgeoisie, it is a mistake of rightist opportunism!' Mao's real targets, beyond pressing for speedier collectivisation, were the two men behind Bo, namely Zhou and Liu. The Chairman adopted a tactic he called 'pitching a stone to cause a ripple', using a proxy to assail the two most powerful men below him.[7]

The Chairman did not relent in the following months, despite Bo Yibo making several self-criticisms. Mao was strengthening his grip over the government even as he undermined his colleagues, demanding in March that 'all major and important directives, policies, plans and events in government work must be reported to the Centre for instruction beforehand'. In May he wrote a menacing note to Liu, insisting that 'all documents and telegrams issued in the name of the Centre can only be issued after I have seen them, *otherwise they are invalid*. Please be careful.' Before the assembled leadership a few weeks later, he reprimanded those who 'do not care so much' about collective leadership, preferring instead to be left alone.[8]

Having put Zhou and Liu on notice, Mao announced a change of speed in the pursuit of socialism at a Politburo meeting on 15 June 1953. Here is how he phrased it in the parlance of Marxism-Leninism:

The general line or the general task of the party for the transition period is basically to accomplish the industrialisation of the country and the socialist transformation of agriculture, handicrafts and capitalist industry and commerce in ten to fifteen years, or a little longer. This general line is a beacon illuminating our work in all fields. Do not depart from this general line, otherwise 'Left' or Right mistakes will occur.[9]

Mao called his speech 'Refute Right Deviationist Views that Depart from the General Line'. Zhou and Liu were never named, but his audience was in no doubt about what was happening. Both had worked hard to maintain the pretence of a New Democracy, used on Stalin's advice to assure entrepreneurs and industrialists that they could continue to run their businesses on a private basis. Mao savaged Zhou Enlai's formulation of 'the social order of New Democracy', and the term would never be used again. Even slogans about 'sustaining private property', according to the Chairman, were manifestations of 'rightism'. Democracy was out, socialism was in. The Chairman proposed the General Line, and in doing so he positioned himself above the party, using it as a yardstick to determine who was a rightist and who was a leftist on the road to socialism. It was a yardstick he would change repeatedly.[10]

Mao also promoted a number of outsiders to senior positions in Beijing as part of his strategy to undermine the tight group of economic managers gathered around Liu Shaoqi and Zhou Enlai. He called this 'putting sand in the mix'. The most important newcomer was Gao Gang, the leader of Manchuria, who arrived in the capital in October 1952 to head the newly created State Planning Commission. He also took responsibility for eight economic ministries, ranging from light industry and fuel to textiles, thus sharing a large portion of what had previously fallen under Zhou Enlai's exclusive purview. Soon he was a fixture at all important leadership meetings. At the party headquarters in Zhongnanhai, the beautifully manicured compound where the empress dowager had lived, he had an office just across the hallway from Mao. His family moved into a spacious residence on Dongjiao Mingxiang, formerly occupied by the French embassy. There was extensive personal contact between the two, with discussions going into the early hours of the night. Gao took cues from the Chairman, laying into Bo Yibo at one of the self-criticism meetings with the minister of finance, carefully reading from notes that Mao had revised and approved beforehand. Gao relished the attack on one of his personal enemies. A year earlier Bo had handed the Chairman a report on corruption in Manchuria, directly implicating Gao. Mao circulated the letter within the higher echelons of the party.[11]

The Chairman was impressed with Gao, and in the summer of 1953 trusted him with another task. He ordered him to investigate Liu Shaoqi's past to find out whether his number two had spied for the nationalists in the 1920s. Gao interpreted this as a sign that the Chairman wanted to get rid of Liu. But Mao was a master of the divide-and-rule game. Just as he held grudges against Liu Shaoqi and Zhou Enlai, he was also wary of Gao Gang. Years earlier, Gao had accompanied Liu to meet Stalin in Moscow. At one meeting that summer of 1949, Gao had floated the idea that Manchuria be declared the seventeenth republic of the Soviet Union to protect it from the United States. Stalin had fixed his eyes on Gao, and after a moment of awkward silence he had shrugged off the idea with a joke. But the proposal prompted Liu to telegraph Mao, demanding that Gao be recalled to Beijing. Mao approved the request, and on 30 July 1949 a defeated Gao went to the airport unaccompanied by other members of the delegation. Months later, when Mao undertook his own pilgrimage to Moscow, Stalin handed him a dossier containing incriminating evidence showing that Gao had personally sent confidential messages to the Soviet leader. Exactly what was in these files remains a mystery, but it did not seem to harm Gao's career. He remained in charge of Manchuria, which soon had thousands of technical advisers from the Soviet Union, working in every capacity from top executives to lowly trackmen on the railways, operated jointly by China and Russia.[12]

Mao tolerated Gao while Stalin was alive. But by bringing him into the Politburo in Beijing in October 1952, the Chairman also removed him from his fiefdom and distanced him geographically from the Soviet Union. He could observe him more closely. Gao did not fare well. He was a talker, and his reputation for shooting off his mouth was confirmed as he met with several Soviet diplomats. He expounded on internal politics. He scoffed about the budget deficit. He provided details about infrastructure projects that had backfired. He ratted on his colleagues.[13]

How much of this Mao knew is unclear, but he sent Gao to Moscow in August 1953 to liaise with the new Soviet leadership. After Stalin had choked to death, his eyes bulging in a last gasp for air, his security boss Lavrenti Beria had been the first to leap forward and kiss his lifeless body. The following day Beria seized power from his terrified colleagues and reigned for a brief two months. On 28 June, Nikita Khrushchev and several others ambushed him and placed him under arrest for 'criminal activities against the party and the state'. Gao met Khrushchev but stayed in Moscow for only two days. He had not been allowed to travel with his own secretary. Ye Zilong, Mao's personal secretary, went along instead, watching Gao's every step. On the way back to Beijing, Gao was reportedly downcast, feeling that 'the clouds were gathering around him, and this trip would bring him nothing good'.[14]

What precisely these worries were is not certain, but in the following months Gao started lobbying for power, hoping to oust Liu Shaoqi as number two. There were endless parties at his residence, as Gao tried to woo potential allies. He was in cahoots with Rao Shushi, the powerful leader who had controlled most of east China. He leaked a highly confidential list of potential members to be considered for a future Politburo. He toured the south to meet military leaders like Lin Biao, who was not on the list, trying to win their support in removing Liu Shaoqi as the Chairman's successor – with a delegation of twenty other regional leaders in tow.

Gao's political fortunes waned dramatically on 17 December after Chen Yun and Deng Xiaoping visited the Chairman to expose his underground activities. They had three lengthy meetings, joined by Zhou Enlai and Peng Dehuai. Mao spoke to other leaders in the following days. He met Gao alone on 23 December. The next day the Chairman assembled his inner circle and warned that there were two headquarters in Beijing, only one of which was under his command: 'In front of No. 8 Dongjiao Mingxiang [Gao's residence], there has been a stream of horses and carriages, while in front of the New China Gate [the formal entrance to the Zhongnanhai compound], it has been so quiet that one can catch sparrows.'[15]

Gao Gang was not named, but the message was unmistakable. Gao broke out in a sweat. Earlier that day, Moscow had announced that Beria and six of his henchmen had been executed after a six-day trial. One of Beria's six accomplices was Sergei Goglidze, who had been chief of security in the Far East. Years later, at the Lushan plenum in September 1959, Mao revealed that Moscow had betrayed a promise not to spy on China by sending Goglidze to collude with Gao Gang.[16]

Gao Gang was purged for 'treachery' and 'splitting the party'. At a tense meeting in February 1954, Zhou Enlai was put in charge of his prosecution in the Chairman's absence. Military security was strengthened around the residences of leaders who might have sided with Gao, while armed guards stood on alert in the conference hall. A tea boy who was allowed into the room was taken aback when he saw Zhou's face 'contorted into a picture of ferocity' as he dressed down Gao. Two days later Gao tried to kill himself with a gun taken from his bodyguard, but in a brief struggle between the two men the bullet missed its target. Half a year later, despite round-the-clock surveillance, he managed to swallow enough sleeping pills to commit suicide. Rao Shushi, for good measure, was also accused of forming an 'anti-party clique' and was locked away. A witch-hunt followed, as other leaders were denounced and packed off to the gulag for scheming against the party.[17]

Mao was the only one who benefited from the whole affair. Gao's purge sent a signal to the Russians that the Chairman would not tolerate any further Soviet meddling in Chinese affairs. Gao had also served the Chairman well as an attack dog against Liu Shaoqi. Liu himself was finally reinstated, but not before grovelling in a lengthy confession at a party convention at which he threw his weight enthusiastically behind the drive to collectivise the country. The road was paved for a Socialist High Tide.[18]

On 15 June 1953 the Chairman had announced that agriculture, commerce and industry would be fully socialised 'in ten to fifteen years', a position he called the General Line. But even as farmers were herded into co-operatives and ever greater amounts of food requisitioned under a grain monopoly introduced later that year, he wanted to whip up the pace of collectivisation. Under the co-operatives, farmers could still hide the grain they were supposed to sell to the state or pretend that the harvest had been

a failure. They still owned the land and were in charge of their own working schedules. What Mao wanted was socialism. And socialism meant
agricultural collectives in which the grain went straight from the fields into
the granaries, all of it under the control of the state. Stalin had accomplished this in the Russian countryside in the early 1930s, and that was
what the Chairman wished to achieve: 'This road travelled by the Soviet
Union is our very model.'[19]

It was not the road favoured by most villagers. As we saw in the preced-
ing chapter, the state took more food in 1954 than ever before, in absolute
numbers and as a proportion of the overall crop. Famine gripped large
parts of the countryside, made worse by a series of devastating floods. In
the autumn of 1954, farmers were once again destroying their tools, felling
trees and slaughtering their livestock. Some openly rebelled, as pitched
battles were fought between villages and the security forces. In the early
months of 1955, Deng Zihui, the man who had calculated that on average
farmers had a third less food than before liberation, started allowing some
co-operatives to disband. He did so as the head of a committee on agriculture, but not before obtaining Mao's full consent. Mao approved some
small adjustments, but he changed his mind in April, as he travelled south
and saw flourishing fields by the side of the railway from the window of his
personal train. In Shanghai he met with the mayor, a tall man with a bouf-
fant hairstyle who lived in awe of Mao. Ke Qingshi told the Chairman
how Deng Zihui had dampened enthusiasm for collectivisation among his
men. Back in Beijing Mao warned Deng to be careful with the dissolution
of co-operatives, 'otherwise you will have to make a self-criticism'.[20]

Over the following weeks Mao continued to attack 'negative attitudes'
towards collectivisation. On 17 May 1955, in a meeting with provincial
leaders in Hangzhou, he suggested that provinces should emulate each
other in the number of new co-operatives they set up. He dismissed
concerns about excessive grain requisitions: 'When it comes to the problem of grain, there is a trend inside and outside the party that says that the
situation is not right. That is wrong. The way I see it, the situation is right,
it's just that there are a few hiccups.' In the margin of a report on co-operatives in Guangxi province, he scribbled that 'Middle peasant claims of
hardship are all fake.' When news of forced procurements in a village in

Guangdong landed on his desk, he wrote: 'Two households who refused to sell their grain have been detained. The co-operatives are very good.'[21]

But the slowdown continued. Some provinces ignored the Chairman's instructions of 17 May and continued to take their cue from Deng Zihui. On 11 July Mao met with Deng and several other senior managers, trying to push for a target of 40 per cent of all villages to be turned into co-operatives by 1957. Deng would not yield. Mao spoke sarcastically: 'You consider yourself to be familiar with peasants but you are also very obstinate!' The meeting lasted for five hours. Still Deng refused to change his views. After the meeting, Mao confided to a colleague that Deng Zihui's ideas 'are so stubborn that they should be bombed by artillery'.[22]

A warning shot across Deng's bows came three weeks later. On 31 July 1955 Mao called for a new campaign to accelerate the transition to socialism, which would now take no more than three years. 'A hurricane in the new socialist mass movement will soon sweep across the villages throughout the country,' the Chairman announced. He added an ominous comment. 'Some of our comrades are tottering along like a woman with bound feet, constantly complaining about the others: too fast, too fast! They think that excessive quibbling, unwarranted complaints, endless worries and countless precepts are the correct policy for guiding the socialist mass movement in the rural areas. No! This is not the correct policy, it is a wrong policy.'[23]

The tone was set. A few weeks later, in the version circulated to a larger audience of party members, the term 'hurricane' was changed to 'high tide'. The chief opponent to the Socialist High Tide, Mao determined, was Deng Zihui, soon to be cast aside as a 'rightist opportunist'. Mao effectively terminated his career when speaking before the assembled heads of all provinces and large cities on 15 August. He condemned Deng's order to slow down the pace of collectivisation as a 'breach of party discipline', as he had issued orders 'without passing through the Centre, which is inappropriate'. 'Zihui has spoken,' Mao asked rhetorically, 'so is his personal decision binding or the one reached by the collective leadership?' The Chairman made clear his views on the road to socialism. 'A tottering pace in collectivisation suits the rich peasants, it conforms to the capitalist road [they want to take].' 'Socialism', he continued, 'must have a dictatorship, it will not work without it . . . This is a war: we are opening fire on peasants with private property. Socialism by half is half a war. This is a war that takes place among a population of 500 million people, it is a war led by the communist party.' Those landlords and rich peasants who sabotaged the co-operatives were counter-revolutionaries who should be sent to labour camps. Intellectuals like Liang Shuming, who had been branded a reactionary three years earlier for writing a letter describing the countryside as the ninth level of hell, were also counter-revolutionaries. In fact, all 'those who complain about the state of the countryside are peasants with excess grain: Liang Shuming, Peng Yihu – there are also those inside the party'.[24]

A high tide rose up and swept away most of the small, privately owned farms in the villages of China. The changes were dramatic. In July 1955 only about 14 per cent of the 120 million families in the countryside were members of a co-operative. Less than a year later, by May 1956, more than 90 per cent belonged to a co-operative. The majority of these were collectives. In the elementary co-operatives, launched in 1953, each farmer nominally shared his patch of land with other members, not unlike a shareholder in a corporation. Sometimes months could be spent trying to evaluate the value of the land and its potential production. Livestock, fishponds, tools and even trees were all assigned a value before being entered into a co-operative. Endless conflicts over these evaluations arose not only between cadres and the farmers, but also between villagers with different class labels. Everywhere, it seemed, poor peasants were discriminated against by those with more assets, as the dispossessed had little to contribute and everything to gain from the co-operatives. In some places bans were passed on blind people joining co-operatives. All these issues were solved by transforming the co-operatives into collectives resembling the farms in the Soviet Union. The collectives took the land from the farmers. They transformed the farmers into agricultural workers who received work points for their labour, which had to be carried out under the orders of a local cadre. This was the last stage of collectivisation. Farmers were now bonded labourers at the beck and call of the state.[25]

More restrictions on private property appeared in March 1956. Farmers who had been enrolled in the collectives had retained the right to cultivate a small plot for their own needs, in their spare time. Now the party reduced these parcels to 5 per cent or less of the overall surface.[26]

The effects of collectivisation on the economy were devastating. The total cropping area for food was reduced by 3 to 4 million hectares. Grain output failed to keep up with population growth. Slaughter of farm animals, which had been a continuous problem in the countryside since liberation, took on unprecedented proportions. And just as in the cities a campaign against counter-revolutionaries unfolded after the arrest of Hu Feng in June 1955, so in the countryside the High Tide unleashed a wave of terror, as local cadres arrested people by the hundreds of thousands. As Mao had made clear over the summer, it was a war on 'peasants with private property'.[27]

But the High Tide was not confined to the countryside alone. In 1956 most of industry and commerce were nationalised. This, too, was accomplished in the midst of terror. Among the party leaders toppled in the wake of the Gao Gang affair was Pan Hannian, the powerful deputy mayor of Shanghai. He and Yang Fan, the chief of security in Shanghai, were arrested in May 1955. Their purge sent shivers through the business community. 'If officials who had been as powerful as he and Yang Fan were unable to command security in the new regime, what chance had we?' wondered Robert Loh. It was well known in the business community that Pan Hannian and other senior officials who vanished overnight had been very close to industrialists like Rong Yiren and Guo Dihuo. They visited each other. They held parties at which musicians were hired, singing along to old tunes of Beijing opera. Pan, 'always well dressed and well mannered', played bridge with Rong. His wife came from a family of bankers closely linked to Guo. All this took place after Mao's attack on the bourgeoisie in 1952, when Rong had been reduced to tears on a public stage, forced to proclaim his shame over his family's exploitative past.[28]

With Pan Hannian and Yang Fan removed, Rong could no longer rely for security on his friendship with high officials. His hand shaking, he went through a photo album taking out every photo that included Pan and burning it. Many others like him were affected, in one way or another, by the removal of hundreds of thousands of people declared in 1955 to be 'counter-revolutionaries'. Just outside the city of Shanghai, in Jiangsu province, over 30,000 people were arrested and a further 15,000 purged for listening to short-wave radios, spreading rumours, hiding weapons, sabotaging work in factories or pasting counter-revolutionary slogans on walls. From top to bottom of the social scale, terror once again gripped the cities.[29]

The time had come for Rong Yiren and others to hand over the keys of their enterprises to the state. But the Chairman wanted them to do so voluntarily. So later in October 1955 he invited representatives of trade and commerce to a meeting in the Yihetang Hall in Zhongnanhai, soliciting their advice. He listened carefully, occasionally expressing concern, as Rong and others begged for a Socialist High Tide in industry. Rong gave a long speech, reviewing the history of his own textile mills, which would have been doomed had it not been for liberation. Whatever reservations he and others had harboured against state intervention in the following years had been completely misplaced. Rong was full of hope for the future of the People's Republic under the correct guidance of the Communist Party of China. There was only one snag. Rong felt frustrated by his inability to contribute more to the cause of socialism. 'Although my enterprise is already under joint private–state ownership, I am not satisfied. I want to go further on the road to ownership by the whole people . . . We want to walk towards communism.' More speeches by other captains of industry followed. Mao smiled. The occasion was followed by a dinner.[30]

Back in Shanghai, Rong, who was one of the leaders of the All-China Federation of Industry and Commerce, prepared his fellow industrialists for nationalisation. When they were ready, the Chairman came through Shanghai. To mark the occasion, Rong offered his Shenxin Number Nine Mill to the Chairman. Mao was delighted. Then came a meeting with eighty leading businessmen at the Sino-Soviet Friendship Hall, the gleaming new structure towering above all other buildings in Shanghai. This occasion, too, was full of gravitas, as the doors swung open and the Chairman slowly walked into the hall, his face beaming with a benevolent smile. The audience gasped, stiffening with surprise. 'He smiles often, and his expression is usually friendly and mild. He gives the impression of being a kindly, simple, honest peasant.' The Chairman puffed occasionally on his cigarette. The entrepreneurs were nervous, but Mao put them at their ease. 'Why don't you smoke?' he asked them calmly. 'It won't hurt you. Church-ill has smoked throughout his long life and he is in good health. In fact, the only man I know who doesn't smoke but has lived long is Chiang Kai-shek.' They all laughed. The tension dissipated. 'Now I have come from Beijing to seek your advice,' he went on. Many businessmen, he said, had been requesting that the socialist transformation of private enterprise should be hastened, lest the national bourgeoisie lag behind in progress towards socialism. Robert Loh, who was in the audience, describes what happened next: 'One by one, responding to the cues of the Chairman, the leading industrialists asked that socialism be introduced with the least delay possi-ble. They vied to outdo each other in flattery. Mao listened for two hours.'[31]

Mao left, promising to give serious thought to their opinions. But he warned them that he would have to consider carefully their best interests before deciding to accelerate the pace of nationalisation. A few weeks after the meeting, the authorities announced that the transformation to social-ism was to be accomplished not in six years, as most had anticipated, but in a mere six days. Shock teams were sent around the city to nationalise all industry, forcing businessmen to give up their enterprises and become members of the Federation of Industry and Commerce. Most did so out of fear, but they had to demonstrate wild enthusiasm in public. The reason for this was simple. Every entrepreneur knew that, once his property had been handed over to the state, his only means of livelihood would depend on the whim of the party. And many remembered the brutality of the campaign against them in 1952. This time an impression of joy was created: 'When we found that in the campaign we were to be heroes instead of victims, we were almost dizzy with relief. Thus some of our joy was genuine, although none of it came from "entering socialism" as the propaganda claimed.'[32]

A parade was staged, with banners, bands, drums, gongs, firecrackers and large crowds. 'Encouragement stations' were placed along the route of the march. As the entrepreneurs approached the Sino-Soviet Friendship Hall, the crowd started shouting slogans such as 'Salute the Patriotic National Capitalists Who are Marching Bravely towards Socialism' or 'Welcome our National Capitalist Friends to Join our Socialist Family'.

Young girls gave them flowers and refreshments. The entrepreneurs carried stacks of large red envelopes which contained their formal applications for full nationalisation. After they had presented these to Chen Yi, the mayor of Shanghai, delegations representing workers, peasants and students burst into the hall to congratulate the business community.

The vast fortunes that some families had accumulated over many generations vanished overnight. Small shopowners also lost everything, as they were organised into co-operatives. Throughout the country more than 800,000 owners of private enterprises, big or small, were voluntarily stripped of their property rights. All commerce and industry became functions of the state.

The government expropriated private enterprise under a so-called 'redemption-purchase policy', although the policy entailed neither purchase nor redemption. Only token compensation was offered, often about one-fifth of the real value of each property. Each owner was also to be credited 5 per cent per year of the assessed value of the property, although this interest would be paid for seven years only. Even this promise would not last.

Small shopowners were ruined. Many used their business premises as living quarters for themselves and their families, paying for their living expenses out of the till. But now their personal possessions were taken away by the state, sometimes down to their pots and pans and even the baby's crib. The compensation was barely sufficient to pay for cigarettes. Those who were lucky were allowed to continue running their shops as state employees at 20 yuan a month. But many now faced starvation. If they tried to find a job elsewhere, they discovered that they were classified as capitalists, meaning that they were denied the benefits that gave ordinary workers some semblance of security. As in 1952, a wave of suicides followed, although this time the authorities intervened quickly. Many younger entrepreneurs were taken from their families and sent to the border wastelands to work on socialist projects. Older men received some financial assistance from a mutual fund, set up with the money from the more solvent firms. Many of the wealthier businessmen were paid in government bonds. They were non-negotiable, and when they became due, the principal and accrued interest were reinvested in more bonds.

But in most cases the owners of big industries were not concerned with compensation. They wanted a job from the state. Many were relatively well off, and some even retained their titles as managers or department heads. A select few fared particularly well, having courted the leadership and taken the lead in offering their holdings to the state. They were appointed to prestigious committees, sometimes even sent to serve in the capital. One such was Rong Yiren, who had publicly donated his whole enterprise to the state. Soon Mao promoted him to become deputy mayor of Shanghai. Although the regime would catch up with most of them during the Cultural Revolution, Rong survived the tumult thanks to the protection of Zhou Enlai, living in Zhongnanhai as an adviser to the textile ministry.[33]

12

The Gulag

The lives of millions were swallowed up by a vast array of prison camps scattered across the length and breadth of the country. This network is sometimes referred to as the *laogai*, an abbreviation for *laodong gaizao*, or 'reform through labour'. Its origins date back to the early days of the communist party, when prisoners were put to work to help meet the cost of their incarceration. Like everyone else, they were also supposed to reform themselves through endless study sessions and indoctrination meetings.

Already during the civil war, as huge stretches of the countryside were liberated, there were too few prisons to keep up with a swelling number of convicts. Temples, guilds, schools and factories were requisitioned. Chain gangs were used on public works, from road maintenance to dyke construction. Large labour camps, many of them holding thousands of inmates, sprang up across the countryside. In the areas of Shandong controlled by the communist party, almost every district boasted a camp, each holding up to 3,000 inhabitants. The prisoners were made to reclaim wasteland, grow wheat, extract minerals or make bricks. Many did not have shoes, even in the depth of winter, while hunger was pervasive. Those who tilled the fields supplemented their diet with weeds like dandelions, while a few lucky ones caught frogs.[1]

The fall of the cities did nothing to alleviate the pressure. The nationalists had a sophisticated network of prisons, many built and run according to the highest standards current in Europe and the United States at the time. But they never had more than 90,000 convicts, as they used fines, short sentences, general amnesties, remission of sentence and parole to keep people out of gaol. An extra 120 penitentiaries formerly run by the nationalists barely dented the shortfall in prison capacity.[2]

Unlike its predecessors, the new regime did not hesitate to imprison people for a very long time, often for the slightest misdemeanour. Su Wencheng was sentenced to fifteen years in Beijing for robbing graves in December 1949. Others in the capital faced a spell of five to ten years for stealing a pair of trousers or a bicycle. These were common criminals, but there was a growing list of political crimes which seemed to warrant a term of ten years or more. The catch-all term of 'counter-revolutionary' was common, covering just about anything from listening to foreign radio to slacking at work, but other charges included having worked for military organisations or civil organisations in the previous regime and betraying the nation or the party.[3]

The prison population reached crisis point soon after the Great Terror was launched in October 1950. Within half a year well over a million people were languishing in gaol. A whole new incarceration system had to be devised. In Hubei, where tens of thousands were held, progressively larger camps appeared at every level of the administrative hierarchy, stretching from 150 inmates in each county and 500 in each large city to a thousand for entire regions, while at the top the provincial security bureau 'administers ten labour camps for more than 10,000 inmates'. In Guangxi, where a ferocious campaign unfolded, more than 80,000 people were behind bars. So crowded was the county gaol in Xingye that the standard width of an inmate's sleeping space was no more than 20 centimetres. In Pingnan they were not allowed to wash more than once a week, despite soaring temperatures and high humidity. The stench was repulsive. Nine out of ten inmates suffered from skin disease. Over a hundred died each month.[4]

So dire were the facilities in some improvised gaols in Sichuan that prisoners excreted in their trousers, their bottoms covered in maggots. In the county prison in Chongqing, a fifth of the inmates died within half a year. Most of the others were sick. The head of the Public Security Bureau refused to improve the situation. His motto was that 'it is better for prisoners to die than for them to flee'. All over south-west China thousands of prisoners were buried every month. In the north, which had been under communist control for much longer, the situation was no better. In Cangxian county, Hebei, a third of all inmates were sick, leading to dozens of deaths. Scabies, lice and cockroaches were common. Here too the air was so rank that guards refused to approach the prisoners. Quentin Huang, a bishop who refused to relinquish his faith, was locked up in a wooden cage with eighteen other convicts. It had bars about 10 centimetres in diameter each and about 5 centimetres apart. The door was locked and chained. The cage was about 2 by 2.5 metres in dimension, situated at the dark, damp end of a long room. The other end of the room was used as quarters for the guards who watched the prisoners. 'Neglect and delay, particularly with diarrhoea cases, soon turned a part of the wooden cage into a natural latrine, filthy and foul smelling with lice, fleas, and hungry rats, both big and small, running hither and thither even in the daytime, from the farther corners of the muddy walls just next to the wooden cage.'[5]

In the spring of 1951 the leadership decided to alleviate the pressure by putting more prisoners to work, using them to build roads, dig reservoirs or bring fallow land under cultivation. Mao even opined that if the executions stopped at two per thousand and everyone above that quota were sentenced to a life of hard labour, this would amount to a formidable workforce. 'But of course it is troublesome to carry out these ideas in practice, it is not quite as straightforward as killing the lot,' he mused. Nonetheless, taking the Soviet Union as his inspiration, he proposed a quota of 0.5 per thousand, or 300,000 prisoners.[6]

Luo Ruiqing, as head of public security, was tasked with the logistics of the operation. It soon ran into difficulties. Transporting a third of a million people all over the country was no small feat, even for a one-party state. And once they arrived at their respective destinations, often by lorry, sometimes by train, the inmates had to be housed, fed and clothed. Of the 60,000 victims earmarked for hard labour in the ore, coal and tin mines spread across the mountains in Yunnan, barely 3,000 could be accommodated. Plans to deploy a docile labour force of 200,000 on irrigation projects were even more challenging, as very few inmates could be effectively supervised in the open.[7]

But the new regime was not one to abandon a plan that looked good on paper merely because it ran into difficulties on the ground, so a constellation of labour camps, stretching across the country's most inhospitable border regions, began taking shape. In Manchuria there existed a vast, swampy expanse infected with mosquitoes called the Great Northern Wilderness. Further west, in Qinghai, labour camps appeared in a bleak expanse pockmarked by salt marshes and surrounded by arid mountains. In the south there was a string of salt, tin and uranium mines, while brick factories, state farms and irrigation projects appeared almost everywhere. By the end of 1951 more than 670,000 people had been sent to these camps (by now the total prison population had doubled to 2 million). Many inmates were exhausted even before they arrived. Hard labour finished off many of them. In a salt mine in Hebei, prisoners slept on rough mats strewn directly on a humid floor. There was not even enough water to drink, let alone food, and a hundred died each month, many from dysentery. Elsewhere prisoners died of cold. In Sichuan the inmates worked along the railway without any trousers in the middle of the winter. Fourteen from a unit of 300 froze to death. In Yan'an, the erstwhile red capital, close to 200 died of cold. In the tin mines of Lianxian, Guangdong, prisoners were so badly treated that one in three committed suicide or died of disease within a year. And despite all the work they were forced to perform, each prisoner still cost the state far more than the centrally allocated quota had anticipated. On top of this, more than 1.2 million inmates did not contribute to their own upkeep.[8]

Over the following years the overall population in the gulag did not increase substantially, hovering around 2 million, although an ever greater proportion of prisoners was forced to work. For every man or woman who died of disease or maltreatment, another one entered a camp. By 1955 more than 1.3 million people were at work, contributing over 700 million yuan in industrial products as well as 350,000 tons of grain to the state. They came from all walks of life, as the gulag became a microcosm of the wider population outside the camps. On the lowest rung of the social hierarchy were poor farmers, sent to the gulag because they could not repay their loans to the state. At the top were more than 3,000 doctors, engineers and technical experts, rounded up in 1955 as part of the hunt for counter-revolutionary cliques. In between were priests, monks, teachers, students, journalists, entrepreneurs, clerks, pedlars, fishermen, musicians, bankers, prostitutes and soldiers.[9]

Nine out of ten were political prisoners. Many were not formally

sentenced for several years after their arrest. The case of Duan Kewen, who
had worked for the nationalists, took two years. He wore chains for five
years, even as he worked in a brick factory. He was hardly unique. By 1953
roughly 300,000 new cases were brought every year, even though there were
only 7,000 judges in the whole country. The backlog amounted to an estimated 400,000 to 500,000 cases. This did not include many farmers who
were sent to prison without a trial at the village level. And when a court hearing came, the hastily convened People's Tribunals dispensed rough justice. A
powerful inspectorate, set up by the party, examined thousands of cases and
concluded that only 90 per cent were 'correct'. Tens of thousands of victims
ended up in the gulag for no reason, even by the standards of the regime
itself, as 'innocent people are arrested, imprisoned or shot, families are
broken up and lives are destroyed'. In some counties where random checks
were carried out, for instance in Gansu and Ningxia provinces, as many as
28 per cent of inmates had been wrongly accused of a crime.[10]

Their experiences varied enormously, if only because the sprawling
gulag itself was so diverse, but by all accounts the inmates lived in fear of
violence. Next to the wooden cage used to lock up Quentin Huang was a
pile of ropes, shackles and handcuffs. Some victims spent years in chains,
for instance Duan Kewen and Harriet Mills. Many tightening devices
were also very heavy, digging into the skin and lacerating the flesh. Beatings were common, administered with bamboo sticks, leather belts, heavy
clubs or bare knuckles. Sleep deprivation was widely used. Other forms of
torture were more ingenious, and came with poetic titles drawn from
traditional literature. 'Dipping the Duckling into the Water' meant
suspending a victim upside down with bound hands. 'Sitting on the Tiger
Bench' consisted of fastening somebody's knees to a small iron bench with
his hands cuffed behind the back. Bricks were inserted under the tied legs,
causing them to bend unnaturally, eventually breaking at the knees. There
was an extensive repertoire of torture methods, as ever more ingenious
ways of degrading other human beings were developed. In Beijing some
victims had their feet shackled to the window until they fainted. Salt was
rubbed into their wounds. Some had to squat on the bucket used for
excrement and hold a spittoon for hours without moving. Others were
sodomised. In the south the guards sometimes built crude electric machines

with a battery in a wooden box and a wheel on the outside. Two cords were attached to the victim's hands or other body parts and then the wheel was turned to generate an electric shock.[11]

The list could go on. But by all accounts the most dreaded aspect of incarceration was not the frequent beatings, the hard labour or even the grinding hunger. It was thought reform, referred to by one victim as a 'carefully cultivated Auschwitz of the mind'. As Robert Ford, an English radio operator, put it after a four-year spell in prison, 'When you're being beaten up, you can turn into yourself and find a corner of your mind in which to fight the pain. But when you're being spiritually tortured by thought reform, there's nowhere you can go. It affects you at the most profound, deepest levels and attacks your very identity.' The self-criticism and indoctrination meetings lasted for hours on end, day in, day out, year after year. And unlike those on the outside, once the group discussions were over, the others were still in the same cell. They were encouraged to examine, question and denounce each other. Sometimes they had to take part in brutal struggle meetings, proving on whose side they stood by beating a suspect. 'By the time you got through such a meeting you would, if you were a conscientious person at all, suffer terribly mentally and groan for days. Silence and distress were the outcome.' Every bit of human dignity was stripped away as victims tried to survive by killing their former selves. Wang Tsunming, a nationalist officer captured in 1949, came to the conclusion that thought reform was nothing less than the 'physical and mental liquidation of oneself by oneself'. Those who resisted the process committed suicide. Those who survived it renounced being themselves.[12]

While the total population in the gulag stood at roughly 2 million in the early years of the regime, it ballooned in 1955. That year another purge of counter-revolutionaries was launched, reaching far beyond the Hu Feng case. More than 770,000 people found themselves under arrest. It was more than the existing labour camps could bear. A whole new dimension was added to the world of incarceration, swallowing up 300,000 new inmates. It was called 're-education through labour', or *laojiao*. In contrast to 'reform through labour', or *laogai*, it dispensed with judicial procedures altogether, holding any undesirable element indefinitely – until deemed fully 're-educated'. These camps were organised not by the Ministry of Public

Security, but by the police and even the local militia. This shadow world formally received the seal of approval in January 1956 and was designed for those who did not qualify for a term of hard labour yet were not deemed worthy of liberty either. People could now be arrested and disappear without any form of trial. Its use would expand dramatically after August 1957.[13]

Not every suspect was sent to the gulag. One response to prison congestion was to place convicts under the 'supervision of the masses' (*guanzhi*). This meant being at the beck and call of local cadres, who controlled every aspect of the lives of these victims. They served as scapegoats and were paraded through the villages during every major campaign, in some cases as many as two or three hundred times even before the Cultural Revolution started in 1966. They were forced to carry out the most demeaning jobs, from carrying manure to working on public roads. They were fed scraps of food or mere leftovers.

The numbers were substantial. By 1952, in parts of Sichuan, over 3 per cent of the population ended up under some form of judicial control. This was the case, for instance, for several villages in Qingshen county. The victims included anyone considered to be a social misfit, from opium smokers and petty thieves to mere vagrants passing through. In Shandong up to 1.4 per cent of villagers were placed under supervision, the majority without any form of approval by the Public Security Bureau. In Changwei county, supervision was used 'randomly and chaotically'. The local militia locked up anybody deemed to be troublesome. One example was a man who made the mistake of talking back to a cadre.

Those caught up in the punitive wheels of the system were routinely tortured. Some were forced to kneel on broken stones, others had to bend forward in the so-called aeroplane position. A few had to go through mock executions. In Yidu entire families were put under surveillance; some of their daughters were raped. Extortion was rife. 'Similar examples are too numerous to be enumerated,' concluded the authors of an investigative report. Luo Ruiqing himself wrote of the pain and humiliation with which the system was shot through. In You county, he stressed, every breach of discipline was met with punishment, whether speaking at work or being absent from work for more than an hour. Some were beaten, others were stripped of their trousers, a few were given *yin* and *yang* haircuts, as one half of the head was shaved.[14]

In the cities too, people could be placed under public supervision, although this was relatively rare. In one case a graduate of Stanford University who worked as dean of a law college in Shanghai was picked up one morning during the Great Terror of 1951. The only charges brought against him were that he was a 'lackey of the rich and an oppressor of the poor' and that he had a brother in the Taiwanese government. For this he was sentenced to be kept under surveillance for three years.

He was made into a janitor at the trade association he had previously headed. He was paid 18 yuan a month and could live only by selling his household furnishings. His employers addressed him only to give him orders and wrote weekly reports on his behavior. He himself had to go once a week to the police with a written expression of his gratitude to the party for the leniency of the people's justice; if his gratitude was not expressed in terms sufficiently abject, he was made to rewrite his paper until it was found acceptable. No one else dared speak to him, let alone try to help or comfort him.

After sixteen months he threw himself into a river.[15]

How many found themselves in a similar situation? Luo Ruiqing estimated that some 740,000 people were under public supervision in 1953, but from his desk in Beijing he could barely capture the extent to which people were detained locally without ever being reported to the higher authorities. A glimpse of this underground world comes from an investigation report on Sichuan filed in 1952. It noted that in four villages in Xinjin county ninety-six people were formally placed under supervision, but a further 279 found themselves in the same type of bonded labour without any form of judicial process. Nobody knows how many other people across the country were detained by local cadres, but the system must have added at least another 1 to 2 million to the captive population.[16]

With collectivisation in the countryside, the difference between a prisoner sent to a labour camp, a convict placed under supervision and a free farmer tilling his own plot became less and less obvious. This was particularly true with conscripted labour. Right from the start the regime had little hesitation in rounding up villagers to work on large projects carried out for the greater good. And from the beginning this spelt misery for those unfortunate enough to be drafted. In Suqian county in 1950 dozens of ordinary people died of cold, hunger and exhaustion, forced to work outside in subzero temperatures clothed in rags. Hunger was widespread, as they were fed mere scraps.[17]

These were not the teething pains of a new regime unaccustomed to organising corvée labour. The longer in power, the bigger the vision, as massive projects spread hunger and misery to millions of conscripted labourers. One of the biggest plans was to tame the Huai River, which flowed through the northern plain from south Henan towards north Jiangsu, where it joined the Yangzi River. It was notoriously vulnerable to flooding. By the winter of 1949, hundreds of thousands of paupers were sent to work along the Huai River. Instead of draining the waterlogged areas to make sure that the flow of the river could scour away its load of silt, they were compelled to build dykes and embankments. The plan had been conceived by party officials who had never even set foot in the area. When the snow melted the following spring, the river flooded some 130,000 hectares in the region around Suxian county alone, creating a lot of misery.[18]

After the flooding had been blamed on nature, Mao announced a programme to 'Harness the Huai River' with dams on the upper reaches and upstream reservoirs for storing floodwater. The project would last several decades. People were drafted by the hundreds of thousands, toiling in the icy water bare-legged, or lugging wet sand and earth in baskets suspended on shoulder-poles. They were housed far away from their homes, in tiny sheds built of bamboo, reed or corn stalks. Many had to travel for days to reach the river, carrying with them their own tools, clothes, stoves, quilts and mats. In 1951 the alarm was raised, as local cadres conscripted neighbouring farmers without any regard for agricultural production. When rain followed snow, week after week, food reserves quickly ran out, pushing many of the villages along the Huai River into famine.[19]

By 1953 the situation was even worse. Few farmers were given adequate food. Many survived on a watery concoction dished out three times a day. Some were fed nothing but sorghum, a monotonous diet that caused excruciating constipation, so much so that 'blood is everywhere in the toilets'. In Suxian county some young workers lay prostrate on the ground, crying with hunger, while others fought each other for an extra portion. Several wrote letters to their families pleading for help: 'Think of a way to come and rescue a crowd of hungry ghosts!' Some hanged themselves in despair. Discipline was relentless, all the more since many of the conscripted villagers were outcasts, classified as family members of 'landlords', 'rich farmers', 'counter-revolutionaries' and 'criminals'. Some cadres pinned red and white strips on the workers, distinguishing 'glorious' from 'shameless' ones. Those who spent more than three minutes in the toilet were punished. Tai Shuyi, a ruthless leader, forced his team to work throughout the night on several occasions. Within three days, over a hundred people were spitting blood. Accidents were common all along the river, as dykes subsided, structures collapsed and dynamite was exploded without proper control, killing hundreds. Tens of thousands were seriously ill but received no medical treatment. Those who could tried to escape. In some places, for instance the reservoir at Nanwan in Henan province, 3,000 of a total labour force of 10,000 managed to abscond.[20]

The situation was no better elsewhere. In Hubei, the villagers rounded up to work on a dam were not even provided with makeshift huts. They slept outside in the bitterly cold winter. One in twenty became severely ill, some dying as cadres just stood by and seemed 'not to care'. Up further north in Zhouzhi county, a region of Shaanxi covered in mountain forests, a massive water-conservancy project compelled close to a million people to work for the state in 1953. Poverty was everywhere, forcing some families to give away their children as 'the majority of workers lack food'. It was a taste of the future. In 1958, during the Great Leap Forward, villagers would be herded into giant People's Communes where food was distributed according to merit. Hundreds of millions would be forced to work on giant water-conservancy projects far from home, as the country became one enormous labour camp.[21]

The boundaries between the free and the unfree were also porous in the most remote border region of the country, namely the north-west. In 1949, as Chapter 3 explained, hundreds of thousands of demobilised soldiers, petty thieves, beggars, vagrants and prostitutes were sent to help develop and colonise the Muslim belt which ran through Gansu, Ningxia, Qinghai and Xinjiang. The trend continued unabated in the following years, as batch after batch of migrants was sent from the interior provinces, often alongside convoys of political prisoners. Migration was supposed to be voluntary, but as with everything else in the People's Republic, quotas had to be met. All too often tales of piped water, electricity and tables laden with fresh fruit enticed credulous people seeking a better life. The reality was a far cry from the propaganda. After a long train journey followed by several days cramped in the back of a lorry, they were confronted with misery. The first contingents of settlers had to dig holes in the ground and sleep on rough mats on the floor, sheltered from the sand storms by a sheet of tarpaulin. Work consisted of levelling dunes, cutting shrubbery, planting trees and digging irrigation ditches. Many escaped and returned home. As rumours spread about the dire conditions in the north-west, the people most at risk of relocation – the poor, the unemployed and the politically undesirable – tried to avoid face-to-face encounters with the cadres in charge of recruitment. In Beijing they placed children at key intersections to warn them of their arrival. Those who genuinely volunteered or could not avoid relocation found themselves in holding centres without beds, sleeping on straw laid over a moist earthen floor. Some cried themselves to sleep, others absconded in the dead of night.[22]

By 1956 four out of five migrants to Gansu province faced hunger, with insufficient food to tide them over the spring. Their clothes were threadbare, while some children had no trousers and walked to school barefoot. There was no money to buy salt, edible oil, vegetables or even a needle to patch up their rags. The noble idea of reclaiming land from the desert ran into problems, as the sand was poor in nutrients. It never rained enough to grow much besides some wheat and a few vegetables. Li Shuzhen, who wormed her way back to the capital, wrote to the People's Congress: 'The government there only looks after you for three months, then it washes its hands of you. After the fields were ruined by hail, my father died of hunger.' Liu Jincai also complained: 'I spent more than two years there and did not even earn enough to buy a pair of cotton trousers.' And if that was not enough, the local population also discriminated against the migrants. Sometimes tensions over scarce resources degenerated into fist-fights, as migrants were beaten unconscious. They were aliens in a foreign land, unable to speak the local language. So bad was the situation across the entire region that in December 1956 the minister of domestic affairs temporarily halted all migration.[23]

But one region was a success, and that was Xinjiang. After its annexation by Peng Dehuai in 1949, over 100,000 soldiers from the First Field Army stayed behind to prevent any secession. They cultivated the soil and protected the border. In 1954 they became part of a large development corporation called the Xinjiang Production and Construction Corps. Tens of thousands of demobilised soldiers, political prisoners and migrants from the east joined its ranks, building irrigation canals, roads and telephone lines. They planted walls of trees to protect their camps from the sand. They grew cotton and wheat in giant collective farms around the desert oases. Soon the Corps developed into the biggest landowner and largest employer in the region. Its tentacles spread everywhere, operating factories, roads, canals, railways, mines, forests and reservoirs. It had its own schools, hospitals, laboratories, police force and courts – not to mention a vast network of prisons and labour camps. It was a state within the state. In 1949 the Chinese accounted for no more than 3 per cent of the local population. Within half a decade the Corps had created 'an army of Han Chinese colonists'. Few settlers were volunteers, least of all the political prisoners, but all were better off than the Uighurs and Muslims around them. Penal exile in Xinjiang was the foundation of one of the most successful programmes of colonisation in modern history.[24]

PART FOUR

BACKLASH (1956–57)

13

Behind the Scenes

By 1956 China stood proud and triumphant. War was a distant memory. Inflation had been brought under control. Unemployment, seemingly, had been solved. Industry was churning out ever increasing amounts of iron and steel. The international prestige of the regime was at a zenith. No longer was China the sick man of Asia, as the People's Republic had fought the Americans to a standstill in the Korean War. And after the death of Stalin, no other communist leader enjoyed more prestige than Mao, the philosopher, poet and statesman in Beijing. Such was his standing that the Chairman increasingly assumed the mantle of leadership for developing countries around the world.

Ostensibly, the regime stood for values that had universal appeal: freedom, equality, peace, justice and democracy (albeit under the dictatorship of the proletariat). It promised security from hunger and want, with jobs and housing for all. Unlike liberal democracy, it proposed a unique social experiment to achieve these ideals, as people would merge into a classless society of plenty for all in which the state would wither away. Like the Soviet Union after the Bolshevik Revolution, the regime excelled at mesmerising very different audiences on the road to utopia. It offered economic equality to the discontents of capitalism. It whispered freedom to those liberals outraged by authoritarian governments. 'It flaunts patriotism before the nationalist, dedication before the devout, and revenge before the oppressed.' Communism, in short, was all things to all men.[1]

The People's Republic widely advertised its success. It built up a glowing image with a profusion of statistics. Everything, apparently, was measurable in the New China, from the latest coal output and grain production to the number of square metres of housing built since liberation. Whatever the object of measurement, the trend was always upwards, even though the figures were sometimes rather vague. Percentages, for instance, were always favoured. Lump sums were not broken down. Categories were rarely defined, indices often came without items, and price base periods shifted erratically. Sometimes they vanished altogether. Cost and labour seemed irrelevant, and were excluded from accounting. The ways in which the data were collected and the methods used to produce the official statistics were never published. Sceptical statisticians found huge discrepancies. But dreamers around the world were dazzled. In every domain, it seemed, the People's Republic was surging forward.[2]

Besides mere numbers, the very imagery of revolution had romantic appeal. There were mass rallies on Tiananmen every year, as the regime paraded its resources in iron, steel, flesh and blood. Tanks and rocket launchers rumbled by, with fighter jets screaming overhead, as a never-ending procession of drummers, dancers and workers waved olive branches or released doves and coloured balloons. 'Even the tiny Mongol ponies of the Cavalry trotted precisely in step, like an articulated clock-work toy,' noted one foreign visitor in sheer amazement, standing in the midst of an ecstatic crowd. And a sea of red could be seen even outside mass parades in Beijing. Scarlet, the symbol of a revolution for basic rights and equality, was everywhere, on banners, flags, scarves, ties and armbands. The iconography of socialism was simple and enduring, with its sheaths of wheat, its rising sun in gold and its ubiquitous red star. Workers and peasants, with raised hands or clenched fists, seemed almost to jump out of the posters so liberally plastered on the walls of many buildings. What could be more evocative of progress than the image of a young girl with pigtails proudly driving a tractor through the fields? When Cai Shuli and thirty other graduates from a high school in Beijing heard of a young girl named Liu Ying, resolutely steering a tractor through the fields of the Great Northern Wilderness, their imaginations were so fired that they volunteered to go north: 'The stirring in our hearts is impossible to describe,' she wrote to Mayor Peng Zhen, 'and we have decided to offer our youth to the Great Northern Wilderness to reclaim the rich soil together with comrade Liu Ying.'[3]

There was also a flow of reports, statements and announcements from the leadership, not to mention the writings of the Chairman himself. These could be impenetrable to outsiders, replete as they were with Marxist-Leninist jargon, not to mention cryptic hints at changes in the power structure of the communist party. But they also conveyed a sense of purpose and commitment, pledging better wages for workers, promising more homes for the disabled or resolving to fight for the dignity of ethnic minorities. There was no end to statements of good intent, accompanied by ever more decrees, rules and regulations that would nudge China forward on the road to communism. It was all about the world in the making, not the world as it was. It was a world of plans, blueprints and models. Even more prominent than the official literature were the many slogans intended to galvanise a broader audience. Mao himself was a master of powerful, stirring quotations that found their way into every household in China, whether it was 'Women Hold up Half the Sky', 'Revolution is Not a Dinner Party' or 'Imperialism is a Paper Tiger'. His was the motto 'Serve the People', calling out from posters and placards everywhere, the white characters written in a flamboyant hand against a red background.

Like Cai Shuli, who pledged to help reclaim the Great Northern Wilderness, plenty of party members looked past the misery of the present to see a radiant future beckoning ahead. Dan Ling, who had joined the party as a schoolboy just before liberation, was still imbued with the idealism of youth several years later, despite his doubts over some of the campaigns against enemies of the state. Li Zhisui, now working as the Chairman's doctor, had also grown wiser since setting foot on shore with his wife in 1949, but he remained an ardent believer. Even outside the privileged ranks of the party, the whole idea of 'building socialism' was taken to heart, especially by a younger generation that went through the new schools set up after liberation. A sense of adventure combined with boundless idealism when young students volunteered to go off as pioneers to border regions or distant irrigation projects. The key to understanding the appeal of communism, despite the grim reality on the ground, lay in the fact that it allowed so many followers to believe that they were participants in an historic process of transformation, contributing to something much bigger and better than themselves, or anything that had come before. In a world full of workers who set new records and soldiers who used their bodies to block enemy fire, everyone was encouraged to become a hero. The propaganda machine ceaselessly glorified heroic workers, peasants and soldiers, held up as so many models for emulation.[4]

Just as there were model workers and soldiers, there were model schools, hospitals, factories, offices, prisons, homes and co-operatives. These offered a glimpse of the future, a vision of the world to be. By 1956 thousands of foreign visitors were carefully selected by the regime and taken on guided tours to visit these showcase sites, all expenses paid, surrounded by minders who controlled their every movement. One guest wrote that 'one gets to feel something like an infant in transit from one country to another and being passed from one hand to another'. But many were happy to be herded around, all too ready to help dispel the misinformation and hostile stereotypes that existed abroad about communism in the People's Republic.[5]

Foreign pilgrims were allowed to interview only the most loyal and tested party members. Rong Yiren, who could no longer rely on the protection of senior leaders after the purge of Pan Hannian in Shanghai, decided to join the show. It was one way to become indispensable to the regime. He turned himself into a showcase industrialist, paid to conjure up a world of illusions. Foreign visitors to his home would find his wife contentedly knitting a sweater. Two dogs frisked about merrily in the garden, where a nurse in uniform could be seen wheeling a baby across the lawn. 'On a wall, a crucifix discreetly suggested freedom of worship. The bookshelves showed Shakespeare as well as Marx.' In an adjacent room his daughter practised the piano. Most of the conversation was about his garden, as if he had nothing more to worry about than the correct fertiliser for his peonies. One French visitor who witnessed this touching tableau was truly awed: 'I have never seen a more contented family,' she said. Rong had an answer to every question. When pressed and asked how he could be so happy, he would purse his lips and consider the question gravely: 'I *was* worried at first,' he would confess. 'When the Communists liberated Shanghai, we were apprehensive, if not for our lives, at least for our property.' Then he would look his guest in the eye, his voice ringing with sincerity. 'But the Communists have kept their promise. We have come to realise that the Chinese Communists never deceive people.'[6]

Throughout the country, countless shows were put on for the benefit of foreign journalists, visiting statesmen, ranking leaders, student groups and, of course, the Chairman himself. As hundreds of Buddhist temples were destroyed, large sums of money were lavished on a handful of structures where showpiece monks could lecture about a religious renaissance in the New China. In model factories equipped with the latest technology, workers were carefully picked and trained to illustrate the triumphs of the planned economy. Around all major cities, model villages were selected to showcase the benefits of collectivisation. Everywhere, or so it appeared, people worked hard and were enthusiastic, never tiring of praising the party. In the propaganda state nothing was as it seemed.[7]

China was a theatre. Even outside the tourist circuit, people were required to smile. When farmers were asked to surrender a greater share of their crop, they had to do so enthusiastically, with fanfare. When shopkeepers were required to hand over their assets to the state, they had to do so voluntarily, with beaming faces. A smile, in China as in other parts of Asia, did not always mean joy; it could convey embarrassment or hide pain and anger. But, more importantly, nobody wished to be accused of dragging their feet. Most people depended on the state for their livelihood. And all had spent countless hours in study sessions since liberation, learning how to parrot the party line, provide the correct answers and create the illusion of consent. Ordinary people may not all have been great heroes, but many were great actors.

Huge resources were poured into this giant Potemkin village. One lasting result was the immense strides made in transportation. A network of communications tied the country together as never before. Highways reached out to every destination, many of them paved by conscript labour and chain gangs. Trains ran on time, as exclusive sleeping berths with dining facilities delivered foreign guests and leading officials to their destinations. Many cities were spruced up, the drains cleaned and the roads swept regularly.

In the capital splendid public buildings shot up like mushrooms after the rain, rising far above a sea of grey roofs of courtyard houses and the rose-red walls of the imperial city. Ministries, institutes and museums appeared in the centre and on the outskirts, some with vast curving roofs of glazed tiles, others with plain flat ones, but all inspired by a Russian predilection for monumental proportions. In one district alone, dozens of buildings sprang up, seemingly within the space of a few months, from the Institute of Aeronautics and the Oil Institute to the Institute of Metallurgy, all with spacious forecourts and extensive wings. Outside Xizhimen, the north-western gate of the ancient city wall, a Soviet Union Exhibition Hall soon appeared. Rumours circulated about the amount of pure gold used to gild its towering spire. In the heart of the capital, Tiananmen Square was cleared of many of its ancient structures to make way for the annual parades. Most of the city wall that hindered traffic was dismantled.[8]

Big, tangible symbols of power also went up in other cities, as the machinery of the central government was duplicated at the provincial level, complete with all the showcase buildings and prestige projects that accompanied an expanding state. In Chongqing, a sprawling city built on hills often veiled in drizzle and mist, a beautiful concert hall was erected in the middle of the People's Cultural Park. A large sports stadium soon followed, as well as an Assembly Hall. A huge and ornate building with three circular tiers of green-glazed roof, the latter cost an estimated 100,000 yuan per year to maintain, although it was apparently seldom used. Many other new buildings stood empty, as Chongqing was no longer the capital of Sichuan. Further north, in Zhengzhou, an entirely new city seemed to rise out of the wheat fields, far away from the old town, with a broad boulevard flanked by large administrative buildings, all with their own gardens and dormitories. In Lanzhou, the arid capital of Gansu, new government offices appeared for several kilometres on either side of the Yangzi, almost doubling the area of the city with new institutes, hospitals, factories and residential blocks. The new streets, built by pick and shovel, were wide enough to have lanes on both sides for slower-moving traffic. They were straight as an arrow, cutting through older thoroughfares without any regard for the past.[9]

Everywhere the speed of construction was startling. The leadership was in a rush to catch up with the future. As a result, many buildings were erected in a 'haphazard, wild manner', without much planning. As local leaders tried to outdo each other in building ever larger facilities, many new structures came without running water and sewerage facilities. Where cities were built outside the centre, as in Zhengzhou, the cost of building roads and services sank a hole in the budget. And in the haste to catapult the country into communism, the most basic steps such as surveys of the local topography, the composition of the soil and the distribution of water were ignored, resulting in costly errors. In some cases newly built roads were ceaselessly torn up, as different local authorities became locked in legal battles to extract compensation from each other. Even in Beijing, the foundations of entire factories subsided, while load-bearing beams warped and split. The waste was enormous. In the empire of central planning, nothing seemed planned.[10]

As a result, even some centrepieces of the Potemkin project, designed to awe and woo foreign guests, were deeply flawed. Behind a gleaming façade of socialist modernity lay a ramshackle world of shoddy construction. The Qianmen Hotel in Beijing was one of three new venues built to host foreign delegations. By 1956 it was a favourite haunt of goodwill visitors. The taps dripped, leaving stains in sinks and tubs. Water in the toilets ran constantly, sometimes overflowing the tanks. Doors did not fit properly, light bulbs flickered, windows refused to close.[11]

As vast amounts of money were ploughed into prestige buildings, the housing of ordinary people was neglected – with the exception of model dormitories built for show, for instance student accommodation at Peking University or the People's Mansion in Xi'an. Factories and dormitories were jumbled together, often with no regard for basic standards of hygiene. Local people often complained that 'the dead and the living are being continuously evicted'. Much housing was drab, built like military barracks, with row after row of low units, all identical and more often than not without any leisure facilities. It was badly constructed too. In the suburbs of the capital, away from the public gaze, housing for workers was built with reject material. Walls moved when they were touched, door frames collapsed after one storm, and rain dripped through the roof. In Nanyuan, a suburb about 13 kilometres south of the Imperial Palace, water dripped from the walls in new residential units. Some houses came without doors. This, too, was a conscious choice. As Liu Shaoqi put it in his instructions to the Ministry of Textile Industry in February 1956, 'You must build single-storey dormitories for the workers, not multi-storey ones. Our workers are not necessarily used to multi-storey buildings, in future we can build good multi-storey buildings. And you don't necessarily have to build those structures very well, if they are slightly better than temporary sheds then it should be acceptable, anyway in future they will be demolished.' A few trees he deemed acceptable, but ponds, rockeries, flowers and grass were unnecessary. Even providing workers with teacups, as was the habit in the Capital Number Two Cotton Mill, was 'too good'. This was part of a new drive for austerity, as the government periodically had to cut back on spending.[12]

The housing problem was compounded by the fact that local governments, in thrall to gigantism, were keen to eliminate their existing stock. The scale of destruction was staggering. According to Li Fuchun, housing with a total surface area of over 2 million square metres had been erased in Beijing, Wuhan, Taiyuan and Lanzhou since 1949, at a cost of 60 million yuan. A fifth of Taiyuan and Lanzhou was wiped from the map. In Sichuan, from the provincial capital down to county seats, up to 40 per cent of the urban surface was reduced to rubble. The local people compared the land to tofu, the party to a sharp knife: it cut off whichever portion it wanted. Those who were evicted were often left with no accommodation, even in Beijing. Residents cleared from the area around the Dongjiao Railway Station were put up in temporary sheds for ten months. Some of them cried as they shivered in the snow. Everywhere there was a housing shortage.[13]

Many workers therefore lived in appalling conditions. In Anshan, the site of a sprawling iron and steel complex in Manchuria where the glow from the blast furnaces turned the night an eerie red, the dormitories were so inadequate that families of six had to share one bed. Occasionally a roof caved in or a wall collapsed, forcing workers to live in animal pens or dark caves on the eastern fringes of the city, in the mountains where the coal and iron was mined. Some went hungry, and could be seen shuffling along the streets at the end of their shift, begging for food. Lack of clothing and heating was widespread, even though temperatures plunged to an average of minus 20 degrees Celsius in the winter. When an icy blanket of snow covered the city, the cold seeped through flimsy buildings, threadbare blankets and torn quilts, freezing some babies to death – or so the Anshan Party Committee wrote in a confidential report.[14]

Further south, in Nanjing, the workforce had more than doubled since liberation, but overall living space had failed to keep pace, meaning that each worker had to be content with an average of 2 square metres. Dormitories often lacked ventilation, so people woke up with headaches caused by lack of oxygen. But they were the lucky ones, as government accommodation was reserved for single workers. Families lived outside the factory premises, often up to 25 kilometres away, meaning that many hours were wasted on the daily commute – not counting the expense of 40 cents a day for a mere dozen kilometres, a rate that would have exhausted the entire monthly allowance of 10 per cent of the population in just over a week.[15]

Just south of Nanjing, in the industrial city of Ma'anshan, lying on the bank of the Yangzi River, workers were sick for months on end, unable to afford even basic medical care. The dormitories were crowded, although pressure on housing also meant that some families lived in sheds so exposed to the elements that even in winter a fire could not be started. Ragged urchins were seen begging in the streets. Some workshops even lacked drinking water. There were no toilets. Leading cadres were too busy meeting production targets to care about the workforce. As the workers put it, 'they do not send us hardship funds, they send us only burial fees'. [16]

More detailed studies show that the average space per worker shrank inexorably after liberation, sometimes by half (see Table 2, p. 269). In Wuhan it was 2.4 metres, although this figure excluded a quarter of the workforce who lived in sheds and huts. The city that was home to 1.9 million people had 80,000 workers without a roof above their heads. These were the numbers crunched by the Bureau for Statistics. According to the Bureau for Labour, everywhere ordinary people suffered from a chronic shortage of housing.[17]

People beamed with health, at least when they appeared in propaganda posters, peering confidently into the future. The numerous statistics that the regime churned out on every aspect of health and hygiene, from the number of flies that had been swatted to the incidence of cholera in the countryside, encouraged an image of unceasing progress. Health campaigns punctuated daily life, as people were mobilised at intervals to sweep the streets, remove rubbish, kill rats or fill cesspools. During the Patriotic Health Campaign in 1952, as the country was on a war footing against enemy germs, battalions of conscripted citizens had disinfected entire cities. Much of the campaign, as the Ministry of Health admitted, turned out to be wasteful, as Chapter 7 showed.

But there were real gains. China had always had huge health-care problems, in particular in the countryside where schistosomiasis (an intestinal disease which attacked the liver and spleen), hookworm and beriberi were common. Infant mortality was high before liberation, and there were few modern doctors, except in the big cities. Some improvements of the 1950s were due to new medical breakthroughs. After the Second World War, for instance, mass production of penicillin began in many countries, bringing a steady decline in the number of bacterial infections. The end of more than a decade of war helped other aspects of public health in China. Piles of garbage that had accumulated in many cities during the civil war were removed. Streets were cleaned, trenches filled, drainage improved. Inoculation became widespread, even if it was forcibly performed by cadres keen to fill their quotas. Most of all, the one-party state mobilised its resources against devastating epidemics, many of which were brought under control soon after they appeared.

But health care was not free. The much flaunted barefoot doctors, trained to bring basic health care to the countryside, only appeared years later during the Cultural Revolution. And much medical help that farmers would have received from non-governmental sources before liberation vanished, sometimes overnight. Hundreds of mission hospitals scattered throughout the countryside were liquidated. Taoist and Buddhist temples, along with other religious or charitable institutions, were closed down, except for a few under government control. Everywhere pharmacists, doctors and nurses had to jump through the hoops, demonstrating their allegiance to the new regime as one campaign of thought reform succeeded another. And everywhere, by 1956, the state had taken over most companies, including retail pharmacies and private clinics.

Whatever improvements may have followed liberation, health was soon on the decline. Published reports and newspaper articles described great strides in health care, but far more critical surveys, quietly filed away in the archives, reveal a picture of chronic malnutrition and poor health. This was true not only of the countryside, where collectivisation had reduced the farmers to the status of serfs, but also of the cities. One reason was the decline in income for most workers across the country. Just as farmers had to live on increasingly smaller rations of grain, workers had to make do with dwindling salaries. But health care involved considerable costs, and medicine was expensive. The Bureau for Labour, which studied hundreds of factories in 1956, concluded that 'over the past few years the real income of workers has followed a downward trend'. Inflation outpaced wages. About half of all workers in heavy industry failed to make even 50 yuan a month. The proportion was higher in light industry. In Beijing one in six workers barely managed to scrape a living, making less than 10 yuan a month for basic expenses. And below them, in the shadowy world of construction, dwelled an underclass of paupers who made up 40 per cent of the workforce. Health everywhere was on the decline, as disease rates inched up year after year. By 1955 almost one in every twenty workers had to take sick leave for more than six months. In some factories 40 per cent of workers suffered from a serious chronic illness, although few could afford to take rest – despite the propaganda about workers' sanatoria and holiday retreats.[18]

Conditions were much worse outside the capital. In Nanjing a worker earning less than 20 yuan a month for himself was unable to afford anything beyond the most basic daily necessities. But in 1956 one in ten people throughout the city lived in sheer destitution, making no more than 7 yuan a month. This was despite the forced removal of hundreds of thousands of undesirables in the years after liberation. Half of these paupers were people impoverished as a result of collectivisation. They ranged from unemployed rickshaw pullers and small shopkeepers hounded out of their trade to the family members of victims denounced as counter-revolutionaries. Some were workers fired from state enterprises, often for the slightest infraction of labour discipline. These people were marked for life, becoming untouchables, pariahs living on the margins of society, unable to find another job.

Among workers in Nanjing, more than 7 per cent suffered from tuberculosis, 6 per cent had stomach ailments, another 6 per cent high blood pressure. Poisoning and work accidents were common. In the Nanjing Chemical Factory the concentration of harmful particles in the air exceeded the Soviet Union's limit by a factor of 36. In the workshop dealing with saltpetre, '100 per cent of the workers, to varying degrees, suffer from poisoning,' some of the worst cases causing an enlarged liver and spleen. Lungs infected with siliceous dust were common in glass and cement factories, while the number of trachoma and nose infections was 'serious'.[19]

Comparisons with the years before liberation are fraught with difficulty, if only because so few detailed studies based on archival evidence are available. But the regime itself was keen to compare itself with its predecessor, and it enrolled its statisticians to come up with detailed, inflation-adjusted studies that went back to 1937, the peak of the nationalist era just before the onset of the Japanese invasion. Most were never published, and for good reason. They showed that in many cases life had been better two decades earlier. Workers in the Shenxin Textile Factory in Hankou, for instance, saw a steep decline in the amount of grain, pork and oil they could consume as well as the quantity of cloth they could buy after the revolution. By 1957, on average, a worker had an extra 6 kilos of grain per year, but almost half less pork, a third less edible oil and a fifth less cloth when compared with 1937. Many were malnourished. As Table 2 shows, the situation was hardly unique to that single factory, as workers were badly fed, badly clothed and badly housed, often in conditions not even equivalent to 1948, the height of the civil war.

Table 2: Average Annual Consumption and Living Space for Workers in Wuhan, 1937–57

	Grain (kilos)	Pork (kilos)	Oil (kilos)	Cloth (metres)	Housing (square metres)
Zhenyi Cotton Mill					
1937	157	8.8	7	10.6	6.5
1948	150	2.8	4.5	4.2	2.7
1952	161	7.8	7.3	8.7	3.9
1957	147	5.2	5	6	3.9
Hankou Battery Factory					
1937	170	12.5	8.5	8	4
1948	164	10.7	7.7	8.3	2.8
1952	153	7.2	6.6	5.8	2.1
1957	135	5	4.3	3.9	2.8
Wuchang Power Engine Factory					
1937	172	6.7	5.9	7.2	4.6
1948	197	6.6	4.1	4.6	3.9
1952	151	7.8	9.3	6	4.4
1957	127	5	3.9	4.7	4.1
Wuchang Shipyard					
1937	159	8	5.5	7	5
1948	146	6.5	7	4.7	4
1952	167	6.5	6.5	10	4
1957	146	5	4	7	4

Source: Hubei, 28 March 1958, SZ44-2-158, pp. 24, 38, 47 and 59

Even when by 1952 workers had witnessed some improvements, conditions invariably went downhill in the following five years. But these statistics mentioned only consumption, not the overall cost of living. From 1952 to 1957 living expenses went resolutely upwards. For the workers in the Shenxin Textile Factory mentioned above, the rent increased from 88 yuan a year in 1952 to 400 yuan five years later. In every factory surveyed by the Bureau for Statistics the trend was clear: average living space shrank while the rent crept up. In the Wuchang Shipyard, included in Table 2, rent rose from 271 yuan in 1948 to 361 yuan in 1952, then doubled to 721 yuan in 1955 and reached a phenomenal 990 yuan in 1957.[20]

Malnourishment and poor health were also common in schools. The Youth League, after a wide-ranging survey of middle-school students, declared that 'their health is very bad'. In Wuhan, each received 300 grams of vegetables and 150 grams of bean products a month. Rough grains and sweet potatoes constituted the rest of the diet. In the entire province of Henan, no vegetables were served for a full month, with the food consisting of nothing but noodles. In Mianyang, Sichuan, students captured their diet in a popular ditty: 'Rice is rare, it's soup we get, the more you eat, the slimmer you get, the food is bad, the taste the same, there is no salt and there is no oil.' In Liaoning province, one in three students was undernourished. In Yingkou, the busy port where the province's maize, soybeans, apples and pears left by sea, students would regularly faint with hunger in physical education classes. Strict rationing was justified in the name of morality, as 'eating too much grain is wasteful and lacking in communist virtue'. Those who went hungry were told to drink water: 'boiled water also contains calories'. In Xinmin, a city just outside the provincial capital Shenyang, four out of ten students suffered from night blindness, a condition caused by malnutrition, in particular lack of vitamin A found in fish oils and dairy products. Some classes were held in temples or abandoned churches, although there never seemed to be enough light. Even in daytime, it could be 'as dark as in a prison'.[21]

There were other setbacks. The regime was determined to eradicate disease and eliminate all pests, but this laudable goal was not always well served by mass campaigns that mobilised millions across the country. When people were given a quota of rat tails to be delivered to the authorities, they started breeding the rodents. The whole idea of a military campaign against epidemics, in which people were deployed in battalions, banners unfurled and bugles blaring, ran against common medical practice. This was the case with the drive to eliminate schistosomiasis. The number of people infected by the parasite increased every year after liberation, especially in parts of east China. The leadership ignored the issue. They were more interested in fighting the wasps and butterflies suspected of being infected with germs by enemy agents during the Korean War. Only after the Chairman had been shown the debilitating effects of schistosomiasis during a visit to Zhejiang province in November 1955 did the disease finally win attention from the party. Mao wrote a poem, grandly titled 'Farewell to the Plague Spirit', and in February 1956 he gave the order to start a mass campaign: 'Schistosomiasis must be eliminated!'[22]

Millions of farmers were taken to lakes, crawling through the mud to catch the snails which transmitted the infection. But, all along, leading medical authorities had warned that any attempt to eradicate the disease simply by collecting snails was hopeless. The snails were merely the host of shistosome worms invisible to the human eye. Farmers and cattle who came into contact with the worms were at risk of infection, as the worms propagated themselves in the veins and liver of a parasitised body. Human and animal waste laden with worm eggs was then released back into the lakes, where the cycle was completed as the eggs hatched inside the bodies of the snails. The advice of experts was dismissed at best, denounced as bourgeois at worst. Snails were dug out and collected by hand by whole platoons of villagers. New irrigation canals were opened up in order to block existing ones and bury the snails. The campaign relied on huge manpower, but as soon as it came to an end people were sent back to work in infected lakes to cut grass or collect reeds.[23]

This happened in Hubei, a central province along the Yangzi studded with a thousand lakes with dabbling ducks, lotus and water chestnuts. A third of the population there remained at risk. Despite glowing reports from local cadres bidding farewell to the plague spirit, more than 1.5 million people were still infected. In Hanchuan county, some 700 cases were cured during the campaign, but over a thousand new cases appeared immediately afterwards. In other provinces too, the archives show that the campaign barely dented the incidence of schistosomiasis. This was a country run by slogans and quotas, with one campaign following on the heels of another. There was little room for patient work in controlling the many dimensions of the disease, including better disposal of human waste. Collectivisation did not help, as people in co-operatives tended to care less for animals that did not belong to them, including the proper disposal of manure. Traditional rules of hygiene, including drinking boiled water and eating hot food, also suffered when people lived at the beck and call of party officials.[24]

In some cases a more frightening gap appeared between the world of propaganda and the reality on the ground. The People's Republic enacted a stream of praiseworthy policies for the victims of leprosy, including the provision of leper colonies fitted with every possible amenity. Eliminating leprosy would have been an enormously complex task for any government at the time, all the more so since lepers were widely stigmatised. But in the People's Republic local cadres could barely feed their own workforce. They had many other priorities, lowest among which were disfigured people suffering from a disease erroneously thought to be highly infectious. Prejudice was rampant, and a few educational pamphlets on the disease, distributed by the health authorities, were not about to change that situation overnight. A great deal of evidence buried in the party archives suggests that the situation actually became worse in the years following liberation, if only because the one-party state vested so much more power in local cadres than would ever have been possible in the past.

As missionaries were forced out of the country, sometimes existing leper colonies found themselves cut off from foreign funds. In Moxi, a deprived area high up in the mountains in Sichuan, they abandoned not only a church that proudly displayed its colourful bell tower, but also a leper colony with 160 patients, who were left to fend for themselves. Nobody came to their rescue, despite pleas for help. Soon some patients started leaving the colony to beg along the twisted, rutted mountain roads. Few were welcome. Some were hounded and beaten by frightened villagers. Several were buried alive. A report from the provincial health authorities stated: 'Again one leper was buried alive in the summer of 1954 in Yongding county; similar circumstances also appeared in other counties.' This was not confined to Sichuan alone. In neighbouring Guizhou, often rocked by rebellions from the minority people who lived in the hills and highlands that dominate the province, the number of infections increased sharply after liberation. As panic spread through the villages, some of the local cadres decided to burn the victims to death. This occurred on more than one occasion, one of the worst cases being a village where eight lepers perished at the stake. In some cases the militia acted on the orders of the local authorities: 'The militia tied up a leper and burned him to death. His parents cried all day and night.'[25]

But the worst episode was probably in Yongren county, Yunnan, where a hundred lepers were set alight in June 1951. The idea was first proposed in a conference held by the county party committee a month earlier. Ma Xueshou, a high-ranking cadre in charge of rural affairs, proposed: 'The lepers from the hospital in the fourth district often come out to wash and run about, it creates a bad impression among the masses, and they demand that they be burned.' 'We cannot burn them,' answered the county party secretary. But Ma insisted, and a month later he volunteered to take full responsibility: 'If the masses want to burn them, then let's burn them, we should do it for the masses, it is their request, just do it and I will assume responsibility.' Several others agreed. So the militia assembled all the lepers, locked them in the hospital and set the building on fire. The victims screamed for help, to no avail. Only six of 110 victims survived.[26]

Even when lepers received care, funds mysteriously disappeared. Who, after all, could call to account a few cadres looking after lepers in colonies far from the party centre? In Yanbian, Sichuan, the men in charge appropriated most of the available funds to build themselves spacious mansions. The mud huts for the patients, several kilometres further inland against the mountains, were so ramshackle that they were in imminent danger of collapse. But the problem was also one of scale. In all Guangdong province, by 1953 there were an estimated 100,000 lepers, although the medical authorities could afford to take care of only 2,000 cases.[27]

Lepers were among the most vulnerable members of society, and their needs were not served well by a one-party state that sought to control everyone but answered to nobody. But there were many other needy members of society whose fates came to lie entirely in the hands of local cadres. In some orphanages taken over from non-governmental organisations, the death rate stood at 30 per cent. The blind and the elderly found it difficult to fit into a new society where so much depended on the ability to take orders and earn work points. With the gradual stripping away of most basic liberties – freedom of expression, belief, assembly, association and movement – the majority of ordinary people became increasingly defenceless, as very little stood between them and the state.[28]

———————

By 1956 many of the hopes that sprang from liberation years earlier had been dashed. Instead of treating people with respect, the state viewed them as mere digits on a balance sheet, a resource to be exploited for the greater good. Farmers had lost their land, their tools and their livestock in the name of collectivisation. They were forced to deliver ever larger shares of the crop to the state, answering the call of the bugle in the morning to follow orders from local cadres. In factories and shops in the cities, employees were treated more like bonded labour than the working-class heroes featured in official propaganda. They were pressed into working ever longer hours, chasing one production record after another even as their benefits steadily declined. Everybody, except those inside the party, had to tighten their belts in the pursuit of utopia. China was a country seething with discontent. Social strains were about to explode into open opposition to the regime.

14

Poisonous Weeds

A turning point in the communist world came in the early morning of 25 February 1956. On the final day of the Twentieth Congress, as foreign delegates were busy packing their bags, Nikita Khrushchev assembled the Soviet representatives for an unscheduled secret session in the Great Kremlin Palace, the Moscow residence of the Russian tsars. In a four-hour speech delivered without interruption, Khrushchev denounced the regime of suspicion, fear and terror created by Stalin. Launching a devastating attack on his former master, he accused him of being personally responsible for brutal purges, mass deportations, executions without trial and the torture of innocent party loyalists. Khrushchev further assailed Stalin for his 'mania for greatness' and the cult of personality he had fostered during his reign. Members of the audience listened in stunned silence. There was no applause at the end, as many of the delegates left in a state of shock.[1]

Copies of the speech were sent to foreign communist parties. It set off a chain reaction. In Beijing the Chairman was forced on to the defensive. Mao was China's Stalin, the great leader of the People's Republic. The secret speech could only raise questions about his own leadership, in particular the adulation surrounding him. DeStalinisation was nothing short of a challenge to Mao's own authority. Just as Khrushchev pledged to return his country to the Politburo, Liu Shaoqi, Deng Xiaoping, Zhou Enlai and others in Beijing spoke out in favour of the principles of collective leadership. At the Eighth Party Congress in September 1956, a reference to Mao Zedong Thought was removed from the party charter, collective leadership was lauded and the cult of personality decried. Hemmed in by Khrushchev, Mao had little choice but to put a brave face on these measures, even contributing to them in the months prior to the

congress. But the Chairman did not hide his anger when he spoke to Li
Zhisui, accusing Liu Shaoqi and Deng Xiaoping of taking control of the
agenda and pushing him into the background.[2]

Khrushchev also accused Stalin of ruining agriculture in the 1930s,
even though he 'never went anywhere, never met with workers and collective farmers' and knew the country only from 'films that dressed up and
prettified the situation in the countryside'. This, too, must have been too
close to the bone for a Chairman who viewed the country from the comfort
of his private train, passing through stations emptied of all but security
personnel. Khrushchev's scathing comments on the failure of collective
farming seemed like unintended criticism of the Socialist High Tide. Zhou
Enlai and Chen Yun listened to the prompts from Moscow and tried to
slow down the pace of collectivisation, calling in the summer of 1956 for
an end to 'rash advances'. They reduced the size of collective farms, reverted
to a limited free market and allowed greater scope for private production.
Mao saw this as a personal challenge. Atop an editorial of the *People's Daily*
criticising the High Tide for 'attempting to do all things overnight',
forwarded to him for his approval, Mao angrily scrawled, 'I will not read
this.' He later wondered, 'Why should I read something that abuses me?'
In a severe personal setback, the Socialist High Tide was scrapped at the
Eighth Party Congress.[3]

The secret speech also prompted calls for reform in Eastern Europe.
In Poland, workers took to the streets in Poznań, protesting over higher
work quotas and demanding better wages. In June 1956 a large crowd
of over 100,000 gathered near the Imperial Castle occupied by the
secret police and overwhelmed the premises, freeing all prisoners and
seizing firearms. The headquarters of the communist party was
ransacked. Soviet forces were called in, including tanks, armoured cars
and field guns as well as more than 10,000 soldiers. Shots were fired at
the demonstrators, killing up to a hundred and injuring many more.
But the Polish United Workers' Party, as the communist party was
named, soon turned to conciliation under the leadership of Władysław
Gomułka, raising wages and promising other political and economic
reforms. It was the start of an era known as the Gomułka thaw, as
communists tried to find a 'Polish way to socialism'.

A few months later a rebellion broke out in Hungary, with thousands of students marching through the streets of Budapest. As a delegation tried to enter the radio building of the parliament to broadcast their demands to the nation, they were shot at by the public security police. Violence erupted throughout the country, as pitched battles took place between demonstrators and the police. Moscow tried to restore order by sending thousands of Soviet troops and tanks to the capital. Incensed, the population took to the streets and turned against the regime. In the narrow, cobbled streets of Budapest, rebels fought the tanks with Molotov cocktails. Revolutionary councils appeared across Hungary, seizing power from local authorities and clamouring for a general strike. Everywhere the insurgents smashed the hallowed symbols of communism, burning books, stripping red stars from buildings and tearing down memorials from their pedestals, including the large bronze statue of Stalin in Városliget, the main park in Budapest. By the end of the month, most Soviet troops had been forced to withdraw from the city. Imre Nagy, the new premier, formed a coalition government. Political prisoners were released. Non-communist parties that had been banned were now allowed and joined the coalition.

For a few brief days, Moscow appeared to tolerate the new government. But on 31 October Hungary declared that it intended to leave the Warsaw Pact. The same day violence erupted again near the party headquarters in Budapest, as a crowd grabbed members of the secret police and hung them from lampposts. The scene was shown on Soviet newsreels a few hours later. Khrushchev, who was spending the week in Stalin's dacha in the comfortable Lenin Hills overlooking downtown Moscow, agonised all night, fearful that the rebellion might spread to neighbouring countries and prompt the collapse of the Soviet bloc. He and his colleagues reversed their decision. On 4 November a large Soviet force invaded Hungary, killing thousands of rebels. Over 200,000 refugees fled across the border. Mass arrests were carried out over several months, as all public opposition was suppressed.

The events triggered by deStalinisation were eagerly followed in China. In October 1956, Gomułka gave a dramatic speech that was reproduced in full in Beijing, promising 'socialism with freedom'. He revealed that collectives in Poland produced much less than privately owned farms. But, for

many readers in China, Gomułka's remarks about the Soviet Union were
the real bombshell. Poland was in debt because it had been forced to sell
cheaply to the Soviet Union but pay dearly for imports. It seemed that the
Russians were guilty of 'imperialist exploitation'. And just when speculation over the Polish situation reached its height, news came of the
Hungarian revolt, creating even more excitement in China. 'For the first
time,' observed Robert Loh, 'newspapers were read avidly. Previously, we
had been forced to read them because the official press items were used as
discussion topics in our regular mass organization meetings. Now, however,
absenteeism soared while workers waited in block-long queues for a chance
to buy a paper.' People had to read between the lines, as the news was
severely censored, but workers started invoking the example of Hungary in
acts of defiance against the state.[4]

Discontented people in all walks of life started taking to the streets.
They were fed up, striking, demonstrating or petitioning the government
for a whole variety of reasons. Students boycotted classes in schools and
institutes of higher learning throughout the country. In the Nanjing Institute of Aeronautics and Astronautics, built in 1952 on the site of an old
Ming palace, over 3,000 students went on strike for a month in the autumn
of 1956. The college had advertised itself as a leading university but was no
more than a middle-ranking technical institute. A few streets away, in
Nanjing Normal University, the situation also took a turn for the worse
after the Public Security Bureau sheltered six students guilty of beating up
a young man who had accidentally bumped into them. Soon calls for
justice rang out from the campus. The police threatened to arrest the
demonstrators for 'starting a rebellion', prompting 480 students to gather
in front of the mayor's office chanting slogans in favour of democracy and
human rights. Nanjing was not the only city rocked by unrest. Until the
archives are fully open, nobody will know for certain the extent of student
discontent, but in just one medium-sized city – Xi'an – workers and
students petitioned or went on strike on no fewer than forty separate occasions. By early 1957 over 10,000 students were up in arms all across the
country.[5]

Workers went on strike in unprecedented numbers. The Ministry of
Industry counted more than 220 cases in 1956, the majority having started

after October. Demonstrations in Shanghai attracted thousands of followers. A few were even led by party officials or members of the Youth League.
Most of the workers protested against decreasing real income, poor housing
and dwindling welfare benefits. Grievances had been mounting for many
years, but what caused the explosion of discontent was the collectivisation
of private enterprises under the Socialist High Tide. Outside Shanghai
strikes also paralysed entire sectors of the economy. In Manchuria, 2,000
workers in grain transportation deliberately slowed their pace or petitioned
the government for pay increases. When party officials retaliated by threatening to treat them as counter-revolutionaries, the strikers became even
more determined. In Fuzhou, along the coast opposite Taiwan, workers
petitioned the municipal government on sixty occasions.[6]

In the countryside too, discontent with collectivisation mounted
throughout 1956. The state had begun to introduce some reforms, reducing the size of collective farms and allowing villagers to trade some produce
grown on their own private plots. Farmers, however, wanted the right to
leave the collectives altogether. After a disastrous harvest in the autumn of
1956, everywhere in Xianju county, Zhejiang, villagers started making
trouble. They withdrew from the collectives, clamoured against the party
and beat up local cadres who stood in their way. Over a hundred collectives collapsed altogether. In Tai county, Jiangsu, thousands of petitioners
approached the party headquarters with grievances, as whole parts of the
economy in the region reverted back to barter trade in the wake of collectivisation. Villagers left the collectives in droves, some with their own
cattle, seed and tools, determined to make it on their own.[7]

In Guangdong tens of thousands of farmers were leaving the collectives
by the winter of 1956–7, with the damage most pronounced in Zhongshan and Shunde counties. In some of the Shunde villages, up to a third of
the people forcibly took back the land and started planting their own
crops. They beat cadres who tried to intervene. In the Zhanjiang region,
covering several counties, one out of every fifteen villagers was courageous
enough to quit, in the full knowledge that they would become the target
of violence from the militia, who dragged away their cattle and refused
their children access to schools. Some were not even allowed to walk on
the main streets. In Xinyi county irate farmers destroyed collective

property, set fire to grain stores and even took knives to collective meetings, threatening party officials who refused to let them go.[8]

Some of the local cadres even started speaking out against collectivisation. 'Life in a co-operative is worse than in a labour camp,' opined one.
In Shantou, also in Guangdong, some party officials described the grain
monopoly as a system of exploitation worse than the feudalism of the past.
In Bao'an county, 60 per cent of cadres opposed the monopoly. A deputy
secretary of Luoding county said the following about the collectives:
'Before I went to the countryside I believed in the superiority of the
co-operatives, but once I got there and ate gruel I became so hungry that
my head spun, so I no longer feel that there is anything superior about it.'
At a party meeting in Yingde county, several participants openly expressed
the view that the economy had been in better shape before 1949. In Yaxian
county (Sanya), over forty leading cadres and their families followed the
farmers in refusing to join the co-operatives. One head of a co-operative in
Yangjiang county accused the party of having failed to provide farmers
with anything more than gruel in the three years since the monopoly had
been introduced. At a higher level, among the 14,264 cadres of eleven
counties which made up the Huiyang region, over 10,000 were described
as 'confused' in their thinking.[9]

Some villagers – with or without the connivance of local cadres – made
it all the way to the capital, despite the restrictions the household-registration system imposed on their freedom of movement. At any one time
there were dozens of petitioners gathered outside the State Council, seeking redress in an act of last resort. In one case a woman with four emaciated
infants approached the main gate with a sign strapped to her body: it read
'starvation', a stark term of accusation against a regime that had promised
that nobody would die of hunger. On another occasion a man lit a lantern
in broad daylight and approached the main gate of the party headquarters
at Zhongnanhai seeking an audience with Chairman Mao. His unmistakable message was that the communist party was an agent of darkness which
had shrouded the land.[10]

Other groups of protesters reached the capital. Since liberation, 5.7
million soldiers had been demobilised, but they harboured many grievances. At best they were abandoned to their own fate in the countryside,

but during collectivisation many were treated like pariahs, unable as they were to earn their keep. Half a million suffered from chronic diseases, although the regime showed little interest in their medical needs. Their anger spilled over in the winter of 1956–7, as large groups congregated in the cities to put pressure on the local authorities. A few organised revolutionary committees, promising with some bravado to launch a guerrilla campaign. Chen Zonglin, who hailed from a region ravaged by famine in Anhui, argued loudly: 'if the government does not give us jobs we will fight them to the end!' On five separate occasions groups of veterans camped in front of the State Council to press their demands.[11]

Observing the strikes in Shanghai, Robert Loh felt that 'One could feel new life flowing back into the beaten-down people, and it was indescribably exhilarating. Equally indescribable was the changed attitude of the communist officials. They were confused as well as frightened, and their arrogance was gone. They tried to placate everyone, especially the workers whom always they seemed to fear the most.' For good reason, the cadres were in no position to suppress the strikes. The Chairman himself defended the democratic right of students, workers and peasants to express themselves and take to the streets. He had become a champion of the people, allowing a hundred flowers to bloom.[12]

———

After Khrushchev had delivered his secret speech in February 1956, Mao spent two months carefully considering his position. He had to be cautious with Khrushchev. Not only was he the powerful head of the Soviet bloc, but he had also increased aid to the People's Republic, trying to put relations with Beijing on a new footing after Stalin's death. A year earlier Khrushchev had even promised to provide China with the expertise necessary to make an atomic bomb. The Chairman's hands were also tied as his colleagues proposed to cut back on industrial projects and slow the pace of collectivisation, invoking Khrushchev to rein in his policies.

Mao's response to deStalinisation came on 25 April, when he addressed an enlarged meeting of the Politburo in a speech entitled 'On the Ten Great Relationships'. China, he announced, was ready to strike out on its own, finding a Chinese way to socialism. The Chairman was scathing about those who 'copy everything indiscriminately and transplant it mechanically'. Instead of slavishly following the old Stalinist model, with its lopsided emphasis on heavy industry, China should develop its own version of socialism. The Soviet Union had made a grave mistake by taking too much from the peasants through a system of compulsory sales, but China, he explained, took into account the interests of both peasants and the state by having a very low agricultural tax. He believed that 'We have done better than the Soviet Union and a number of East European countries,' where agriculture and light industry had been neglected. In developing its own road to socialism, China should even learn from capitalist countries. But those who followed Khrushchev in rejecting every aspect of Stalin's legacy were also wrong: 'When the north wind is blowing, they join the north; tomorrow, when there is a west wind blowing, they switch to the west.' 'In the Soviet Union,' he added, 'those who once extolled Stalin to the skies have now in one swoop buried him thirty kilometres deep in the ground.' Mao saw himself as occupying the middle ground, declaring that Stalin was a great Marxist who was 70 per cent right and 30 per cent wrong.

The Chairman was seeking consensus, trying to rally his colleagues around him by accommodating many of the objections that had been raised against collectivisation. He stole their agenda by proposing a balance between heavy industry on the one hand and light industry and agriculture on the other. This was necessary 'to ensure the livelihood of the people'. The 'pressing problems in their work and daily life' must be addressed and wages adjusted. Mao championed the ordinary man.

But he went much further than merely making concessions on the economy. Seeking to reclaim moral leadership over the party, he tried to do so by posing as a protector of democratic values. He admonished his colleagues, placing himself above them: 'The Communist Party fears two things: first it fears the people noisily crying like a baby, and secondly it fears the democrats making comments. If what they say makes sense, how can you not listen?' Less than a year earlier, Mao had denounced Liang Shuming and Peng Yihu as 'counter-revolutionaries'. Now he praised them as the guardians of democracy: 'We have deliberately kept the democratic parties, we have not knocked them down, nor have we knocked down

Liang Shuming or Peng Yihu. We should unite all the people around us, let them abuse us and oppose us. As long as their abuse is reasonable, no matter who says what, we can accept it, it is very useful for the party, the people and socialism.' He embraced other parties: 'We should hail two parties, long live the Communist Party, and long live the Democratic Party, but we should not hail the capitalist class, they should have no more than two or three years left.'[13]

Mao outdid Khrushchev. Months earlier he had been forced on the defensive, looking like an ageing leader out of touch with reality and clinging to a model that had failed in the past. Now he, rather than Khrushchev, was the true rebel, striking a far more liberal and conciliatory tone than his counterpart in Moscow. A week later, on 2 May, he encouraged freedom of expression among intellectuals, asking the party to 'let a hundred flowers bloom, let a hundred schools contend'.

But Mao was still annoyed with his colleagues. He had been compelled to endorse spending cuts and other economic reforms, and there was nothing he could do to block a return to the principles of collective leadership. A few days later he boarded a plane and travelled to the south, trying to bolster support from regional leaders. At the end of May, he sent a warning signal to his inner circle by swimming in the muddy, dangerous Yangzi, the mightiest river in China. He did so on three occasions, despite strong currents and whirlpools, surrounded by his security men. Dr Li Zhisui had to use all his energy to stay afloat. He was a fast learner. He turned around and soon floated along with the Chairman, basking in the sun. By braving the Yangzi, the Chairman had demonstrated his determination to his colleagues. A poem soon followed:

> I don't care whether the winds thrash me or the waves pound me,
> I meet them all, more leisurely than strolling in the garden court.[14]

Over the following months Mao continued to approve popular unrest and open discussion of the country's problems. He kept quiet during the Eighth Party Congress, which dropped the Socialist High Tide, deleted all reference to Mao Zedong Thought from the constitution and denounced the cult of personality. He appeared conciliatory, biding his time.

The Hungarian revolt provided him with an opportunity to reclaim the initiative. As Soviet troops crushed the rebels in Budapest in early November, the Chairman faulted the Hungarian Communist Party for having become an 'aristocratic stratum divorced from the masses', allowing complaints among the people to fester and run out of control. Mao wanted a purge of the ranks in its Chinese counterpart to avoid a similar fate. What he proposed was nothing less than a new Rectification Campaign, invoking the days of Yan'an when he had compelled every party member to go through the wringer, ferreting out spies and enemy agents. The real dangers, Mao opined in a meeting with his top echelon, were not workers and students demonstrating on the streets, but 'dogmatism', 'bureaucratism' and 'subjectivism' inside the party itself. 'The party needs to be given some lessons. It is a good thing that students demonstrate against us.' In 1942, Mao had asked young, idealistic volunteers to attack 'dogmatism' inside the party, trying to use them against his rivals. Now he wanted the Chinese Communist Party to welcome critical views from outsiders in a great reckoning: 'Those who insult the masses should be liquidated by the masses.' Mao was using the students and workers on strike everywhere in the country as a way of putting his comrades on notice.[15]

There was, of course, the danger that some intellectuals would voice counter-revolutionary ideas. In 1942, instead of following the Chairman's cues, the young volunteers had savaged the way in which the red capital was run. Mao turned against them with a vengeance, forcing them to denounce each other in endless struggle meetings. But fourteen years later the Chairman was confident that this would not happen again. Repeated campaigns of thought reform had produced a pliant intelligentsia. Only a year earlier 770,000 people had been arrested as counter-revolutionaries. Mao assured his doubtful colleagues that they had nothing to fear, as 'right now nine and a half out of ten counter-revolutionaries have already been cut out'. This was confirmed by security boss Luo Ruiqing two weeks later. During the Hungarian uprising a few weeks earlier, he reported, some people had written anonymously to advocate the overthrow of the party. A few even wanted to get rid of the Chairman. But these were isolated voices, as all the hotbeds of counter-revolution had been successfully wiped out the previous year.[16]

Still, few among Mao's colleagues relished the prospect of another Rectification Campaign, let alone one in which non-party members were allowed openly to voice their discontent. The Chairman sugared the pill by promising a 'gentle breeze and mild rain', as those who had strayed from the path would face ideological education rather than disciplinary punishment. Even then, senior leaders like Liu Shaoqi and Peng Zhen feared that the situation might spiral out of control if people were encouraged to air their grievances openly.

Many inside the party preferred a clampdown on all popular opposition. The Chairman had to do the rounds. A few counter-revolutionaries might take centre stage, he ventured on 18 January 1957, but repression would only make matters worse. 'Don't be afraid of disturbances, the bigger and the longer, the better,' he said a few days later. 'Let the demons and ogres come out, let everybody have a good look at them . . . let those bastards come out.' They were nothing but a few poisonous weeds that appeared among fragrant flowers, and they were bound to grow every year, no matter how often they were pulled up. Then, on 27 January, he wondered: 'Even if mistakes in the party line were made and the country were to descend into chaos, even if several counties and provinces were occupied, with rebel troops all the way up to West Chang'an Avenue in Beijing, would the country collapse? Not as long as the army is reliable.'[17]

Mao's big day came on 27 February 1957, almost exactly one year after Khrushchev's secret speech, as he addressed an enlarged session of the Supreme State Council Conference. His speech was entitled 'On the Correct Handling of Contradictions among the People'. In Hungary, Mao explained, people had taken to the streets four months earlier, but most of them were not counter-revolutionaries. The fault lay with the party, in particular bureaucratic cadres who failed to distinguish between legitimate concerns expressed by the people and more malicious threats posed by enemies of the regime. The result was that force instead of persuasion had been used. In China too, Mao acknowledged, mistakes had occurred in the past, for instance during the political campaigns of 1951 and 1952. Many of those sentenced to labour camps, he reassured his audience, would soon benefit from an amnesty. He even expressed regret at the loss of innocent lives. He also warned that if legitimate complaints by ordinary people were badly handled, China could go the way of Hungary, as contradictions among the people would turn into contradictions between the people and the party, making the use of force necessary. The Chairman rang with sincerity, as he enumerated examples of serious errors made by the Chinese Communist Party. He was harsh with the party bureaucracy. He announced that a Rectification Campaign would soon be inaugurated to help party members improve their work. The public at large were required to help the Chinese Communist Party by airing their grievances so that social injustices could be redressed. No retaliation would be taken against those who spoke out. Again came the Chairman's dramatic call to 'let a hundred flowers bloom, let a hundred schools contend'. Mao ended his speech by comparing himself to a star in an opera, growing too old to continue playing the leading role. He hinted that he might soon step back from the stage.[18]

The speech was a tremendous achievement. Mao came across as an earnest proponent of a more humane form of socialism, departing radically from past tradition. The Chairman did what he did best: rally a majority around him with promises of a better future. The meeting was attended not only by ranking party leaders and government officials, but also by members of organisations outside the party. It was taped and played to select audiences around the country. Robert Loh, who listened to the speech with 200 other delegates in Shanghai, was convinced that Mao was utterly sincere. For more than a year he had been preparing his escape to Hong Kong, but now he was dazed. 'After Mao's speech everything seemed possible. For the first time in many years, I allowed myself to hope.'[19]

———

Criticisms were slow in coming. In Beijing, the mayor Peng Zhen used his clout to control the official newspapers, including the *People's Daily*, and hold back the campaign.[20] Again, Mao took to the roads, travelling south to drum up support. On the one hand, he used all his charm to cultivate intellectuals and democrats, urging them to overcome their hesitations and speak out. On the other hand, he met army and party cadres, telling them that he understood why they were itching to repress the students who were on strike. 'An intellectual has a tail just like a dog,' he explained, 'if you pour some cold water on it, he will tuck it between his legs, but if you try a different attitude he will wag it high in the air, and he will look quite cocky. Just because he has read a couple of books he feels quite cocky. When working people see his cocky air, when they see that attitude, they feel a little uncomfortable.'[21]

Mao himself was deeply suspicious of intellectuals, but he hoped that the true followers would take up the gauntlet by speaking out against the party bureaucracy. It was a high-risk gamble. After Mao had used all his influence to have the full weight of the propaganda machine finally move behind the campaign in late April, some mild rebukes were offered at first. But in May the tone became more strident. Soon a torrent of criticism burst out.

Big posters were glued on the walls of factories, dormitories and offices, as people wrote their views on bright sheets of pink, yellow and green paper. Some wrote pithy slogans in favour of democracy and human rights, others offered lengthy essays presenting probing analyses of the role of democracy in a socialist state, the existence of glaring social disparities in a system premised on equality or the existence of corruption inside the party ranks. Students protested against the tight control that the party maintained over culture and the arts. They railed against past injustices and the harshness of the early campaigns against counter-revolutionaries, speaking up in favour of Hu Feng. Wu Ningkun, whose house had been ransacked at Nankai University a year earlier during the hunt for Hu Feng sympathisers, called the whole campaign 'unjustifiable and preposterous'. 'A flagrant violation of civil rights, a premeditated official lynching', he continued. 'The campaign itself was a mistake, an attempt to stamp out freedom of thought and speech on the model of the Stalinist purges, which have already been exposed and denounced by Khrushchev.' Wu confidently waited for an apology from Nankai University.[22]

Another target of popular ire was Moscow, as people took the party to task for slavishly emulating the Soviet Union. And everybody, it seemed, denounced poor housing and low wages, contrasting a falling standard of living to the privileges that party members enjoyed. A few penned long diatribes against the entire system, attacking the communist party and Mao Zedong in person, comparing the Chairman to the pope. Under

Chiang Kai-shek, one critic wrote, there had been more freedom of speech than in New China. Even the state-controlled press carried searing indictments of the communist party. In an article entitled 'The Party Dominates the World', Chu Anping, who had studied at the London School of Economics under Harold Laski, took Mao Zedong to task for thinking that the world belonged to him. Chu Anping was a member of the Democratic League, as were Zhang Bojun and Luo Longji, who organised a series of meetings with democrats with no party affiliation. Many demanded that party representatives withdraw from schools, state organs and joint enterprises, while a few mocked the Chairman himself. Particularly hurtful must have been Luo Longji's comment that Mao was an 'amateur intellectual' of the proletariat trying to lead professional intellectuals of the bourgeoisie.[23]

A few took up the farmers' cause. Dai Huang, a committed party member and celebrated war correspondent, was taken aback by the lavish banquets and fine houses enjoyed by local cadres in the countryside, when life for most farmers was little better than before liberation. He wrote a long letter to the Chairman offering his suggestions. Fei Xiaotong, a sociologist who had made his name studying the countryside before liberation, published his account of a visit to a remote village in Jiangsu he knew from the 1930s. As soon as he had arrived, several elderly women approached him to complain about food shortages. He wrote a mildly critical report, pointing out that it was 'simple-minded' to believe that collectivisation would solve every problem.[24]

Much more violent confrontations took place in closed forums attended by party officials. In Shanghai the deputy mayor welcomed 250 students who had returned from abroad after liberation. The meeting was held in the Culture Club, the art deco building that had once housed the prestigious French Club. There were graduates from some of the best universities around the world, and when asked to speak out they did so with extraordinary vehemence, blasting the lies and broken promises of the regime. They assailed the arbitrary and unjust treatment of intellectuals, and were incensed by the brutal repression that had accompanied every campaign for thought reform. But most of all they were embittered by the waste of their talents in New China. Dozens yelled simultaneously, their voices

shrill with emotion. The deputy mayor soon lost his poise, and sweat
started running down his face. His hair was untidy, his uniform wrinkled.
'He sat gripping the arms of his chair and his eyes darted from one shouting member of the audience to another.'

The climax of the meeting came when an engineer complained that he
had given up a US$800-a-month job in order to return and serve the
motherland. He had not been allowed to do anything useful ever since,
as even minor technical suggestions he made were rejected as 'bourgeois'.
He had been transferred four times since coming back from abroad in
1951. Each time his salary had been readjusted downwards, and now he
was paid a mere pittance. The engineer became angrier and angrier, and
suddenly he took off his jacket and rushed up to the deputy mayor to
shake the coat in his face. 'For six years I have not bought a single
garment,' he shouted. 'For six years I have not been allowed to use my
ability or my training. Because of what I have endured I've lost thirty
pounds. Why? Why? How long do you expect us to put up with your
stupidity, your indifference? Do you think we will all sit back quietly and
let you Communists grow fat and insolent?' By now everyone in the
audience was screaming wildly.[25]

There were small victories. In Shanghai the mayor apologised publicly
to a professor who had been unjustly persecuted as an anti-party element.
After the apology, other wrongly accused intellectuals were released from
prison. Among them was Henry Ling, who had been the president of
Shanghai University from 1945 to 1949. The experience of six years behind
bars was visible in his emaciated frame, but he was delighted to be free and
keen to follow the country's new path.[26]

Students had been striking and demonstrating sporadically since the
summer of 1956, but now tens of thousands took to the streets. On 4 May
1957, some 8,000 of them converged on Beijing, marking the anniversary
of the May Fourth Movement, an abortive student uprising dating back to
1919. They created a 'Democracy Wall' covered with posters and slogans
charging the communist party with 'suppression of freedom and democracy in all the country's educational institutions'. They called for a
nationwide movement of protest, and liaised with demonstrators in other
cities. In Chengdu and Qingdao students turned violent, beating up local

officials and ransacking party premises. A full-scale riot broke out in Wuhan, as students from a middle school who were furious about enrolment policy stormed the party headquarters, breaking down doors and rummaging through the files. Several party officials were tied up and marched through the streets.[27]

Workers, too, took to the streets. Like the students, they had been active in strikes for almost a year, paralysing parts of the economy in Manchuria, Tianjin, Wuhan and Shanghai, but now matters came to a head. In Shanghai alone, major labour disturbances involving over 30,000 workers erupted at more than 580 enterprises, dwarfing anything the country had ever seen, even during the heyday of the nationalist regime in the 1930s. Minor incidents were also registered at another 700 factories, including walkouts and organised slowdowns in production.[28]

Some workers turned violent, tearing slogans and posters about increased production from the walls. Daring denunciations of communism appeared instead. Party officials were heckled at packed meetings, as workers made long and bitter complaints. In one incident, disgruntled workers frogmarched a local official to the Huangpu River, where they dunked his head in the water at two- to three-minute intervals. After an hour the man's face was covered with mud and blood, and he jumped into the river in an effort to swim away. A bystander who offered help was stoned by the workers. In Shanghai and elsewhere, the sight of terrified and cringing party cadres became common. 'Several times, in the streets,' reported Robert Loh, 'I saw cadres being reviled, insulted and jeered at by angry mobs.' In the words of another protagonist, Tommy Wu, the art student who had taken part in Tiger-Hunting Teams years earlier, 'it was truly a public catharsis'.[29]

Robert Loh himself was bemused by the whole situation and preferred to keep a low profile, despite exhortations from party officials to speak out. He escaped to Hong Kong a few weeks later. Others, too, were prudent. Yue Daiyun, the party member who had tried to protect an impoverished tailor from the execution squad during land reform, was equally guarded: 'Despite my sympathy with those who were speaking out, some sense of inner caution prevented me from joining this chorus of critical voices. I felt it prudent to wait and see what would happen before commenting

openly myself.' Instead she decided to participate in the campaign by joining together with other young teachers, discussing the publication of a
new literary magazine.[30]

———

Around the country party officials were taken aback by the torrent of criticism unleashed by the Hundred Flowers. In Beijing the Chairman himself
was in a state of shock. He had badly miscalculated. 'He stayed in bed,' his
doctor Li Zhisui noted, 'depressed and apparently immobilised, sick with
the cold that called me back, as the attacks grew ever more intense. He was
rethinking his strategy, plotting the revenge.'[31]

On 15 May 1957, Mao wrote an article entitled 'Things are Changing'.
It was distributed to leaders within the party. Mao told them: 'We shall let
the rightists run amok for a time and let them reach their climax. The more
they run amok, the better for us. Some say they are afraid of being hooked
like a fish, and others say they are afraid of being lured in deep, rounded up
and annihilated. Now that large numbers of fish have come to the surface of
themselves, there is no need to bait the hook.' Mao was planning a counter-
attack, and asked the propaganda machine to encourage more people to
come out and criticise the party. He was particularly infuriated with members
of the democratic parties who had proved themselves to be so unreliable.
'They are nothing but a bunch of bandits and whores,' he told his doctor.[32]

Behind the scenes the *People's Daily* was told to prepare to attack those
the Chairman now dubbed 'rightists'. A hint came on 8 June, when an
editorial by Mao accused a small number of people of attempting to assail
the party and overthrow the government. On 11 June the speech he had
given on 'Contradictions among the People' several months earlier was
finally published, but its conciliatory tone was completely reversed. The
article had been carefully rewritten to make it appear as if a trap had been
laid for opponents of the regime all along, designed to 'lure the snakes of
reaction out of their holes'. Everything was turned on its head, making it
seem that the Chairman's encouragement of debate had been nothing but
a cunning strategy to unmask all the enemies of revolution.

The period of blooming and contending was over. Mao was forced
back into a temporary alliance with his opponents inside the party.

Assailed from all sides, they, too, found unity behind their Chairman. Deng Xiaoping and Peng Zhen, who had had their doubts all along, pressed for sweeping measures against all rightists. The Chairman put Deng in charge of the campaign, which targeted hundreds of thousands of individuals. On 15 May Mao had opined that the number of rightists was '1, 3, 5 or up to 10 per cent, as the case may be'. As the months went by, the number of victims gradually increased, eventually reaching over half a million people.[33]

The democrats whom Mao had described as 'bandits and whores' were accused of having followed an 'anti-communist, anti-people, anti-socialist bourgeois line'. Chu Anping, who had denounced the party for thinking that it dominated the world, was expelled from the party and forced to confess in one meeting after another. Others were harassed by student activists, who organised themselves spontaneously into hunting squads. On two occasions loyal students from the People's University burst into the office of Zhang Bojun, then minister of communications, while Luo Longji, soon labelled 'China's Number One Rightist', was hounded at his own home. As leaders of the Democratic League, they were accused of heading a secret 'Zhang–Luo Anti-Party Alliance' and stripped of all their positions.[34]

Much harsher measures were invoked against those who had joined in riots. In Wuhan, several middle-school students were executed before a crowd of 10,000 people. They, too, were accused of taking orders from the 'Zhang–Luo Anti-Party Alliance'.[35]

People turned against each other. Zhang Bojun and Luo Longji themselves tried to discredit each other. At one point Luo walked up to Zhang's residence and smashed his walking stick against the front door in a fit of anger. Other members of the Democratic League, including Wu Han, a historian and head of the Beijing branch of the league, did not want to lag behind, joining a chorus of accusations against both Zhang and Luo. Sometimes the politics of denunciation ripped apart entire families. Dai Huang, who had spoken out on behalf of the farmers, was taken to task by his own wife, who put up a wall poster accusing him of plotting against the party. Fei Xiaotong was forced to repudiate his report on the countryside and debase himself in a confession to the National People's Congress, accepting that he had supported the 'Zhang–Luo Anti-Party Alliance' and had 'opposed the goals of socialism'.[36]

Many victims initially thought that the anti-rightist campaign had nothing to do with them, since they had only answered the call of the party when airing their views. This was the case with Wu Ningkun. But as the faculty at his university spent weeks studying party directives and newspaper editorials, he was soon made to recant and confess to being a bourgeois rightist. Colleagues and friends shunned him. He sat through meetings like a criminal awaiting his sentence, almost relieved when he was finally sent away to a labour camp in the Great Northern Wilderness.[37]

Even party members who were convinced that they had played it safe found themselves facing inquisitorial meetings, with rows of stern committee members subjecting their victims to endless interrogations and denunciations. This was the case with Yue Daiyun, who was put in charge of a committee tasked with denouncing five people as rightists. She spent all summer poring over the records of dozens of colleagues. Then came her turn to face accusations of rightism. 'Surely such a serious accusation could not be applied to me, I reasoned; surely the error would be quickly corrected.' She had to face her entire department, as eight to nine people stood up, one after the other, calling her a traitor and a counter-revolutionary. Some of the most vicious accusations came from a young teacher who had also been labelled a rightist, as he was eager for a chance to prove himself to the party.[38]

Some meetings degenerated into shouting sessions during which the victims were physically abused, with their hair grabbed and their heads pressed down on to the stage. This happened to several university professors in Beijing. In one case a participant was so furious that he shattered a teacup on the head of a victim at the Beijing Institute of Politics and Law. But intellectuals were still relatively safe from the physical violence that would erupt during the Cultural Revolution in 1966.[39]

Far more distressing was the arbitrary nature of the campaign. Mao had set a quota on the number of rightists and every unit in the country had to meet it. The criteria for identifying a rightist were so vague that they could potentially include almost anyone who had ever voiced an opinion. 'Opposing socialist culture', 'opposing socialist economic and political systems', 'opposing the fundamental policies of the state', 'denying the achievements of the people's democratic revolution, the socialist revolution and socialist construction' and 'opposing the leadership of the Communist Party' were all fatal mistakes.

Even with these sweeping criteria, many of the victims were merely 'accidental dissidents', to use the expression of historian Wang Ning. In some places the cadres simply ticked names off a list to fill their quota. In one theatre employees were asked to draw lots. One cashier was selected as the token rightist. Qian Xinbo, a journalist in the Central People's Broadcast Service, was approached by a cadre and asked how he felt about being named as a rightist, since several of his friends had already been denounced. 'I don't have a lot to say, let the party decide,' Qian answered meekly, knowing that the party committee had already determined his fate. One young woman aged seventeen was packed off to the gulag for displaying 'blind faith in foreign imperialist things': she had praised shoe polish made in the United States.[40]

Jealousy and personal animosity, as always, played a role. One young man was brought down for rising too quickly in the ranks. As He Ying explained:

> I became a rightist at the age of nineteen. I was the youngest editor in a literature journal in Jilin, and was well known in the literary circle of the province. I got higher pay than many of my colleagues, and I became a focus of public attention. So sometimes I was overconfident and arrogant. Many of my colleagues were jealous and wanted to see me brought down. I kept quiet about politics during the Hundred Flowers, but they convinced the party secretary to label me a rightist when the campaign started.

The story told by Yin Jie is strikingly similar: 'When I was studying at college, I got a higher allowance than many of my fellow students . . . In addition, I did not study hard but always got good marks. Therefore I became a target of jealousy. Some people really hated me. When the campaign started, they urged the head of my department to label me as a rightist.'[41]

One response to false accusations was suicide. Cong Weixi witnessed how a victim jumped to his death in the middle of a denunciation meeting. 'As the high pitch of condemnation echoed around the hall, a man sitting a couple of rows in front of me suddenly stood up. Before I realised what was happening, he quickly went for the balcony of the fourth floor and dived . . . Blood! I saw blood when I looked out. I covered my eyes as I did not have the courage to look any more.' There were thousands of similar cases, and always suicide was interpreted as a final act of betrayal of the people. Hu Sidu, who had denounced his father Hu Shi in 1950 and striven to join the communist party, was hounded to his death after he had put forward suggestions to improve the quality of teaching in his college.[42]

At the other extreme were those who not only accepted the party's judgement, but actually volunteered to go to the Great Northern Wilderness to seek introspection and self-renewal. Ding Ling, who had been the star of leftist literature in the 1930s, agreed with her husband that they should 'renew themselves' and carve out a new road ahead by following the values of the Chinese Communist Party. Some intellectuals had tied their own destinies so closely to the party that they simply could not envisage life without it.[43]

More than half a million people were labelled during the anti-rightist campaign, including intellectuals like Ding Ling who had devoted their entire careers to the party. The leadership itself had been put on notice, knowing that Mao could call upon the people to attack them. Many party leaders fell into line, no longer daring to question the Chairman's policies. The cautious views of Zhou Enlai and Chen Yun on the economy were pushed aside. Mao was ebullient. Less than a decade after liberation, he was ready to push for a new, bold experiment that would propel China to the forefront of the socialist camp. Mao called it the Great Leap Forward, as the country would accelerate the pace of collectivisation and soar into a communist utopia of plenty for all. Over the next four years, tens of millions of people would be worked, starved or beaten to death in the greatest man-made catastrophe the country had ever seen.

Notes

For abbreviations used in the Notes, please see Bibliography, p. 399.

1: Siege

1   Jiang Yanyan, 'Changchun yixia shuiguandao gongdi wachu shuqian ju shigu' (Thousands of skeletons excavated at a construction site), *Xin wenhua bao*, 4 June 2006.

2   Zhang Zhenglong, *Xuebai xuehong* (Snow is white but blood is red), Hong Kong: Dadi chubanshe, 1991, p. 441.

3   'Northern Theater', *Time*, 2 June 1947.

4   Cable by Li Keting to Chiang Kai-shek, 11 June 1948, Guoshiguan, file 002080200330042.

5   Order from Chiang Kai-shek, 12 June 1948, Guoshiguan, file 0020601 0000240012; Fred Gruin, '30,000,000 Uprooted Ones', *Time*, 26 July 1948.

6   Zhang, *Xuebai xuehong*, p. 469; Wang Junru interviewed by Andrew Jacobs, 'China is Wordless on Traumas of Communists' Rise', *New York Times*, 1 Oct. 2009.

7   Cable from Li Keting, 24 June 1948, Guoshiguan, file 002080200331025; cable from Li Keting, 14 Aug. 1948, Guoshiguan, file 002090300188346; Duan Kewen, *Zhanfan zishu* (Autobiography of a war criminal), Taipei: Shijie ribaoshe, 1976, p. 3.

8   Cable to Chiang Kai-shek, 26 Aug. 1948, Guoshiguan, file 002020400016104; order from Chiang Kai-shek to Zheng Guodong, 17 Aug. 1948, Guoshiguan, file 002080200426044; 'Time for a Visit?', *Time*, 1 Nov. 1948; Henry R. Lieberman, 'Changchun Left to Reds by Chinese', *New York Times*, 7 Oct. 1949.

9   Cable from Li Keting, 13 July 1948, Guoshiguan, file 002090300187017; Zhang Yinghua interviewed by Andrew Jacobs, 'China is Wordless'; Song Zhanlin interviewed by Zhang Zhenglong, *Xuebai xuehong*, p. 474.

10 Zheng Dongguo, *Wo de rongma shengya: Zheng Dongguo huiyi lu*, Beijing: Tuanjie chubanshe, 1992, ch. 7; Duan, *Zhanfan zishu*, p. 5; Wang Daheng, *Wo de bange shiji* (The first half-century of my life), online publication,

Qing pingguo dianzi tushu xilie, pp. 7–8; see also Zhang Zhiqiang and Wang Fang (eds), *1948, Changchun: Wei neng jichu de jiaxin yu zhaopian* (1948, Changchun: The family letters and photos that were never sent), Jinan: Shandong huabao chubanshe, 2003.

11 'Time for a Visit?', *Time*, 1 Nov. 1948; Zhang, *Xuebai xuehong*, p. 446; cable by Li Keting to Chiang Kai-shek, 2 Sept. 1948, Guoshiguan, file 002090300191009.

12 'Time for a Visit?', *Time*, 1 Nov. 1948.

13 Zhang, *Xuebai xuehong*, p. 467.

2: War

1 Theodore H. White and Annalee Jacoby, *Thunder out of China*, London: Victor Gollancz, 1947, p. 259, with a minor stylistic change; 'Victory', *Time*, 20 Aug. 1945; 'Wan Wan Sui!', *Time*, 27 Aug. 1945.

2 Diana Lary and Stephen MacKinnon (eds), *Scars of War: The Impact of Warfare on Modern China*, Vancouver: University of British Columbia Press, 2001; Sheldon H. Harris, *Factories of Death: Japanese Biological Warfare 1932–45 and the American Cover-Up*, London: Routledge, 1994; Konrad Mitchell Lawson, 'Wartime Atrocities and the Politics of Treason in the Ruins of the Japanese Empire, 1937–1953', doctoral dissertation, Harvard University, 2012.

3 Stephen MacKinnon, 'Refugee Flight at the Outset of the anti-Japanese War', in Lary and MacKinnon, *Scars of War*, pp. 118–35; see also R. Keith Schoppa, *In a Sea of Bitterness: Refugees during the Sino-Japanese War*, Cambridge, MA: Harvard University Press, 2011.

4 'I am Very Optimistic', *Time*, 3 Sept. 1945.

5 White and Jacoby, *Thunder out of China*, p. 263.

6 C. K. Cheng, *The Dragon Sheds its Scales*, New York: New Voices Publishing, 1952, p. 122.

7 Stalin's requirements on seven typescript pages are mentioned in John R. Deane, *The Strange Alliance: The Story of our Efforts at Wartime Cooperation with Russia*, New York: Viking Press, 1947, p. 248; see also David M. Glantz, *The Soviet Strategic Offensive in Manchuria, 1945: 'August Storm'*, London: Frank Cass, 2003, p. 9, and Robert H. Jones, *The Roads to Russia: United States Lend-Lease to the Soviet Union*, Norman: University of Oklahoma Press, 1969, pp. 184–5.

8 'To the Bitter End', *Time*, 20 Aug. 1945.

9 Michael M. Sheng, *Battling Western Imperialism: Mao, Stalin, and the United States*, Princeton: Princeton University Press, 1997, pp. 103 and 156.

10 Jay Taylor, *The Generalissimo: Chiang Kai-shek and the Struggle for Modern China*, Cambridge, MA: Harvard University Press, 2009, p. 317.

11 Ibid., pp. 321–3.

12 'The Short March', *Time*, 17 Dec. 1945.

13 Yang Kuisong, *Mao Zedong yu Mosike de enen yuanyuan* (Mao and Moscow),

Nanchang: Jiangxi renmin chubanshe, 1999, ch. 8; Yang Kuisong, *'Zhongjian didai' de geming: Guoji da beijing xia kan Zhonggong chenggong zhi dao*, Taiyuan: Shanxi renmin chubanshe, 2010, p. 474; essential on the relationship between Mao and Stalin is Dieter Heinzig, *The Soviet Union and Communist China 1945–1950: The Arduous Road to the Alliance*, Armonk, NY: M. E. Sharpe, 2004.

14 Taylor, *The Generalissimo*, pp. 323–4.

15 James M. McHugh, letter to his wife dated 30 June 1946, Cornell University Library, Division of Rare and Manuscript Collections, quoted in Hannah Pakula, *The Last Empress: Madame Chiang Kai-shek and the Birth of Modern China*, New York: Simon & Schuster, 2009, p. 530; 'Wounds', *Time*, 18 March 1946; William Gray, 'Looted City', *Time*, 11 March 1946; Taylor, *The Generalissimo*, p. 327; see also 'Soviet Removals of Machinery', 8 July 1947, US Central Intelligence Agency Report, CIA-RDP82-00457D000070010002-5, National Archives at Park College.

16 Zhang Baijia, 'Zhou Enlai and the Marshall Mission', in Larry I. Bland (ed.), *George C. Marshall's Mediation Mission to China, December 1945–January 1947*, Lexington, VA: George C. Marshall Foundation, 1998, pp. 213–14; Simei Qing, 'American Visions of Democracy and the Marshall Mission to China', in Hongshan Li and Zhaohui Hong (eds), *Image, Perception, and the Making of U.S.–China Relations*, Lanham, MA: University Press of America, 1998, p. 283; Taylor, *The Generalissimo*, p. 346.

17 Zhang, *Xuebai xuehong*, pp. 170–1; Marshall to Truman, *Foreign Relations of the United States*, 1946, vol. 9, p. 510, quoted in Chang Jung and Jon Halliday, *Mao: The Unknown Story*, London: Jonathan Cape, 2005, p. 295.

18 Chang and Halliday, *Mao*, p. 297; Sheng, *Battling Western Imperialism*, p. 156; Steven I. Levine, *Anvil of Victory: The Communist Revolution in Manchuria, 1945–1948*, New York: Columbia University Press, 1987, p. 178.

19 Taylor, *The Generalissimo*, p. 358; Freda Utley, *The China Story*, Chicago: H. Regnery, 1951, ch. 2.

20 Suzanne Pepper, *Civil War in China: The Political Struggle, 1945–1949*, Berkeley: University of California Press, 1978, pp. 242–3.

21 Carsun Chang, *The Third Force in China*, New York: Bookman Associates, 1952, p. 172.

22 Associated Press Report, 24 July 1947, quoted in Michael Lynch, *Mao*, London: Routledge, 2004, p. 141; 'Report on China', *Time*, 13 Oct. 1947.

23 Utley, *The China Story*, ch. 2.

24 Taylor, *The Generalissimo*, pp. 378–9.

25 'Worse & Worse', *Time*, 26 Jan. 1948.

26 'Sick Cities', *Time*, 21 June 1948.

27 'Next: The Mop-Up', *Time*, 23 Feb. 1948; 'Rout', *Time*, 8 Nov. 1948; Henry R. Lieberman, '300,000 Starving in Mukden's Siege', *New York*

Times, 2 July 1948; Seymour Topping, *Journey between Two Chinas*, New York: Harper & Row, 1972, p. 312.

28   Frederick Gruin, '30,000,000 Uprooted Ones', *Time*, 26 July 1948.

29   Taylor, *The Generalissimo*, pp. 385–9.

30   Doak Barnett, letter no. 25, 'Communist Siege at Peiping', 1 Feb. 1949, Institute of Current World Affairs; 'One-Way Street', *Time*, 27 Dec. 1948.

31   Taylor, *The Generalissimo*, p. 396; Chang and Halliday, *Mao*, pp. 308–9.

32   Derk Bodde, *Peking Diary: A Year of Revolution*, New York: Henry Schuman, 1950, pp. 100–1; Doak Barnett, letter no. 25, 'Communist Siege at Peiping', 1 Feb. 1949, Institute of Current World Affairs; 'Defeat', *Time*, 7 Feb. 1949; Jia Ke interviewed by Jane Macartney in 'How We Took Mao Zedong to the Gate of Heavenly Peace, by Jia Ke, 91', *The Times*, 12 Sept. 2009.

33   Sun Youli and Dan Ling, *Engineering Communist China: One Man's Story*, New York: Algora Publishing, 2003, pp. 10–11.

34   Arne Odd Westad, *Decisive Encounters: The Chinese Civil War, 1946–1950*, Stanford: Stanford University Press, 2003, p. 259; Bo Yibo, *Ruogan zhongda shijian yu juece de huigu* (Recollections of several important decisions and events), Beijing: Zhonggong zongyang dangxiao chubanshe, 1997, vol. 1, pp. 160–1.

35   'To Defend the Yangtze', *Time*, 20 Dec. 1948; Roy Rowan, *Chasing the Dragon: A Veteran Journalist's Firsthand Account of the 1946–9 Chinese Revolution*, Guilford, CT: Lyons Press, 2004, p. 146.

36   Frederick Gruin, 'Eighteen Levels Down', *Time*, 20 Dec. 1948; Su Yu, *Su Yu junshi wenji* (Collected military writings by Su Yu), Beijing: Jiefangjun chubanshe, 1989, p. 455, quoted in Luo Pinghan, *Dangshi xijie* (Details in the history of the Communist Party), Beijing: Renmin chubanshe, 2011, p. 150; 'Or Cut Bait', *Time*, 29 Nov. 1948.

37   Long Yingtai, *Da jiang da hai 1949* (Big river, big sea: Untold stories of 1949), Hong Kong: Tiandi tushu youxian gongsi, 2009, p. 221.

38   Topping, *Journey between Two Chinas*, p. 29.

39   Ibid., p. 43.

40   'Sunset', *Time*, 31 Jan. 1949.

41   'Shore Battery', *Time*, 2 May 1949; Rowan, *Chasing the Dragon*, pp. 195–6.

42   Topping, *Journey between Two Chinas*, pp. 64–7; Robert Doyle, 'Naked City', *Time*, 2 May 1949.

43   Topping, *Journey between Two Chinas*, pp. 64–7.

44   Ibid., p. 73; Robert Doyle, 'Naked City', *Time*, 2 May 1949; Jonathan Fenby, *Modern China: The Fall and Rise of a Great Power, 1850 to the Present*, New York: Ecco, 2008, p. 346.

45   'Swift Disaster', *Time*, 2 May 1949; Rowan, *Chasing the Dragon*, p. 201.

46   'The Weary Wait', *Time*, 23 May 1949; Rowan, *Chasing the Dragon*, pp. 198–9; Jack Birns, *Assignment Shanghai: Photographs on the Eve of Revolution*, Berkeley: University of California Press, 2003.

47   'Will They Hurt Us', *Time*, 16 May 1949.

48   Mariano Ezpeleta, *Red Shadows over Shanghai*, Quezon City: Zita, 1972, p. 185.

49   Christopher Howe, *Shanghai: Revolution and Development in an Asian Metropolis*, Cambridge: Cambridge University Press, 1981, p. 43.

50   Feng Bingxing interviewed by the Shanghai Daily, 'Shanghai Celebrates its 60th year of Liberation', *Shanghai Daily*, 28 May 2009.

51   'The Communists Have Come', *Time*, 6 June 1949; Rowan, *Chasing the Dragon*, pp. 198–9.

52   Dwight Martin, 'Exile in Canton', *Time*, 17 April 1949.

53   'Next: Chungking', *Time*, 24 Oct. 1949.

54   Doak Barnett, letter no. 17, 'Sinkiang Province', 9 Sept. 1948, Institute of Current World Affairs.

55   Doak Barnett, letter no. 21, 'Kansu, Sinkiang, Chinghai, Ninghsia', 15 Oct. 1948, Institute of Current World Affairs.

56   Doak Barnett, letter no. 20, 'Kansu, Province, Northwest China', 8 Oct. 1948, Institute of Current World Affairs.

57   On the history of Xinjiang, see Andrew D. W. Forbes, *Warlords and Muslims in Chinese Central Asia: A Political History of Republican Sinkiang, 1911–1949*, Cambridge: Cambridge University Press, 1986; see also the memoirs of Sheng Shicai in Allen S. Whiting and General Sheng Shih-tsai, *Sinkiang: Pawn or Pivot?*, East Lansing, MI: Michigan State University Press, 1958; letter from Peng Dehuai to Mao Zedong, 29 Dec. 1949, RGASPI, 82-2-1241, pp. 194–7; Trade Agreement with Peng Dehuai for Xinjiang, 5 Jan. 1950, RGASPI, 82-2-1242, pp. 20–39; on Russian troops in December 1949 see O. C. Ellis, Report from Tihwa, 15 Nov. 1950, PRO, FO371-92207, p. 7; on the communist conquest and subsequent rule of Xinjiang, one should also read James Z. Gao, 'The Call of the Oases: The "Peaceful Liberation" of Xinjiang, 1949–53', in Jeremy Brown and Paul G. Pickowicz (eds), *Dilemmas of Victory: The Early Years of the People's Republic of China*, Cambridge, MA: Harvard University Press, 2008, pp. 184–204.

58   On Tibet see Tsering Shakya, *The Dragon in the Land of Snows*, New York: Columbia University Press, 1999; see also Chen Jian, 'The Chinese Communist "Liberation" of Tibet, 1949–51', in Brown and Pickowicz, *Dilemmas of Victory*, pp. 130–59.

59   The formulation is taken from Christian Tyler, *Wild West China: The Taming of Xinjiang*, London: John Murray, 2003, p. 131.

3: Liberation

1   Kang Zhengguo, *Confessions: An Innocent Life in Communist China*, New York: Norton, 2007, p. 5. On the rice-sprout song, see Hung Chang-tai, 'The Dance of Revolution: *Yangge* in Beijing in the Early 1950s', *China Quarterly*, no. 181 (2005), pp. 82–99; David Holm, 'Folk Art as Propaganda: The *Yangge* Movement in Yan'an', in Bonnie S. McDougall (ed.),

Popular Chinese Literature and Performing Arts in the People's Republic of China, 1949–1979, Berkeley: University of California Press, 1984, pp. 3–35.

2   'Reds in Shanghai Show off Might', *New York Times*, 8 July 1949; Ezpeleta, *Red Shadows over Shanghai*, p. 191; Robert Guillain, 'China under the Red Flag', in Otto B. Van der Sprenkel, Robert Guillain and Michael Lindsay (eds), *New China: Three Views*, London: Turnstile Press, 1950, p. 101.

3   Wu Hung, *Remaking Beijing: Tiananmen Square and the Creation of a Political Space*, London: Reaktion Books, 2005.

4   Sun and Dan, *Engineering Communist China*, p. 12.

5   Li Zhisui, *The Private Life of Chairman Mao: The Memoirs of Mao's Personal Physician*, New York: Random House, 1994, pp. 51–2.

6   Bodde, *Peking Diary*, pp. 13–14; Sun and Dan, *Engineering Communist China*, pp. 11–12; a video clip of the 1949 parade in Beijing appears in the digital version of Sang Ye and Geremie R. Barmé, 'Thirteen National Days, a Retrospective', *China Heritage Quarterly*, no. 17, March 2009.

7   Sun and Dan, *Engineering Communist China*, pp. 7–13.

8   Li, *The Private Life of Chairman Mao*, pp. 37–41.

9   Frances Wong, *China Bound and Unbound. History in the Making: An Early Returnee's Account*, Hong Kong: Hong Kong University Press, 2009, pp. 47–50.

10 Edvard Hambro, 'Chinese Refugees in Hong Kong', *Phylon Quarterly*, 18, no. 1 (1957), p. 79; see also Glen D. Peterson, 'To Be or Not to Be a Refugee: The International Politics of the Hong Kong Refugee Crisis, 1949–55', *Journal of Imperial and Commonwealth History*, 36, no. 2 (June 2008), pp. 171–95.

11 The story, with many others, is told by Ying Meijun's daughter, Long Yingtai, in *Da jiang da hai*; see also Glen D. Peterson, 'House Divided: Transnational Families in the Early Years of the People's Republic of China', *Asian Studies Review*, no. 31 (March 2007), pp. 25–40; Mahlon Meyer, *Remembering China from Taiwan: Divided Families and Bittersweet Reunions after the Chinese Civil War*, Hong Kong: Hong Kong University Press, 2012.

12 Kang, *Confessions*, pp. 6–7.

13 Frederic Wakeman, ' "Cleanup": The New Order in Shanghai', in Brown and Pickowicz, *Dilemmas of Victory*, pp. 37–8.

14 Guillain, 'China under the Red Flag', pp. 85–6.

15 Wakeman, ' "Cleanup" ', pp. 42–4.

16 Ji Fengyuan, *Linguistic Engineering: Language and Politics in Mao's China*, Honolulu: University of Hawai'i Press, 2004, p. 68; James L. Watson, *Class and Social Stratification in Post-Revolution China*, Cambridge: Cambridge University Press, 1984, p. 143.

17 Ezpeleta, *Red Shadows over Shanghai*, p. 198; p. 41; Paolo A. Rossi, *The Communist Conquest of Shanghai: A Warning to the West*, Arlington, VA: Twin Circle, 1970, p. 41.

18 Otto B. Van der Sprenkel, 'Part I', in Van der Sprenkel, Guillain and Lindsay (eds), *New China: Three Views*, p. 9.

19 Ezpeleta, *Red Shadows over Shanghai*, p. 191.

20 Shanghai, 1951, B1-2-1339, pp. 9-14; Statistics on counter-revolutionaries, 1962, Hebei, 884-1-223, p. 149.

21 Guillain, 'China under the Red Flag', pp. 91–2.

22 Report on attitudes towards the goverment among ordinary people, 5 July 1950, Nanjing, 4003-1-20, p. 143.

23 Bodde, *Peking Diary*, p. 67; Beijing, July 1949, 2-1-55, p. 2; Beijing, Dec. 1949, 2-1-125, p. 3; Beijing, 30 Dec. 1949, 2-1-55, pp. 43–55.

24 Report from the social services quoted, with slight stylistic changes, in Aminda M. Smith, 'Reeducating the People: The Chinese Communists and the "Thought Reform" of Beggars, Prostitutes, and other "Parasites" ', doctoral dissertation, Princeton University, 2006, pp. 150 and 158.

25 Report on the Branch Reformatory of the Western Suburbs, 24 Oct. 1952, Beijing, 1-6-611, pp. 13–16.

26 Wakeman, ' "Cleanup" ', p. 47; Frank Dikötter, *Crime, Punishment and the Prison in Modern China*, New York: Columbia University Press, 2002, pp. 365–6.

27 Frank Dikötter, *Exotic Commodities: Modern Objects and Everyday Life in China*, New York: Columbia University Press, 2006, pp. 51–2.

28 Van der Sprenkel, 'Part I', pp. 17–18.

29 Beijing, 30 Dec. 1949, 2-1-55, p. 45; Smith, 'Reeducating the People', pp. 99 and 108.

30 The list is in Shanghai, 1950, Q131-4-3925, entire file; the details about the brothels are in Christian Henriot, ' "La Fermeture": The Abolition of Prostitution in Shanghai, 1949–1958', *China Quarterly*, no. 142 (June 1995), pp. 471–80.

31 Smith, 'Reeducating the People', pp. 122–3 and 165, quoting reports from the Bureau for Civil Affairs in Beijing; Henriot, ' "La Fermeture" ', p. 476.

32 Report on the refugee problem, 27 April 1949, Shanghai, B1-2-280, pp. 43–4.

33 Report on attitudes towards the goverment among ordinary people, 5 July 1950, Nanjing, 4003-1-20, p. 143; Nanjing, 30 Aug. 1951, 5012-1-7, pp. 1–3, 26–8, 39–40, 52–5; Nanjing, Nov. 1952, 5012-1-12, pp. 21 and 42.

34 Beijing, Dec. 1949, 2-1-125, p. 3; Smith, 'Reeducating the People', pp. 151 and 156–7.

35 Zhang Lü and Zhu Qiude, *Xibu nüren shiqing: Fu Xinjiang nübing rensheng mingyun gushi koushu shilu* (Oral histories of women soldiers sent to Xinjiang), Beijing: Jiefangjun wenyi chubanshe, 2001, p. 110.

36 Newspaper quoted in Richard Gaulton, 'Political Mobilization in Shanghai, 1949–1951', in Howe, *Shanghai*, p. 46.

37 Shanghai, 12 Sept., 12 Oct. and 18 Nov. 1950, B1-2-280, pp. 98, 117 and 178.

38 On workers in Shanghai see Elizabeth J. Perry, 'Masters of the Country? Shanghai Workers in the Early People's Republic', in Brown and Pickowicz, *Dilemmas of Victory*, pp. 59–79.

39 An excellent description of the salvage in Tianjin appears in Van der

Sprenkel, 'Part I', pp. 36–7.

40 Guillain, 'China under the Red Flag', p. 103.

41 Barnett, letter no. 37, 'Communist Economic Policies and Practices', 14 Sept. 1949.

42 Ezpeleta, *Red Shadows over Shanghai*, p. 204.

43 Guillain, 'China under the Red Flag', pp. 118–19.

44 Ibid., p. 110; Perry, 'Masters of the Country?'

45 Report on tax, 1950, Beijing, 1-9-95, pp. 10, 40 and 63; *Neibu cankao*, 11 May 1950, p. 10; speech by Bo Yibo at the third plenum of the Seventh Central Committee of the CPC, 9 June 1950, Hubei, SZ1-2-15, pp. 13–18.

46 Ezpeleta, *Red Shadows over Shanghai*, p. 205.

47 Shandong, 18 May 1949, A1-2-7, p. 49; *Neibu cankao*, 11 Sept. 1950, pp. 58–9; on Hangzhou and liberation more generally, one should read James Zheng Gao, *The Communist Takeover of Hangzhou: The Transformation of City and Cadre, 1949–1954*, Honolulu: University of Hawai'i Press, 2004.

48 Robert Doyle, 'The Ideal City', *Time*, 29 Aug. 1949; Financial Bulletin, 20 April 1950, PRO, FO371-83346, pp. 31–3.

49 'Shanghai Express', *Time*, 19 June 1950; *Neibu cankao*, 19 May 1950, pp. 48–50; *Neibu cankao*, 1 June 1950, pp. 4–5; *Neibu cankao*, 24 May 1950, p. 73.

50 Beijing, Dec. 1949, 1-9-47, p. 3; 10 Dec. 1953, 1-9-265, p. 7; Report on unemployment in Shanghai circulated by the central government, 30 Aug. 1950, Gansu, 91-1-97, p. 3.

51 *Neibu cankao*, 24 Aug. 1950, pp. 67–9; *Neibu cankao*, 6 June 1950, p. 23; *Neibu cankao*, 10 Aug. 1950, p. 13; Nanjing, Report on Industry, 1951, 5034-1-3, pp. 31–2; Telegram from Chen Yi to Mao Zedong, 10 May 1950, Sichuan, JX1-807, pp. 29–31.

52 'Shanghai Express', *Time*, 19 June 1950.

53 Ezpeleta, *Red Shadows over Shanghai*, p. 209; Randall Gould, 'Shanghai during the Takeover, 1949', *Annals of the American Academy of Political and Social Science*, no. 277 (Sept. 1951), p. 184; Barnett, letter no. 26, 'Communist "Administrative Take Over" of Peiping', 28 Feb. 1949, and letter no. 36, 'Communist Propaganda Techniques', 12 Sept. 1949.

54 Guillain, 'China under the Red Flag', p. 105; Gould, 'Shanghai during the Takeover, 1949', p. 184; Barnett, letter no. 26, 'Communist "Administrative Take Over" of Peiping', 28 Feb. 1949, and letter no. 36, 'Communist Propaganda Techniques', 12 Sept. 1949.

55 Esther Y. Cheo, *Black Country Girl in Red China*, London: Hutchinson, 1980, p. 77; Li, *The Private Life of Chairman Mao*, pp. 41 and 44.

4: The Hurricane

1 'Coolies Rule by Terror', *New York Times*, 11 May 1927; Chang and Halliday, *Mao*, pp. 40–1.

2   *New York Times*, 15 May 1927; Mao Zedong, 'Report on an Investigation of the Peasant Movement in Hunan', March 1927, *Selected Works of Mao Zedong*, Beijing: Foreign Languages Press, 1965, vol. 1, pp. 23–4.

3   Mao, 'Report on an Investigation of the Peasant Movement in Hunan', March 1927, *Selected Works of Mao Zedong*, vol. 1, pp. 23-4.

4   On Zhou Libo and his novel, see Brian J. DeMare, 'Turning Bodies and Turning Minds: Land Reform and Chinese Political Culture, 1946–1952', doctoral dissertation, University of California, Los Angeles, 2007, pp. 64–7; David Der-wei Wang, *The Monster that is History: History, Violence, and Fictional Writing in Twentieth-Century China*, Berkeley: University of California Press, 2004, pp. 166–7.

5   In Russian the vocabulary was *kulak* for rich peasants, *serednyak* for middle-income peasants, *bedniak* for the poor and *batrak* for labourers. The term for landlord was Mao's invention, as we see below.

6   Some remarkable insights into these conversions come from missionaries, who rarely failed to point out the parallels between Christian and communist doctrines; see for instance Robert W. Greene, *Calvary in China*, New York: Putnam, 1953, pp. 77–9.

7   All the quotations are from interviews in the documentary directed by Chen Xiaoqing, *Baofeng zhouyu* (The hurricane), China Memo Films, 2006; on the lack of revolutionary fervour in Manchuria, see Levine, *Anvil of Victory*, p. 199.

8   See, among others, Anne Osborne, 'Property, Taxes, and State Protection of Rights', in Madeleine Zelin, Jonathan Ocko and Robert Gardella (eds), *Contract and Property in Early Modern China*, Stanford: Stanford University Press, 2004, pp. 120–58; Li Huaiyin, *Village Governance in North China, 1875–1936*, Stanford: Stanford University Press, 1995, pp. 234–49.

9   Doak Barnett, letter no. 37, 'Communist economic policies and practices', 14 Sept. 1949; Zhang, *Xuebai xuehong*, pp. 433–6.

10 DeMare, 'Turning Bodies and Turning Minds', pp. 152–3; Philip C. Huang, *The Peasant Economy and Social Change in North China*, Stanford: Stanford University Press, 1985, p. 71; S. T. Tung, 'Land Reform, Red Style', *Freeman*, 25 Aug. 1952, quoted in Richard J. Walker, *China under Communism: The First Five Years*, New Haven: Yale University Press, 1955, p. 131.

11 John L. Buck, *Land Utilization in China*, Nanjing: University of Nanking, 1937; Jack Gray, *Rebellions and Revolutions: China from the 1800s to the 1980s*, Oxford: Oxford University Press, 1990, p. 160.

12 Sun Nainai, Xushui, interviewed in 2006; the practice of burying people alive in the region was also noted by Raymond J. de Jaegher, *The Enemy Within: An Eyewitness Account of the Communist Conquest of China*, Garden City, NY: Doubleday, 1952, pp. 112–14; Liu Shaoqi reprimanded his colleagues for the practice in 1947, as we see below on p. 73.

13 Jack Belden, *China Shakes the World*, New York: Harper, 1949, p. 33.

14 John Byron and Robert Pack, *The Claws of the Dragon: Kang Sheng, the Evil Genius behind Mao and his Legacy of Terror in People's China*, New York: Simon & Schuster, 1992, pp. 125–6; Roger Faligot and Rémi

Kauffer, *The Chinese Secret Service*, New York: Morrow, 1989, pp. 103–4 and 115–18.

15 Zhang Yongdong, *Yijiusijiu nianhou Zhongguo nongcun zhidu biange shi* (A history of changes in the Chinese countryside after 1949), Taipei: Ziyou wenhua chubanshe, 2008, pp. 23–4; Luo Pinghan, *Tudi gaige yundong shi* (A history of the campaign for land reform), Fuzhou: Fujian renmin chubanshe, 2005, pp. 182–4 and 205; on land reform as a political device to overthrow traditional elites one should also read the many essays of Qin Hui, for instance Bian Wu (Qin Hui), 'Gongshe zhi mi: Nongye jituanhua de zai renshi' (The myth of the commune: Revisiting the collectivisation of agriculture), *Ershiyi shiji*, no. 48 (Aug. 1998), pp. 22–36, and Qin Hui, *Nongmin Zhongguo: Lishi fansi yu xianshi xuanze* (Peasant China: Historical reflections and realistic choices), Zhengzhou: Henan renmin chubanshe, 2003.

16 Report by Liu Shaoqi at the National Conference on Land Reform, Aug. 1947, Hebei, 572-1-35, two versions of the same speech in documents 1 and 3, pp. 33–4; this report is also quoted in a much more detailed context in a chapter on land reform by Yang Kuisong, *Zhonghua renmin gongheguo jianguo shi yanjiu* (Studies on the history of the founding of the People's Republic of China), Nanchang: Jiangxi renmin chubanshe, 2009, vol. 1, p. 55.

17 Zhang Mingyuan, 'Wo de huiyi' (My recollections), p. 259, quoted in Zhang Ming, 'Huabei diqu tudi gaige yundong de zhengzhi yunzuo (1946–1949)' (Land reform in North China, 1946–1949), *Ershiyi shiji*, no. 82 (April 2003), pp. 32–41; on Shandong, see Zhang Xueqiang, *Xiangcun bianqian yu nongmin jiyi: Shandong laoqu Junan xian tudi gaige yanjiu* (Village change and peasant memory: Studies on land reform in Junan county, Shandong), Beijing: Shehui kexue wenxian chubanshe, 2006.

18 Liu Tong, *Zhongyuan jiefang zhanzheng jishi* (A historical record of the civil war in the central plains), Beijing: Renmin chubanshe, 2003, pp. 317–18, quoted in Luo, *Tudi gaige yundong shi*, p. 273.

19 *Renmin ribao*, 30 March 1951, p. 2, quoted in DeMare, 'Turning Bodies and Turning Minds', p. 5.

20 Brian Crozier, *The Man who Lost China: The First Full Biography of Chiang Kai-shek*, New York: Scribner, 1976, p. 352.

21 Bo, *Ruogan zhongda shijian yu juece de huigu*, vol. 1, pp. 115–28.

22 Mao Zedong quoted in a speech by Deng Zihui on the spirit of the Third Plenum of the Seventh Central Committee of the CPC, 10 July 1950, Hubei, SZ1-2-15, p. 29.

23 On Guangdong see Shaanxi, 9 Sept. 1950, 123-1-83, p. 164; on the south-west see *Neibu cankao*, 27 July 1950, pp. 93–4; the numbers for tax collection are in *Neibu cankao*, 14 Sept. 1950, p. 67.

24 Reports on grain requisitions, 3 and 8 Feb., 13 and 19 March and 3 May 1950, Hubei, SZ1-2-32, pp. 33, 36, 66–7, 69–70, 72–4 and 83–4; Report on land reform by the South China Bureau, 13 Dec. 1951, Gansu, 91-18-532, pp. 22–5; on Guizhou, see the pioneering

article by Wang Haiguang, 'Zhengliang, minbian yu "feiluan"' (Grain procurements, popular revolts and 'bandit disorder'), *Zhongguo dangdaishi yanjiu*, no. 1 (Aug. 2011), pp. 229–66.

25 *Neibu cankao*, 2 Sept. 1950, pp. 7–8.

26 Shaanxi, 1 Feb. 1951, 123-1-151, pp. 33–8.

27 Report from the East China Bureau, 5 May 1950, Shaanxi, 123-1-83, pp. 1–7.

28 In the case of Hubei, the provincial party committee expressed the need to carry out land reform as a specific strategy to cope with popular rebellion in a series of documents in Hubei, 3 and 8 Feb., 13 and 19 March and 3 May 1950, SZ1-2-32, pp. 33, 36, 66–7, 69–70, 72–4 and 83–4.

29 Sichuan, 12 Sept. 1951, JX1-177, p. 18; Report on land reform from the Teng County Party Committee, 27 Jan. and 2 Feb. 1951, Shandong, A1-2-68, pp. 61 and 64–5.

30 Report from Guizhou, 12 April 1951, Sichuan, JX1-839, pp. 127–8.

31 *Neibu cankao*, 2 June 1950, p. 10.

32 Cheo, *Black Country Girl in Red China*, pp. 161–2; Old Sun, born 1918, Xushui, Henan, interviewed in 2006.

33 Reports on Yunyang, 12 and 30 May and 10 June 1951, Hubei, SZ1-5-75, pp. 37–8, 41–4, 58–60; *Neibu cankao*, 24 Aug. 1950, pp. 65–6; *Neibu cankao*, 9 Sept. 1950, pp. 46–7; Report on land reform by the South China Bureau, 13 Dec. 1951, Gansu, 91-18-532, pp. 22–5.

34 Sichuan, 9 Dec. 1951, JX1-168, p. 72; 4 Nov. 1951, JX1-168, pp. 16–17; 5 March 1951, JX1-837, pp. 124–5.

35 Instructions from Li Jingquan, 21 April 1951, Sichuan, JX1-842, p. 3.

36 Report from Luotian, 1 Aug. 1951, Hubei, SZ1-2-60, pp. 79–85.

37 Yang Li, *Dai ci de hong meigui: Gudacun chenyuan lu* (Thorny rose: The tragedy of Gudacun), Guangzhou: Zhonggong Guangdong shengwei dangshi yanjiushi, 1997, pp. 100–16; Zheng Xiaofeng and Shu Ling, *Tao Zhu zhuan* (A biography of Tao Zhu), Beijing: Zhonggong dangshi chubanshe, 2008, pp. 230–1; Yang, *Zhonghua renmin gongheguo jianguo shi yanjiu*, vol. 1, p. 150; Yue Sai, 'Wo qinxian qinjian de Zhonggong tugai zhenfan sharen shishi' (I personally witnessed killings by the communist party during land reform and the campaign to suppress counter-revolutionaries), *Kaifang*, March 1999; on overseas Chinese in Guangdong see Glen D. Peterson, 'Socialist China and the *Huaqiao*: The Transition to Socialism in the Overseas Chinese Areas of Rural Guangdong, 1949–1956', *Modern China*, 14, no. 3 (July 1988), pp. 309–35.

38 Shandong, October 1948, G26-1-37, doc. 2, pp. 49–50; Financial report on Shandong by Kang Sheng, 1 Jan. and 4 Sept. 1949, Shandong, A1-2-19, pp. 68–9 and 119; Report on the Jiluyu region, 1 Feb. 1949, Shandong, G52-1-194, doc. 5, p. 7; on the impoverishment following land distribution, see also Gao Wangling and Liu Yang, 'Tugai de jiduanhua' (The radicalization of the land reform movement), *Ershiyi shiji*, no. 111 (Feb. 2009), pp. 36–47.

39 Report from the South-west Bureau, 27 June 1951, Sichuan, JX1-809, pp. 42–4.

40 Correspondence between the Ministry of Culture and the Provincial Bureau for Cultural Affairs, Shandong, 19 Sept. 1951, A27-1-230, pp. 69–72.

41 Frederick C. Teiwes, 'The Establishment and Consolidation of the New Regime, 1949–57', in Roderick MacFarquhar (ed.), *The Politics of China: The Eras of Mao and Deng*, New York: Cambridge University Press, 1997, p. 36; see also David Shambaugh, 'The Foundations of Communist Rule in China: The Coercive Dimension', in William C. Kirby (ed.), *The People's Republic of China at 60: An International Assessment*, Cambridge, MA: Harvard University Asia Center, 2011, pp. 21–3.

5: The Great Terror

1 Mao Zedong quoted in a speech by Deng Zihui on the spirit of the Third Plenum of the Seventh Central Committee of the CPC, 10 July 1950, Hubei, SZ1-2-15, pp. 19–47; needless to say, these uncensored quotations are substantially different from the published speech in Mao's collected writings.

2 Mao Zedong, 'Don't Hit Out in All Directions', 6 June 1950, *Selected Works of Mao Zedong*, vol. 5, p. 34.

3 Report from the South China Bureau, 21 Dec. 1950, Guangdong, 204-1-34, p. 50; Report on Guangxi, March 1951, Guangdong, 204-1-34, pp. 16–24; the quotation is from Mao Zedong, 'A Single Spark Can Start a Prairie Fire', 5 Jan. 1930, *Selected Works of Mao Zedong*, vol. 1, p. 124.

4 Instructions from Mao Zedong, 3 Jan. 1951, Sichuan, JX1-836, p. 10; Report on Guangxi from inspection team, March 1951, Guangdong, 204-1-34, pp. 16–24 and 69–70; the telegram Tao wired to Mao is quoted in Yang, *Dai ci de hong meigui*, p. 111; while this telegram may be apocryphal, the figure of 430,000 pacified and 40,000 killed appears in Report from Guangxi Provincial Party Committee, 7 July 1951, Sichuan, JX1-836, pp. 78–82.

5 Report by Luo Ruiqing, 23 Aug. 1952, Shaanxi, 123-25-2, p. 357.

6 The quotation comes from Zhang Guotao, an ex-Politburo member and military leader who fell foul of Mao and was interviewed in Hong Kong in 'High Tide of Terror', *Time*, 5 March 1956; on Dzerzhinsky, see Faligot and Kauffer, *The Chinese Secret Service*, p. 345.

7 Hubei, 21 Nov. 1950, SZ1-2-32, pp. 7–13; Report on Labour Camps, 8 June 1951, and Report from Li Xiannian on the Campaign against Counter-Revolutionaries, 1951, Hubei, SZ1-2-60, pp. 51 and 115; Report by Luo Ruiqing, 23 Aug. 1952, Shaanxi, 123-25-2, p. 357.

8 Orders from Ye Jianying to Tao Zhu and Chen Manyuan, 10 May 1951, Guangdong, 204-1-34, pp. 1–5 (Ye Jianying was Tao Zhu's immediate superior as leader of the Central and South China Bureau); Mao Zedong to Deng Xiaoping, Rao Shushi, Deng Zihui, Ye Jianying, Xi Zhongxun and Gao Gang, 20 April 1951, Sichuan, JX1-834, pp. 75–7.

9 Mao's Comments on Report from Henan, 11 March 1951, Sichuan, JX1-836, p. 17; Mao's instructions to Luo Ruiqing, 30 Jan. 1951, Sichuan, JX1-834, p. 9; see also Comments by Mao, 20 Jan. 1951, Shaanxi, 123-25-2, p. 40.

10 Orders by Mao Zedong transmitted to Li Jingquan, 18 Feb. 1951, Sichuan, JX1-807, pp. 89–91; this form of government in Nazi Germany has been called 'working towards the Führer' by Ian Kershaw, and Roderick MacFarquhar and Michael Schoenhals have proposed calling it 'working towards the Chairman' in the case of the Cultural Revolution, Roderick MacFarquhar and Michael Schoenhals, *Mao's Last Revolution*, Cambridge, MA: Belknap Press of Harvard University Press, 2006.

11 Order from Mao, 14 April 1951, Shandong, A1-5-29, p. 124; this comment is different from the version printed in Mao Zedong, *Jianguo yilai Mao Zedong wengao* (Mao Zedong's manuscripts since the founding of the People's Republic), Beijing: Zhongyang wenxian chubanshe, 1987–96, vol. 2, pp. 215–16, as is the case in many other of Mao's directives used in this chapter; the central directive dated 21 May 1951 is in Mao, *Jianguo yilai*, vol. 2, p. 319.

12 Mao Zedong to Deng Xiaoping, Rao Shushi, Deng Zihui, Ye Jianying, Xi Zhongxun and Gao Gang, 20 April 1951, Sichuan, JX1-834, pp. 75–7; the exact formulation is three out of five military regions that encompassed several provinces each; in Guizhou the number given was 29,000; see Investigation Report on Guizhou, 7 July 1951, Sichuan, JX1-839, pp. 250–2.

13 Minutes of the Third National Conference on Public Security, 16 and 22 May 1951, Shandong, A1-4-9, p. 38; see also Shandong, A51-1-28, p. 215; Luo Ruiqing's talk at the Government Administration Council, 3 Aug. 1951, Shandong, A51-1-28, p. 212.

14 Sichuan, 20 March 1953, JK1-729, p. 29; this document is dated 1953, when the judicial authorities looked into some of the most egregious abuses that took place during the terror in 1951.

15 Report from Qian Ying, secretary of the Central Commission for Discipline Inspection, to Zhu De, 25 March 1953, Sichuan, JK1-730, p. 35.

16 Report on infringements against minority policy, Sichuan, 24 July 1952, JX1-880, pp. 82–3.

17 Statistics and detailed examples about false arrests in Guizhou can be found in a report circulated in Sichuan, 18 June 1951, JX1-839, pp. 227–9.

18 Sichuan, 25 April 1951, JX1-839, pp. 159–60; Report by Deng Xiaoping to Mao Zedong, 13 March 1951, Shandong, A1-5-20, pp. 16–19.

19 Report from Yunnan, 29 April 1951, Sichuan, JX1-837, p. 74.

20 Hu Yaobang, Report on West Sichuan, 29 April 1951, Sichuan, JX1-837, p. 190.

21 Sichuan, 28 May 1951, JX1-837, pp. 105–8; Report by Luo Zhimin, Sichuan, July 1951, JX1-37, pp. 1–2.

22 Comments by Mao, 16 May 1951, Shandong, A1-5-20, p. 134; see also Mao, *Jianguo yilai*, vol. 2, p. 306.

23 Report from Fuling, 5 April and 28 May 1951, Sichuan, JX1-837,

pp. 141–2 and 147–8; Report on capital executions in Wenjiang, 28 June 1951, Sichuan, JX1-342, p. 115; Report from the East China Bureau, including details on west Sichuan, 12 May 1951, Shandong, A1-5-29, p. 189; on mass killings in west Sichuan, including Dayi, Mianyang and other counties, see also Sichuan, JX1-342, 7 June 1951, p. 32.

24 Guo Ya, 'Kaifeng de zhenya' (The campaign to suppress counter-revolutionaries in Kaifeng), in Jiao Guobiao, *Hei wulei jiyi* (Memories from the five black categories), 2010, vol. 8, Beijing: Jiao Guobiao, pp. 57–8.

25 Greene, *Calvary in China*, p. 96.

26 Zhang Yingrong interviewed by Liao Yiwu, *God is Red: The Secret Story of How Christianity Survived and Flourished in Communist China*, New York: HarperCollins, 2011, pp. 121–2; Zhang was classified as a landlord because his eldest brother had been a county chief under the nationalist government.

27 Instructions from the Provincial Party Committee, 3 April 1951, Hebei, 855-1-137, p. 23; Zhang Mao'en interviewed by Liao Yiwu, *God is Red*, p. 136.

28 Instructions from the Provincial Party Committee, 3 April 1951, Hebei, 855-1-137, p. 23; Sichuan, 25 Feb. 1953, JK1-745, p. 67.

29 Report on the killing of Huang Zuyan, 12 April 1951, Comments by Mao Zedong, Shandong, 19 April 1951, A1-5-20, pp. 38–43; a witness at the time also sees this incident as critical in the triggering of 'revenge killings' by Mao: see Li Changyu, 'Mao's "Killing Quotas"', *China Rights Forum*, no. 4 (2005), pp. 41–4.

30 Comments by Mao, 18 March 1951, Shandong, A1-5-20, pp. 63–4; also in Mao, *Jianguo yilai*, vol. 2, pp. 168–9.

31 Reports from Shandong with Comments by Mao, 3, 4 and 7 April 1951, Shandong, A1-4-14, pp. 30, 43 and 50; the reference to 'faint-hearted comrades' is not included in the *Jianguo yilai*, vol. 2, pp. 225–6; Report from Jinan to the Centre, 13 April 1951, Sichuan, JX1-835, pp. 33–4.

32 Report on Preparations for the Raid from the East China Bureau to the Centre, 27 April 1951, Sichuan, JX1-834, pp. 83–4; Robert Loh, *Escape from Red China*, London: Michael Joseph, 1962, pp. 65–6.

33 Loh, *Escape from Red China*, pp. 65–6 and 68.

34 Noel Barber, *The Fall of Shanghai*, New York: Coward, McCann & Geoghegan, 1979, p. 223.

35 'Speech by Mayor Peng Zhen', *Renmin ribao*, 22 June 1951, p. 1; the original is much longer and is abbreviated here.

36 Cheo, *Black Country Girl in Red China*, p. 60.

37 Chow Ching-wen, *Ten Years of Storm: The True Story of the Communist Regime in China*, New York: Holt, Rinehart & Winston, 1960, p. 110; Instructions from the Provincial Party Committee, 3 April 1951, Hebei, 855-1-137, p. 23.

38 Instructions from Mao, 30 April 1951, Sichuan, JX1-834, pp. 92–3; see also Mao, *Jianguo yilai*, vol. 2, pp. 267–8.

39 Luo Ruiqing's report to Mao Zedong, 20 March 1951, Sichuan, JX1-834, pp. 50–2.

40   Kou Qingyan, Report on Border Defence and the Campaign against Counter-Revolutionaries, 28 Oct. 1951, Guangdong, 204-1-27, pp. 152–5; Report by Wang Shoudao to the Centre, 26 Dec. 1952, Shandong, A1-5-85, pp. 120–5.

41   Report by Luo Ruiqing, 2 Jan. 1953, Shandong, A1-5-85, pp. 49 and 62; see also Report by Luo Ruiqing, 22 April 1953, Shandong, A1-5-85, p. 43.

42   Report by Luo Ruiqing, 23 Aug. 1952, Shaanxi, 123-25-2, p. 357.

43   Report from Fuling, 5 April and 28 May 1951, Sichuan, JX1-837, pp. 141–2 and 147–8; Report on capital executions in Wenjiang, 28 June 1951, Sichuan, JX1-342, pp. 113–14; General report by Deng Xiaoping, 30 Nov. 1951, Sichuan, JX1-809, p. 32.

44   Report from the Eastern China region, Shandong, 12 May 1951, A1-5-29, pp. 183–4.

45   Report on counter-revolutionaries, Hebei, 1962, 884-1-223, p. 149.

46   Minutes of the Third National Conference on Public Security, 16 and 22 May 1951, Shandong, A1-4-9, p. 14.

47   Liu Shaoqi, Report at the Fourth Plenum of the Seventh Central Committee, 6 Feb. 1954, Guangdong, 204-1-203, pp. 3–8; Mao Zedong, 'On the Ten Great Relationships', 25 April 1956, circulated on 16 May 1956, Shandong, A1-2-387, pp. 2–17; this figure was probably based on the statistics gathered by Xu Zirong, the deputy minister for public security, and submitted in a report dated 14 January 1954. The report is referred to in Yang Kuisong's article entitled 'Reconsidering the Campaign to Suppress Counterrevolutionaries', *China Quarterly*, no. 193 (March 2008), pp. 102–21.

48   Georg Paloczi-Horvath, *Der Herr der blauen Ameisen: Mao Tse-tung*, Frankfurt am Main: Scheffler, 1962, p. 249.

49   On the outcasts and their social function see Yang Su, *Collective Killings in Rural China during the Cultural Revolution*, Cambridge: Cambridge University Press, 2011, pp. 114–20.

50   Loh, *Escape from Red China*, p. 70.

51   Li, 'Mao's "Killing Quotas"', p. 41.

52   Cheo, *Black Country Girl in Red China*, p. 73.

6: The Bamboo Curtain

1   Peter Lum, *Peking, 1950–1953*, London: Hale, 1958, p. 84; Peter Lum was the pen name of Eleanor Peter Crowe, the wife of Colin Crowe and sister of Catherine Lum, Antonio Riva's wife; 'Old Hands, Beware!', *Time*, 27 Aug. 1951; see also L. H. Lamb, British Embassy Report, 29 Aug. 1951, PRO, FO371-92332, p. 155.

2   'Old Hands, Beware!', *Time*, 27 Aug. 1951; the drawing and other evidence of the affair appear in PRO, FO371-92333, pp. 2–25.

3   Lum, *Peking, 1950–1953*, pp. 90–2.

4   Hao Yen-p'ing, *The Commercial Revolution in Nineteenth-Century China:*

The Rise of Sino-Western Mercantile Capitalism, Berkeley: University of California Press, 1986; Philip Richardson, *Economic Change in China, c. 1800–1950*, Cambridge: Cambridge University Press, 1999, p. 42.

5   On the foreign community in the republican era, see Frank Dikötter, *China before Mao: The Age of Openness*, Berkeley: University of California Press, 2008; a wonderful book on the expatriate communities is Frances Wood, *No Dogs and Not Many Chinese: Treaty Port Life in China, 1843–1943*, London: John Murray, 1998; see also Nicholas R. Clifford, *Spoilt Children of Empire: Westerners in Shanghai and the Chinese Revolution of the 1920s*, Hanover, NH: University Press of New England, 1991; John K. Fairbank, *Chinabound: A Fifty-Year Memoir*, New York: Harper & Row, 1982, p. 51.

6   See the seminal work of Albert Feuerwerker, *The Foreign Establishment in China in the Early Twentieth Century*, Ann Arbor: University of Michigan Press, 1976, pp. 106–7.

7   Elden B. Erickson interviewed by Charles Stuart Kennedy, 25 June 1992, The Association for Diplomatic Studies and Training Foreign Affairs Oral History Project; 'Angus Ward Summarizes Mukden Experiences', *Department of State Bulletin*, 21, no. 547 (26 Dec. 1949), p. 955, quoted in Herbert W. Briggs, 'American Consular Rights in Communist China', *American Journal of International Law*, 44, no. 2 (April 1950), p. 243; see also, among others, Sergei N. Goncharov, John W. Lewis and Xue Litai, *Uncertain Partners: Stalin, Mao, and the Korean War*, Stanford: Stanford University Press, 1993, pp. 33–4.

8   Mao Zedong, 'Farewell, John Leighton Stuart', 18 Aug. 1949, *Selected Works of Mao Zedong*, vol. 4, p. 433.

9   David Middleditch interviewed by Beverley Hooper, 21 Aug. 1971, quoted in Beverley Hooper, *China Stands Up: Ending the Western Presence, 1948–1950*, London: Routledge, 1987, p. 47; on the emergency evacuation see also Hooper, *China Stands Up*, p. 48.

10 Ezpeleta, *Red Shadows over Shanghai*, p. 173; Eleanor Beck, 'My Life in China from 2 January 1946 to 25 September 1949', unpublished manuscript quoted in Hooper, *China Stands Up*, pp. 47–9.

11 Hooper, *China Stands Up*, p. 50.

12 Van der Sprenkel, 'Part I', pp. 5–6.

13 Hooper, *China Stands Up*, pp. 73–4.

14 Ibid., pp. 57 and 77; Edwin W. Martin, *Divided Counsel: The Anglo-American Response to Communist Victory in China*, Lexington: University Press of Kentucky, 1986, p. 42.

15 Doak Barnett, letter no. 38, 'Chinese Communists: Nationalism and the Soviet Union', 16 Sept. 1949, Institute of Current World Affairs; Bodde, *Peking Diary*, pp. 219–20; David Middleditch interviewed by Beverley Hooper, 21 Aug. 1979, in Hooper, *China Stands Up*, p. 73.

16 Hooper, *China Stands Up*, pp. 78–9, quoting Beck, 'My Life in China'.

17 Ibid., pp. 80–1.

18 American Embassy to Foreign Service, 15 March 1951, PRO, FO371-92331, pp. 29–34; Control of American Assets, Jan. 1951, PRO, FO371-92294, pp. 81–7.

19   William G. Sewell, *I Stayed in China*, London: Allen & Unwin, 1966, p. 126.

20   Rossi, *The Communist Conquest of Shanghai*, pp. 100–1; Liliane Willens, *Stateless in Shanghai*, Hong Kong: China Economic Review Publishing, 2010, pp. 253–4.

21   Godfrey Moyle interviewed by Barber, *The Fall of Shanghai*, p. 226.

22   Memorandum and Letter from the British Consulate General in Shanghai, 2 and 6 March 1951, PRO, FO371-92260 pp. 99–101 and 128–9.

23   Rossi, *The Communist Conquest of Shanghai*, pp. 72–3; see also Aron Shai, 'Imperialism Imprisoned: The Closure of British Firms in the People's Republic of China', *English Historical Review*, 104, no. 410 (Jan. 1989), pp. 88–109.

24   Rossi, *The Communist Conquest of Shanghai*, pp. 67–70.

25   Peitaiho Beach, 11 Sept. 1952, PRO, FO371-99238, pp. 13–15, and British Embassy to Foreign Office, 21 Jan. 1952, PRO, FO371-99345, p. 31.

26   On Harriet Mills, who later wrote about her experience and became a sinologist, see J. M. Addis, Conversation with Sardar Panikkar, 4 Dec. 1951, PRO, FO371-92333, pp. 135–6; Testimony by Father Rigney, 7 March 1956, PRO, FO371-121000, pp. 26–7; in an interesting case of Stockholm syndrome, Harriet Mills proclaimed after her deportation from the country in 1955 that 'New China is a peace-loving nation' and stuck to her official confession as a spy as well as to her denunciations of several other Americans; see Arrests and Trials in China, 1955, PRO, FO371-115182, pp. 54–70; the Ricketts also justified their incarceration; see Allyn and Adele Rickett, *Prisoners of Liberation*, New York: Cameron Associates, 1957; both cases gave rise to allegations of brainwashing; on the sweep see Lum, *Peking, 1950–1953*, p. 71.

27   Orders on the Treatment of Foreigners, Shandong, 14 Aug. 1951, A1-4-9, p. 85; Lum, *Peking, 1950–1953*, p. 21.

28   Lum, *Peking, 1950–1953*, p. 99.

29   Walker, *China under Communism*, p. 19; on the pitiable state of many White Russians in 1953, see Parliamentary Question, 28 Jan. 1953, PRO, FO371-105338, pp. 61–2 and 116–22.

30   '14 Chinese Trappists Dead, 274 are Missing', *Catholic Herald*, 19 Dec. 1947; R. G. Tiedemann, *Reference Guide to Christian Missionary Societies in China: From the Sixteenth to the Twentieth Century*, Armonk, NY: M. E. Sharpe, 2009, p. 25; Theresa Marie Moreau, *Blood of the Martyrs: Trappist Monks in Communist China*, Los Angeles: Veritas Est Libertas, 2012; Hooper, *China Stands Up*, p. 38.

31   Creighton Lacy, 'The Missionary Exodus from China', *Pacific Affairs*, 28, no. 4 (Dec. 1955), pp. 301–14; 'New China Hands?', *Time*, 17 Jan. 1949.

32   Hooper, *China Stands Up*, p. 115.

33   British Legation to the Holy See, 22 Aug. 1950, FO371-83535, p. 70.

34   Foreign Office, The Treatment of Christian Institutions under the Present Regime in China, 29 Aug. 1951, PRO, FO371-92368, pp. 112–17.

35   International Fides Service, 22 Sept. 1951, PRO, FO371-92333, pp. 29–32; Rossi, *The Communist Conquest of Shanghai*, pp. 137–8.

36 Orders from the Bureau of Public Security, Shandong, 14 Aug. 1951, A1-4-9, p. 85; on Mao's fascination with the Vatican, see Chang and Halliday, *Mao*, p. 327; see also Rossi, *The Communist Conquest of Shanghai*, pp. 144–5.

37 W. Aedan McGrath, *Perseverance through Faith: A Priest's Prison Diary*, ed. Theresa Marie Moreau, Bloomington, IN: Xlibris Corporation, 2008.

38 'On the King's Highway', *Time*, 15 Sept. 1952; 'US Bishop Died in Red Jail', *New York Times*, 3 Sept. 1952; see also Jean-Paul Wiest, *Maryknoll in China: A History, 1918–1955*, Armonk, NY: M. E. Sharpe, 1988, pp. 395–400.

39 A. Olbert, 'Short Report about the Diocese of Tsingtao', 17 July 1953, AG SVD, Box 616, pp. 4440–6; 'The Struggle of the Archbishop of Lan Chow', 1953, AG SVD, Box 631, pp. 5878–86.

40 'The Suspicious Butterflies', *Time*, 3 Nov. 1952; China Missionary Newsletters, Oct. 1952, PRO, FO137-105336, p. 9.

41 Hooper, *China Stands Up*, p. 119.

42 Christianity in Communist China, 1954, PRO, FO371-110371, p. 43; Arrest of Canadian Nuns at Canton, 20 April 1951, PRO, FO371-92331, pp. 49–54; Foreign Office, 19 Dec. 1951, PRO, FO371-92333 p. 130; André Athenoux, *Le Christ crucifié au pays de Mao*, Paris: Alsatia, 1968, pp. 127–8.

43 *Catholic Herald*, 14 Dec. 1941, p. 1; Walker, *China under Communism*, p. 191; see also Arrest of Canadian Nuns at Canton, 20 April 1951, PRO, FO371-92331, p. 49.

44 Christianity in Communist China, 1954, PRO, FO371-110371, pp. 43–5; the 1954 numbers are from Report from the Centre, Shandong, A14-1-16, 7 May 1954, p. 2; Letter from Qingdao missionaries in Hong Kong to Rome, 23 March 1953, AG SVD, Box 616, p. 4424.

45 Barnett, letter no. 38, 'Chinese Communists'; Knight Biggerstaff, *Nanking Letters, 1949*, Ithaca, NY: China–Japan Program, Cornell University, 1979, pp. 50–1; the monument in Shenyang went up in 1946; see Gray, 'Looted City', *Time*, 11 March 1946, and also J. A. L. Morgan, Journey to Manchuria, 30 Nov. 1956, PRO, FO371-120985, p. 129; 'Leaning to One Side', *Time*, 19 Sept. 1949.

46 Mao Zedong, 'On the People's Democratic Dictatorship: In Commemoration of the 28th Anniversary of the Communist Party of China, June 30, 1949', in *Selected Works of Mao Zedong*, vol. 4, p. 423; 'Mao Settles the Dust', *Time*, 11 July 1949; Chang and Halliday, *Mao*, p. 323.

47 The exact amounts of funding for the Long March are in Taylor, *The Generalissimo*, p. 111; 'On the Ten Major Relationships', 25 April 1956, *Selected Works of Mao Tse-tung*, vol. 5, p. 304.

48 The propaganda against Tito was noted repeatedly by Barnett, letter no. 38, 'Chinese Communists'.

49 Paul Wingrove, 'Gao Gang and the Moscow Connection: Some Evidence from Russian Sources', *Journal of Communist Studies and Transition Politics*, 16, no. 4 (Dec. 2000), p. 93.

50 Philip Short, *Mao: A Life*, London: Hodder & Stoughton, 1999, p. 422;

the best article on Mao's trip is Paul Wingrove, who uses archives from the Ministry of Foreign Affairs: Paul Wingrove, 'Mao in Moscow, 1949–50: Some New Archival Evidence', *Journal of Communist Studies and Transition Politics*, 11, no. 4 (Dec. 1995), pp. 309–34; David Wolff, '"One Finger's Worth of Historical Events": New Russian and Chinese Evidence on the Sino-Soviet Alliance and Split, 1948–1959', *Cold War International History Project Bulletin*, Working Paper no. 30 (Aug. 2002), pp. 1–74; Sergey Radchenko and David Wolff, 'To the Summit via Proxy-Summits: New Evidence from Soviet and Chinese Archives on Mao's Long March to Moscow, 1949', *Cold War International History Project Bulletin*, no. 16 (Winter 2008), pp. 105–82; see also Heinzig, *The Soviet Union and Communist China 1945–1950*.

51   Report of Negotiation between Zhou, Mikoyan and Vyshinsky to Stalin, 2 and 3 Feb. 1950, RGASPI, 82-2-1247, pp. 1–6, 68–93.

52   Wingrove, 'Mao in Moscow', p. 331.

53   Financial Bulletin, 20 April 1950, PRO, FO371-83346, p. 33; see also Interrogation Reports, Jan. 1952, PRO, FO371-99364, p. 19; Rossi, *The Communist Conquest of Shanghai*, p. 91.

54   Interrogation Reports, Jan. 1952, PRO, FO371-99364, p. 138; Interrogation Report, 31 May 1951, PRO, FO371-92353, p. 2.

55   Interrogation Reports, Jan. 1952, PRO, FO371-99364, pp. 24 and 138; Loh, *Escape from Red China*, p. 148; Willens, *Stateless in Shanghai*, p. 222; Hong Kong Interrogation Reports 726 and 863, 10 June and 26 Nov. 1954, RG59, Box 5, 903069, Lot 56D454, National Archives at College Park.

56   T. G. Zazerskaya, *Sovetskie spetsialisty i formirovanie voenno-promyshlennogo kompleksa Kitaya (1949–1960 gg.)*, St Petersburg: Sankt Peterburg Gosudarstvennyi Universitet, 2000; Shen Zhihua, *Sulian zhuanjia zai Zhongguo* (Soviet experts in China), Beijing: Xinhua chubanshe, 2009; Deborah A. Kaple, 'Soviet Advisors in China in the 1950s', in Odd Arne Westad (ed.), *Brothers in Arms: The Rise and Fall of the Sino-Soviet Alliance, 1945–1963*, Washington: Woodrow Wilson Center Press, 1998, pp. 117–40; see also '150,000 Big Noses', *Time*, 16 Oct. 1950.

57   RGASPI, 25 June 1950, 17-137-402, pp. 114 and 221–30; 18 Dec. 1950, 17-137-403, pp. 215–24.

58   Ministry of Foreign Affairs, Beijing, 6 Sept. 1963, 109-3321-2, pp. 66–8; a much more detailed account of exports to the Soviet Union from 1949 to 1962 appears in Frank Dikötter, *Mao's Great Famine: The History of China's Most Devastating Catastrophe, 1958–1962*, London: Bloomsbury, 2010, pp. 73–7.

59   Hua-yu Li, 'Instilling Stalinism in Chinese Party Members: Absorbing Stalin's *Short Course* in the 1950s', in Thomas P. Bernstein and Hua-yu Li (eds), *China Learns from the Soviet Union, 1949–Present*, Lanham, MD: Lexington Books, 2009, pp. 107–30; Esther Holland Jian, *British Girl, Chinese Wife*, Beijing: New World Press, 1985, p. 134.

60   K. E. Priestley, 'The Sino-Soviet Friendship Association', *Pacific Affairs*, 25, no. 3 (Sept. 1952), p. 289; Paul Clark, *Chinese Cinema: Culture and*

Politics since 1949, Cambridge: Cambridge University Press, 1987, pp. 40–1.

7: War Again

1   Andrei Lankov, *From Stalin to Kim Il Sung: The Formation of North Korea, 1945–1960*, London: Hurst, 2002; see also Jasper Becker, *Rogue Regime: Kim Jong Il and the Looming Threat of North Korea*, New York: Oxford University Press, 2005.

2   Chen Jian, *China's Road to the Korean War*, New York: Columbia University Press, 1996, p. 110; Goncharov, Lewis and Xue, *Uncertain Partners*, pp. 142–5.

3   Shen Zhihua, 'Sino-North Korean Conflict and its Resolution during the Korean War', *Cold War International History Project Bulletin*, nos 14–15 (Winter 2003–Spring 2004), pp. 9–24; Shen Zhihua, 'Sino-Soviet Relations and the Origins of the Korean War: Stalin's Strategic Goals in the Far East', *Journal of Cold War Studies*, 2, no. 2 (Spring 2000), pp. 44–68.

4   Max Hastings, *The Korean War*, New York: Simon & Schuster, 1987, p. 53.

5   Chang and Halliday, *Mao*, p. 360.

6   Alexandre Y. Mansourov, 'Stalin, Mao, Kim, and China's Decision to Enter the Korean War, Sept. 16–Oct. 15, 1950: New Evidence from the Russian Archives', *Cold War International History Project Bulletin*, nos 6–7 (Winter 1995), p. 114.

7   Nie Rongzhen, 'Beijing's Decision to Intervene', and Peng Dehuai, 'My Story of the Korean War', in Xiaobing Li, Allan R. Millett and Bin Yu (eds), *Mao's Generals Remember Korea*, Lawrence: University Press of Kansas, 2001, pp. 31 and 41.

8   The episode is recounted on the basis of detailed archival sources in Chang and Halliday, *Mao*, p. 364.

9   Quoted in Matthew Aid and Jeffrey T. Richelson, 'U.S. Intelligence and China: Collection, Analysis, and Covert Action', Digital National Security Archive Series, p. 3 (online publication).

10   David Halberstam, *The Coldest Winter: America and the Korean War*, London: Macmillan, 2008, p. 372.

11   Shu Guang Zhang, *Mao's Military Romanticism: China and the Korean War, 1950–1953*, Lawrence: University Press of Kansas, 1995, p. 126; Richard Peters and Xiaobing Li (eds), *Voices from the Korean War: Personal Stories of American, Korean, and Chinese Soldiers*, Lexington: University Press of Kentucky, 2004; see also interrogation reports of prisoners of war, for instance KG0876, Li Shu Sun, 27 Nov. 1951; KG0896, Chang Hsin Hua, 21 Dec. 1951; KG0915, K'ang Wen Ch'eng, 29 Dec. 1951; KG0937, Chou Shih Ch'ang, 9 Jan. 1952; all in Assistant Chief of Staff G2, RG319, Box 332, 950054 ATIS Interrogation Reports, National Archives at College Park.

12   Li Xiu interviewed by Max Hastings, *The Korean War*, p. 172.

13   The details of Mao's repeated interventions are in Zhang, *Mao's Military Romanticism*, p. 137.

14   Mao, *Jianguo yilai*, vol. 2, p. 152.

15   Chang and Halliday, *Mao*, p. 367.

16   International Committee of the Red Cross, Geneva, 'Refusal of Repatriation', 25 July 1951, BAG 210-056-003.03, pp. 70–4; on the POWs see David Cheng Chang, 'To Return Home or "Return to Taiwan": Conflicts and Survival in the "Voluntary Repatriation" of Chinese POWs in the Korean War', doctoral dissertation, University of California, San Diego, 2011.

17   Peters and Li (eds), *Voices from the Korean War*, p. 178.

18   Pete Schulz, letter to Max Hastings, quoted in *The Korean War*, p. 196.

19   The numbers vary and these are the most accepted ones, quoted for instance in Chang and Halliday, *Mao*, p. 378.

20   Loh, *Escape from Red China*, pp. 56–7; Report on attitudes towards the government among ordinary people, Nanjing, 4003-1-20, 5 July 1950, p. 143; *Neibu cankao*, 13 July 1950, pp. 41–2.

21   *Neibu cankao*, 7 Nov. 1950, p. 23; Opinion Survey, Nanjing, 22 Nov. 1950, 4003-3-89, pp. 72–7.

22   *Neibu cankao*, 30 Nov. 1950, pp. 151–7.

23   *Nanfang ribao*, translated in *Current Background*, no. 55, American Consulate-General, Hong Kong, 22 Jan. 1951, quoted in Walker, *China under Communism*, p. 302, with a few stylistic changes.

24   Walker, *China under Communism*, pp. 302–5; Lum, *Peking, 1950–1953*, p. 62.

25   Central Directive, 19 Dec. 1950, Guangdong, 204-1-245, p. 101.

26   Loh, *Escape from Red China*, pp. 57–8.

27   Gansu, Report on the Hate America, Aid Korea Campaign, 25 March 1951, 91-1-314, p. 13; Guangdong, 1 April 1951, 204-1-36, pp. 41–2; Guangdong, 1 April 1951, 204-1-36, p. 51.

28   Loh, *Escape from Red China*, p. 59.

29   Report from the North-east China Bureau, 9 Oct. 1951, Gansu, 91-1-244, pp. 80–90; Report at the Politburo by Deng Xiaoping, Sichuan, 6 Nov. 1951, JX1-809, p. 41.

30   *Neibu cankao*, 16 July 1951, p. 92; 30 Aug. 1951, pp. 102–3.

31   *Neibu cankao*, 31 Aug. 1951, p. 108; 16 July 1951, p. 92; 23 Oct. 1951, p. 60.

32   *Neibu cankao*, 30 Aug. 1951, pp. 102–3.

33   *Neibu cankao*, 18 Sept. 1951, p. 90; 25 July 1951, p. 148.

34   Guangdong, 1 April 1951, 204-1-36, pp. 41–2; Li, *The Private Life of Chairman Mao*, p. 56.

35   Jilin, 16 March 1951, 2-7-56, p. 15; Report by the Wendeng County Party Committee, Shandong, 28 Sept. 1951, A1-2-74, pp. 106–8; Report from the North China Region, Hebei, 10 May 1951, 855-1-84, pp. 77–8.

36   Report from the North China Region, Hebei, 10 May 1951, 855-1-84, pp. 77–8; the case from Yueyang is in *Neibu cankao*, 23 July 1951, p. 140.

37   Report from the North China Region, Hebei, 10 May 1951, 855-1-84, pp. 77–8; *Neibu cankao*, 23 July 1951, p. 140.

38   Shandong, 5 Dec. 1951, A1-4-9, pp. 122–5.

39   Report to the People's Congress, Jilin, 30 Dec. 1950, 2-7-47, pp. 59–60;

Reports on Cooperativisation, Jilin, 19 Jan., 16 and 22 March and 23 June 1951, 2-7-56, pp. 2, 14–15, 26 and 84.

40   Jilin, 20 Feb., 25 March and 5 Aug. 1952, 1-1(8)-37, pp. 1, 2 and 14–15; Jilin, 2 and 29 Feb. 1952, 2-8-32, pp. 91–4 and 107.

41   *Neibu cankao*, 28 May 1951, pp. 47–8; 3 June 1951, p. 36; General report by Deng Xiaoping, Sichuan, 30 Nov. 1951, JX1-809, p. 31; *Neibu cankao*, 18 March 1952, pp. 155–7; 24 March 1952, pp. 227–8; 7 April 1952, pp. 68–9.

42   Kenneth G. Lieberthal, *Revolution and Tradition in Tientsin, 1949–1952*, Stanford: Stanford University Press, 1980, pp. 98–9.

43   Report on Germ Warfare from the Centre, Shandong, 2 April 1952, A1-5-58, p. 104.

44   On the Needham expedition, see Ruth Rogaski, 'Nature, Annihilation, and Modernity: China's Korean War Germ-Warfare Experience Reconsidered', *Journal of Asian Studies*, 61, no. 2 (May 2002), p. 382; when interviewed by Jonathan Mirsky in 1961, Needham admitted not having seen any evidence at all, but added that he trusted what he was told by Chinese bacteriologists; Jonathan Mirsky, email correspondence, 28 June 2012.

45   Lum, *Peking, 1950–1953*, p. 122.

46   'Transfusions of Hate', *Time*, 23 June 1952; Raja Hutheesing, *Window on China*, London: Derek Verschoyle, 1953, pp. 169–70.

47   Frank Moraes is quoted extensively in 'Transfusions of Hate', *Time*, 23 June 1952; on Unit 731 and the United States see Stephen L. Endicott, 'Germ Warfare and "Plausible Denial": The Korean War, 1952–1953', *Modern China*, 5, no. 1 (Jan. 1979), pp. 79–104; Li, *The Private Life of Chairman Mao*, p. 56.

48   Waldemar Kaempffert, 'Science in Review', *New York Times*, 6 April 1952; *Neibu cankao*, 14 March 1952, p. 111; 24 March 1952, pp. 220 and 222.

49   *Neibu cankao*, 24 March 1952, pp. 220–2; 6 May 1952, p. 31; 28 March 1952, p. 275.

50   *Neibu cankao*, 6 May 1952, pp. 30–3; on Dehui, see Jilin, 22 April 1951, 2-7-56, pp. 14–15; on the recurrence of cases of holy water after 1952 one should read Steve A. Smith, 'Local Cadres Confront the Supernatural: The Politics of Holy Water (*Shenshui*) in the PRC, 1949–1966', *China Quarterly*, no. 188 (2006), pp. 999–1022.

51   Rogaski, 'Nature, Annihilation, and Modernity', p. 384.

52   Report by the Shandong Commission for Discipline Inspection, 17 Nov. 1952, Sichuan, JK1-729, p. 5; Report from the Shaanxi Provincial Party Committee, 13 Oct. 1953, Shandong, A1-5-75, p. 220.

53   Lum, *Peking, 1950–1953*, p. 124; on Tianjin, see Rogaski, 'Nature, Annihilation, and Modernity', p. 394.

54   On the impact of the campaign on the urban landscape, see Rogaski, 'Nature, Annihilation, and Modernity', p. 394.

55   William Kinmond, *No Dogs in China: A Report on China Today*, New York: Thomas Nelson, 1957, p. 164.

56   Lum, *Peking, 1950–1953*, p. 125; Report to Zhu De from Qian Ying, Secretary of the Central Commission for Discipline Inspection, 25 March

1953, Sichuan, JK1-730, p. 31; Ministry of Health to Mao Zedong, Report on achievements in health care of the past four years, 10 Oct. 1953, Gansu, 91-2-185, pp. 37–8.

57 Report on hygiene circulated by the Centre, 7 Jan. 1953, Shandong, A1-5-84, pp. 63 and 74–5; Ministry of Health to Mao Zedong, Report on achievements in health care of the past four years, 10 Oct. 1953, Gansu, 91-2-185, pp. 37–8; Report from the Shaanxi Provincial Party Committee, 13 Oct. 1953, Shandong, A1-5-75, p. 220.

58 Rowan, *Chasing the Dragon*, p. 50; *Renmin ribao*, 12 Sept. 1949, p. 5; 27 Dec. 1950, p. 6; Lum, *Peking, 1950–1953*, pp. 100 and 121; Confidential letter from the British Embassy, 8 May 1952, PRO, FO371-99236, p. 137; Cheo, *Black Country Girl in Red China*, pp. 46–8.

59 Lum, *Peking, 1950–1953*, p. 129; Cheo, *Black Country Girl in Red China*, pp. 46–8.

60 Cheo, *Black Country Girl in Red China*, pp. 46–8.

61 Report from Qian Ying, secretary of the Central Commission for Discipline Inspection, to Zhu De, Sichuan, 25 March 1953, JK1-730, p. 32; Report from People's Council, Shandong, 16 Dec. 1952, A101-3-228, p. 59; Shandong, 6 Dec. 1954, A101-3-318, pp. 81–4.

62 Zhang, *Mao's Military Romanticism*, pp. 181–3; Chen, *China's Road to the Korean War*; Kathryn Weathersby, 'Deceiving the Deceivers: Moscow, Beijing, Pyongyang, and the Allegations of Bacteriological Weapons Use in Korea', *Cold War International History Project Bulletin*, no. 11 (1998), pp. 181 and 183; see also Milton Leitenberg, 'New Russian Evidence on the Korean War Biological Warfare Allegations: Background and Analysis', *Cold War International History Project Bulletin*, no. 11 (1998), pp. 185–99; Milton Leitenberg, 'The Korean War Biological Weapon Allegations: Additional Information and Disclosures', *Asian Perspective*, 24, no. 3 (2000), pp. 159–72.

8: The Purge

1 Bing Lu, *Xin Zhongguo fan fubai diyi da'an: Qiangbi Liu Qingshan, Zhang Zishan jishi* (New China's first big case against corruption: The execution of Liu Qingshan and Zhang Zishan), Beijing: Falü chubanshe, 1990; a copy of the report on Zhang Zishan and Liu Qingshan by Bo Yibo and Liu Lantao to Mao Zedong, which triggered the Three-Anti Campaign, is in Gansu, 91-13-19, 29 Nov. 1951, p. 10.

2 Bo, *Ruogan zhongda shijian yu juece de huigu*, vol. 1, pp. 157–8.

3 Ibid., pp. 160–1.

4 Geremie Barmé, *The Forbidden City*, Cambridge, MA: Harvard University Press, 2008, p. 144.

5 Gao Hua, *Hong taiyang shi zenyang shengqi de. Yan'an zhengfeng yundong de lailong qumai* (How did the red sun rise over Yan'an? A history of the Rectification Campaign), Hong Kong: Chinese University Press, 2000, pp. 1, 530, 580 and 593; see also David E. Apter and Tony

Saich, *Revolutionary Discourse in Mao's Republic*, Cambridge, MA: Harvard University Press, 1994; Chen Yung-fa, *Yan'an de yinying* (Yan'an's Shadow), Taipei: Institute of Modern History, Academia Sinica, 1990.

6   Orders from the Centre on the Three-Anti Campaign, Hebei, 1 Dec. 1951, 855-1-75, pp. 73–4; Mao, *Jianguo yilao*, vol. 2, p. 528.

7   Instruction by Mao to all local units, Sichuan, 30 Dec. 1951, JX1-813, p. 56; on Zhou, see the seminal article of Michael M. Sheng, 'Mao Zedong and the Three-Anti Campaign (November 1951 to April 1952): A Revisionist Interpretation', *Twentieth-Century China*, 32, no. 1 (Nov. 2006), pp. 56–80; see also Zhang Ming, 'Zhizheng de daode kunjing yu tuwei zhi dao: Sanfan wufan yundong jiexi' (Analysis of the Three-Anti and Five-Anti Campaign), *Ershiyi shiji*, no. 92 (Dec. 2005), pp. 46–58.

8   Mao, *Jianguo yilai*, vol. 2, p. 535.

9   Directives from the Centre, 9 Jan. 1952, Guangdong, 204-1-278, pp. 23–8; partially reprinted in Mao, *Jianguo yilai*, vol. 3, pp. 30–1; Directives from the Centre, 5 and 11 Feb. 1952, Guangdong, 204-1-278, pp. 148–53; these reports are partially reproduced, without some of the figures, in Mao, *Jianguo yilai*, vol. 3, pp. 154–5 and 192; Report from Bo Yibo, 28 Feb. 1952, Guangdong, 204-1-253, pp. 33–5.

10   Tommy Jieqin Wu, *A Sparrow's Voice: Living through China's Turmoil in the 20th Century*, Shawnee Mission, KS: M.I.R. House International, 1999, pp. 91–2.

11   Sun and Dan, *Engineering Communist China*, pp. 17–18.

12   Chow, *Ten Years of Storm*, pp. 126–7.

13   Report from the North China Region, Hebei, 15 April 1952, 888-1-13, pp. 98–9; Report by Luo Ruiqing and Directives from the Centre, 8 and 9 Jan. 1952, Guangdong, 204-1-278, pp. 99–105; Report from Bo Yibo, Hebei, 3 Jan. 1952, 888-1-1, pp. 21–4; Report from Bo Yibo, Hebei, 20 Jan. 1952, 888-1-1, p. 32.

14   Report from Xi Zhongxun and Instructions from the Centre, 11 and 13 Dec. 1951, Guangdong, 204-1-253, pp. 5–6; Report from Jinan, 27 Dec. and 4 Jan. 1952, Guangdong, 204-1-278, pp. 32–4.

15   Loh, *Escape from Red China*, p. 82; Chow, *Ten Years of Storm*, p. 125; Li, *The Private Life of Chairman Mao*, p. 64.

16   Report from the North China Region, Hebei, 8 Feb. 1952, 888-2-8, pp. 19–20; Report from the North China Region, Hebei, 29 Feb. and 12 Oct. 1952, 888-1-22, pp. 44 and 77.

17   Report from the North China Region, Hebei, 20 Feb. 1952, 888-1-24, p. 23; Gansu, 23 March 1952, 91-18-540, p. 33.

18   Loh, *Escape from Red China*, p. 82; Li, *The Private Life of Chairman Mao*, p. 64.

19   Report by An Ziwen, Hebei, 18 Oct. 1952, 888-1-1, pp. 136–8.

20   Report on relationships between Liu Qingshan, Zhang Zishan and the Tianjin Special District, Hebei, 1952, 888-1-92, pp. 134–41; Chow, *Ten Years of Storm*, p. 125.

21   Mao, *Jianguo yilai*, vol. 3, p. 21; Sheng, 'Mao Zedong and the Three-Anti Campaign', p. 32.

22   Alec Woo interviewed by Jasper Becker, *C. C. Lee: The Textile Man*, Hong Kong: Textile Alliance, 2011, p. 56; Pepper, *Civil War in China*, pp. 118–25.

23   Wong Siu-lun, *Emigrant Entrepreneurs: Shanghai Industrialists in Hong Kong*, Hong Kong: Oxford University Press, 1988; Becker, *C. C. Lee*, pp. 55–63.

24   Hugh Seton-Watson noted how there were three stages in East Europe, namely a 'genuine coalition' with some other forces, a 'bogus coalition' with those not directly controlled by the communist party, and finally a 'monolithic regime' as everything outside the party was brought to heel; see Hugh Seton-Watson, *The East European Revolution*, London: Methuen, 1950, pp. 167–71.

25   Huang Kecheng, *Huang Kecheng zishu* (The autobiography of Huang Kecheng), Beijing: Renmin chubanshe, 1994, p. 217; Mao Zedong, 'Report to the Second Plenary Session of the Seventh Central Committee of the Communist Party of China', 5 March 1949, *Selected Works of Mao Zedong*, vol. 4, p. 364.

26   For a more upbeat assessment, see Marie-Claire Bergère, 'Les Capitalistes shanghaïens et la période de transition entre le régime Guomindang et le communisme (1948–1952)', *Etudes Chinoises*, 8, no. 2 (Autumn 1989), p. 22.

27   Rossi, *The Communist Conquest of Shanghai*, p. 65; 'Merchants and the New Order', *Time*, 17 March 1952; John Gardner, 'The Wu-fan Campaign in Shanghai', in Doak Barnett, *Chinese Communist Policies in Action*, Seattle: University of Washington Press, 1969, pp. 477–53.

28   Loh, *Escape from Red China*, pp. 85–9.

29   Report by Luo Ruiqing, 24 Feb. 1952, Sichuan, JX1-812, p. 29; *Changjiang ribao*, 12 March 1952, quoted in Theodore Hsi-en Chen and Wen-hui C. Chen, 'The "Three-Anti" and "Five-Anti" Movements in Communist China', *Pacific Affairs*, 26, no. 1 (March 1953), p. 15.

30   Loh, *Escape from Red China*, pp. 85–9, 95 and 97; Bo Yibo, Report from Shanghai, Hebei, 12 April 1952, 888-1-10, pp. 27–8; Report on a denunciation meeting, Shanghai, 4 April 1952, B182-1-373, pp. 183–5.

31   Chow, *Ten Years of Storm*, p. 125; Report on a denunciation meeting, 15 April 1952, Shanghai, B182-1-373, pp. 232–5; Sichuan, 12 May 1952, JX1-420, p. 30; Guangdong, 1952, 204-1-69, pp. 73–4; Guangdong, 10 Oct. 1952, 204-1-69, pp. 45–7 and 55–9; *Neibu cankao*, 5 Feb. 1952, p. 31.

32   Loh, *Escape from Red China*, p. 98; Chow, *Ten Years of Storm*, p. 133.

33   Loh, *Escape from Red China*, p. 98; Shanghai, 27 March 1952, B182-373, p. 144; on the campaign in Shanghai, one should read Yang, *Zhonghua renmin gongheguo jianguo shi yanjiu*, pp. 260–307.

34   Instructions from the Centre and Report from Tianjin, Hebei, 15 Feb. 1952, 888-1-10, p. 31; Report by Beijing to the Centre, 13 Feb. 1952, Sichuan, JX1-420, p. 6; Shanghai, July 1952, B13-2-287, p. 20.

35   Hutheesing, *Window on China*, p. 165.

36   Gardner, 'The Wu-fan Campaign in Shanghai', p. 524; Loh, *Escape from Red China*, p. 117; Walker, *China under Communism*, p. 108.

37 Instructions from the Centre and Report from Tianjin, Hebei, 15 Feb.
    1952, 888-1-10, pp. 31–5; Report by Tan Zhenlin to Mao Zedong,
    Sichuan, 5 May 1952, JX1-812, pp. 180–1; on the collapse of tax income,
    blamed on the Three-Anti and Five-Anti campaigns, see for instance
    Report from the North-east Tax Bureau to the Centre, 31 Oct. 1952,
    Gansu, 91-1-495, pp. 82–91.

38 Report on Trade, 10 Jan. 1953, Zhejiang, J125-2-29, pp. 1–3; Report by
    Tan Zhenlin to Mao Zedong, Sichuan, 5 May 1952, JX1-812, pp. 180–1;
    Report from the South China region, March 1953, Guangdong, 204-1-
    91, p. 12; Guangdong, 1 March 1953, 204-1-91, pp. 118–20.

39 Report by Tan Zhenlin to Mao Zedong, Sichuan, 5 May 1952, JX1-812,
    pp. 180–1; Report by South China to Mao Zedong, Sichuan, 19 Feb.
    1952, JX1-812, pp. 16–22; Report from Subei to Mao Zedong, Sichuan,
    19 March 1952, JX1-812, p. 106; *Neibu cankao*, 22 Feb. 1952, pp. 167–8.

40 Report by South China to Mao Zedong, Sichuan, 19 Feb. 1952, JX1-812,
    pp. 16–22; Report by Tan Zhenlin to Mao Zedong, Sichuan, 5 May 1952,
    JX1-812, pp. 180–1; Instructions from the Centre, Sichuan, March 1953,
    JX1-813, pp. 44–5; *Neibu cankao*, 25 Feb. 1952, pp. 192–3.

9: Thought Reform

1 Michael Bristow, 'Hu Warns Chinese Communist Party', *BBC News*,
   30 June 2011.

2 Chang and Halliday, *Mao*, pp. 193–4 and 238–40.

3 Ibid., p. 242; on Wang Shiwei, see also Huang Changyong, *Wang Shiwei
   zhuan* (A biography of Wang Shiwei), Zhengzhou: Henan renmin
   chubanshe, 2000; Dai Qing, *Wang Shiwei and 'Wild Lilies': Rectification
   and Purges in the Chinese Communist Party, 1942–1944*, Armonk, NY: M.
   E. Sharpe, 1994.

4 Chang and Halliday, *Mao*, pp. 240–6; Gao, *Hong taiyang*, pp. 304–5; see
   also Cheng Yinghong, *Creating the 'New Man': From Enlightenment Ideals
   to Socialist Realities*, Honolulu: University of Hawai'i Press, 2009.

5 Mao Zedong, 'Cast Away Illusions, Prepare for Struggle', 14 Aug. 1949,
   Selected Works of Mao Zedong, vol. 4, p. 428.

6 Cheng Yuan interviewed by Wang Ying, 7 Nov. 2008, Wang Ying, 'Gaizao
   sixiang: Zhengzhi, lishi yu jiyi (1949–1953)' (Reforming thoughts: Politics, history and memory, 1949–1953), doctoral dissertation, Beijing:
   People's University, 2010, pp. 121–2.

7 Liu Xiaoyu interviewed by Wang Ying, Beijing, 27 Nov. 2008, Wang,
   'Gaizao sixiang', pp. 150–5.

8 Wang, 'Gaizao sixiang', pp. 111–12; Mao Zedong, 'Letter to Feng Youlan',
   13 Oct. 1949, in Michael Y. M. Kau and John K. Leung (eds), *The Writings of Mao Zedong: 1949–1976*, Armonk, NY: M. E. Sharpe, 1986, vol. 1,
   p. 17; Pei Yiran, 'Zijie peijian: Fanyou qian zhishifenzi de xianluo' (The
   'disarmament' of Chinese intellectuals before the anti-rightist campaign),
   Ershiyi shiji, no. 102 (Aug. 2007), p. 35.

9   Mao Zedong, 'Report on an Investigation of the Peasant Movement in Hunan', March 1927, *Selected Works of Mao Zedong*, vol. 1, p. 24.

10 Liu Yufen interviewed by Wang Ying, Beijing, 19 Nov. 2008, in Wang, 'Gaizao sixiang', pp. 83–7.

11 Ibid.

12 Reports on land reform from the Democratic League, Hubei, SZ37-1-7, 11 Aug. 1950; *Neibu cankao*, 28 Aug. 1950, pp. 88–9; 21 Dec. 1951, pp. 92–3; an example of opposition to land reform appears in the fictionalised account of S. T. Tung, *Secret Diary from Red China*, Indianapolis: Bobbs-Merrill, 1961; Yue Daiyun, *Siyuan, shatan, Weiminghu: 60 nian Beida shengya (1948–2008)* (Sixty years at Beijing University, 1948–2008), Beijing: Beijing daxue chubanshe, 2008, quoted in Wang, 'Gaizao sixiang', pp. 88–9.

13 DeMare, 'Turning Bodies and Turning Minds', pp. 289–90; Wang, 'Gaizao sixiang', p. 93; Mao, *Jianguo yilai*, vol. 2, p. 198.

14 DeMare, 'Turning Bodies and Turning Minds', pp. 298 and 93.

15 Philip Pan, *Out of Mao's Shadow: The Struggle for the Soul of a New China*, Basingstoke: Picador, 2009, pp. 31–2; Lin Zhao, like so many others, later became a victim of the regime. Arrested as a counter-revolutionary in 1960, she was secretly executed eight years later after writing hundreds of pages critical of Mao Zedong in prison, some of them in her own blood.

16 On the direct continuation of the Yan'an tradition after 1949, see Gao, *Hong taiyang*, p. 388; I have taken Mao's pronouncement from Loh, *Escape from Red China*, p. 78; a more formal translation appears in Cheng, *Creating the 'New Man'*, p. 70; Wu Ningkun and Li Yikai, *A Single Tear: A Family's Persecution, Love, and Endurance in Communist China*, London: Hodder & Stoughton, 1993, p. 7.

17 Wu and Li, *A Single Tear*, p. 5; Cheng, *Creating the 'New Man'*, p. 65.

18 Loh, *Escape from Red China*, pp. 78–81.

19 Instructions from the Centre and Report from Nanjing, 17 and 18 Feb. 1952, Guangdong, 204-1-253, pp. 28–31; Mao's endorsement appears in Mao, *Jianguo yilai*, vol. 3, p. 232, but without the report; on Chengde, see Report from the Centre, Shandong, 11 July 1953, A1-5-49, p. 19.

20 Pei, 'Zijie peijian', p. 36.

21 Loh, *Escape from Red China*, pp. 78–81.

22 Liu Xiaoyu interviewed by Wang Ying, Beijing, 27 Nov. 2008, Wang, 'Gaizao sixiang', pp. 152–3.

23 Pei, 'Zijie peijian', p. 37.

24 Instructions from the Ministry of Education, Shandong, 7 Feb. 1952, A29-2-35, pp. 1–4; Report from the Centre, Shandong, 23 June 1953, A1-5-49, p. 8; Report to and from the Centre and the Ministry of Education, 14 May, 9 June, 13 Sept. and 8 Oct. 1953, Shaanxi, 123-1-423, entire folder.

25 Cheng, *Creating the 'New Man'*, p. 75; Loh, *Escape from Red China*, pp. 71 and 78–9.

26 Loh, *Escape from Red China*, p. 82.

27 'No Freedom of Silence', *Time*, 2 Oct. 1950; the story about Mao trying

to audit Hu Shi's course comes from a witness, the librarian Tchang Fou-jouei, as told to Jean-Philippe Béjà; on Hu Shi and his son Hu Sidu, see Shen Weiwei, 'The Death of Hu Shi's Younger Son, Sidu', *Chinese Studies in History*, 40, no. 4 (Summer 2007), pp. 62–77.

28   Report from the Centre and Letter from Liang Shuming, Hebei, 30 Jan. 1952, 888-1-10, pp. 18–19; Mao Zedong, 'Criticism of Liang Shuming's Reactionary Ideas', 16–18 Sept. 1953, *Selected Works of Mao Zedong*, vol. 5, p. 121; the exchanges between Mao and Liang in September 1953 are in Dai Qing, 'Liang Shuming and Mao Zedong', *Chinese Studies in History*, 34, no. 1 (Autumn 2000), pp. 61–92, although this article does not mention the 1952 confrontation which set the stage for the dispute a year later.

29   Kirk A. Denton, *The Problematic of Self in Modern Chinese Literature: Hu Feng and Lu Ling*, Stanford: Stanford University Press, 1998, p. 88.

30   See Merle Goldman, 'Hu Feng's Conflict with the Communist Literary Authorities', *China Quarterly*, no. 12 (Oct. 1962), pp. 102–37; Andrew Endrey, 'Hu Feng: Return of the Counter-Revolutionary', *Australian Journal of Chinese Affairs*, 5 (Jan. 1981), pp. 73–90; Yu Fengzheng, *Gaizao: 1949–1957 nian de zhishifenzi* (Reform: Intellectuals from 1949 to 1957), Zhengzhou: Henan renmin chubanshe, 2001, pp. 358–427.

31   Wu and Li, *A Single Tear*, pp. 35–8.

32   Charles J. Alber, *Embracing the Lie: Ding Ling and the Politics of Literature in the People's Republic of China*, London: Praeger, 2004; Pei, 'Zijie peijian', p. 40.

33   Sun and Dan, *Engineering Communist China*, pp. 23–4.

34   Yearly report from the Ministry of Public Security, Shandong, 28 April 1956, A1-1-233, pp. 57–60; Report from the Provincial Party Committee's Five-Man Team to the Central Ten-Man Team, Hebei, 22 Sept. 1955, 886-1-5, p. 31; the overall number of arrests in 1955 was much higher, as we see in the chapter on the gulag.

35   Lu Dingyi, in his report at a conference of eighteen provinces, reported 500 suicide attempts: Shandong, 4 Aug. 1955, A1-2-1377, p. 21; Luo Ruiqing, who knew better, put the figure at 4,200: Report by Luo Ruiqing, Hebei, 16 July 1956, 886-1-17, pp. 30–1; Wu and Li, *A Single Tear*, p. 40; Pei, 'Zijie peijian', p. 37; Report by Luo Ruiqing, Hebei, 27 April 1955, 855-3-617, pp. 14–17; Report by Luo Ruiqing, Hebei, 20 June 1955, 855-3-617, p. 21.

36   Walker, *China under Communism*, pp. 193–4; Beijing, 14 March and 6 Sept. 1956, 2-8-184, pp. 10 and 40; Beijing, 23 and 27 Oct. 1954, 2-2-40, 50-4; Beijing, 1955, 2-8-186, pp. 43–7.

37   Walker, *China under Communism*, pp. 193–4.

38   Ibid., pp. 195–6; *Renmin ribao*, 29 July 1953, p. 3; on restrictions in the use of gold, see Instructions from the People's Bank of China, 10 June 1954, Shandong, A68-2-920, pp. 4–6.

39   Maria Yen, *The Umbrella Garden: A Picture of Student Life in Red China*, New York: Macmillan, 1953, p. 171.

40   Kang, *Confessions*, pp. 17–19.

41 Walker, *China under Communism*, p. 199.

42 Dikötter, *China before Mao*, pp. 78–80.

43 Yen, *The Umbrella Garden*, pp. 173–5; Mark Tennien, *No Secret is Safe: Behind the Bamboo Curtain*, New York: Farrar, Straus & Young, 1952, pp. 119–20.

44 Beijing, 2-5-32, 7 Oct. 1953, p. 1; 31 March 1954, p. 6; 23 Aug. 1954, p. 20.

45 Yen, *The Umbrella Garden*, pp. 166–7.

46 He Qixin, 'China's Shakespeare', *Shakespeare Quarterly*, 37, no. 2 (Summer 1986), pp. 149–59; Simon S. C. Chau, 'The Nature and Limitations of Shakespeare Translation', in William Tay et al. (eds), *China and the West: Comparative Literature Studies*, Hong Kong: Chinese University Press, 1980, p. 249.

47 Willens, *Stateless in Shanghai*, p. 228; on revolutionary theatre in the 1950s, see Constantine Tung, 'Metamorphosis of the Hero in Chairman Mao's Theater, 1942–1976', unpublished manuscript.

48 Dikötter, *Exotic Commodities*, pp. 252–5.

49 Priestley, 'The Sino-Soviet Friendship Association', p. 289; Clark, *Chinese Cinema*, pp. 40–1; Yen, *The Umbrella Garden*, pp. 178–9; see also Julian Ward, 'The Remodelling of a National Cinema: Chinese Films of the Seventeen Years (1949–66)', in Song Hwee Lim and Julian Ward (eds), *The Chinese Cinema Book*, London: British Film Institute, 2011, pp. 87–94.

50 Hu Qiaomu, Talk at the United Front Work Department, 1 Feb. 1951, Guangdong, 204-1-172, pp. 118–19.

51 Holmes Welch, *Buddhism under Mao*, Cambridge, MA: Harvard University Press, 1972, pp. 1 and 69–70; Richard C. Bush, *Religion in Communist China*, Nashville: Abingdon Press, 1970, p. 299.

52 Peter Goullart, *Forgotten Kingdom*, London: John Murray, 1957, pp. 291–9.

53 Report from the South-west China Region's Party Committee, Shandong, 31 Dec. 1952, A1-5-78, pp. 48–50.

54 Walker, *China under Communism*, pp. 188–9; Welch, *Buddhism under Mao*, pp. 48–9.

55 Welch, *Buddhism under Mao*, pp. 68 and 80; Report by Wang Feng, Shandong, 18 March 1955, A14-1-21, pp. 32–7.

56 James Cameron, *Mandarin Red: A Journey behind the 'Bamboo Curtain'*, London: Michael Joseph, 1955, pp. 104–6; Welch, *Buddhism under Mao*, p. 150 and ch. 6; the role of the United States in forcing China to tolerate some religion is stated in Report by Wang Feng, Shandong, 18 March 1955, A14-1-21, pp. 32–7.

57 Report from the Centre, 17 April 1953, Jilin, 1-7(2)-7, pp. 101–4 and 120–5; Report by Wang Feng, Shandong, 18 March 1955, A14-1-21, pp. 32–7.

58 C. K. Yang, *A Chinese Village in Early Communist Transition*, Cambridge, MA: Harvard University Press, 1959, pp. 194–6.

59 Hebei, 15 Feb. and 2 March 1951, 855-1-137, pp. 2 and 9; Bush, *Religion in Communist China*, pp. 386–8; Kou Qingyan, Report on Border

Defence and the Campaign against Counter-Revolutionaries, 28 Oct.
1951, Guangdong, 204-1-27, pp. 152–5; Report by Luo Ruiqing, 18 Feb.
1953, Shandong, A1-5-85, pp. 10–11.

60 C. K. Yang, *Religion in Chinese Society: A Study of Contemporary Social
Functions of Religion and Some of their Historical Factors*, Berkeley: University of California Press, 1961, p. 400; Sichuan, 4 Aug. 1955, JX1-418,
pp. 117–18; *Neibu cankao*, 3 Jan. 1955, pp. 2–4.

61 Walker, *China under Communism*, p. 190.

62 Bush, *Religion in Communist China*, p. 113; Zhang Yinxian interviewed
by Liao Yiwu, *God is Red*, pp. 18–19.

63 Order from the Provincial Party Committee, Shandong, 24 June 1952,
A1-5-59, pp. 115–16.

64 Bush, *Religion in Communist China*, p. 116; Cameron, *Mandarin Red*,
p. 190.

65 The numbers are from Report from the Centre, 7 May 1954, Shandong,
A14-1-16, p. 2; the revival of religion is in Shandong, 28 Sept. 1955,
A14-1-21, pp. 39–42; Sichuan, 4 Aug. 1955, JX1-418, pp. 117–18.

66 Bush, *Religion in Communist China*, pp. 124–7.

67 Report on religion from the Sichuan Provincial Party Committee, Shandong, 1952, A1-5-78, pp. 75–7.

68 *Neibu cankao*, 26 June 1950, pp. 97–101; 123-1-83, Zhang Desheng,
Report on Pingliang Rebellion, Shaanxi, 24 June 1950, 123-1-83,
pp. 92–6.

69 On Ningding see Sichuan, 6 Feb. 1952, JX1-879, pp. 3–6; on other uprisings see Shandong, A1-5-78, entire file.

70 Bush, *Religion in Communist China*, p. 269; Tyler, *Wild West China*,
pp. 138–40.

71 Bush, *Religion in Communist China*, pp. 274–5 and 281; James A. Millward, *Eurasian Crossroads: A History of Xinjiang*, New York: Columbia
University Press, 2007, pp. 248–9.

72 Willard A. Hanna, 'The Case of the Forty Million Missing Muslims',
20 Sept. 1956, Institute of Current World Affairs.

10: The Road to Serfdom

1 Mao Zedong, 'On the People's Democratic Dictatorship: In Commemoration of the 28th Anniversary of the Communist Party of China, June
30, 1949', *Selected Works of Mao Zedong*, vol. 4, p. 419.

2 There is an abundant secondary literature based on published statistics
that shows how grain output increased gradually between 1949 and 1958
(one good example is Carl Riskin, *China's Political Economy: The Quest for
Development since 1949*, Oxford: Oxford University Press, 1987). While
the more optimistic of these accounts can be disputed on the basis of
archival evidence, the point of this chapter and the following one is that
even moderate growth in grain output is only part of the story, as the
obsessive pursuit of more grain was carried out at the expense of other

economic activities, was achieved only thanks to huge inputs of manpower and ultimately did not benefit the countryside as ever larger proportions of the crop were procured by the state. This chapter also highlights the other social and economic costs of collectivisation.

3   Report from Yichang County, Hubei, 5 and 15 April 1952, SZ1-2-100, pp. 58–60.

4   Tung, *Secret Diary*, pp. 94–5.

5   Sichuan, 20 March 1953, JK1-729, pp. 26–7; Sichuan, 23 Feb. 1953, JK1-729, pp. 56–7.

6   Guangdong, June 1953, 204-1-94, pp. 122–8.

7   Ibid.; Report by the Provincial Party Committee's Bureau for Policy Research, 1952, Hubei, SZ1-2-114, pp. 53–4.

8   Jilin, 19 Jan., 16 and 22 March and 23 June 1951, 2-7-56, pp. 2, 14–15, 26 and 84.

9   Report from the Ministry of Internal Affairs, Sept. 1952, Zhejiang, J103-4-71, pp. 42–5.

10 Ibid., pp. 44–5; Report from the Ministry of Agricultural Work, 28 Aug. and 18 Sept. 1953, Jilin, 1-7(2)-7, pp. 101–4 and 107–9; Jilin, 20 Nov. 1950 and 7 Aug. 1951, 2-7-47, pp. 23–4 and 127–8; Reports on the Three-Anti Campaign by the East China Region, Shandong, 1 July and 29 Aug. 1952, A1-1-45, pp. 13 and 81.

11 Sichuan, 21 June 1953, JK1-13, p. 42.

12 Shaanxi, 24 June 1950, 123-1-83, pp. 152–4; Hubei, 1951, SZ37-1-39, n.p.; for a long-term analysis of the decline of sideline occupations, see Gao Wangling, *Lishi shi zenyang gaibian de: Zhongguo nongmin fanxingwei, 1950–1980* (How history is changed: Acts of resistance among the farmers in China, 1950–1980), Hong Kong: Chinese University of Hong Kong Press, 2012.

13 Hubei, 23 May 1952, SZ37-1-174, n.p., and Hubei, 30 May 1951, SZ1-5-75, p. 60; Hubei, 1951, SZ37-1-39, n.p.

14 *Neibu cankao*, 25 March 1953, p. 605; 4 April 1953, p. 83; 9 April 1953, p. 185; 20 April 1953, p. 417; 29 April 1953, p. 559; 22 June 1953, pp. 354–5; Report from the Ministry of Agricultural Work, 28 Aug. and 18 Sept. 1953, Jilin, 1-7(2)-7, pp. 101–4 and 107–9.

15 Report from the Shandong Provincial Party Committee, 4 Oct. 1953, Jilin, 1-7(2)-7, pp. 69–70; the amounts required to get sufficient calories are in Jean C. Oi, *State and Peasant in Contemporary China: The Political Economy of Village Government*, Berkeley: University of California Press, 1989, pp. 48–9; Urgent Telegram to the Centre, 17 Feb. 1955, Jilin, 1-1(11)-81, pp. 1–3; on Nanhe, see Report from the Centre, 28 Aug. 1953, Jilin, 1-7(2)-7, pp. 101–4 and 117–18.

16 Report on the western region of Guangdong, June 1953, Guangdong, 204-1-94, pp. 73–7; Jilin, 15 and 30 Dec. 1954, 1-1(10)-74, pp. 33 and 34.

17 Report on the western region of Guangdong, June 1953, Guangdong, 204-1-94, pp. 73–7.

18 Jilin, 12 May 1953, 55-7-2, p. 45; Sichuan, 23 Feb. 1953, JK1-729, p. 57.

19 Jilin, 12 Oct. 1954, 1-7(3)-2, p. 4; 24 Feb. 1955, 1-7(4)-1, p. 5; Zhang, *Yijiusijiu nianhou Zhongguo nongcun zhidu biange shi*, pp. 111–12.

20 See, for instance, Report from the Henan Party Committee's Financial Committee, Shandong, 6 March 1953, A1-2-138, pp. 7–14, and Guangdong, Aug. 1953, 204-1-95, pp. 31–7.

21 Report by Cao Juru at Second National Conference on Finances, 28 July 1953, Shandong, A1-2-143, pp. 138–40; Bo, *Ruogan zhongda shijian yu juece de huigu*, vol. 1, pp. 267–80.

22 The shortfall in foreign trade stood at 140 million: see Report from Cao Juru at Second National Conference on Finances, 28 July 1953, Shandong, A1-2-143, pp. 138–40; Report from the People's Government on Foreign Trade, Aug. 1953, Shandong, A1-2-138, pp. 70–1.

23 Minutes of conversation between Stalin and Zhou Enlai, 3 Sept. 1952, Archives of the President, Russian Federation, 45-1-329, pp. 75–87, quoted and translated in *Cold War International History Project Bulletin*, nos 6–7 (Winter 1995–6), pp. 10–17.

24 Li Fuchun, Report on the Soviet Union's reactions to the Five-Year Plan, Shandong, 21 June 1953, A1-2-144, pp. 67–87, quotation on p. 73; Mao's Instructions on the 1953 Plan, 1953, Hubei, SZ1-2-115, pp. 7–10; see also Zhang Shu Guang, *Economic Cold War: America's Embargo against China and the Sino-Soviet Alliance, 1949–1963*, Stanford: Stanford University Press, 2001, pp. 109–10; for the background on how Stalin returned to the first Five-Year Plan in the months before his death in March 1953, see memoirs of Yuan Baohua, 'Fu Sulian tanpan de riri yeye' (The days and nights of negotiation during my visit to Moscow), *Dangdai Zhongguo shi yanjiu*, Jan. 1996, pp. 17–22, and Li Yuran, 'Woguo tong Sulian shangtan' (Our country's negotiations with the Soviet Union), in Pei Jianzhang, *Xin Zhongguo waijiao fengyun* (The shifting winds of new China's foreign relations), Beijing: Shijie zhishi, 1991, vol. 2, pp. 15–18; Bo, *Ruogan zhongda shijian yu juece de huigu*, vol. 1, pp. 305–9.

25 On the decisions and debates behind the monopoly, see the memoirs of one of the key players, Bo, *Ruogan zhongda shijian yu juece de huigu*, vol. 1, pp. 267–80.

26 Ibid., pp. 267–72.

27 Guangdong, 1954, 204-1-122, pp. 19–21 and 31–3; Guangdong, Dec. 1953, 204-1-222, pp. 69 and 113; An Pingsheng, Report on Procurements in East Guangdong region, 8 Jan. 1954, 204-1-337, pp. 89–91.

28 Report by Li Tingxu on the Situation in Jiangxi, 15 Feb. 1954, Shaanxi, 123-1-1203, pp. 10–11.

29 Report by the Jingzhou Public Security Bureau, 28 Feb. 1954, Shaanxi, 123-1-1203, pp. 23–5; Sichuan, 4 Aug. 1955, JX1-418, pp. 115–16.

30 Guangdong, 1954, 204-1-122, pp. 19–21 and 31–3; Guangdong, Dec. 1953, 204-1-222, pp. 69 and 113; An Pingsheng, Report on Procurements in East Guangdong, 8 Jan. 1954, 204-1-337, pp. 89–91; Reports from the North-west Region, Gansu Provincial Party Committee and the Gannan Region, 21 and 29 Jan. and 1 Feb. 1954, Shaanxi, 123-1-1204, pp. 2–11; Hebei, 19 Nov. 1953, 25 and 26 Dec. 1953 and 13 March 1954, 855-2-420, pp. 2, 17, 26, 29 and 40–7.

31   Report from South China region, Hebei, 19 Feb. 1955, 855-3-605;
     Report by Luo Ruiqing at the National Conference on Public Security,
     Shandong, 13 June 1955, A1-2-1377, pp. 66–7 and 72; Sichuan, 4 Aug.
     1955, JX1-418, pp. 115–16.

32   Reports from the North-west Region, Gansu Provincial Party Committee
     and the Gannan Region, 21 and 29 Jan. and 1 Feb. 1954, Shaanxi, 123-1-
     1204, pp. 2–11, quotation on p. 8.

33   Guangdong, 1954, 204-1-122, pp. 19–21 and 31–3; Guangdong, Dec.
     1953, 204-1-222, pp. 69 and 113; An Pingsheng, Report on Procure-
     ments in East Guangdong, 8 Jan. 1954, 204-1-337, pp. 89–91; Report by
     the Jiangxi Provincial Party Committee, 4 March 1954, Shaanxi, 123-1-
     1203, pp. 3–10.

34   Joseph Needham and Francesca Bray, *Science and Civilisation in China*,
     vol. 6: *Biology and Biological Technology*, part 2: *Agriculture*, Cambridge:
     Cambridge University Press, 1984, p. 401.

35   Oi, *State and Peasant in Contemporary China*, p. 75.

36   Shandong, 2 Feb. 1954, A1-2-236, pp. 12–15; Tung, *Secret Diary*, p. 142.

37   Report from the Bureau for Grain, 4 June 1963, Shandong, A131-1-70;
     Hebei, 10 Oct. 1956, 855-3-889, p. 36; Shaanxi, 1965, 231-1-703, entire
     table; Urgent Telegram to the Centre, 17 Feb. 1955, Jilin, 1-1(11)-81,
     pp. 1–3.

38   Oi, *State and Peasant in Contemporary China*, pp. 48–9; Talk by Deng
     Zihui, 15 July 1954, Guangdong, 209-1-22, pp. 1–5.

39   Instructions from the Centre on the grain monopoly, 2 Jan. 1954, Guang-
     dong, 204-1-337, p. 46; the reports on famine are in *Neibu cankao*,
     7, 9 and 12 April 1954, pp. 70–1, 88–9 and 126; *Neibu cankao*, 13 and 14
     May 1954, pp. 174–5; 186–7; *Neibu cankao*, 30 June 1954, pp. 371–2;
     Neibu cankao, 7 July 1954, pp. 117–18.

40   Instructions from the Centre, 28 Aug. 1954, Guangdong, 204-1-333,
     pp. 167–9; Hebei, 3 March and 3 Aug. 1955, 855-3-605, pp. 39 and
     68–75; on the monopoly on cotton and oil, see Zhang, *Yijiusijiu nianhou
     Zhongguo nongcun zhidu biange shi*, p. 101.

41   Background information in Tiejun Cheng and Mark Selden, 'The Origins
     and Social Consequences of China's *Hukou* System', *China Quarterly*,
     no. 139 (Sept. 1994), pp. 644–68; Shandong, 12 April 1954, A1-2-236,
     p. 14; Ministry of Labour, Report on Migration from the Countryside,
     4 Dec. 1953, Gansu, 91-2-201, pp. 1–6; *Neibu cankao*, 5 Aug. 1954,
     pp. 76–7.

42   Cheng and Selden, 'The Origins and Social Consequences of China's
     Hukou System', pp. 644–68.

11: High Tide

 1   Lum, *Peking, 1950–1953*, pp. 164–5.
 2   Telegram from Stalin to Mao, 20 April 1948, Archive of the President of the
     Russian Federation, quoted in Andrei M. Ledovsky, 'Marshall's Mission in

the Context of U.S.S.R.–China–U.S. Relations', in Larry I. Bland (ed.), *George C. Marshall's Mediation Mission to China, December 1945–January 1947*, Lexington, VA: George C. Marshall Foundation, 1998, p. 435; Bo, *Ruogan zhongda shijian yu juece de huigu*, vol. 1, pp. 115–28.

3   Gao Wenqian, *Zhou Enlai: The Last Perfect Revolutionary*, New York: Public Affairs, 2007, pp. 87–8.

4   Gao, *Hong taiyang*, pp. 491–5.

5   On Mao's insomnia, see Li, *The Private Life of Chairman Mao*, pp. 107–13; on Mao's erratic and shifting attitude towards government affairs and his ignorance of economics, see Michael M. Sheng, 'Mao and Chinese Elite Politics in the 1950s: The Gao Gang Affair Revisited', *Twentieth-Century China*, 36, no. 1 (Jan. 2011), p. 77.

6   Chang and Halliday, *Mao*, pp. 385–6.

7   Bo, *Ruogan zhongda shijian yu juece de huigu*, vol. 1, pp. 241–2; Jin Chongji and Chen Qun (eds), *Chen Yun zhuan* (A biography of Chen Yun), Beijing: Zhongyang wenxian chubanshe, 2005, p. 880; the whole affair is recounted in detail in Sheng, 'The Gao Gang Affair Revisited', and Frederick C. Teiwes, *Politics at Mao's Court: Gao Gang and Party Factionalism in the Early 1950s*, Armonk, NY: M. E. Sharpe, 1990, pp. 52–78.

8   Sheng, 'The Gao Gang Affair Revisited', p. 79; Note to Liu Shaoqi dated 19 May 1953 in Mao, *Jianguo yilai*, vol. 4, p. 229 (the emphasis is from Mao).

9   Mao Zedong, 'Refute Right Deviationist Views that Depart from the General Line', 15 June 1953, *Selected Works of Mao Zedong*, vol. 5, p. 93.

10   For the abandonment of the New Democracy, see Lin Yunhui, *Xiang shehuizhuiyi guodu, 1953–55* (The transition to socialism, 1953–55), Hong Kong: Chinese University Press, 2009.

11   Dai Maolin and Zhao Xiaoguang, *Gao Gang zhuan* (A biography of Gao Gang), Xi'an: Shaanxi renmin chubanshe, 2011, pp. 306–7.

12   Goncharov, Lewis and Xue, *Uncertain Partners*, p. 68.

13   Wingrove, 'Gao Gang and the Moscow Connection', pp. 95–7.

14   Stalin's death is described in Simon Sebag Montefiore, *Stalin: The Court of the Red Tsar*, New York: Knopf, 2004, p. 649; on Gao's visit to Moscow see Dai and Zhao, *Gao Gang zhuan*, p. 310; Andrei Ledovsky spoke to Gao Gang on the plane back to Beijing, and is quoted in Wingrove, 'Gao Gang and the Moscow Connection', p. 100.

15   Zhao Jialiang and Zhang Xiaoji, *Gao Gang zai Beijing*, Hong Kong: Dafeng chubanshe, 2008, p. 188.

16   On Beria's execution see William Taubman, *Khrushchev: The Man and his Era*, London, Free Press, 2003, p. 256; Mao's comment about Sergei Goglidze is in his speech at Lushan on 11 September 1959, Gansu, 91-18-494, p. 126.

17   Gao's death as well as security arrangements in the capital are described by his secretary in Zhao and Zhang, *Gao Gang zai Beijing*, pp. 201 and 210; the tea boy appears in Chang and Halliday, *Mao*, p. 388.

18   Wingrove, 'Gao Gang and the Moscow Connection', pp. 100–3.

19   Mao Zedong, On the Cooperative Transformation of Agriculture,

Shandong, 31 July 1955, A1-2-292, pp. 19–42; a translated version, from which the quotation is taken, appears in Kau and Leung, *The Writings of Mao Zedong, 1949–1976*, vol. 1, 603.

20 Liu Jianhui and Wang Hongxu, 'The Origins of the General Line for the Transition Period and of the Acceleration of the Chinese Socialist Transformation in Summer 1955', *China Quarterly*, no. 187 (Sept. 2006), pp. 729–30.

21 Pang Xianzhi and Jin Chongji (eds), *Mao Zedong zhuan, 1949–1976* (A biography of Mao Zedong, 1949–1976), Beijing: Zhongyang wenxian chubanshe, 2003, p. 377; Mao, *Jianguo yilai*, vol. 5, p. 209.

22 Two examples of a provincial party committee that later confessed to ignoring the meeting of 17 May are Jilin and Shandong: see its self-criticism in Jilin, August 1955, 1-7(4)-1, pp. 72–9, and Report from the Provincial Party Committee, 17 Aug. 1955, Shandong, A1-1-188, pp. 204–6; the meeting on 11 July is detailed in Pang and Jin, *Mao Zedong zhuan, 1949–1976*, pp. 380–1; see also Liu and Wang, 'The Origins of the General Line', p. 730.

23 Mao Zedong, On the Cooperative Transformation of Agriculture, Shandong, 31 July 1955, A1-2-292, pp. 19–42.

24 Meeting with Provincial and Municipal Party Secretaries, Shandong, 15 Aug. 1955, A1-2-292, pp. 11–17; Peng Yihu wrote a letter critical of the grain monopoly to the Central Committee.

25 These statistics, as well as the overall development of the co-operatives during the Socialist High Tide, have been provided many times, and I take them from Kenneth R. Walker, 'Collectivisation in Retrospect: The "Socialist High Tide" of Autumn 1955–Spring 1956', *China Quarterly*, no. 26 (June 1966), pp. 1–43; the ban on the blind was passed in Hailong county; see Jilin, 4 Feb. 1956, 2-12-37, pp. 87–90.

26 Instructions from the Centre, 15 March 1956, Guangdong, 217-1-8, p. 2.

27 Li Choh-ming, 'Economic Development', *China Quarterly*, no. 1 (March 1960), p. 42.

28 Loh, *Escape from Red China*, pp. 149–50; Guo Dihuo, 'Wo he Pan Hannian tongzhi de jiaowang', *Shanghai wenshi ziliao xuanji*, vol. 43 (1983), pp. 26–8, quoted in Bergère, 'Les Capitalistes shanghaïens et la période de transition entre le régime Guomindang et le communisme (1948–1952)', p. 29; the reasons behind the arrest of Pan and Yang, who were rehabilitated decades later, are complex, and the most up-to-date guide is Xiaohong Xiao-Planes, 'The Pan Hannian Affair and Power Struggles at the Top of the CCP (1953–1955)', *China Perspectives*, no. 4 (Autumn 2010), pp. 116–27.

29 Report from the Jiangsu Provincial Party Committee, 27 Sept. 1955, Hebei, 855-3-617, pp. 24–31.

30 Pang and Jin, *Mao Zedong zhuan, 1949–1976*, pp. 448–9.

31 Loh, *Escape from Red China*, pp. 179–80.

32 Ibid., p. 188.

33 Ibid., pp. 181–92; Rong Yiren's later career is described in Becker, *C. C. Lee*, p. 63.

12: The Gulag

1   On the early period, the work of Patricia Griffin remains the best on the subject; see Patricia E. Griffin, *The Chinese Communist Treatment of Counterrevolutionaries, 1924–1949*, Princeton: Princeton University Press, 1976; on Shandong, see Frank Dikötter, 'The Emergence of Labour Camps in Shandong Province, 1942–1950', *China Quarterly*, no. 175 (Sept. 2003), pp. 803–17; for a more general history of the Chinese gulag, nothing to date surpasses Jean-Luc Domenach, *L'Archipel oublié*, Paris: Fayard, 1992; in English, the work of Harry Wu is essential: Harry Hongda Wu, *Laogai: The Chinese Gulag*, Boulder: Westview Press, 1992; see also Philip F. Williams and Yenna Wu, *The Great Wall of Confinement: The Chinese Prison Camp through Contemporary Fiction and Reportage*, Berkeley: University of California Press, 2004.

2   Dikötter, *Crime, Punishment and the Prison in Modern China*.

3   Frank Dikötter, 'Crime and Punishment in Post-Liberation China: The Prisoners of a Beijing Gaol in the 1950s', *China Quarterly*, no. 149 (March 1997), pp. 147–59; the terms for these political crimes were *juntong, zhongtong, Guomindang, hanjian* and *pandang*.

4   The figure of over 1 million appears in Report from the Third Conference on Public Security, 1 June 1951, Sichuan, JX1-834, p. 101; on Hunan see Report on Labour Camps, 8 June 1951 and Report from Li Xiannian on the Campaign against Counter-Revolutionaries, 1951, Hubei, SZ1-2-60, pp. 51, 79–85 and 115; Report from the Guangxi Provincial Party Committee, 7 July 1951, Sichuan, JX1-836, pp. 78–82, also Hebei, 7 July 1951, 684-1-59, pp. 12–15.

5   Sichuan, 1951, JX1-839, pp. 486–7; Inspection Report on the Chongqing County Prison, 24 July 1951, Sichuan, JX1-342, pp. 33–4; see also Public Security Bureau Report on Prisons in Western Sichuan, 1951, Sichuan, JX1-342, pp. 92–3; on death rates in south-west China see Sichuan, 5 Sept. 1951, JX1-839, pp. 386–7; Hebei, 31 May 1951, 855-1-137, p. 47; Quentin K. Y. Huang, *Now I Can Tell: The Story of a Christian Bishop under Communist Persecution*, New York: Morehouse-Gorham, 1954, p. 22.

6   Mao Zedong to Deng Xiaoping, Rao Shushi, Deng Zihui, Ye Jianying, Xi Zhongxun and Gao Gang, 20 April 1951, Sichuan, JX1-834, pp. 75–7.

7   The decision to put 300,000 prisoners to work is in Minutes of the Third National Conference on Public Security, Shandong, 16 and 22 May 1951, A1-4-9, pp. 14, 38 and 43; Report by Luo Ruiqing, Shandong, 4 June 1951, A1-5-20, pp. 149–51.

8   Report from Luo Ruiqing to Mao Zedong, 5 Dec. 1951, Sichuan, JX1-834, pp. 240–5; the tin mines at Lianxian are mentioned in Report from Qian Ying, secretary of the Central Commission for Discipline Inspection, to Zhu De, 25 March 1953, Sichuan, JK1-730, p. 36.

9   Yearly report from the Ministry of Public Security, 28 April 1956, Shandong, A1-1-233, pp. 57–60; Sichuan, 21 June 1953, JK1-13, pp. 40–1; the experts in the gulag are mentioned in Order from Deng Xiaoping, 24 July and 13 Aug. 1956, Shandong, A1-1-233, pp. 74–5.

10 Duan, *Zhanfan zishu*; Report from the Inspectorate, 14 March 1953, Hebei, 855-2-298, pp. 16–27; Report from North-west China to the Centre, 21 March 1953, Hebei, 855-2-298, p. 30.

11 Sichuan, 20 March 1953, JK1-729, p. 29; Report on the Three-Anti Campaign in Judicial System, 16 March 1953, Beijing, 2-5-18, p. 6; the electric device is described in Huang, *Now I Can Tell*, pp. 22–7 and 89.

12 The comment about the Auschwitz of the mind is from Harry Wu, who is quoted alongside Robert Ford and Wang Tsunming in Kate Saunders, *Eighteen Layers of Hell: Stories from the Chinese Gulag*, London: Cassell Wellington House, 1996, p. 73; a good description of cellmates being forced to beat each other appears in Harold W. Rigney, *Four Years in a Red Hell: The Story of Father Rigney*, Chicago: Henry Regnery, 1956, p. 156; see also Huang, *Now I Can Tell*, pp. 106–10; Simon Leys commented a long time ago on the two alternatives facing anyone caught up in the gulag, one being suicide, the other a complete renunciation of one's former self: see Simon Leys, *Broken Images: Essays on Chinese Culture and Politics*, New York: St Martin's Press, 1980, p. 146.

13 Report on Re-education through Labour Camps, 10 Jan. 1956, Shandong, A1-1-233, pp. 33–7; the figure of 300,000 comes from the Third National Conference of the Ministry of Public Security on Reform through Labour, 27 Oct. 1955, Shandong, A1-1-233, p. 39.

14 Report on Western Sichuan to the Fourth National Conference on Public Security, 19 July 1952, Sichuan, JX1-843, pp. 53–5; Report by Changwei County Party Committee, 22 May and 1 June 1953, Shandong, A1-5-85, pp. 86 and 992–4; Report by Luo Ruiqing, 6 Feb. 1953, Shandong, A1-5-85, pp. 20–3.

15 Loh, *Escape from Red China*, p. 69.

16 Report by Luo Ruiqing, 6 Feb. 1953, Shandong, A1-5-85, pp. 20–3.

17 *Neibu cankao*, 27 May 1950, pp. 80–1.

18 Report on the Huai River, 14 Oct. 1950, Nanjing, 4003-3-84, pp. 143–4.

19 *Neibu cankao*, 24 March 1951.

20 *Neibu cankao*, 23 March 1953, pp. 548–55.

21 Report on the Jingzhou region, 15 Dec. 1951, Hubei, SZ37-1-63, p. 3; Shaanxi, 27 Dec. 1953, 123-1-490, n.p., first document in folder.

22 Beijing, 30 March 1956, 2-8-58, p. 17.

23 Beijing, 1 Dec. 1956, 2-8-58, p. 34; Report by Xie Juezai on Migration, 27 July 1956, Beijing, 2-8-47, p. 4; Letters from the Public, 8 Dec. 1956, Beijing, 2-8-247, pp. 113–14.

24 Tyler, *Wild West China*, pp. 192–5.

13: Behind the Scenes

1 Valentin Chu, *The Inside Story of Communist China: Ta Ta, Tan Tan*, London: Allen & Unwin, 1964, pp. 13–14.

2 Ibid., pp. 37–48.

3 Cameron, *Mandarin Red*, pp. 33–5; see also Hung Chang-tai, *Mao's New*

World: Political Culture in the Early People's Republic, Ithaca, NY: Cornell University Press, 2011, pp. 92–108; letter fom Cai Shuli, 24 April 1957, Beijing, 2-9-230, p. 58; Liang Jun, one of China's first female tractor drivers, was eulogised in posters, novels and films after 1953 (later she appeared on 1-yuan banknotes).

4 Some wonderful pages on this sense of idealism appear in Sheila Fitzpatrick, *Everyday Stalinism: Ordinary Life in Extraordinary Times: Soviet Russia in the 1930s*, New York: Oxford University Press, 1999, pp. 67–72.

5 Kinmond, *No Dogs in China*, pp. 27 and 171; see also the chapter on China in the excellent book by Paul Hollander, *Political Pilgrims: Western Intellectuals in Search of the Good Society*, Piscataway, NJ: Transaction Publishers, pp. 278–346.

6 Loh, *Escape from Red China*, pp. 161–2.

7 Some of the best pages on the tourist circuit are in Chu, *The Inside Story of Communist China*, pp. 256–61; see also Hollander, *Political Pilgrims*.

8 Peter Schmid, *The New Face of China*, London: Harrap, 1958, p. 52; Wu, *Remaking Beijing*, p. 105; on Beijing, see also Wang Jun, *Beijing Record: A Physical and Political History of Planning Modern Beijing*, London: World Scientific, 2011; Hung, *Mao's New World*, pp. 25–50.

9 J. M. Addis and Douglas Hurd, 'A Visit to South-West China' and 'A Visit to North-West China', 25 Oct. to 21 Nov. 1955, FO371-115169, pp. 4, 16 and 29; Kinmond, *No Dogs in China*, p. 113.

10 Sun Jingwen, Report at the First National Conference on City Building, 14 June 1954, Shandong, A107-2-307, pp. 49–67; Report by Gao Gang on capital construction at the Second National Conference on Financial and Economic Work, 29 June 1953, Shandong, A1-2-144, pp. 53–9.

11 Kinmond, *No Dogs in China*, p. 26.

12 Sun Jingwen, Report at the First National Conference on City Building, 14 June 1954, Shandong, A107-2-309, pp. 49–67, quotation on p. 55; see also the report on urban planning by the Soviet expert Balakin, 15 June 1954, Shandong, A107-2-309, pp. 68–89; besides these official reports, complaints about housing figure prominently in letters from the public written to the People's Congress, for instance in Beijing, 27 Dec. 1956, 2-8-247, pp. 125–6 and 181; Instructions by Liu Shaoqi to the Ministry of Textile Industry, 22 Feb. 1956, Shandong, A1-2-387, p. 72; the Dongjiao Railway Station is mentioned in Beijing, 10 Nov. 1956, 2-8-247, p. 52.

13 Li Fuchun, Report at the First National Design Conference, 24 Sept. 1957, Shandong, A107-1-67, pp. 138–47.

14 Report from Anshan Party Committee, 22 March 1956, Shandong, A1-2-393, pp. 42–3.

15 Report from the Workers' Union, 25 June 1956, Nanjing, 4003-1-107, pp. 370–6.

16 Report on labour conditions circulated by the Centre, 22 March 1956, Nanjing, 4003-1-107, pp. 364–5.

17 Hubei, May 13 Aug. 1956, SZ29-1-13, pp. 2–3; Hubei, May 1956, SZ29-1-144, pp. 14–35; Report from the Federation of Trade Unions to the

Centre, 29 May 1956, Shandong, A1-2-393, pp. 54–8; also in Nanjing, 4003-1-108, pp. 54–60.

18 Report from the Federation of Trade Unions to the Centre, 29 May 1956, Shandong, A1-2-393, pp. 54–8; also in Nanjing, 4003-1-108, pp. 54–60.

19 Report from the Workers' Union, 25 June 1956, Nanjing, 4003-1-107, pp. 370–6; Nanjing, 4 Feb. 1956, 4003-1-107, p. 48; Nanjing, 20 Feb. 1957, 4003-1-122, p. 25; Survey of Health Conditions in Factories, 1954, Nanjing, 5065-2-142, pp. 52–3.

20 Hubei, 28 March 1958, SZ44-2-158, pp. 16–59.

21 Report by the Youth League, 5 Aug. 1956, Shandong, A1-2-393, pp. 103–5.

22 Kawai Fan and Honkei Lai, 'Mao Zedong's Fight against Schistosomiasis', *Perspectives in Biology and Medicine*, 51, no. 2 (Spring 2008), pp. 176–87.

23 The medical debates are reported by David M. Lampton, *The Politics of Medicine in China: The Policy Process, 1949–1977*, Folkestone, Kent: Dawson, 1977, pp. 48 and 64–5; see also Miriam D. Gross, 'Chasing Snails: Anti-Schistosomiasis Campaigns in the People's Republic of China', doctoral dissertation, University of California, San Diego, 2010.

24 Report on Eradication Work in the Last Half of 1957, 11 Sept. 1957, Hubei, SZ1-2-405, pp. 25–36.

25 Report on Leprosy in Xikang Province, 22 Aug. 1951, Sichuan, JK32-158, pp. 1–2; Report on Leprosy in Xikang Province, 1955, Sichuan, JK32-36, p. 8; *Neibu cankao*, 18 Dec. 1952, pp. 256–7; see also JK16-83, 1953, p. 3; Inspection Report on the Leper Colony at Yanbian, 1954, Sichuan, JK16-241, pp. 6–8.

26 *Neibu cankao*, 13 May 1953, pp. 168–70.

27 Inspection Report on the Leper Colony at Yanbian, 1954, Sichuan, JK16-241, pp. 6–8; on Guangdong, see *Neibu cankao*, 14 April 1953, pp. 282–3.

28 *Neibu cankao*, 3 April 1953, pp. 59–61.

14: Poisonous Weeds

1 Taubman, *Khrushchev*, pp. 271–2.

2 Pang and Jin (eds), *Mao Zedong zhuan, 1949–1976*, p. 534; Li, *The Private Life of Chairman Mao*, pp. 182–4.

3 Taubman, *Khrushchev*, p. 272; Wu Lengxi, *Yi Mao zhuxi: Wo qinshen jingli de ruogan zhongda lishi shijian pianduan* (Remembering Chairman Mao: Fragments of my personal experience of certain important historical events), Beijing: Xinhua chubanshe, 1995, p. 57.

4 Loh, *Escape from Red China*, pp. 229–30.

5 Nanjing, 1957, Nanjing, 4003-1-122, p. 103; Report from the Federation of Labour Unions, 22 Feb. 1957, Nanjing, 4003-1-122, pp. 83–7; the figure of over 10,000 students appears in Report from the Centre, 25 March 1957, Nanjing, 4003-1-122, pp. 78–82.

6 Report from the Ministry of Industry, 19 Feb. 1957, Guangdong, 219-2-112, pp. 99–100; Report from the Federation of Labour Unions, 22 Feb.

1957, Nanjing, 4003-1-122, pp. 83–7; Jilin, 20 May 1957, 1-1(13)-50, p. 4; *Neibu cankao*, 24 Sept. 1956, pp. 615–16; 15–16 Nov. 1956, pp. 367–8 and 401–2; 17 Dec. 1956, pp. 342–3.

7 Yang Xinpei, Report on Xianju County, 13 Aug. 1957, Shandong, A1-1-318, pp. 93–8; Report from the Jiangsu Provincial Party Committee, 20 May 1957, Shandong, A1-1-318, p. 87.

8 Guangdong, 23 May 1957, 217-1-30, pp. 10–12; Report from the Shunde County Party Committee, 24 April 1957, Guangdong, 217-1-371, pp. 21–4; Report from the Xinyi County Party Committee, 6 March 1957, Guangdong, 217-1-408, pp. 16–18.

9 Guangdong, 15 Sept. 1957, 217-1-30, pp. 90–3.

10 Sichuan, 28 May to 15 July 1957, JC1-1155, p. 24.

11 Report from the Ministry of Domestic Affairs, 27 Feb. 1957, Nanjing, 4003-1-122, pp. 66–7; Shandong, 9 March 1957, A1-1-318, p. 108; on the miserable world of veterans, see Neil J. Diamant, *Embattled Glory: Veterans, Military Families, and the Politics of Patriotism in China, 1949–2007*, Lanham, MD: Rowman & Littlefield, 2009.

12 Loh, *Escape from Red China*, p. 231.

13 On the Ten Great Relationships, 25 April 1956, circulated on 16 May 1956, Shandong, A1-2-387, pp. 2–17.

14 Li, *The Private Life of Chairman Mao*, p. 163; Chang and Halliday, *Mao*, p. 401.

15 Closing Speech at the Second Plenum of the Eighth Central Committee, 15 Nov. 1956, Gansu, 91-18-480, pp. 74–6.

16 Interjections by Mao at the Second Plenum of the Eighth Central Committee, 10-15 Nov. 1956, Gansu, 91-18-480, p. 60; Speech by Luo Ruiqing, 27 Nov. 1956, Hebei, 886-1-18, pp. 45–55.

17 Speech by Mao Zedong, 18 Jan. 1957, Gansu, 91-3-57, pp. 57–63; Interjection by Mao, 19 Jan. 1957, Gansu, 91-3-57, p. 77; Interjection by Mao, 23 Jan. 1957, Gansu, 91-3-57, p. 84; Speech by Mao, 27 Jan. 1957, Gansu, 91-3-57, pp. 71–2.

18 Speech to Enlarged Session of China's Supreme State Conference, 27 Feb. 1957, Gansu, 91-3-57, pp. 1–41; a translation of a virtually identical version appears in Roderick MacFarquhar, Timothy Cheek and Eugene Wu (eds), *The Secret Speeches of Chairman Mao: From the Hundred Flowers to the Great Leap Forward*, Cambridge, MA: Harvard University Press, 1989, pp. 131–89; see also Loh, *Escape from Red China*, pp. 289–2.

19 Loh, *Escape from Red China*, p. 293; on other enthusiastic reactions to the speech, see Eddy U, 'Dangerous Privilege: The United Front and the Rectification Campaign of the Early Mao Years', *China Journal*, no. 68 (July 2012), pp. 50–1.

20 On Peng Zhen and the *People's Daily*, see Roderick MacFarquhar, *The Origins of the Cultural Revolution*, vol. 1: *Contradictions among the People, 1956–1957*, London: Oxford University Press, 1974, especially p. 193.

21 A good example is his meeting with democrats and representatives of trade and industry, 7 Dec. 1956, Shandong, A1-2-387, p. 71; the

quotation about intellectuals is from Mao's speech in Nanjing, 20 March 1957, Shandong, A1-1-312, pp. 2–17.

22   The colours of the posters are mentioned in Yue Daiyun, *To the Storm: The Odyssey of a Revolutionary Chinese Woman*, Berkeley: University of California Press, 1985, p. 7; Wu, *A Single Tear*, p. 54.

23   Dai Qing, *Liang Shuming, Wang Shiwei, Chu Anping*, Nanjing: Jiangsu wenyi chubanshe, 1989, pp. 236–8; see also Zhang Yihe, *Wangshi bingbu ruyan* (Do not let bygones be bygones), Beijing: Renmin wenxue chubanshe, 2004; Luo's remark was so hurtful that Mao even commented on it at the summing-up of the Third Plenum of the Eighth Central Committee, 9 Oct. 1957, Shandong, A1-1-315, p. 15.

24   Dai Huang, 'Righting the Wronged', in Zhang Lijia and Calum MacLeod (eds), *China Remembers*, Oxford: Oxford University Press, 1999, p. 66; James P. McGough, *Fei Hsiao-t'ung: The Dilemma of a Chinese Intellectual*, White Plains, NY: M. E. Sharpe, 1979, pp. 61–2.

25   Loh, *Escape from Red China*, pp. 304–5.

26   Ibid., p. 301.

27   Ibid., p. 298; on Wuhan, see Roderick MacFarquhar (ed.), *The Hundred Flowers Campaign and the Chinese Intellectuals*, New York: Octagon Books, 1974, pp. 143–53.

28   Elizabeth J. Perry, 'Shanghai's Strike Wave of 1957', *China Quarterly*, no. 137 (March 1994), pp. 1–27.

29   Ibid., p. 13; Loh, *Escape from Red China*, p. 300.

30   Yue, *To the Storm*, p. 7.

31   Li, *The Private Life of Chairman Mao*, p. 200.

32   'Things are Beginning to Change', *Selected Works of Mao Zedong*, vol. 5, pp. 441–2.

33   The official number is 552,877 rightists (Henry Yuhuai He, *Dictionary of the Political Thought of the People's Republic of China*, Armonk, NY: M. E. Sharpe, 2001, p. 115), but experts on the campaign believe that this does not take into account unofficial persecutions, which would bring the total to over 650,000; see, for instance, Hua Min, *Zhongguo da nizhuan: 'Fanyou' yundong shi* (China's great reversal: A history of the anti-rightist campaign), Flushing, NY: Mingjing, 1996, p. 148; on the role of Deng Xiaoping, see Chung Yen-lin, 'The Witch-Hunting Vanguard: The Central Secretariat's Roles and Activities in the Anti-Rightist Campaign', *China Quarterly*, no. 206 (June 2011), pp. 391–411; there is a wealth of evidence in Song Yongyi (ed.), *Chinese Anti-Rightist Campaign Database*, Hong Kong: Universities Service Center for China Studies, 2010.

34   Report by the Beijing Municipal Party Committee, 7 July 1957, Gansu, 91-1-19, pp. 145–8; on the presumed alliance, see Frederick C. Teiwes, *Politics and Purges in China: Rectification and the Decline of Party Norms*, Armonk, NY: M. E. Sharpe, 1993, pp. 235–40; see also Zhu Zheng, *Fan youpai douzheng shimo* (The history of the anti-rightist campaign), Hong Kong: Mingbao chubanshe youxian gongsi, 2004, pp. 275–313.

35   MacFarquhar, *The Hundred Flowers Campaign and the Chinese Intellectuals*, p. 264.

36 Zhu, *Fan youpai douzheng shimo*, pp. 275–313; Zhang, *Wangshi bingbu ruyan*; Dai, 'Righting the Wronged', p. 66; McGough, *Fei Hsiao-t'ung*, pp. 79–82.

37 Wu, *A Single Tear*, p. 64.

38 Yue, *To the Storm*, pp. 7 and 32.

39 Report by the Beijing Municipal Party Committee, 7 July 1957, Gansu, 91-1-19, pp. 145–8; on the presumed alliance, see Teiwes, *Politics and Purges in China*, pp. 235–40.

40 Wang Ning, 'The Great Northern Wilderness: Political Exiles in the People's Republic of China', University of British Columbia, doctoral dissertation, 2005, p. 33; Qian Xinbo, 'Jiaoxin cheng "youpai"' (Becoming a rightist by opening one's heart), in Niu Han and Deng Jiuping (eds), *Jingji lu: Jiyi zhong de fanyoupai yundong* (The thorny path: The anti-rightist campaign in memory), Beijing: Jingji ribao chubanshe, 1998, pp. 401–4; Dai, 'Righting the Wronged', p. 67.

41 He Ying interviewed by Wang, 'The Great Northern Wilderness', p. 48, with a few stylistic changes.

42 Cong Weixi, *Zouxiang hundun: Cong Weixi huiyilu* (Towards chaos: Reminiscences of Cong Weixi), Guangzhou: Huacheng chubanshe, 2007, pp. 5–6, quoted in Wang, 'The Great Northern Wilderness', p. 137; Shen, 'The Death of Hu Shi's Younger Son, Sidu'.

43 Ding Ling, 'Dao Beidahuang qu' (To the Great Northern Wilderness), in Niu Han and Deng Jiuping (eds), *Yuan shang cao: Jiyi zhong de fanyoupai yundong* (Grass on the land: The anti-rightist campaign in memory), Beijing: Jingji ribao chubanshe, 1998, p. 318.

Select Bibliography

Archives

Non-Chinese Archives
AG SVD – Archivum Generale of the Societas Verbi Divini, Rome
Guoshiguan – National Archives, Hsin-tien, Taiwan
ICRC – International Committee of the Red Cross, Geneva
National Archives at College Park – National Archives, Washington
PCE – Archives of the Presbyterian Church of England, SOAS, London
PRO – The National Archives, London
RGASPI – Rossiiskii Gosudarstvennyi Arkhiv Sotsial'no-Politicheskoi Istorii, Moscow

Central Archives
Ministry of Foreign Affairs – Waijiaobu Dang'anguan, Beijing

Provincial Archives
Gansu – Gansu sheng dang'anguan, Lanzhou
91 Zhonggong Gansu shengwei (Gansu Provincial Party Committee)
96 Zhonggong Gansu shengwei nongcun gongzuobu (Gansu Provincial Party Committee Department for Rural Work)

Guangdong – Guangdong sheng dang'anguan, Guangzhou
204 Huanan xingzheng weiyuanhui (Administrative Committee for South China)
217 Guangdong sheng nongcunbu (Guangdong Provincial Bureau for Rural Affairs)

Hebei – Hebei sheng dang'anguan, Shijiazhuang

572 Zhongguo gongchandang zhongyang weiyuanhui (Central Committee of the CCP)

684 Zhonggong Rehe shengwei (Rehe Provincial Party Committee)

855 Zhonggong Hebei shengwei (Hebei Provincial Party Committee)

856 Zhonggong Hebei shengjiwei (Hebei Provincial Committee for Inspecting Discipline)

879 Zhonggong Hebei shengwei nongcun gongzuobu (Hebei Provincial Party Committee Department for Rural Work)

886 Hebei shengwei wuren xiaozu bangongshi (Office of the Hebei Provincial Party Committee Five-Man Team)

888 Hebei shengwei jieyue jiancha bangongshi (Thrift Investigation Office of the Provincial Party Committee)

942 Hebei sheng tongjiju (Hebei Province Office for Statistics)

979 Hebei sheng nongyeting (Hebei Province Agricultural Bureau)

Hubei – Hubei sheng dang'anguan, Wuhan

SZ1 Zhonggong Hubei sheng weiyuanhui (Hubei Provincial Party Committee)

SZ18 Zhonggong Hubei sheng weiyuanhui nongcun zhengzhibu (Hubei Provincial Party Committee Department for Rural Politics)

SZ29 Hubei sheng zonggonghui (Hubei Province Federation of Trade Unions)

SZ34 Hubei sheng renmin weiyuanhui (Hubei Provincial People's Congress)

SZ37 Hubei sheng renmin zhengfu tudi gaige weiyuanhui (Hubei Committee for Land Reform)

SZ44 Hubei sheng tongjiju (Hubei Province Office for Statistics)

SZ107 Hubei sheng nongyeting (Hubei Province Agricultural Bureau)

Jilin – Jilin sheng dang'anguan, Changchun

1 Zhonggong Jilin shengwei (Jilin Provincial Party Committee)

2 Jilin sheng renmin zhengfu (Jilin Provincial People's Government)

55 Jilin sheng nongyeting (Jilin Province Agricultural Bureau)

Shaanxi – Shaanxi sheng dang'anguan, Xi'an

123 Zhonggong Shaanxi shengwei (Shaanxi Provincial Party Committee)

Shandong – Shandong sheng dang'anguan, Jinan

G26 Zhonggong Bohaiqu wei (Bohai Region Party Committee)

G52 Jinluyu bianqu wenjian huiji (Documents from the Jinluyu Base Area)

A1 Zhonggong Shandong shengwei (Shandong Provincial Party Committee)

A14 Shandong sheng renmin zhengfu zongjiao shiwuhu (Office for Religious Affairs of the Shandong Municipal People's Government)

A29 Shangdong sheng jiaoyuting (Shandong Province Education Bureau)

A51 Shandong sheng gaoji renmin fayuan (Shandong Higher People's Court)

A68 Zhongguo renmin yinhang Shandong fenhang (Shangdong Branch of the People's Bank of China)

A101 Shandong sheng renmin zhengfu (Shandong Municipal People's Government)

Sichuan – Sichuan sheng dang'anguan, Chengdu

JC1 Zhonggong Sichuan shengwei (Sichuan Provincial Party Committee)

JX1 Zhonggong Jianxi xingshu weiyuanhui (Party Committee of the West Sichuan Region)

JK1 Zhonggong Xikang shengwei (Xikang Provincial Party Committee)

JK16 Xikang sheng minzhengting (Xikang Province Bureau for Civil Affairs)

JK32 Xikang sheng weishengting (Xikang Province Bureau for Health and Hygiene)

Zhejiang – Zhejiang sheng dang'anguan, Hangzhou

J007 Zhejiang shengwei nongcun gongzuobu (Zhejiang Provincial Party Committee's Department for Rural Work)

J103 Zhenjiang shengwei minzhengting (Zhejiang Provincial Party Committee's Bureau for Civil Affairs)

Municipal Archives

Beijing – Beijing shi dang'anguan, Beijing

1 Beijing shi weiyuanhui (Beijing Municipal Party Committee)

2 Beijing shi renmin weiyuanhui (Beijing Municipal People's Congress)

14 Beijing shi renmin zhengfu zhengfa weiyuanhui (Committee for Law and Politics of the Beijing Municipal People's Congress)

Nanjing – Nanjing shi dang'anguan, Nanjing, Jiangsu
4003 Nanjing shiwei (Nanjing Municipal Party Committee)
5012 Nanjing shi minzhengju (Nanjing Municipal Bureau for Civil Affairs)
5034 Nanjing shi gongyeju (Nanjing Municipal Bureau for Industry)
5065 Nanjing shi weishengju (Nanjing Municipal Bureau for Health and Hygiene)

Shanghai – Shanghai shi dang'anguan, Shanghai
A2 Shanghai shiwei bangongting (Office of the Shanghai Municipal Party Committee)
A36 Shanghai shiwei gongye zhengzhibu (Shanghai Municipal Party Committee's Bureau for Industry and Politics)
A71 Shanghai shiwei funü lianhehui (Shanghai Municipal Party Committee's All-China Women's Federation)
B1 Shanghai shi renmin zhengfu (Shanghai Municipal People's Government)
B2 Shanghai shi renmin weiyuanhui zhengfa bangongting (Office for Law and Politics of the Shanghai Municipal People's Congress)
B13 Shanghai shi zengchan jieyue weiyuanhui (Shanghai Municipal Committee on Increased Production and Economic Thrift)
B31 Shanghai shi tongjiju (Shanghai Municipal Bureau for Statistics)
B182 Shanghai shi gongshanghang guanliju (Shanghai Municipal Bureau for Supervision of Business)
B242 Shanghai shi weishengju (Shanghai Municipal Bureau for Health and Hygiene)
C1 Shanghai shi zonggonghui (Shanghai Municipal Federation of Trade Unions)

Published Works

Apter, David E. and Tony Saich, *Revolutionary Discourse in Mao's Republic*, Cambridge, MA: Harvard University Press, 1994.
Athenoux, André, *Le Christ crucifié au pays de Mao*, Paris: Alsatia, 1968.

Barber, Noel, *The Fall of Shanghai*, New York: Coward, McCann & Geoghegan, 1979.

Barnett, A. Doak, *China on the Eve of Communist Takeover*, New York: Praeger, 1963.

Barnett, A. Doak, *Communist China: The Early Years 1949–55*, New York: Praeger, 1965.

Becker, Jasper, *C. C. Lee: The Textile Man*, Hong Kong: Textile Alliance, 2011.

Becker, Jasper, *Rogue Regime: Kim Jong Il and the Looming Threat of North Korea*, New York: Oxford University Press, 2005.

Belden, Jack, *China Shakes the World*, New York: Harper, 1949.

Bergère, Marie-Claire, 'Les Capitalistes shanghaïens et la période de transition entre le régime Guomindang et le communisme (1948–1952)', *Etudes Chinoises*, 8, no. 2 (Autumn 1989), pp. 7–30.

Biggerstaff, Knight, *Nanking Letters, 1949*, Ithaca, NY: China–Japan Program, Cornell University, 1979.

Bing Lu, *Xin Zhongguo fan fubai diyi da'an: Qiangbi Liu Qingshan, Zhang Zishan jishi* (New China's first big case against corruption: The execution of Liu Qingshan and Zhang Zishan), Beijing: Falü chubanshe, 1990.

Birns, Jack, *Assignment Shanghai: Photographs on the Eve of Revolution*, Berkeley: University of California Press, 2003.

Bo Yibo, *Ruogan zhongda shijian yu juece de huigu* (Recollections of several important decisions and events), Beijing: Zhonggong zongyang dangxiao chubanshe, 1997.

Bodde, Derk, *Peking Diary: A Year of Revolution*, New York: Henry Schuman, 1950.

Briggs, Herbert W., 'American Consular Rights in Communist China', *American Journal of International Law*, 44, no. 2 (April 1950), pp. 243–58.

Brown, Jeremy and Paul G. Pickowicz (eds), *Dilemmas of Victory: The Early Years of the People's Republic of China*, Cambridge, MA: Harvard University Press, 2008.

Bush, Richard C., *Religion in Communist China*, Nashville: Abingdon Press, 1970.

Byron, John and Robert Pack, *The Claws of the Dragon: Kang Sheng, the*

Evil Genius behind Mao and his Legacy of Terror in People's China, New York: Simon & Schuster, 1992.

Cameron, James, *Mandarin Red: A Journey behind the 'Bamboo Curtain'*, London: Michael Joseph, 1955.

Chang, David Cheng, 'To Return Home or "Return to Taiwan": Conflicts and Survival in the "Voluntary Repatriation" of Chinese POWs in the Korean War', doctoral dissertation, University of California, San Diego, 2011.

Chang Jung and Jon Halliday, *Mao: The Unknown Story*, London: Jonathan Cape, 2005.

Chao, Kang, *Agricultural Production in Communist China, 1949–1965*, Madison: University of Wisconsin Press, 1970.

Chen Jian, *China's Road to the Korean War*, New York: Columbia University Press, 1996.

Chen Jian, 'The Chinese Communist "Liberation" of Tibet, 1949–51', in Jeremy Brown and Paul G. Pickowicz (eds), *Dilemmas of Victory: The Early Years of the People's Republic of China*, Cambridge, MA: Harvard University Press, 2008, pp. 130–59.

Chen Jian, *Mao's China and the Cold War*, Chapel Hill: University of North Carolina Press, 2001.

Chen, Theodore Hsi-en and Wen-hui C. Chen, 'The "Three-Anti" and "Five-Anti" Movements in Communist China', *Pacific Affairs*, 26, no. 1 (March 1953), pp. 3–23.

Chen Yung-fa, *Yan'an de yinying* (Yan'an's shadow), Taipei: Institute of Modern History, Academia Sinica, 1990.

Chêng, C. K., *The Dragon Sheds its Scales*, New York: New Voices Publishing, 1952.

Cheng, Tiejun and Mark Selden, 'The Origins and Social Consequences of China's *Hukou* System', *China Quarterly*, no. 139 (Sept. 1994), pp. 644–68.

Cheng Yinghong, *Creating the 'New Man': From Enlightenment Ideals to Socialist Realities*, Honolulu: University of Hawai'i Press, 2009.

Cheo, Esther Y., *Black Country Girl in Red China*, London: Hutchinson, 1980.

Chow Ching-wen, *Ten Years of Storm: The True Story of the Communist Regime in China*, New York: Holt, Rinehart & Winston, 1960.

Chu, Valentin, *The Inside Story of Communist China: Ta Ta, Tan Tan*, London: Allen & Unwin, 1964.

Chung Yen-lin, 'The Witch-Hunting Vanguard: The Central Secretariat's Roles and Activities in the Anti-Rightist Campaign', *China Quarterly*, no. 206 (June 2011), pp. 391–411.

Clark, Paul, *Chinese Cinema: Culture and Politics since 1949*, Cambridge: Cambridge University Press, 1987.

Clifford, Nicholas R., *Spoilt Children of Empire: Westerners in Shanghai and the Chinese Revolution of the 1920s*, Hanover, NH: University Press of New England, 1991.

Crozier, Brian, *The Man who Lost China: The First Full Biography of Chiang Kai-shek*, New York: Scribner, 1976.

Dai Huang, 'Righting the Wronged', in Zhang Lijia and Calum MacLeod (eds), *China Remembers*, Oxford: Oxford University Press, 1999, pp. 63–72.

Dai Maolin and Zhao Xiaoguang, *Gao Gang zhuan* (A biography of Gao Gang), Xi'an: Shaanxi renmin chubanshe, 2011.

Dai Qing, 'Liang Shuming and Mao Zedong', *Chinese Studies in History*, 34, no. 1 (Autumn 2000), pp. 61–92.

Dai Qing, *Liang Shuming, Wang Shiwei, Chu Anping*, Nanjing: Jiangsu wenyi chubanshe, 1989.

Dai Qing, *Wang Shiwei and 'Wild Lilies': Rectification and Purges in the Chinese Communist Party, 1942–1944*, Armonk, NY: M. E. Sharpe, 1994.

de Jaegher, Raymond J., *The Enemy Within: An Eyewitness Account of the Communist Conquest of China*, Garden City, NY: Doubleday, 1952.

Deane, John R., *The Strange Alliance: The Story of our Efforts at Wartime Cooperation with Russia*, New York: Viking Press, 1947.

DeMare, Brian J., 'Turning Bodies and Turning Minds: Land Reform and Chinese Political Culture, 1946–1952', doctoral dissertation, University of California, Los Angeles, 2007.

Denton, Kirk A., *The Problematic of Self in Modern Chinese Literature: Hu Feng and Lu Ling*, Stanford: Stanford University Press, 1998.

Diamant, Neil J., *Embattled Glory: Veterans, Military Families, and the Politics of Patriotism in China, 1949–2007*, Lanham, MD: Rowman & Littlefield, 2009.

Dikötter, Frank, *China before Mao: The Age of Openness*, Berkeley: University of California Press, 2008.

Dikötter, Frank, 'Crime and Punishment in Post-Liberation China: The Prisoners of a Beijing Gaol in the 1950s', *China Quarterly*, no. 149 (March 1997), pp. 147–59.

Dikötter, Frank, *Crime, Punishment and the Prison in Modern China*, London: Hurst; New York: Columbia University Press, 2002.

Dikötter, Frank, 'The Emergence of Labour Camps in Shandong Province, 1942–1950', *China Quarterly*, no. 175 (Sept. 2003), pp. 803–17.

Dikötter, Frank, *Exotic Commodities: Modern Objects and Everyday Life in China*, New York: Columbia University Press, 2006.

Dikötter, Frank, *Mao's Great Famine: The History of China's Most Devastating Catastrophe, 1958–1962*, London: Bloomsbury, 2010.

Domenach, Jean-Luc, *L'Archipel oublié*, Paris: Fayard, 1992.

Dransard, Louis, *Vu en Chine*, Paris: Téqui, 1952.

Duan Kewen, *Zhanfan zishu* (Autobiography of a war criminal), Taipei: Shijie ribaoshe, 1976.

Endicott, Stephen L., 'Germ Warfare and "Plausible Denial": The Korean War, 1952–1953', *Modern China*, 5, no. 1 (Jan. 1979), pp. 79–104.

Endrey, Andrew, 'Hu Feng: Return of the Counter-Revolutionary', *Australian Journal of Chinese Affairs*, 5 (Jan. 1981), pp. 73–90.

Ezpeleta, Mariano, *Red Shadows over Shanghai*, Quezon City: Zita, 1972.

Faligot, Roger and Rémi Kauffer, *The Chinese Secret Service*, New York: Morrow, 1989.

Fan, Kawai and Honkei Lai, 'Mao Zedong's Fight against Schistosomiasis', *Perspectives in Biology and Medicine*, 51, no. 2 (Spring 2008), pp. 176–87.

Fenby, Jonathan, *Modern China: The Fall and Rise of a Great Power, 1850 to the Present*, New York: Ecco, 2008.

Figes, Orlando, *A People's Tragedy: The Russian Revolution, 1891–1924*, London: Jonathan Cape, 1996.

Fitzpatrick, Sheila, *Everyday Stalinism: Ordinary Life in Extraordinary Times: Soviet Russia in the 1930s*, New York: Oxford University Press, 1999.

Forbes, Andrew D. W., *Warlords and Muslims in Chinese Central Asia: A*

Political History of Republican Sinkiang, 1911–1949, Cambridge: Cambridge University Press, 1986.

Gao Hua, *Hong taiyang shi zenyang shengqi de. Yan'an zhengfeng yundong de lailong qumai* (How did the red sun rise over Yan'an? A history of the Rectification Movement), Hong Kong: Chinese University Press, 2000.

Gao, James Z., 'The Call of the Oases: The "Peaceful Liberation" of Xinjiang, 1949–53', in Jeremy Brown and Paul G. Pickowicz (eds), *Dilemmas of Victory: The Early Years of the People's Republic of China*, Cambridge, MA: Harvard University Press, 2008, pp. 184–204.

Gao, James Zheng, *The Communist Takeover of Hangzhou: The Transformation of City and Cadre, 1949–1954*, Honolulu: University of Hawai'i Press, 2004.

Gao Wangling, *Lishi shi zenyang gaibian de: Zhongguo nongmin fanxing-wei, 1950–1980* (How history is changed: Acts of resistance among the farmers in China, 1950–1980), Hong Kong: Chinese University of Hong Kong Press, 2012.

Gao Wangling and Liu Yang, 'Tugai de jiduanhua' (The radicalization of the land reform movement), *Ershiyi shiji*, no. 111 (Feb. 2009), pp. 36–47.

Gao Wenqian, *Zhou Enlai: The Last Perfect Revolutionary*, New York: PublicAffairs, 2007.

Gardner, John, 'The Wu-fan Campaign in Shanghai', in Doak Barnett, *Chinese Communist Policies in Action*, Seattle: University of Washington Press, 1969, pp. 477–53.

Glantz, David M., *The Soviet Strategic Offensive in Manchuria, 1945: 'August Storm'*, London: Frank Cass, 2003.

Goldman, Merle, 'Hu Feng's Conflict with the Communist Literary Authorities', *China Quarterly*, no. 12 (Oct. 1962), pp. 102–37.

Goncharov, Sergei N., John W. Lewis and Xue Litai, *Uncertain Partners: Stalin, Mao, and the Korean War*, Stanford: Stanford University Press, 1993.

Gould, Randall, 'Shanghai during the Takeover, 1949', *Annals of the American Academy of Political and Social Science*, no. 277 (Sept. 1951), pp. 182–92.

Goullart, Peter, *Forgotten Kingdom*, London: John Murray, 1957.

Gray, Jack, *Rebellions and Revolutions: China from the 1800s to the 1980s*, Oxford: Oxford University Press, 1990.

Greene, Robert W., *Calvary in China*, New York: Putnam, 1953.

Gross, Miriam D., 'Chasing Snails: Anti-Schistosomiasis Campaigns in the People's Republic of China', doctoral dissertation, University of California, San Diego, 2010.

Halberstam, David, *The Coldest Winter: America and the Korean War*, London: Macmillan, 2008.

Hambro, Edvard, 'Chinese Refugees in Hong Kong', *Phylon Quarterly*, 18, no. 1 (1957), pp. 69–81.

Hao Yen-p'ing, *The Commercial Revolution in Nineteenth-Century China: The Rise of Sino-Western Mercantile Capitalism*, Berkeley: University of California Press, 1986.

Harris, Sheldon H., *Factories of Death: Japanese Biological Warfare 1932–45 and the American Cover-Up*, London: Routledge, 1994.

Hastings, Max, *The Korean War*, New York: Simon & Schuster, 1987.

He, Henry Yuhuai, *Dictionary of the Political Thought of the People's Republic of China*, Armonk, NY: M. E. Sharpe, 2001.

He Qixin, 'China's Shakespeare', *Shakespeare Quarterly*, 37, no. 2 (Summer 1986), pp. 149–59.

Heinzig, Dieter, *The Soviet Union and Communist China 1945–1950: The Arduous Road to the Alliance*, Armonk, NY: M. E. Sharpe, 2004.

Henriot, Christian, '"La Fermeture": The Abolition of Prostitution in Shanghai, 1949–1958', *China Quarterly*, no. 142 (June 1995), pp. 467–86.

Holm, David, 'Folk Art as Propaganda: The *Yangge* Movement in Yan'an', in Bonnie S. McDougall (ed.), *Popular Chinese Literature and Performing Arts in the People's Republic of China, 1949–1979*, Berkeley: University of California Press, 1984, pp. 3–35.

Hooper, Beverley, *China Stands Up: Ending the Western Presence, 1948–1950*, London: Routledge, 1987.

Hua Min, *Zhongguo da nizhuan: 'Fanyou' yundong shi* (China's great reversal: A history of the anti-rightist campaign), Flushing, NY: Mingjing, 1996.

Huang Changyong, *Wang Shiwei zhuan* (A biography of Wang Shiwei), Zhengzhou: Henan renmin chubanshe, 2000.

Huang, Quentin K. Y., *Now I Can Tell: The Story of a Christian Bishop under Communist Persecution*, New York: Morehouse-Gorham, 1954.

Huang Zheng, *Liu Shaoqi yisheng* (Liu Shaoqi: A life), Beijing: Zhongyang wenxian chubanshe, 2003.

Huang Zheng, *Liu Shaoqi zhuan* (A biography of Liu Shaoqi), Beijing: Zhongyang wenxian chubanshe, 1998.

Huang Zheng, *Wang Guangmei fangtan lu* (A record of conversations with Wang Guangmei), Beijing: Zhongyang wenxian chubanshe, 2006.

Hung Chang-tai, 'The Dance of Revolution: *Yangge* in Beijing in the Early 1950s', *China Quarterly*, no. 181 (2005), pp. 82–99.

Hung Chang-tai, 'Mao's Parades: State Spectacles in China in the 1950s', *China Quarterly*, no. 190 (June 2007), pp. 411–31.

Hung Chang-tai, *Mao's New World: Political Culture in the Early People's Republic*, Ithaca, NY: Cornell University Press, 2011.

Hutheesing, Raja, *Window on China*, London: Derek Verschoyle, 1953.

Ji Fengyuan, *Linguistic Engineering: Language and Politics in Mao's China*, Honolulu: University of Hawai'i Press, 2004.

Jiang Weiqing, *Qishi nian zhengcheng: Jiang Weiqing huiyilu* (A seventy-year journey: The memoirs of Jiang Weiqing), Nanjing: Jiangsu renmin chubanshe, 1996.

Jin Chongji and Chen Qun (eds), *Chen Yun zhuan* (A biography of Chen Yun), Beijing: Zhongyang wenxian chubanshe, 2005.

Jin Chongji and Huang Zheng (eds), *Liu Shaoqi zhuan* (A biography of Liu Shaoqi), Beijing: Zhongyang wenxian chubanshe, 1998.

Jones, Robert H., *The Roads to Russia: United States Lend-Lease to the Soviet Union*, Norman: University of Oklahoma Press, 1969.

Kang Zhengguo, *Confessions: An Innocent Life in Communist China*, New York: Norton, 2007.

Kaple, Deborah A., 'Soviet Advisors in China in the 1950s', in Odd Arne Westad (ed.), *Brothers in Arms: The Rise and Fall of the Sino-Soviet Alliance, 1945–1963*, Washington: Woodrow Wilson Center Press, 1998, pp. 117–40.

Kau, Michael Y. M. and John K. Leung (eds), *The Writings of Mao Zedong: 1949–1976*, Armonk, NY: M. E. Sharpe, 1986–92.

Khrushchev, Nikita, *Vremia, liudi, vlast'* (Time, people, power), Moscow: Moskovskiye Novosti, 1999.

Kinmond, William, *No Dogs in China: A Report on China Today*, New York: Thomas Nelson, 1957.

Lacy, Creighton, 'The Missionary Exodus from China', *Pacific Affairs*, 28, no. 4 (Dec. 1955), pp. 301–14.

Ladany, Laszlo, *The Communist Party of China and Marxism, 1921–1985: A Self-Portrait*, London: Hurst, 1988.

Ladany, Laszlo, *Law and Legality in China: The Testament of a China-Watcher*, London: Hurst, 1992.

Lampton, David M., *The Politics of Medicine in China: The Policy Process, 1949–1977*, Folkestone, Kent: Dawson, 1977.

Lankov, Andrei, *From Stalin to Kim Il Sung: The Formation of North Korea, 1945–1960*, London: Hurst, 2002.

Lary, Diana, *China's Republic*, Cambridge: Cambridge University Press, 2006.

Lawson, Konrad Mitchell, 'Wartime Atrocities and the Politics of Treason in the Ruins of the Japanese Empire, 1937–1953', doctoral dissertation, Harvard University, 2012.

Ledovsky, Andrei M., 'Marshall's Mission in the Context of U.S.S.R.–China–U.S. Relations', in Larry I. Bland (ed.), *George C. Marshall's Mediation Mission to China, December 1945–January 1947*, Lexington, VA: George C. Marshall Foundation, 1998, pp. 423–44.

Leitenberg, Milton, 'The Korean War Biological Weapon Allegations: Additional Information and Disclosures', *Asian Perspective*, 24, no. 3 (2000), pp. 159–72.

Leitenberg, Milton, 'New Russian Evidence on the Korean War Biological Warfare Allegations: Background and Analysis', *Cold War International History Project Bulletin*, no. 11 (1998), pp. 185–99.

Leys, Simon, *Broken Images: Essays on Chinese Culture and Politics*, New York: St Martin's Press, 1980.

Li Changyu, 'Mao's "Killing Quotas"', *China Rights Forum*, no. 4 (2005), pp. 41–4.

Li Choh-ming, 'Economic Development', *China Quarterly*, no. 1 (March 1960), pp. 35–50.

Li Hua-yu, 'Instilling Stalinism in Chinese Party Members: Absorbing Stalin's *Short Course* in the 1950s', in Thomas P. Bernstein and Hua-yu

Li (eds), *China Learns from the Soviet Union, 1949–Present*, Lanham, MD: Lexington Books, 2009, pp. 107–30.

Li Hua-yu, *Mao and the Economic Stalinization of China, 1948–1953*, Cambridge, MA: Harvard University Press, 2006.

Li Huaiyin, 'Confrontation and Conciliation under the Socialist State: Peasant Resistance to Agricultural Collectivization in China in the 1950s', *Twentieth-Century China*, 33, no. 2 (2007), pp. 73–99.

Li Huaiyin, *Village Governance in North China, 1875–1936*, Stanford: Stanford University Press, 1995.

Li Xiaobing, Allan R. Millett and Bin Yu (eds), *Mao's Generals Remember Korea*, Lawrence: University Press of Kansas, 2001.

Li Zhisui, *The Private Life of Chairman Mao: The Memoirs of Mao's Personal Physician*, New York: Random House, 1994.

Liao Yiwu, *God is Red: The Secret Story of How Christianity Survived and Flourished in Communist China*, New York: HarperCollins, 2011.

Lieberthal, Kenneth G., *Revolution and Tradition in Tientsin, 1949–1952*, Stanford: Stanford University Press, 1980.

Lin Yunhui, *Xiang shehuizhuiyi guodu, 1953–55* (The transition to socialism, 1953–55), Hong Kong: Chinese University Press, 2009.

Liu Jianhui and Wang Hongxu, 'The Origins of the General Line for the Transition Period and of the Acceleration of the Chinese Socialist Transformation in Summer 1955', *China Quarterly*, no. 187 (Sept. 2006), pp. 724–31.

Liu Shaw-tong, *Out of Red China*, Boston: Little, Brown, 1953.

Loh, Robert, *Escape from Red China*, London: Michael Joseph, 1962.

Long Yingtai, *Da jiang da hai 1949* (Big river, big sea: Untold stories of 1949), Hong Kong: Tiandi tushu youxian gongsi, 2009.

Lu Xiaobo, *Cadres and Corruption: The Organizational Involution of the Chinese Communist Party*, Stanford: Stanford University Press, 2000.

Lum, Peter, *Peking, 1950–1953*, London: Hale, 1958.

Luo Pinghan, *Dangshi xijie* (Details in the history of the Communist Party), Beijing: Renmin chubanshe, 2011.

Luo Pinghan, *Tudi gaige yundong shi* (A history of the campaign for land reform), Fuzhou: Fujian renmin chubanshe, 2005.

Lüthi, Lorenz M., *The Sino-Soviet Split: Cold War in the Communist World*, Princeton: Princeton University Press, 2008.

Lynch, Michael, *Mao*, London: Routledge, 2004.

MacFarquhar, Roderick (ed.), *The Hundred Flowers Campaign and the Chinese Intellectuals*, New York: Octagon Books, 1974.

MacFarquhar, Roderick, *The Origins of the Cultural Revolution*, vol. 1: *Contradictions among the People, 1956–1957*, London: Oxford University Press, 1974.

MacFarquhar, Roderick, Timothy Cheek and Eugene Wu (eds), *The Secret Speeches of Chairman Mao: From the Hundred Flowers to the Great Leap Forward*, Cambridge, MA: Harvard University Press, 1989.

MacFarquhar, Roderick and Michael Schoenhals, *Mao's Last Revolution*, Cambridge, MA: Belknap Press of Harvard University Press, 2006.

McGough, James P., *Fei Hsiao-t'ung: The Dilemma of a Chinese Intellectual*, White Plains, NY: M. E. Sharpe, 1979.

McGrath, W. Aedan, *Perseverance through Faith: A Priest's Prison Diary*, ed. Theresa Marie Moreau, Bloomington, IN: Xlibris Corporation, 2008.

Mansourov, Alexandre Y., 'Stalin, Mao, Kim, and China's Decision to Enter the Korean War, Sept. 16–Oct. 15, 1950: New Evidence from the Russian Archives', *Cold War International History Project Bulletin*, nos 6–7 (Winter 1995), pp. 94–119.

Mao Zedong, *Jianguo yilai Mao Zedong wengao* (Mao Zedong's manuscripts since the founding of the People's Republic), Beijing: Zhongyang wenxian chubanshe, 1987–96.

Mao Zedong, *Mao Zedong waijiao wenxuan* (Selection of writings on foreign affairs by Mao Zedong), Beijing: Zhongyang wenxian chubanshe, 1994.

Martin, Edwin W., *Divided Counsel: The Anglo-American Response to Communist Victory in China*, Lexington: University Press of Kentucky, 1986.

Meyer, Mahlon, *Remembering China from Taiwan: Divided Families and Bittersweet Reunions after the Chinese Civil War*, Hong Kong: Hong Kong University Press, 2012.

Millward, James A., *Eurasian Crossroads: A History of Xinjiang*, New York: Columbia University Press, 2007.

Moreau, Theresa Marie, *Blood of the Martyrs: Trappist Monks in Communist China*, Los Angeles: Veritas Est Libertas, 2012.

Näth, Marie-Luise (ed.), *Communist China in Retrospect: East European Sinologists Remember the First Fifteen Years of the PRC*, Frankfurt: P. Lang, 1995.

Niu Han and Deng Jiuping (eds), *Yuan shang cao: Jiyi zhong de fanyoupai yundong* (Grass on the land: The anti-rightist campaign in memory), Beijing: Jingji ribao chubanshe, 1998.

Niu Han and Deng Jiuping (eds), *Jingji lu: Jiyi zhong de fanyoupai yundong* (The thorny path: The anti-rightist campaign in memory), Beijing: Jingji ribao chubanshe, 1998.

Oi, Jean C., *State and Peasant in Contemporary China: The Political Economy of Village Government*, Berkeley: University of California Press, 1989.

Osborne, Anne, 'Property, Taxes, and State Protection of Rights', in Madeleine Zelin, Jonathan Ocko and Robert Gardella (eds), *Contract and Property in Early Modern China*, Stanford: Stanford University Press, 2004, pp. 120–58.

Pakula, Hannah, *The Last Empress: Madame Chiang Kai-shek and the Birth of Modern China*, New York: Simon & Schuster, 2009.

Pan, Philip, *Out of Mao's Shadow: The Struggle for the Soul of a New China*, Basingstoke: Picador, 2009.

Pang Xianzhi, Guo Chaoren and Jin Chongji (eds), *Liu Shaoqi*, Beijing: Xinhua chubanshe, 1998.

Pang Xianzhi and Jin Chongji (eds), *Mao Zedong zhuan, 1949–1976* (A biography of Mao Zedong, 1949–1976), Beijing: Zhongyang wenxian chubanshe, 2003.

Pasqualini, Jean, *Prisoner of Mao*, Harmondsworth: Penguin, 1973.

Pei Yiran, 'Zijie peijian: Fanyou qian zhishifenzi de xianluo' (The 'disarmament' of Chinese intellectuals before the anti-rightist campaign), *Ershiyi shiji*, no. 102 (Aug. 2007), pp. 34–45.

Peng Dehuai, *Peng Dehuai zishu* (Autobiography of Peng Dehuai), Beijing: Renmin chubanshe, 1981.

Peng Dehuai zhuan (Biography of Peng Dehuai), Beijing: Dangdai Zhongguo chubanshe, 1993.

Perry, Elizabeth J., 'Masters of the Country? Shanghai Workers in the

Early People's Republic', in Jeremy Brown and Paul G. Pickowicz (eds), *Dilemmas of Victory: The Early Years of the People's Republic of China*, Cambridge, MA: Harvard University Press, 2008, pp. 59–79.

Perry, Elizabeth J., 'Shanghai's Strike Wave of 1957', *China Quarterly*, no. 137 (March 1994), pp. 1–27.

Peters, Richard and Xiaobing Li (eds), *Voices from the Korean War: Personal Stories of American, Korean, and Chinese Soldiers*, Lexington: University Press of Kentucky, 2004.

Peterson, Glen D., 'House Divided: Transnational Families in the Early Years of the People's Republic of China', *Asian Studies Review*, no. 31 (March 2007), pp. 25–40.

Peterson, Glen D., 'Socialist China and the *Huaqiao*: The Transition to Socialism in the Overseas Chinese Areas of Rural Guangdong, 1949–1956', *Modern China*, 14, no. 3 (July 1988), pp. 309–35.

Peterson, Glen D., 'To Be or Not to Be a Refugee: The International Politics of the Hong Kong Refugee Crisis, 1949–55', *Journal of Imperial and Commonwealth History*, 36, no. 2 (June 2008), pp. 171–95.

Pipes, Richard, *A Concise History of the Russian Revolution*, New York: Knopf, 1995.

Priestley, K. E., 'The Sino-Soviet Friendship Association', *Pacific Affairs*, 25, no. 3 (Sept. 1952), pp. 287–92.

Qin Hui (Bian Wu), 'Gongshe zhi mi: Nongye jituanhua de zai renshi' (The myth of the commune: Revisiting the collectivisation of agriculture), *Ershiyi shiji*, no. 48 (Aug. 1998), pp. 22–36.

Qin Hui, *Nongmin Zhongguo: Lishi fansi yu xianshi xuanze* (Peasant China: Historical reflections and realistic choices), Zhengzhou: Henan renmin chubanshe, 2003.

Qing Simei, 'American Visions of Democracy and the Marshall Mission to China', in Hongshan Li and Zhaohui Hong (eds), *Image, Perception, and the Making of U.S.–China Relations*, Lanham, MA: University Press of America, 1998, pp. 257–312.

Radchenko, Sergey and David Wolff, 'To the Summit via Proxy-Summits: New Evidence from Soviet and Chinese Archives on Mao's Long March to Moscow, 1949', *Cold War International History Project Bulletin*, no. 16 (Winter 2008), pp. 105–82.

Richardson, Philip, *Economic Change in China, c. 1800–1950*, Cambridge: Cambridge University Press, 1999.

Rickett, Allyn and Adele, *Prisoners of Liberation*, New York: Cameron Associates, 1957.

Rigney, Harold W., *Four Years in a Red Hell: The Story of Father Rigney*, Chicago: Henry Regnery, 1956.

Riskin, Carl, *China's Political Economy: The Quest for Development since 1949*, Oxford: Oxford University Press, 1987.

Rogaski, Ruth, 'Nature, Annihilation, and Modernity: China's Korean War Germ-Warfare Experience Reconsidered', *Journal of Asian Studies*, 61, no. 2 (May 2002), pp. 381–415.

Rossi, Paolo A., *The Communist Conquest of Shanghai: A Warning to the West*, Arlington, VA: Twin Circle, 1970.

Rowan, Roy, *Chasing the Dragon: A Veteran Journalist's Firsthand Account of the 1946–9 Chinese Revolution*, Guilford, CT: Lyons Press, 2004.

Salisbury, Harrison E., *The New Emperors: China in the Era of Mao and Deng*, Boston: Little, Brown, 1992.

Sang Ye, *China Candid: The People on the People's Republic*, Berkeley: University of California Press, 2006.

Saunders, Kate, *Eighteen Layers of Hell: Stories from the Chinese Gulag*, London: Cassell Wellington House, 1996.

Schama, Simon, *Citizens: A Chronicle of the French Revolution*, New York: Knopf, 1989.

Schoppa, R. Keith, *In a Sea of Bitterness: Refugees during the Sino-Japanese War*, Cambridge, MA: Harvard University Press, 2011.

Sebag Montefiore, Simon, *Stalin: The Court of the Red Tsar*, New York Knopf, 2004.

Service, Robert, *Comrades: A History of World Communism*, Cambridg MA: Harvard University Press, 2007.

Seton-Watson, Hugh, *The East European Revolution*, London: Methu 1950.

Sewell, William G., *I Stayed in China*, London: Allen & Unwin, 196

Shai, Aron, 'Imperialism Imprisoned: The Closure of British Firms People's Republic of China', *English Historical Review*, 104, n (Jan. 1989), pp. 88–109.

Shakya, Tsering, *The Dragon in the Land of Snows*, New York: Columbia University Press, 1999.

Shambaugh, David, 'The Foundations of Communist Rule in China: The Coercive Dimension', in William C. Kirby (ed.), *The People's Republic of China at 60: An International Assessment*, Cambridge, MA: Harvard University Asia Center, 2011, pp. 19–24.

Shen Zhihua, *Sikao yu xuanze: Cong zhishifenzi huiyi dao fanyoupai yundong (1956–1957)* (Reflections and choices: The consciousness of intellectuals and the anti-rightist campaign, 1956–1957), Hong Kong: Xianggang Zhongwen daxue dangdai Zhongguo wenhua yanjiu zhongxin, 2008.

Shen Zhihua, 'Sino-North Korean Conflict and its Resolution during the Korean War', *Cold War International History Project Bulletin*, nos 14–15 (Winter 2003–Spring 2004), pp. 9–24.

Shen Zhihua, 'Sino-Soviet Relations and the Origins of the Korean War: Stalin's Strategic Goals in the Far East', *Journal of Cold War Studies*, 2, no. 2 (Spring 2000), pp. 44–68.

Shen Zhihua, *Sulian zhuanjia zai Zhongguo* (Soviet experts in China), Beijing: Xinhua chubanshe, 2009.

Sheng, Michael M., *Battling Western Imperialism: Mao, Stalin, and the United States*, Princeton: Princeton University Press, 1997.

Sheng, Michael M., 'Mao and Chinese Elite Politics in the 1950s: The Gao Gang Affair Revisited', *Twentieth-Century China*, 36, no. 1 (Jan. 2011), pp. 67–96.

Sheng, Michael M., 'Mao Zedong and the Three-Anti Campaign (November 1951 to April 1952): A Revisionist Interpretation', *Twentieth-Century China*, 32, no. 1 (Nov. 2006), pp. 56–80.

Short, Philip, *Mao: A Life*, London: Hodder & Stoughton, 1999.

Smith, Aminda M., 'Reeducating the People: The Chinese Communists and the "Thought Reform" of Beggars, Prostitutes, and Other "Parasites"', doctoral dissertation, Princeton University, 2006.

Smith, Steve A., 'Fear and Rumour in the People's Republic of China in the 1950s', *Cultural and Social History*, 5, no. 3 (2008), pp. 269–88.

Smith, Steve A., 'Local Cadres Confront the Supernatural: The Politics of

Holy Water (*Shenshui*) in the PRC, 1949–1966', *China Quarterly*, no. 188 (2006), pp. 999–1022.

Song Yongyi (ed.), *Chinese Anti-Rightist Campaign Database*, Hong Kong: Universities Service Center for China Studies, 2010.

Strauss, Julia, 'Morality, Coercion and State Building by Campaign in the Early PRC: Regime Consolidation and After, 1949–1956', *China Quarterly*, no. 188 (2006), pp. 891–912.

Strauss, Julia, 'Paternalist Terror: The Campaign to Suppress Counterrevolutionaries and Regime Consolidation in the People's Republic of China, 1950–1953', *Comparative Studies in Society and History*, 44 (2002), pp. 80–105.

Su, Yang, *Collective Killings in Rural China during the Cultural Revolution*, Cambridge: Cambridge University Press, 2011.

Sun Youli and Dan Ling, *Engineering Communist China: One Man's Story*, New York: Algora Publishing, 2003.

Szonyi, Michael, *Cold War Island: Quemoy on the Front Line*, Cambridge: Cambridge University Press, 2008.

Tao Lujia, *Yige shengwei shuji huiyi Mao Zedong* (A provincial party secretary remembers Mao Zedong), Taiyuan: Shanxi renmin chubanshe, 1993.

Taubman, William, *Khrushchev: The Man and his Era*, London, Free Press, 2003.

Taylor, Jay, *The Generalissimo: Chiang Kai-shek and the Struggle for Modern China*, Cambridge, MA: Harvard University Press, 2009.

Teiwes, Frederick C., 'The Establishment and Consolidation of the New Regime, 1949–57', in Roderick MacFarquhar (ed.), *The Politics of China: The Eras of Mao and Deng*, New York: Cambridge University Press, 1997, pp. 5–86.

Teiwes, Frederick C., *Politics and Purges in China: Rectification and the Decline of Party Norms*, Armonk, NY: M. E. Sharpe, 1993.

Teiwes, Frederick C., *Politics at Mao's Court: Gao Gang and Party Factionalism in the Early 1950s*, Armonk, NY: M. E. Sharpe, 1990.

Tennien, Mark, *No Secret is Safe: Behind the Bamboo Curtain*, New York: Farrar, Straus & Young, 1952.

Tharp, Robert N., *They Called Us White Chinese: The Story of a Lifetime of*

Service to God and Mankind, Charlotte, NC: Eva E. Tharp Publications, 1994.

Townsend, James R. and Brantly Womack, *Politics in China*, Boston: Little, Brown, 1986.

Tung, Constantine, 'Metamorphosis of the Hero in Chairman Mao's Theater, 1942–1976', unpublished manuscript.

Tung, S. T., *Secret Diary from Red China*, Indianapolis: Bobbs-Merrill, 1961.

Tyler, Christian, *Wild West China: The Taming of Xinjiang*, London: John Murray, 2003.

U, Eddy, 'Dangerous Privilege: The United Front and the Rectification Campaign of the Early Mao Years', *China Journal*, no. 68 (July 2012), pp. 32–57.

U, Eddy, *Disorganizing China: Counter-Bureaucracy and the Decline of Socialism*, Stanford: Stanford University Press, 2007.

U, Eddy, 'The Making of Chinese Intellectuals: Representations and Organization in the Thought Reform Campaign', *China Quarterly*, no. 192 (2007), pp. 971–89.

Volland, Nicolas, 'Translating the Socialist State: Cultural Exchange, National Identity, and the Socialist World in the Early PRC', *Twentieth-Century China*, 33, no. 2 (April 2008), pp. 51–72.

Wakeman, Frederic, ' "Cleanup": The New Order in Shanghai', in Jeremy Brown and Paul G. Pickowicz (eds), *Dilemmas of Victory: The Early Years of the People's Republic of China*, Cambridge, MA: Harvard University Press, 2008, pp. 21–58.

Walker, Kenneth R., 'Collectivisation in Retrospect: The "Socialist High Tide" of Autumn 1955–Spring 1956', *China Quarterly*, no. 26 (June 1966), pp. 1–43.

Walker, Richard J., *China under Communism: The First Five Years*, New Haven: Yale University Press, 1955.

Wang, David Der-wei, *The Monster that is History: History, Violence, and Fictional Writing in Twentieth-Century China*, Berkeley: University of California Press, 2004.

Wang Haiguang, 'Zhengliang, minbian yu "feiluan" ' (Grain procurements, popular revolts and 'bandit disorder'), *Zhongguo dangdaishi yanjiu*, no. 1 (Aug. 2011), pp. 229–66.

Wang Jun, *Beijing Record: A Physical and Political History of Planning Modern Beijing*, London: World Scientific, 2011.

Wang Ning, 'The Great Northern Wilderness: Political Exiles in the People's Republic of China', doctoral dissertation, University of British Columbia, 2005.

Wang Ying, 'Gaizao sixiang: Zhengzhi, lishi yu jiyi (1949–1953)' (Reforming thoughts: Politics, history and memory, 1949–1953), doctoral dissertation, Beijing: People's University, 2010.

Watson, George, *The Lost Literature of Socialism*, Cambridge: Lutterworth Press, 2010.

Watson, James L., *Class and Social Stratification in Post-Revolution China*, Cambridge: Cambridge University Press, 1984.

Weathersby, Kathryn, 'Deceiving the Deceivers: Moscow, Beijing, Pyongyang, and the Allegations of Bacteriological Weapons Use in Korea', *Cold War International History Project Bulletin*, no. 11 (1998), pp. 176–84.

Welch, Holmes, *Buddhism under Mao*, Cambridge, MA: Harvard University Press, 1972.

Westad, Odd Arne, *Brothers in Arms: The Rise and Fall of the Sino-Soviet Alliance, 1945–1963*, Washington: Woodrow Wilson Center Press, 1998.

Westad, Odd Arne (ed.), *Decisive Encounters: The Chinese Civil War, 1946–1950*, Stanford: Stanford University Press, 2003.

Whiting, Allen S. and General Sheng Shih-tsai, *Sinkiang: Pawn or Pivot?*, East Lansing, MI: Michigan State University Press, 1958.

Wiest, Jean-Paul, *Maryknoll in China: A History, 1918–1955*, Armonk, NY: M. E. Sharpe, 1988.

Willens, Liliane, *Stateless in Shanghai*, Hong Kong: China Economic Review Publishing, 2010.

Williams, Philip F. and Yenna Wu, *The Great Wall of Confinement: The Chinese Prison Camp through Contemporary Fiction and Reportage*, Berkeley: University of California Press, 2004.

Wingrove, Paul, 'Gao Gang and the Moscow Connection: Some Evidence from Russian Sources', *Journal of Communist Studies and Transition Politics*, 16, no. 4 (Dec. 2000), pp. 88–106.

Wingrove, Paul, 'Mao in Moscow, 1949–50: Some New Archival Evidence', *Journal of Communist Studies and Transition Politics*, 11, no. 4 (Dec. 1995), pp. 309–34.

Wolff, David, '"One Finger's Worth of Historical Events": New Russian and Chinese Evidence on the Sino-Soviet Alliance and Split, 1948–1959', *Cold War International History Project Bulletin*, Working Paper no. 30 (Aug. 2002), pp. 1–74.

Wong, Frances, *China Bound and Unbound: History in the Making: An Early Returnee's Account*, Hong Kong: Hong Kong University Press, 2009.

Wong Siu-lun, *Emigrant Entrepreneurs: Shanghai Industrialists in Hong Kong*, Hong Kong: Oxford University Press, 1988.

Wood, Frances, *No Dogs and Not Many Chinese: Treaty Port Life in China, 1843–1943*, London: John Murray, 1998.

Wu, Harry Hongda, *Laogai: The Chinese Gulag*, Boulder: Westview Press, 1992.

Wu Lengxi, *Shinian lunzhan: 1956–1966 Zhong Su guanxi huiyilu* (Ten years of theoretical disputes: My recollection of Sino-Soviet relationships), Beijing: Zhongyang wenxian chubanshe, 1999.

Wu Lengxi, *Yi Mao zhuxi: Wo qinshen jingli de ruogan zhongda lishi shijian pianduan* (Remembering Chairman Mao: Fragments of my personal experience of certain important historical events), Beijing: Xinhua chubanshe, 1995.

Wu Ningkun and Li Yikai, *A Single Tear: A Family's Persecution, Love, and Endurance in Communist China*, London: Hodder & Stoughton, 1993.

Wu, Tommy Jieqin, *A Sparrow's Voice: Living through China's Turmoil in the 20th Century*, Shawnee Mission, KS: M.I.R. House International, 1999.

Xiao-Planes, Xiaohong, 'The Pan Hannian Affair and Power Struggles at the Top of the CCP (1953–1955)', *China Perspectives*, no. 4 (Autumn 2010), pp. 116–27.

Xiong Huayuan and Liao Xinwen, *Zhou Enlai zongli shengya* (The life of Zhou Enlai), Beijing: Renmin chubanshe, 1997.

Yan Yunxiang, *Private Life under Socialism: Love, Intimacy and Family Change in a Chinese Village, 1949–1999*, Stanford: Stanford University Press, 2003.

Yang, C. K., *A Chinese Village in Early Communist Transition*, Cambridge, MA: Harvard University Press, 1959.

Yang, C. K., *Religion in Chinese Society: A Study of Contemporary Social Functions of Religion and Some of their Historical Factors*, Berkeley: University of California Press, 1961.

Yang Kuisong, 'Reconsidering the Campaign to Suppress Counterrevolutionaries', *China Quarterly*, no. 193 (March 2008), pp. 102–21.

Yang Kuisong, *Zhonghua renmin gongheguo jianguo shi yanjiu* (Studies on the history of the founding of the People's Republic of China), Nanchang: Jiangxi renmin chubanshe, 2009.

Yang Nianqun, 'Disease Prevention, Social Mobilization and Spatial Politics: The Anti-Germ Warfare Incident of 1952 and the Patriotic Health Campaign', *Chinese Historical Review*, 11, no. 2 (Autumn 2004), pp. 155–82.

Yen, Maria, *The Umbrella Garden: A Picture of Student Life in Red China*, New York: Macmillan, 1953.

Yu Fengzheng, *Gaizao: 1949–1957 nian de zhishifenzi* (Reform: Intellectuals from 1949 to 1957), Zhengzhou: Henan renmin chubanshe, 2001.

Yue Daiyun, *To the Storm: The Odyssey of a Revolutionary Chinese Woman*, Berkeley: University of California Press, 1985.

Zazerskaya, T. G., *Sovetskie spetsialisty i formirovanie voenno-promyshlennogo kompleksa Kitaya (1949–1960 gg.)*, St Petersburg: Sankt Peterburg Gosudarstvennyi Universitet, 2000.

Zhang Jiabai, 'Zhou Enlai and the Marshall Mission', in Larry I. Bland (ed.), *George C. Marshall's Mediation Mission to China, December 1945–January 1947*, Lexington, VA: George C. Marshall Foundation, 1998, pp. 201–34.

Zhang Lü and Zhu Qiude, *Xibu nüren shiqing: Fu Xinjiang nübing rensheng mingyun gushi koushu shilu* (Oral histories of women soldiers sent to Xinjiang), Beijing: Jiefangjun wenyi chubanshe, 2001.

Zhang Ming, 'Zhizheng de daode kunjing yu tuwei zhi dao: Sanfan wufan yundong jiexi' (Analysis of the Three-Anti and Five-Anti Campaign), *Ershiyi shiji*, no. 92 (Dec. 2005), pp. 46–58.

Zhang Shu Guang, *Economic Cold War: America's Embargo against China and the Sino-Soviet Alliance, 1949–1963*, Stanford: Stanford University Press, 2001.

Zhang Shu Guang, *Mao's Military Romanticism: China and the Korean War, 1950–1953*, Lawrence: University Press of Kansas, 1995.

Zhang Xueqiang, *Xiangcun bianqian yu nongmin jiyi: Shandong laoqu Junan xian tudi gaige yanjiu* (Village change and peasant memory: Studies on land reform in Junan county, Shandong), Beijing: Shehui kexue wenxian chubanshe, 2006.

Zhang Yihe, *Wangshi bingbu ruyan* (Do not let bygones be bygones), Beijing: Renmin wenxue chubanshe, 2004.

Zhang Yongdong, *Yijiusijiu nianhou Zhongguo nongcun zhidu biange shi* (A history of changes in the Chinese countryside after 1949), Taipei: Ziyou wenhua chubanshe, 2008.

Zhang Zhenglong, *Xuebai xuehong* (Snow is white but blood is red), Hong Kong: Dadi chubanshe, 1991.

Zhang Zhiqiang and Wang Fang (eds), *1948, Changchun: Wei neng jichu de jiaxin yu zhaopian* (1948, Changchun: The family letters and photos that were never sent), Jinan: Shandong huabao chubanshe, 2003.

Zhu Zheng, *Fan youpai douzheng shimo* (The history of the anti-rightist campaign), Hong Kong: Mingbao chubanshe youxian gongsi, 2004.

Zubok, Vladislav and Constantine Pleshakov, *Inside the Kremlin's Cold War: From Stalin to Khrushchev*, Cambridge, MA: Harvard University Press, 1996.

Acknowledgements

I acknowledge with gratitude research grant HKU743911H from the Research Grants Council, Hong Kong, and research grant RG016-P-07 from the Chiang Ching-kuo Foundation, Taiwan, which allowed me to carry out the research for this book. A number of people have read and commented on draft versions, in particular Gail Burrowes, May Holdsworth, Christopher Hutton, Françoise Koolen, Jonathan Mirsky, Veronica Pearson, Robert Peckham, Priscilla Roberts, Perry Svensson and Andrew Walder. Jean Hung, at the Universities Service Centre for China Studies at the Chinese University of Hong Kong, was extraordinarily helpful. David Cheng Chang, Deborah Davis, Roderick MacFarquhar, Theresa Marie Moreau, Glen Peterson, Michael Sheng, Constantine Tung, Eddy U and Arthur Waldron were very kind with comments, suggestions and answers to queries. I owe a great deal to Christopher Hutton for ideas and insights on all aspects of the book. Mark Kramer helped me in gaining access to the archives in Moscow, and the custodians of the Society of the Divine Word in Rome generously allowed me to read through their archives. I used several interviews originally collected by Tammy Ho and Chan Yeeshan in 2006 as part of an earlier project on *Mao's Great Famine*. I am grateful to Zhou Xun, who provided files from the Sichuan Provincial Archives. The School of Humanities at the University of Hong Kong, in particular the Department of History, has provided a wonderful research environment, and I am indebted to all my colleagues who supported the project, in particular Daniel Chua and Charles Schencking.

I also received help from friends and colleagues in mainland China, but I prefer not to name them for reasons that seem obvious enough. The endnotes, on the other hand, show how the best and most courageous research on the Mao era often comes from the People's Republic. I am indebted to my publishers, namely Michael Fishwick in London and George Gibson in New York, and my copy-editor Peter James, as well as Anna Simpson, Oliver Holden-Rea, Paul Nash and all the team at Bloomsbury. I would like to convey my gratitude to my literary agent Andrew Wylie in New York and Sarah Chalfant in London. The first sentence in a book always matters a great deal, and so does the last one, in which I would like lovingly to thank my wife Gail Burrowes.

Hong Kong, February 2013

Index

A Note on the Author

Frank Dikötter is Chair Professor of Humanities at the University of Hong Kong. Before moving to Asia in 2006, he was Professor of the Modern History of China at the School of Oriental and African Studies, University of London. He has published nine books about the history of China, including *Mao's Great Famine*, which won the BBC Samuel Johnson Prize for Non-fiction in 2011.

A Note on the Type

The text of this book is set Adobe Garamond. It is one of several versions of Garamond based on the designs of Claude Garamond. It is thought that Garamond based his font on Bembo, cut in 1495 by Francesco Griffo in collaboration with the Italian printer Aldus Manutius. Garamond types were first used in books printed in Paris around 1532. Many of the present-day versions of this type are based on the *Typi Academiae* of Jean Jannon cut in Sedan in 1615.

Claude Garamond was born in Paris in 1480. He learned how to cut type from his father and by the age of fifteen he was able to fashion steel punches the size of a pica with great precision. At the age of sixty he was commissioned by King Francis I to design a Greek alphabet, for this he was given the honourable title of royal type founder. He died in 1561.